CORE CONCEPTS IN CULTURAL ANTHROPOLOGY

THIRD EDITION

Robert H. Lavenda

Emily A. Schultz

St. Cloud State University

Boston Burr Ridge, IL Dubuque, IA Madison, WI New York
San Francisco St. Louis Bangkok Bogotá Caracas Kuala Lumpur
Lisbon London Madrid Mexico City Milan Montreal New Delhi
Santiago Seoul Singapore Sydney Taipei Toronto

The McGraw·Hill Companies

Mc Graw Hill Higher Education

This book is printed on acid-free paper.

1 2 3 4 5 6 7 8 9 0 FGR/FGR 0 9 8 7 6 5

ISBN-13: 978-0-07-305045-4
ISBN-10: 0-07-305045-8

Editor in Chief: *Emily Barrosse*
Publisher: *Phil Butcher*
Sponsoring Editor: *Kevin Witt*
Editorial Coordinator: *Teresa Treacy*
Marketing Manger: *Dan Loch*
Project Manager: *Stacy Shearer*
Design Manager and Cover Designer: *Preston Thomas*
Interior Designer: *Sharon Spurlock*
Art Editor: *Robin Mouat*
Production Supervisor: *Randy Hurst*
Composition: *11/14 Sabon by International Typesetting & Composition*
Printing: *45# New Era Matte, Quebecor World Fairfield*

Library of Congress Cataloging-in-Publication Data

Lavenda, Robert H.
    Core concepts in cultural anthropology / Robert H. Lavenda, Emily A. Schultz.—3rd ed.
    p. cm.
    Includes bibliographical references and index.
    ISBN 0-07-305045-8 (softcover)
    1. Ethnology. 2. Ethnology—Bibliography. I. Schultz, Emily A. (Emily Ann),
    II. Title.
    GN316.L39 2005
    306—dc22   2005051130

The Internet addresses listed in the text were accurate at the time of publication. The inclusion of a Web site does not indicate an endorsement by the authors or McGraw-Hill, and McGraw-Hill does not guarantee the accuracy of the information presented at these sites.

www.mhhe.com

To Jan Beatty

◈ Contents ◈

◈ Preface ◈

THIS BOOK IS A CONCISE introduction to the fundamental key terms and issues of contemporary cultural anthropology. It is not a condensed version of the sixth edition of our textbook *Cultural Anthropology: A Perspective on the Human Condition;* this is something different. Our goal is to provide students with a rapid sketch of the basic ideas and practices of cultural anthropology in a style analogous to a bibliographic essay. A good bibliographic essay prepares its readers to do their own research by giving them an idea of what sources are available and where and how those sources fit into research in that field. So, too, we hope, with this volume: we introduce the core concepts and key terms in cultural anthropology and indicate briefly where they come from and how they are related to one another, in order to provide students with a context for understanding anthropological writing, especially ethnographic writing, when they turn to it.

Our expectation is that this text will be used in conjunction with ethnographies and/or collections of readings during the term. For that reason, we have omitted ethnographic examples and other kinds of details found in our textbook *Cultural Anthropology* (and most introductory texts), and we have concentrated on providing a scaffolding on which students can rely as they begin to read more conventional anthropological texts.

Features

- ◆ *Flexibility.* This text can be used in many different ways. It can be used by itself as a concise introduction to cultural anthropology when the course time that can be devoted to covering the discipline is limited. It can also be used very successfully in conjunction with other readings, either anthologies or ethnographies, or both. *Core Concepts in Cultural Anthropology* may be assigned at the beginning of the term to go along with introductory lectures and be referred to as needed. Another approach, popular with users of earlier editions of *Core Concepts in Cultural Anthropology,* is to assign specific chapters to be read along with particular ethnographies or course topics. To accommodate various uses, we have made each chapter as self-contained as possible. Each chapter has numbered section headings to make it easier for students to navigate the text, and to give instructors additional flexibility should they wish to assign segments of chapters in novel ways best suited for the organization of their courses. We have included cross-references to related topics in other chapters wherever possible. Instructors can feel free to use the chapters and sections in the order that best fits their approach to teaching anthropology.

◆ *Brief and affordable.* What you have in your hands is an unadorned framework or scaffolding for teaching cultural anthropology. Quite intentionally, there are no photographs, no lavish graphics, no elaborate text boxes, no extended ethnographic examples. A consequence of writing a concise introduction is that many of the details and nuances of the field are left out. We assume that instructors will provide favorite ethnographic examples both in class and in other readings to illustrate the issues they raise in class. It is our hope that the brevity and affordability of this text will allow the assignment of additional course readings and will engender lectures and class discussions that bring back the nuance and subtlety that are a part of every human endeavor, including anthropology, teaching, and learning.

◆ *Provides useful study aids.* Each chapter opens with a list of key terms discussed in that chapter. Each chapter ends with a list of suggested readings, which—along with an extensive end-of-book bibliography—directs students to more detailed discussions. The index allows students to quickly find the key terms they need. An online Study Guide provides additional learning help.

◆ *Includes a chapter on theory.* Because all anthropological writing is theoretically situated, we have included a chapter on theory in cultural anthropology. We think it is important for students to get a sense of how the texts they are reading fit into a broader disciplinary context. We also think they need some intellectual tools for interpreting what they are reading: ethnographic writing often refers to alternative theoretical positions, and it is useful for students to know the issues those positions have raised in the course of ongoing anthropological discussion and debate.

◆ *Offers a list of ethnographies in print.* A Web site accompanies the text that lists and plots on a world map a broad selection of ethnographies in print.

A word about the chapters and where to find certain materials: as we put the book together, we found that some important topics fit more easily within certain other, broader topics. For example, discussion of research methods in anthropology will be found in Chapter 1, "Anthropology" and discussion of gender, race, class, ethnicity, and nonkin forms of social organization are found in Chapter 6, "The Dimensions of Social Organization."

What's New in the Third Edition?

◆ Chapter 11, "Globalization," has been extensively revised and reordered. The chapter now contains new or expanded sections on neoliberalism, transnational citizenship, human rights, cultural hybridization, multiculturalism, and cosmopolitanism.

◆ We have added an Appendix with a detailed discussion on how to read ethnography. This will assist students as they move into more advanced anthropological readings.

- A new section on art has been added to Chapter 5 that includes discussions of aesthetics, visual art, music, and dance.

- A discussion of the concept of *relatedness* has been added in Chapter 9, "Kinship and Descent."

- Multisited fieldwork as a contemporary research approach has been added.

- A brief discussion of medical anthropology is found in Chapter 1.

- Chapter 4, "Culture and the Individual," now includes discussions of subjectivity and political power as well as trauma and structural violence.

- A brief discussion of language ideology has been added to the language chapter.

- The discussion of commodity consumption and cultural imperialism has been expanded.

- Suggested readings have been expanded as needed.

Acknowledgments

For valuable suggestions on the Appendix, we would like to thank Tom O'Toole and Katherine Woodhouse Beyer. Our editor at McGraw-Hill, Kevin Witt, has been a pleasure to work with, and we appreciate his insights into the book. We would also like to thank the reviewers of the text who were so generous and careful with their comments.

Martha Kaplan
Vassar College

Shelly Braun
University of Utah

Finally, we would like to thank Jan Beatty, who suggested a book like this to us in the first place. This continues to be an interesting and valuable project for us, as it pushes us to think about the different ways in which cultural anthropology might be presented. We hope that you find it to be an effective tool for teaching anthropology to new generations of students.

1

Anthropology

The key terms and concepts to be covered in this chapter in the order in which they appear:

anthropology
holistic
comparative
evolutionary

biological anthropology
primatologists
paleoanthropologists
forensic anthropologists
medical anthropology

cultural anthropology
culture

fieldwork
informants
participant-observation
monograph

ethnography
ethnology

anthropological linguistics
linguistic anthropology
language
archaeology
prehistory

applied anthropology
development anthropology
objective knowledge

positivism
modernism
postmodernism
reflexive
multisited fieldwork

Anthropology is a discipline that exists at the borders of the social sciences, the humanities, and the biological sciences. The term comes from two Greek words: *anthropos*, meaning "human beings," and *logia*, "the study of." The "study of human beings" would seem to be a rather broad topic for any one field, but anthropologists take the name of their discipline seriously, and anything that has to do with human beings probably is of potential interest to anthropologists. Indeed, **anthropology** can be formally defined as the study of human nature, human society, and the human past. This means that some anthropologists study human origins, others try to understand diverse contemporary ways of life, and some excavate the past or try to understand why we speak the ways we do.

1.1 An Anthropological Perspective

Given its breadth, what coherence anthropology has as a discipline comes from its perspective. Anthropology is holistic, comparative, field based, and evolutionary. For anthropologists, being **holistic** means trying to fit together all that is known about human beings. That is, anthropologists draw on the findings of many different disciplines that study human beings (human biology, economics, and religion, for example), as well as data on similar topics that they have collected, and attempt to produce an encompassing picture of human life. In the same way, when an anthropologist studies a specific group of people, the goal is to produce a holistic portrait of that people's way of life by bringing together information about many different facets of their lives—social, religious, economic, political, linguistic, and so forth—in order to provide a nuanced context for understanding who they are and why they do what they do.

However, to generalize about human nature, human society, and the human past requires information from as wide a range of human groups as possible. Anthropologists realized long ago that the patterns of life common in their own societies were not necessarily followed in other societies. And so, anthropology is a **comparative** discipline: anthropologists must consider similarities and differences in as wide a range of human societies as possible before generalizing about what it means to be human.

Because anthropology is interested in human beings in all places and at all times, anthropologists are curious about how we got to be what we are today. For this reason, anthropology is **evolutionary.** A major branch of anthropology is concerned with *biocultural* the study of the biological evolution of the human species over time, including the study of human origins and genetic variety and inheritance in living human populations. Some anthropologists have also been interested in cultural evolution, looking for patterns of orderly change over time in socially acquired behavior that is not carried in the genes.

1.2 The Subfields of Anthropology

Anthropology in North America historically has been divided into four major subfields: biological anthropology, cultural anthropology, linguistic anthropology, and archaeology.

Biological anthropology is the subfield of anthropology that looks at human beings as biological organisms. Biological anthropologists are interested in many different aspects of human biology, including our similarities to and differences from other living organisms. Those who study the closest living relatives of human beings—the nonhuman primates (chimpanzees and gorillas, for example)—are called **primatologists.** Those who specialize in the study of the fossilized bones and teeth of our earliest ancestors are called **paleoanthropologists.** Other biological anthropologists examine the genetic variation among and within different human populations or investigate variation in human skeletal biology (for example, measuring and comparing the shapes and sizes of bones or teeth using skeletal remains from different human populations). Newer specialties focus on human adaptability in different ecological settings, on human growth and development, and on the connections between a population's evolutionary history and its susceptibility to disease. **Forensic anthropologists** use their knowledge of human anatomy to aid law-enforcement and human-rights investigators by assisting in the identification of skeletal material found at crime or accident sites or at sites associated with possible human-rights violations.

Overlapping biological anthropology and cultural anthropology is the vibrant and relatively new field of **medical anthropology.** Medical anthropologists study the factors that contribute to human disease or illness, as well as the ways in which human groups respond to them. Medical anthropological research covers a vast range of topics, ranging from alcohol use in various societies, to the dimensions of the AIDS pandemic cross-culturally, to social aspects of medical care, to the effects of stress, violence, and social suffering.

Cultural anthropology (sometimes called social anthropology in Great Britain) is another major subfield of anthropology. Cultural anthropologists investigate how variation in the beliefs and behaviors of members of different human groups is shaped by **culture,** sets of learned behaviors and ideas that human beings acquire as members of society. (For a fuller discussion of the concept of culture, see Chapter 2.) Cultural anthropologists specialize in specific domains of human cultural activity. Some study the ways people organize themselves to carry out collective tasks, whether economic, political, or spiritual. Others focus on the forms and meanings of expressive behavior in human societies— language, art, music, ritual, religion, and the like. Still others examine material culture—the things people make and use, such as clothing, housing, and tools, and the techniques they employ to get food and produce material goods. They may also study the ways in which technologies and environments shape each other. For some time, cultural anthropologists have been interested in the way non-Western peoples have responded to the political and economic challenges of European colonialism and the capitalist industrial technology that came with it. They investigate contemporary issues of gender and sexuality, transnational labor migration, and the post–Cold War resurgence of ethnicity and nationalism around the world. And some cultural anthropologists have started to examine the increasing influence of computer technology on the social and cultural life of peoples throughout the world.

In all of these cases, the comparative nature of anthropology requires that what is taken for granted by members of a specific society—the anthropologist's own, as much as any other—must be examined, or "problematized." As a result, there is a double movement in anthropology; anthropologists study other ways of life not only to understand them in their own terms but also to put the anthropologists' own ways of life in perspective.

To make their discipline comparative, cultural anthropologists began to immerse themselves in the lives of other peoples. Traditionally, cultural anthropology is rooted in **fieldwork,** an anthropologist's personal, long-term experience with a specific group of people and their way of life. Where possible, anthropologists try to live for a year or more with the people whose way of life is of concern to them. The result is a fine-grained knowledge of the everyday details of life. Cultural anthropologists get to know people as individuals, not as "data sets." They remember the names and faces of people who, over the course of a year or more, have become familiar to them as complex and complicated men, women, and children. They remember the feel of the noonday sun, the sounds of the morning, the smells of food cooking, the pace and rhythm of life. In this sense, anthropology traditionally has been an *experiential* discipline. This approach does, of course, have drawbacks as well as advantages: Anthropologists are not usually able to make macrolevel generalizations about an entire nation or society, and their attention is not usually directed toward national or international policy-making or data collection. They are often, however, well aware of the *effects* of national or international decisions on the local level. In fact, in recent years, a number of anthropologists have done illuminating work about nations, refugees and migrations, and international and global processes.

People who share information about their way of life with anthropologists traditionally have been called **informants.** In recent years, however, a number of anthropologists have become uncomfortable with that term, which to some conjures up images of police informers and to others seems to reduce fully rounded individuals to the information they provide. But anthropologists have not been able to agree on an expression that might replace informant; some prefer "respondent" or "teacher" or "friend" or simply refer to "the people with whom I work." Regardless of the term, fieldworkers gain insight into another way of life by taking part as fully as they can in a group's social activities, as well as by observing those activities as outsiders. This research method, known as **participant-observation,** is central to cultural anthropology. Cultural anthropologists also use a variety of other research methods, including interviews, censuses, surveys, and even statistical sampling techniques when appropriate.

Cultural anthropologists write about what they have learned in scholarly articles or in books, and sometimes they document the lives of their research subjects on film. The word **monograph** is sometimes used to describe the books that anthropologists write; an ethnographic monograph, or **ethnography,** is a scholarly work about a specific way of life. **Ethnology** is the comparative study of two or more ways of life. Thus, cultural anthropologists who write ethnographies are sometimes called *ethnographers,* and anthropologists who compare ethnographic information on many different ways of life are sometimes called *ethnologists.* The prefix "ethno-" comes from the Greek *ethnos* (people) and is used a great deal by anthropologists to mean "of (or about) a people" or "of (or about) an ethnic group."

A third major subfield of anthropology, called **anthropological linguistics** or **linguistic anthropology,** is the branch of anthropology concerned with the study of human languages. For many people, the most striking cultural feature of human beings is **language,** the system of arbitrary vocal symbols we use to encode our experience of the world and of one another. Anthropological linguists were some of the first people to transcribe non-Western languages and to produce grammars and dictionaries of those languages. They also have worked to show the ways in which a people's language (or languages) serves as the main carrier of important cultural information. In tracing the relationships between language and culture, these anthropologists have investigated a range of topics (see Chapter 3 for details).

In all their research, anthropological linguists seek to understand language in relation to the broader cultural, historical, or biological contexts that make it possible. Modern anthropological linguists are trained in both formal linguistics and anthropology, and some cultural anthropologists study linguistics as part of their professional preparation.

Archaeology, the fourth traditional subfield of North American anthropology, can be defined as a cultural anthropology of the human past, involving the analysis of the material remains of earlier human societies. Through archaeology, anthropologists discover much about human history, particularly **prehistory,** the long stretch of time before the development of writing. Archaeologists look for evidence of past human cultural activity, such as post-holes, garbage heaps, and settlement patterns. Depending on the locations and ages of the sites they are digging, archaeologists may also have to be experts in stone-tool manufacture, metallurgy, or ancient pottery. Because archaeological excavations frequently uncover remains such as bones or plant pollen, archaeologists often work in teams with other scientists who specialize in the analysis of those remains.

The work archaeologists do complements the work done by other kinds of anthropologists. For example, paleontologists may find that archaeological information about successive stone-tool traditions in a particular region may correlate with fossil evidence of prehistoric occupation of that region by ancient human populations. Cultural anthropologists may use the work of archaeologists to help them interpret contemporary patterns of land use or forms of subsistence technology.

While popular media often portray archaeologists as concerned primarily with exotic ancient "stuff" (the "Indiana Jones syndrome," we might call it), archaeologists are usually more interested in seeking answers to cultural questions that can only be addressed properly by considering the passage of time. For example, archaeologists can use dating techniques to establish the ages of artifacts, which then allows them to hypothesize about patterns of sociocultural change in ancient societies. That is, tracing the

TABLE 1.1 The Traditional Subfields of Anthropology

SUBFIELD	DEFINITION
Biological anthropology	the study of human beings as biological organisms
Cultural anthropology	the study of how variation in the beliefs and behavior of members of different human groups is shaped by culture
Linguistic anthropology	the study of human language in cultural context
Archaeology	a cultural anthropology of the past

spread of cultural inventions over time from one site to another allows them to hypothesize about the nature and degree of social contact between different peoples. Some contemporary archaeologists even dig through layers of garbage deposited by people within the past two or three decades, often uncovering surprising information about modern consumption patterns. (Table 1.1 lists the four traditional subfields of anthropology.)

In recent decades, increasing numbers of anthropologists have been using the methods and findings from every subfield of anthropology to address problems in the contemporary world, in what is called **applied anthropology.** This subfield has grown rapidly as an area of involvement and employment for anthropologists. Some applied anthropologists may use a particular group's ideas about illness and health to introduce new public-health practices in a way that makes sense to and will be accepted by members of that group. Others may apply knowledge of traditional social organization to ease the problems of refugees trying to settle in a new land. Still others may tap their knowledge of traditional and Western methods of cultivation to help farmers increase their crop yields. Taken together, these activities are sometimes called **development anthropology** because their aim is to improve people's capacities to maintain their health, produce their food, and otherwise adapt to the challenges of life in the contemporary world.

Applied anthropologists with a background in archaeology may be involved with contract or salvage archaeology, or they may work in cultural resource management to ensure that the human past is not destroyed by, say, the construction of new buildings, highways, or dams. Biological anthropologists may become involved in forensic work, such as the determination of social characteristics of crime or accident victims, or in nutrition.

In recent years, increasing numbers of anthropologists have come to view applied anthropology as a separate field of professional specialization—related to the other four fields but with its own techniques and theoretical questions. More and more universities in the United States have begun to develop courses and programs in applied anthropology.

While anthropology may have begun in Western Europe and the United States more than a century ago, over the course of its history it has become an international discipline. Universities and research institutions in many countries around the world have established anthropology departments, offer courses and degrees, and carry out research, both theoretical and applied. Anthropologists in different countries have established national anthropological associations, and there are also international associations of anthropologists for the dissemination of anthropological research.

1.3 Is Anthropology a Science? Modernism, Postmodernism, and Beyond

At the beginning of the twentieth century, most anthropologists viewed their growing discipline as a science. They agreed that the truth about the world was accessible through the five senses; that a properly disciplined rational mind could derive universal, objective truths from material evidence; and that a single scientific method could be applied to any dimension of reality, from the movement of the planets to human sexual behavior. Such investigation was supposed to produce **objective knowledge**: undistorted, and thus universally valid, knowledge about the world. Anthropologists felt free to apply scientific methods in any area of anthropological interest, from stone tools to religion, confident that the combined results of these efforts would produce a genuine "Science of Man" (as it was then called). This set of ideas and practices is known as **positivism.**

Today, many critical observers of the natural and social sciences connect these ideas to a complex Western cultural ideology called **modernism.** Modernism can be (and has been) viewed in terms of liberation from outdated traditions that prevent people from building better lives for themselves and their children. Critics have argued, however, that modern Western science, rather than being a universal path to objective truth, is itself a culture-bound enterprise connected to a specific definition of progress. Many members of non-Western societies agree with these critics that in their experience, modernist ideas have been used by powerful Western states to dominate them and to undermine their traditional beliefs and practices. From their perspective, Western-style "progress" has meant the loss of political autonomy, an increase in economic impoverishment and environmental degradation, and destruction of systems of social relations and values that clash with the "modern" way of life.

This criticism of modernism, accompanied by an active questioning of all the boundaries and categories that modernists set up as objectively true, has come to be called **postmodernism.** Its plausibility as an intellectual position increased after the end of the Cold War in 1989, when many previously unquestioned cultural and political "truths" about the world seemed to crumble overnight. To be postmodern is to question the universalizing tendencies of modernism, especially of modernist understandings of science. Postmodernists point out that people occupying powerful social positions often are able to pass off their own cultural or political prejudices as universal truths, while dismissing or ignoring alternative views held by powerless groups.

Anthropologists had long considered themselves to be debunkers of distorting Western stereotypes about non-Western peoples. Having frequently defended the integrity of indigenous societies against the onslaughts of modernizing missionaries and "development" experts, they had come to assume that they were on the side of those whose ways of life they studied. From the perspective of some members of those societies, however, as well as from the viewpoint of postmodernists, anthropologists looked just like another group of outside "experts" making their own universal claims about human cultures, behaving no differently from chemists making universal, "expert" claims about molecules.

1.4 Reflexive Anthropology

Postmodern criticism prompted anthropologists to engage in a reappraisal of their discipline and, in particular, to rethink what was involved in fieldwork and the writing of ethnography. While cultural anthropologists continue to value careful observational methods and accurate, systematic data gathering, many of them also take seriously certain parts of the postmodern critique. For example, modeling ethnographers in the field on natural scientists in their laboratories appears problematic once ethnographers grant that the subject matter of anthropology, unlike that of chemistry, consists of human beings, members of the same species as the scientists studying them. Rather than a relationship between a curious human being and inert matter, anthropological fieldwork always involved a social relationship between at least two curious individuals. This meant that the cultural identity and personal characteristics of fieldworkers had to be taken into account when attempting to make sense of their ethnographic writing. Put another way, fieldwork had to become a **reflexive** activity, in which anthropologists carefully scrutinized both their own contribution to fieldwork interactions and the responses these interactions elicited from informants. That is, rather than assuming that they were, for all intents and purposes, invisible to the people they were studying, anthropologists began to consider the effect that they had on the people with whom they were living. They began to recognize that who they were as individuals and as socially-situated actors had an effect on their research. Many contemporary cultural anthropologists have accepted the challenges of doing reflexive fieldwork and are persuaded that such fieldwork produces better, more accurate ethnography than modernist methods ever did. Reflexive fieldworkers are much more explicit about the limitations of their own knowledge and much more generous in the credit they give to their informants. Some have written their ethnographies in new, experimental styles that often read more like novels than scientific texts.

Indeed, many ethnographers today no longer act as outsiders but have taken up the challenge of doing participant-observation in cultural settings to which they belong. They are conscious of potential pitfalls but are convinced that their professional training will help them provide a unique and valuable perspective. Moreover, many have chosen to engage in **multisited fieldwork,** in which the goal is to follow people, or objects, or cultural processes that are not contained by social, national, ethnic, or religious boundaries (see Chapter 2). Working in more than one place, and with persons or institutions that have not traditionally been the focus of ethnographic analysis, they are also revealing interconnections and influences that, in the past, would have escaped the fieldworker's attention. These ethnographers see their task as finding a way to combine the most valuable elements of the postmodern critique of ethnography with a continuing respect for empirical evidence. The challenge of such a task is great and perhaps as paradoxical as the notion of participant-observation, but many ethnographers believe that research undertaken within and across uncomfortable middle ground can yield important insights into human cultural practices, insights that can be secured in no other way.

Indeed, at the beginning of the twenty-first century, many ethnographers (as well as many members of the societies in which they work) have moved beyond the opposition between modernism and postmodernism. They have drawn attention to the ways in which members of non-Western societies selectively incorporate "modern" or "scientific" practices originating in the Western world in order to help them develop their own *alternative modernities.* At the same time, a reconsideration of the nature of "science" by anthropologists and others has shown that the positivist understanding of science may, in fact, offer an incomplete account of scientific successes and failures, not only in the social sciences but also in physical sciences such as physics and biology. This development opens up new and exciting possibilities for alternative understandings of science—and of anthropology as a science—that are yet to be developed.

For Further Reading

BIOLOGICAL ANTHROPOLOGY
Park 1998; Relethford 1996

ARCHAEOLOGY
Ashmore and Sharer 2000

APPLIED ANTHROPOLOGY
Van Willigen 1993

DEVELOPMENT ANTHROPOLOGY
Gardner and Lewis 1996

MEDICAL ANTHROPOLOGY
Baer, Singer and Susser 2003; McElroy and Townsend 2004

FIELD RESEARCH
Agar 1996; Behar 1997; Bernard 1994; Bradburd 1998;
Rabinow 1977; Marcus 1995

2

Culture

The key terms and concepts covered in this chapter, in the order in which they appear:

culture

cultural universals

symbols

ethnocentrism

cultural relativism

cultural hybridization

indigenization

CULTURE HAS LONG BEEN the central concept in anthropology. At its most basic, culture is understood to refer to learned sets of ideas and behaviors that are acquired by people as members of society. Anthropologists have used the concept of culture in a variety of ways over the years, however, and contemporary anthropologists continue to disagree about how it should be defined. Major debates about the culture concept, however, can be connected to particular intellectual and social struggles in which anthropologists have been involved historically.

2.1 Culture Against Racism: The Early Twentieth Century

Culture gained power as an anthropological concept in the early decades of the discipline, around the turn of the twentieth century, in a social and scholarly context in which all important differences between human groups were attributed to differences in the *biology* of the groups, summarized in the concept of *race*. Biological race was thought to be an infallible index for everything else distinctive to a particular human group. Many early physical anthropologists hoped that if they could succeed in accurately identifying the "races of Man," they would be able to specify which languages and customs originated with, belonged to, or were otherwise appropriate for which races. Unfortunately, this search for a scientific definition of race took place in a historical context in which ruling groups in the societies from which the anthropologists came were already convinced of the reality of race and so used race-based distinctions to justify their own domination of darker-skinned peoples around the globe.

In this context, the culture concept was a crucial innovation designed to counteract the racism implicit in nineteenth-century physical anthropology and, more broadly, in nineteenth-century social thought. At the turn of the twentieth century, under the influence of Franz Boas (1858–1942), anthropologists were collecting evidence to show that the diverse beliefs and practices that distinguished different groups of human beings from one another were due to differences in *social learning*, not differences in racial biology. For example, immigrants in the United States were assigned by physical anthropologists to a variety of different "races." Yet Boas and his colleagues were able to show that American-born children of immigrants regularly spoke fluent English, wore the clothing, ate the food, and otherwise adopted ways of life common in the United States. Boas even showed that the head shapes of the children of immigrants differed from the head shapes of their parents, apparently under the influence of nutritional changes.

The so-called races of Man were, in actuality, a single *human* race (or as we would say today, populations of a single human species). As a consequence, all were equipped with the same "pan-human rationality" and were equally capable of creating new cultural traits or adopting cultural traits from others. Another way to emphasize the equal humanity of all human groups was to demonstrate that each of them possessed the same kinds of institutions, or **cultural universals**, designed to achieve the same overall goals for the group's members. This was the path taken by Polish-British anthropologist Bronisław Malinowski (1884–1942), who argued that all human beings everywhere face the same problems of survival or, as he put it, experience the same basic human needs. The members of each society use culture to devise ways of meeting these needs—for food or clothing or shelter or education or reproduction. Different societies meet these needs in different ways, however, and it is the ethnographer's job to catalogue the variety.

Boasians chose a different line of attack, arguing that race, language, and culture were independent phenomena. To show this was to show that the concept of biological race corresponded to no material reality and, thus, explained nothing about variation across human groups. That is, a person's physical attributes—skin color, hair texture, nose shape, stature, or the like—in no way compelled that person to speak or behave in any particular way. Indeed, the rapidity with which people of all "races" could forget old languages and customs and adopt new ones demonstrated the superiority of the culture concept in explaining variation across human groups. Since the capacities to create and learn culture belong to the entire human species, nothing prevents any subgroup from learning languages or beliefs or practices originally developed by some other subgroup.

Boas and his students devoted much effort to documenting an enormous amount of cultural borrowing across social, linguistic, and "racial" boundaries. This work aimed to demolish the concept of biological race for good, and yet at the beginning of the twenty-first century the concept of "race" has not disappeared. Indeed, the concept of culture explains how this can happen: people can invent *cultural* categories based on superficial physical features of human beings, call those categories "races," and then use these categories as building blocks for their social institutions, *even if such categories correspond to no biological reality.* An ongoing challenge within anthropology has been how to deny the reality of race as a biological concept without ignoring the continuing vigor of race as a cultural construction in societies like that of the United States.

Work by Boas and his students suggested strongly that the boundaries between various human groups are fuzzy and fluid and that firm distinctions are difficult to identify, let alone enforce. At the same time, it was apparent that different social groups often lived lives that were quite distinct from those of their neighbors, for several reasons. First, people did, initially at least, learn their native language and the bulk of their culture from those among whom they grew up. Second, social groups often deliberately emphasized unique cultural attributes in order to set themselves apart from their neighbors. Third, many of the groups ethnographers studied had been incorporated into a colonial empire (as in Africa) or within the boundaries of a larger nation-state (as in the United States). In such situations, the sorting of peoples into named societies, each associated with its own way of life, was strongly encouraged by the ruling elites.

2.2 The Evolution of Culture

Anthropologists in the early twentieth century worked within a Darwinian framework and were aware of the discoveries about biological heredity being made by the new science of genetics.

Rather than explaining cultural variation in genetic terms, however, they sought to show the adaptive evolutionary advantages that culture provided for the human species. This theme has been emphasized in recent years by anthropologists known as *cultural inheritance theorists,* who seek to show how the capacity for human culture could have arisen by natural selection. Compared even to our nearest primate relatives, we human beings seem to be born remarkably free of specific "survival instincts," or biological programming designed to secure food, shelter, and mates for us automatically. Instead, as Malinowski suggested, every human group apparently can invent (and modify) its own particular sets of learned cultural traditions in order to solve these problems. Thus, human beings must learn everything necessary to survive and thrive from older, experienced members of their group. In Darwinian terms, they adapt to their environments by learning the culture of those among whom they live.

Such a form of Darwinian adaptation is highly unusual, however. How could it have arisen, and what would be the selective advantage for a species that relied on learned traditions, rather than innate biological programming, for survival? The anthropological answer goes something like this. Human beings are unusually intelligent (witness our large and complex brain). We and our ancestors ranged widely across many different kinds of natural environments, rather than being highly adapted to the resources of a narrow ecological niche, as, for example, are bamboo-eating giant pandas or eucalyptus-leaf-eating koalas. Natural selection for cultural learning in such an intelligent, wide-ranging species might have been favored because it allowed for a much more rapid adaptation to new environmental conditions than does natural selection operating on genes.

For example, human beings were not obliged to wait until natural selection provided them with thick fur before they could survive in cold climates. Instead, they could rely on their cultural capacity to learn to control fire, make warm clothing from skins, invent ways of using cold-adapted plants and animals for food, and so forth. Under such conditions, natural selection would also have favored those human ancestors who learned especially easily from those around them and who were curious and creative in devising cultural solutions for new adaptive problems. Research into human prehistory strongly supports this view of human beings as a species of "weedy generalists," equipped by natural selection with a set of adaptive traits, including a dependence on culture, that has made it possible to survive and thrive in virtually any environment the earth has to offer.

2.3 Culture and Symbolism

Human beings, of course, are not the only animals in the world that learn. Several decades of research, for example, have shown that chimpanzees have invented simple practices of various kinds that other members of their groups acquire through learning, such as fishing for termites with twigs, making leaf sponges to soak up water to drink, cracking nuts open with rocks, and assuming distinctive postures for grooming one another. If culture is defined as practices that are acquired from and shared with other members of one's social group, that mediate one's adaptation to the environment, and that get passed on from generation to generation by means of social learning, then these ape practices certainly can be called culture. At the same time, missing from these forms of ape culture is a key element that is integral to human culture. Unlike the learned behavior of other primates such as chimpanzees, human culture clearly depends on our use of **symbols.**

A symbol is something that stands for something else: "X symbolizes Y." What makes symbols distinct from other forms of representation is that there is *no necessary link* between the symbol (X) and that which it stands for (Y). Put another way, the relationship between a symbol and that which it stands for is conventional and arbitrary. The object you are reading right now is called a "book" because generations of English speakers have agreed to call it that. It could just as easily be called "libro" or "gludge." Apes such as chimpanzees and bonobos do seem to have some rudimentary symbolic capacities, although just how much remains controversial. Nevertheless, these apes do not depend on symbolism to anything like the degree that human beings do. Thus, although learning is not unique to human beings and some learning of shared traditional practices can be found in nonhuman animals, only with human beings do we find a species whose survival depends on its reliance on learned, shared traditions that are *symbolically encoded.*

To depend on symbolic culture is to depend on learning for survival, but it is also much more. Symbols stand for objects, events, and processes in the wider world. But because their link to these phenomena is purely by convention, that which the symbol stands for can never be specified once and for all. The "same" phenomena may be symbolized differently in different societies, or phenomena that are distinguished as "different" in one society may be grouped together as instances of the "same" thing in another. This slippage between symbols and what they stand for makes possible complex human cultural systems, and it enables their remodeling or dismantling under novel conditions. Such slippage also means, however, that effort is constantly required to keep symbolic systems *systemic*—that is, orderly and coherent. Furthermore, nothing guarantees that existing cultural systems will not change over time, due either to internally generated developments or to exposure to new phenomena introduced from outside.

2.4 Ethnocentrism and Cultural Relativism

Still, despite these factors, ethnographers were impressed early on by the high degree of cultural coherence and predictability they regularly encountered while doing field research in non-Western cultures. This was important, because it undermined the racist stereotypes about tribal or non-Western peoples widespread in the early decades of the discipline. In particular, such peoples were regularly portrayed as irrational "savages" or "barbarians" leading lives that were, in the words of seventeenth-century philosopher Thomas Hobbes, "nasty, brutish, and short." Such portrayals of tribal peoples by Western observers were based on the universal human tendency to view one's own way of life as natural and as naturally better than other, different ways of life. Anthropologists call this attitude **ethnocentrism**—that is, using the practices of your own "people" as a yardstick to measure how well the customs of other, different peoples measure up. Inevitably, the ways in which "they" differ from "us" (no matter who "they" and "us" happen to be) are understood, ethnocentrically, in terms of *what they lack*.

Ethnocentric Europeans and North Americans believed that to be "civilized" and "cultured" meant to follow an orderly way of life graced by refinement and harmony. But early anthropologists found that they could use the culture concept to counter these ethnocentric beliefs. They could show that *all* peoples were equally "cultured," because every group's social practices were characterized by order, harmony, and refinement. The particular set of customs one followed depended on the group one was born into, from whose members one learned those customs. Another group's customs might differ from our customs, but each group equally had its own orderly, refined sets of customs. Thus, the child of an aristocratic European family, if brought up among people who hunted and gathered for a living, would learn the language and culture of hunters and gatherers just as easily as one of their children, adopted by the aristocrats, would learn the language and culture proper to aristocratic Europeans. To emphasize that every society (not merely Western European society) had its own integrated culture was a way of emphasizing that each society was human in its own way—indeed, that all human societies were *equally human*.

The term *culture* came to refer to a coherent set of beliefs and customs belonging to a distinct society. Such a view seemed to entail, at the very least, that those who were outsiders to someone else's culture ought to refrain from assuming that difference automatically meant inferiority. A culture could not be fully appreciated, anthropologists argued, until its various beliefs and practices were seen from the point of view of those who lived their lives according to those beliefs and practices. Ethnographic fieldwork introduced anthropologists to peoples about whom they previously lacked firsthand knowledge. By living side by side with people with an unfamiliar set of beliefs and practices for an extended period of time and learning the local language, anthropologists might hope to get a sense of what the world looked like from their hosts' point of view. This perspective on other cultures developed into the position called **cultural relativism,** whereby anthropologists were urged to interpret specific beliefs and practices in the context of the culture to which they belonged. More broadly, anthropologists urged others not to make snap judgments about the value of other peoples' customs but to consider first the role those customs fulfilled within the culture in which they were found. Cultural relativism gave anthropologists (and the members of the societies they studied) ideological ammunition to use against missionaries or colonialists who felt no compunction whatsoever about moving into "primitive" societies and destroying indigenous customs that were not to their liking.

In this sense, cultural anthropologists in the first half of the twentieth century believed that the ethnographic evidence they collected in societies throughout the world supported their claims of equal capacity and equal dignity for all human beings. Knowledge of the orderly, predictable customs and practices characteristic of tribal peoples became well known in Western circles, largely thanks to the work of anthropologists like Margaret Mead (1901–78) in the United States and Malinowski in Britain, who communicated anthropological findings through popular media to a wide audience outside university circles.

Still, not everyone was persuaded by their views. Indeed, new stereotypes about "primitive peoples" emerged that took account of anthropological evidence. It no longer seemed plausible to claim that "savages" and "barbarians" were wild, unruly, and irrational. And so ethnocentric Europeans and North Americans began to argue that "they" were different from "us" because of "their" slavish obedience to tradition, their mindless and uncritical repetition of traditions they'd inherited from their ancestors. People in "modern" Western societies with "scientific" cultures, by contrast, were portrayed as both able and willing to question the validity and rationality of traditional practices and to replace outmoded customs with better-adapted innovations. To view culture as a prison house of custom from which non-Western and tribal peoples were powerless to escape on their own, however, was to take the anthropological concept of culture and apply it in ways that the anthropologists who first developed it had never intended.

2.5 The Boundaries of Culture?

After World War II, European imperial power declined, former colonies were transformed into independent states, and the Civil Rights movement in the United States began to gather momentum. In the context of so many social, cultural, and political changes, and so many challenges to previous authority, the anthropological portrait of a world made up of particular mutually exclusive societies, each with its own, internally consistent culture, increasingly came under scrutiny, both within and outside anthropology.

Some anthropologists had always raised questions about just how sharply bounded, just how internally integrated, any particular culture might be. Boas and his students, as noted previously, had documented much borrowing of cultural objects and practices by one supposedly distinct society from another, suggesting that boundaries between cultural traditions might be rather porous. But if society A borrowed a custom from society B, could that custom ever be made into an "authentic" part of the culture of society A? And if it could be integrated, did that mean that the culture of society A was no longer "authentic"? And who would decide? Furthermore, even if a provisional correspondence could be established between a particular society and a particular set of cultural beliefs and practices, was it plausible to claim that every member of that society shared *every* aspect of its culture—the same beliefs, the same values, the same practices, the same points of view? What if members of the society in question disagreed, say, about how to perform a ritual? Could only one of the parties be correct, and must the others necessarily be wrong? And, again, who would decide?

Ethnographers often sought research settings that seemed to approximate this ideal of cultural uniformity—for example, remote villages or culturally distinct urban neighborhoods. Often they had to acknowledge that this setting was only one part of a larger sociocultural system, even if that larger system was not the focus of their research. This was particularly visible, and problematic, in the case of ethnographic work carried out during the colonial period: the wider imperial setting would be acknowledged briefly, but little or no reference to that setting would be made in the rest of the ethnography.

In recent years, many anthropologists have begun to question the validity of speaking as if a large and complex society could possess a single, uniform "culture." It has also become obvious that even within relatively small homogenous societies, members may disagree with one another about what "their culture" actually is. Anthropologists have become increasingly sensitive to the political issues involved in drawing boundaries around a society or a culture or in taking the views of one subgroup of a larger society as representative of "the culture" as a whole. This is why contemporary anthropologists always acknowledge that social and cultural boundaries are not eternally fixed and why they explicitly question, rather than assume they already know, what any particular set of boundaries means.

2.6 The Concept of Culture in a Global World: Problems and Practices

This has led to rethinking of the way ethnography should be pursued in a world in which local conditions are never isolated from global forces. One solution is to undertake *multisited fieldwork:* doing research not only in a particular local setting (a small village, say) but also in a series of other settings (such as political or corporate centers, whether in the same country or abroad). For example, fieldwork might begin in an urban neighborhood in the United States among a group of immigrants from elsewhere. But it might extend into the urban and national bureaucratic settings in which decisions affecting the immigrant group are made, and it might even continue in the communities abroad from which the immigrants originally came. The advantages and disadvantages of multisited ethnography are still being debated, but the fact that such a research strategy exists testifies to anthropologists' awareness of the often wide-ranging network of complex forces in which any particular local community is enmeshed.

Similarly, contemporary ethnographies are often quite explicit about exactly which members of a group have provided cultural information about a particular issue. Thus, anthropologists are careful to distinguish the opinions of, say, older men from those of women or of younger men, because they have learned that these subgroups regularly have differential access to social power and different interests to defend and so have different interpretations to offer about the cultural institutions and practices in which they are involved.

With this new awareness has come the realization that a concept of culture that emphasizes uniformity of belief and practice is not only not always liberating but can also be used as a way of enforcing inequality. This is clearest when one subgroup within a larger society insists on its version of the tradition as the only correct version and tries to force other subgroups to profess allegiance to that version or else risk persecution. Such practices are perhaps most obvious in those societies that were once colonies but have since become independent states. A common experience in such new states was the discovery that very little, apart from joint opposition to the colonizing power, united the peoples who were citizens of these new states. The ruling groups who had inherited the reins of government following the departure of the colonizer all felt very strongly the need to build some kind of national unity based on a shared "national culture." But the elements of such a national culture could be difficult to find when the only historical experience shared by all the new citizens was the tradition of colonial domination. Sometimes appeal could be made to precolonial customs— religious, economic, or political practices, for example—that were distinct from those that had been introduced by the colonial power. If such practices had once been widely shared, or at least widely recognized, by the bulk of the population, they might become resources on which to build a new national identity. If, however, such practices belonged only to a tiny proportion of the new citizenry— perhaps a powerful tribal group that had come to dominate post-colonial politics, for example—the practices might well be resisted by other groups. Having expelled one colonial power, they would see no advantage in being recolonized by one of their neighbors.

Paradoxically, however, elements of colonial culture often played an important role in the construction of the new national culture. This included not only the bureaucratic apparatus of governmental administration inherited from the colonial past and the new ways of doing business or educating the young introduced during the colonial period but also the language in which all these activities would be carried out. Anthropologists studying the production of national culture have been influenced by the writings of political scientist Benedict Anderson, who argued that nation-states are "imagined communities," most of whose members never see one another face-to-face but who nonetheless experience a sense of fellow feeling for one another. In Anderson's view, much of that fellow feeling in new nation-states develops out of their members' shared experiences of colonial institutions and practices.

Once again, language is a good example. If the peoples who were administered within a single colony came from dozens or hundreds of different ethnic groups, speaking numerous mutually unintelligible languages, any shared sense of belonging to the same nation would likely be very slight. However, once children from all those different groups began to attend colonial schools and learn the colonizer's language, they did have things in common. Moreover, they could then speak with and learn about one another in a way that would not have been possible had they not all learned to speak, say, French in French colonial schools. Again and again, the new nation-states chose the language of their former colonizer as the new national language of government, business, and education. Not only was this "efficient" in that it allowed an important element of continuity in changing circumstances, but it also meant that the official language of the state did not favor any particular indigenous language group over the others.

The culture concept thus can be reformulated to describe an emerging national culture, and attempts can be made to relate that national culture to the local cultures of different groups incorporated within the nation-state. What anthropologists did not expect, however, and what led to their most serious questioning of the traditional culture concept, were cases in which national regimes in various countries did not recognize the existence within their borders of such differentiated and partially overlapping cultures. Thus, if outsiders objected to the way a particular regime was treating its own citizens, spokespersons for the regime might respond that such treatment was "part of their culture" and, as such, beyond the critique of outsiders whose cultures were different. Most notoriously, under apartheid in South Africa, it was official government policy to endorse the notion that each people had its own unique culture. The apartheid regime assigned indigenous African peoples to "homelands" in rural areas far from mines and farms and factories, on the dubious grounds that Africans properly belonged in rural areas, farming the way their ancestors had done, and were not suited to work in, let alone run, modern commercial or industrial institutions in South Africa, because these institutions were part of "European culture."

2.7 Culture: Contemporary Discussion and Debate

What has been the outcome of all this discussion and debate about the culture concept? Some anthropologists assert that the concept of culture has been forever tainted by the older usage that assigned every society its own unique, internally harmonious set of beliefs and practices. Because this use of the concept reflects an outmoded understanding of how societies and cultures relate to one another, they argue, and has permitted culture to be falsely understood as a prison house of custom from which people could never escape, the term should be discarded entirely. They believe that it bears too many traces of the colonial circumstances under which it was developed and to which it proved so useful an intellectual tool in dividing and dominating colonized peoples.

But abandoning the one-society-one-culture model does not mean that the concept of culture needs to be discarded. Many of the anthropologists who reject that model prefer to think of culture as the sum total of all the customs and practices humans have ever produced. They point out that, with the increasing speed and density of communication and travel, nobody anywhere on the face of the earth is isolated from the major flows of information and activity present in our contemporary world. Fast food, rock music, and computers have a worldwide appeal. Because we are a species that needs to learn how to survive and are willing to learn new things from others, people everywhere now seem to be involved in stitching together their own patchwork of beliefs and practices from both local traditions and the wide range of global culture locally available. In situations like this, many contemporary anthropologists argue that what counts as anyone's culture is "up for grabs."

And yet those processes that turn culture into something individuals put together on their own are frequently countered by another process in which groups defend a uniform and closed view of their own culture in the face of potential inundation by global culture. Thus, much like some early anthropologists, contemporary activists in movements of ethnic solidarity defend a monolithic, internally harmonious view of their own culture against "outside" forces claiming to know what is best for them. Such a defense, however, is not without its own paradoxes. For example, in order to present the image of a united front, ethnic activists must downplay the same kinds of internal divisions and disagreements that anthropologists have been criticized for ignoring in traditional ethnographies that emphasize cultural uniformity. Activists may be fully aware of this paradox but still believe that it is justified for political reasons.

At the same time, some individuals defend their right to pick and choose from global culture the customs they want to follow and resist attempts by other members of groups to which they belong to police their beliefs and behavior. More than that, they may challenge those who criticize them for incorporating borrowed cultural practices alongside those they have inherited, asserting that theirs is a living cultural tradition and all living cultural traditions will sometimes change in this way. Put another way, **cultural hybridization**—the mixing and reconfiguring of elements from different cultural traditions—is acknowledged and even celebrated those who creatively recombine local cultural features with features from elsewhere regularly insist that the end result need not be "Westernization" or "Americanization" of their own cultures; rather, they speak of the "Africanization" or "Botswanization" or "Ju/'hoansization"—that is, the **indigenization**—of cultural features that may have originated in the West or in America but have been adopted by local people for local purposes. Because these outside cultural elements are chosen by insiders rather than imposed by outsiders, they are seen to enrich, rather than to destroy or replace, the cultural traditions into which they are being integrated. Prior to the end of the twentieth century, for example, literacy may not have been part of the cultural heritage of southern African foragers like the Ju/'hoansi. But many contemporary Ju/'hoansi who have learned to read and write and transcribe their own language view these as positive changes that strengthen their ongoing, developing cultural tradition. Picking up on these developments, some anthropologists are paying renewed attention to the kinds of cultural borrowing highlighted by the Boasians a century ago, but with a twist. In the contemporary context, anthropologists take for granted that all living cultural traditions are dynamic and open to change. As a result, they draw attention to the deliberation and choice exercised by members of these societies who selectively adopt elements of other cultures, not as a way of rejecting their own tradition for an alien alternative, but in order to reaffirm and strengthen their own evolving cultural identity.

2.8 Culture: A Contemporary Consensus

If there is a contemporary anthropological consensus about the nature of culture, it would seem to involve at least the four following propositions. First, nobody questions that culture is learned, not genetically programmed. Second, many anthropologists would argue that the kind of culture that is learned (and the way it is learned) is never innocent but is always shaped by power relations of some kind. Third, power relations and cultural forms that are global in scope have penetrated local communities and local cultures; the ultimate consequences for anybody's culture are still to be assessed. But fourth, it is incorrect to assume that the penetration of local communities by global culture dooms all local cultural traditions to extinction. On the contrary, local societies can and do indigenize cultural elements that arrive from elsewhere, regularly subverting their homogenizing or "Westernizing" potential and putting them to work in ways that preserve and enhance local goals and interests.

For Further Reading

IDEAS OF CULTURE

Bohannan 1995; Fox and King 2002; Gamst and Norbeck 1976

CONTEMPORARY CRITIQUES

Anderson 1983; Clifford 1988; Hannerz 1996; Marcus and Fischer 1986

THE CONCEPT OF RACE

Contemporary Issues Forum 1998

APE CULTURE

Savage-Rumbaugh et al. 1986

3

Language

The key terms and concepts covered in this chapter, in the order in which they appear:

language
linguistics
anthropological
   linguistics
linguistic
   anthropology

protolanguage
language family

ethnolinguistics

diachronic
synchronic
historical linguistics

grammar
paralanguage
kinesics
code
openness
phonology

phonemes
phonetics
morpheme
morphology

syntagmatic
form class
paradigmatic
frame substitution
syntax
surface structure
deep structure

semantics
linguistic competence
linguistic
   performance
communicative
   competence
Sapir-Whorf hypothesis
ethnosemantics
ethnoscience

etic
emic

speech community
regional dialects
social dialects
registers

sociolinguistics
verbal repertoire
code-switching
diglossia

discourse

pragmatics
ethnopragmatics

pidgin
creole
language ideology
linguistic nationalism

Human beings, alone among all living species, rely on spoken language to communicate with one another. This fact has puzzled and intrigued people in all societies, has played an important role in religious and philosophical reflections on the human condition, and has been a central focus of attention in anthropology from the very beginning. Trying to define language in a clear and unambiguous way, however, has proved surprisingly difficult. Today, most anthropologists would probably agree, minimally, that **language** is a system of arbitrary vocal symbols that human beings use to encode their experience of the world and to communicate with one another. The scholarly discipline that pursues a scientific study of language is called **linguistics.** The terms **anthropological linguistics** and **linguistic anthropology** have been used by anthropologists to refer to the study of language in cultural context.

3.1 Studying Language: A Historical Sketch

The study of language was central to early anthropology because it was a dimension of culture that was easy to observe and study in detail. For example, languages (like the cultures in which they are embedded) show tremendous variation, both over time and across space. The European study of systematic linguistic change over time is usually said to have begun with the work of the British scholar Sir William Jones (1746–94), who studied Sanskrit in India. He pointed out in 1786 that Sanskrit, classical Greek, Latin, and more recent European languages shared numerous similarities, suggesting that they may have all diverged from a common ancestral language, or **protolanguage,** that came to be called *Indo-European.* All languages believed to have descended from a common ancestral language are said to belong to the same **language family.** By 1822, the German scholar Jakob Grimm (of fairy tale fame; 1785–1863) was able to show that regular changes in speech sounds could be traced over succeeding generations of speakers of a single language or among speakers of related languages as they diverged.

In the twentieth century, linguistic anthropologists have been interested in the ways that linguistic change often is triggered by unpredictable and unforeseen cultural and historical events, rather than being generated solely within language itself. The long-standing anthropological focus on the relation between language and culture is sometimes referred to as **ethnolinguistics.**

A major shift in the scholarly approach to language study occurred early in the twentieth century, when scholars turned their attention from studies of language that were **diachronic** (concerned with change over time) to studies of language that were **synchronic** (concerned with the patterns present in a particular language at a particular point in time). The terms *synchronic* and *diachronic* were invented early in the twentieth century by the Swiss scholar Ferdinand de Saussure (1857–1913), one of the architects of this transformation. And from Saussure's time onward, scholars involved in synchronic language studies became known as *linguists*—distinct from *philologists,* who retained a focus on reconstructing linguistic divergence, primarily from written texts. Interest in language history did not disappear, but, influenced by the orientation and practices of scholars like Saussure, it became known as **historical linguistics.** Finally, followers of Saussure called themselves *descriptive* linguists, since their goal was to describe the rules that governed language as people actually spoke it; they contrasted this goal with that of old-fashioned *prescriptive* grammarians, who saw their job as correcting ordinary speech to make it conform to some ideal literary model of proper grammatical usage.

As noted previously, defining language has always been difficult, primarily because it has so many dimensions to which attention might be directed. First, people frequently communicate successfully with one another without using language. Second, people can use language to communicate without actually speaking (they can use gestures or exchange written messages, for example). Linguists traditionally have focused on spoken language, showing how human speech sounds can be grouped into recurring sequences, often called *words,* which are combined into longer utterances according to specific rules. The elements of language and rules for combining words are generally referred to as **grammar.** But much besides grammar is associated with spoken language, such as the various qualities with which we utter our words (volume, pitch, emphasis, speed, and so forth), which linguists call **paralanguage.**

Moreover, grammar and paralanguage do not contain all the meaning we convey when we speak; meaning is also carried by such things as our postures, our facial expressions, and our accompanying gestures. These phenomena, which are sometimes called *body language,* have been studied by anthropologists using a special system of notation called **kinesics.** In addition, we often choose our words carefully, depending on the person we are addressing or the setting in which we are speaking, which highlights the important role context plays in shaping the meaning of our utterances. Finally, as the philologists showed, the language our grandparents (or more distant ancestors) used often differs markedly from the language we use today. So how much of all this should we take into consideration when we study language?

To answer this question, Saussure made an important distinction between what came out of people's mouths when they spoke (which he called *parole*) and the underlying rules that generated that speech (which he called *langue*). In his view, parole varied from speaker to speaker, reflecting each individual's idiosyncratic interests and stylistic preferences, whereas langue referred to the stable, universal rules that all speakers observed. Saussure wanted to define language in a way that would permit him to study it scientifically. Therefore, he recommended paying attention only to the most systematic and unvarying elements of language—that is, to langue, which corresponds to what other linguists call the linguistic **code** or grammar. Saussure argued that langue (the code or grammar shared by all speakers) was a self-contained system and that the significance of any element in the system (such as sounds or words) depended on its relationship with other elements in the system, rather than on some feature of the outside world.

Saussure's approach to language had at least two major consequences. First, it gave linguists a clear-cut object of study, whose intricate details they could probe without distraction; the end result was the birth of the independent discipline of linguistics, which continues this investigation today. Second, it drew attention to the *arbitrariness* of the relationship between the sounds (or words) of language, the meanings they stood for, and the objects in the world to which they referred. Saussure showed convincingly that the sounds of language, by themselves, carried no inherent meaning: a flat-topped piece of furniture with four legs called "table" in English is called "mesa" in Spanish. Subsequent anthropological linguists, like Charles Hockett, would argue that the arbitrariness of the link between sound and meaning in human language was one of a number of related *design features* of language. Furthermore, they would argue that this arbitrariness was a consequence of the design feature Hockett called **openness,** the possibility of using the linguistic code to create totally new combinations of elements in order to articulate meanings never before uttered.

Along with Saussure, Franz Boas often is credited with contributing to the birth of modern linguistics and linguistic anthropology. His focus on language developed as he sought a way of studying culture in a detailed and nuanced way. It seemed clear to him, as it did to other ethnographers of his generation, like Bronislaw Malinowski, that a profound understanding of another culture could not be gained unless the ethnographer knew the language used by members of that culture to articulate their understandings of the world and of themselves. Boas's own observations about language, based on his field experiences, also drew attention to the codelike fashion in which languages were organized.

3.2 The Building Blocks of Language

One tradition of linguistic scholarship that can be traced back to the influence of Boas and Saussure focused on linguistic codes themselves. Early linguists were especially interested in the sound patterns peculiar to particular languages, an area of linguistics that came to be called **phonology.** An important early discovery was that every language has a restricted set of sounds that are recognized by all native speakers and that can be combined according to rules to form all the words of the language. These minimal units of sound recognized by speakers of a particular language, called **phonemes,** are contrasted with the much larger range of speech sounds human beings are theoretically capable of producing and hearing, the scientific study of which is called **phonetics.**

Many early linguists analyzed the sets of phonemes characteristic of particular languages. They were also interested in minimal units of meaning in languages. Although in languages like English such units often correspond to *words,* comparative work in very different languages, such as those of indigenous Americans, demonstrated that not all languages are put together the way English is. And so linguists adopted a new term, **morpheme,** to refer to the minimal unit of meaning in a language and studied the rules for combining morphemes in a branch of linguistics known as **morphology.**

In the first half of the twentieth century, linguists thought of grammar as having two kinds of elements, phonemes and morphemes, each with its own particular set of rules for combination. Following Saussure, these linguists used two procedures to identify rules for combining morphemes. Working with native speakers, they collected texts in the language being studied and examined them for regularities. Saussure conceived of these regularities as falling along two intersecting axes, one vertical and one horizontal. The horizontal, or **syntagmatic,** axis was used to plot the linearity of speech, and many utterances were compared to isolate those grammatical units (traditionally called *parts of speech*) that worked the same way in all utterances. Once the grammatical units had been identified, linguists could then work out which morphemes in the language functioned as which grammatical units. All the morphemes that could substitute for one another at a particular point in the syntagmatic sequence (or sentence) were said to belong to the same **form class** and could be arranged along a vertical, or **paradigmatic,** axis. By leaving a space in the syntagmatic sequence where that form class normally occurred and by asking native speakers of the language which morphemes might properly fill that space, linguists could isolate all the members of a particular form class, a procedure called **frame substitution.** For example, in English, the utterance "The tourist _____ along the sidewalk" is a syntagmatic substitution frame, and all the English words that fit into the empty slot (e.g., *walked, ran,* or *strolled*) belong to the same form class—that is, verbs. All the verbs (including these three) that correctly fill the empty slot of this substitution frame can be aligned along a vertical paradigmatic axis as options that may be grammatically substituted for one another as the speaker chooses.

Working out the syntagmatic structure characteristic of a particular language and using that structure to create substitution frames for eliciting the members of paradigmatic form classes provided a powerful way for descriptive linguists to highlight key features of any language's grammar. But phonological and morphological rules alone could not account for the features of all grammatical sentences, a point forcefully made in 1957 by Noam Chomsky. Chomsky argued that sentences were themselves units of grammatical structure, and he proposed that linguists begin to study **syntax,** the structure of sentences. Chomsky suggested that syntactic relationships could be explained if it were recognized that sentences could be analyzed at two levels: in terms of surface structure and deep structure. **Surface structure** was what came out of people's mouths when they spoke and was the level of structure traditionally studied by descriptive linguists. However, surface structure exhibited a number of peculiarities that could not be explained in terms of the linear sequence of grammatical units and substitutions.

For example, Chomsky observed that native speakers of English were convinced that sentences like "A woman won the contest" and "The contest was won by a woman" were related to one another; grammarians might say they were two versions of a single sentence, the first in active voice and the second in passive voice. Chomsky's syntactic theory built on this intuition of relatedness by claiming that both surface versions of the sentence shared the same **deep structure** and that the passive surface structure was the outcome of the application of a syntactic rule (called the *passive transformation rule*) to the underlying deep syntactic structure of the sentence.

Chomsky later argued that any grammar ought to be a theory of a language, and since all languages were used to convey meanings, every grammar ought to contain a component concerned with how that language dealt with meaning. This justified attention to **semantics,** or the study of meaning, a dimension of language that traditionally had been viewed as too vague and variable to serve as an object of linguistic investigation. The fields of formal syntax and semantics have developed in different directions since the 1960s, but all those developments have roots in the initial orientations provided by Chomsky.

When Chomsky distinguished between deep structure and surface structure, he was building on Saussure's distinction between langue and parole. Like langue, deep structure referred to the stable, unvarying rules of grammar observed by all native speakers of a language; by contrast, like parole, surface structure supposedly varied from speaker to speaker in an unpredictable way. Chomsky also observed that people's actual utterances often were full of errors, hesitations, and false starts that might be the result of physical factors such as sleepiness and thus did not truly represent their underlying grammatical knowledge. And so Chomsky further distinguished between **linguistic competence** (the underlying knowledge of grammatical rules encoded in the brains of all fluent speakers of a language) and **linguistic performance** (the actual things people said, which for the reasons mentioned, might not reflect their actual linguistic competence). Much like Saussure, Chomsky thought linguists should ignore linguistic performance and try to develop theories of linguistic competence.

3.3 Language and Culture

Chomsky's influence in linguistics was nothing short of revolutionary, and it accentuated a split between those linguists who focused on the code alone and other students of language who remained concerned with how speakers used the code in different cultural and social settings. The anthropological linguist Dell Hymes summarized the objections of this latter group when he compared Chomsky's notion of linguistic competence to his own concept of **communicative competence.** Chomsky's focus on the linguistic code led him to define linguistic competence in terms of a speaker's knowledge of the difference between grammatical and ungrammatical sentences in a language.

But Hymes pointed out that successful use of language to communicate with other people requires far more than just grammatical knowledge. It requires speakers to choose vocabulary and topics of speech that are suitable to different audiences in different social settings. For example, fluent speakers of a language might show linguistic competence in their use of casual, grammatically correct linguistic forms in their conversations with friends. But they would betray a colossal lack of communicative competence if they used the same forms when introducing a visiting foreign dignitary in a formal public setting. To identify what constitutes communicative competence, researchers must pay attention to parole, to surface structure, and to actual linguistic performance. According to anthropological linguists like Hymes, these phenomena are not wholly idiosyncratic but show far more culturally shaped regularity than the followers of Saussure or Chomsky have ever acknowledged.

At midcentury, Hymes represented a second tradition of scholarship on language that could be traced back to Boas. Practitioners in this tradition continued to see the study of a particular linguistic code primarily as a means to a more profound understanding of culture, rather than as an end in itself. After Boas, in the 1920s and 1930s, the best-known proponents of this approach were Edward Sapir and Benjamin Whorf. Both were struck by the ways in which linguistic form and cultural meaning shaped each other, and each in his own way tried to characterize that relationship. Whorf's analyses of the grammatical codes of indigenous North American languages like Hopi attracted attention (and eventual notoriety) both within and outside anthropology. In several controversial articles, he seemed to be claiming that every language had a unique, self-contained grammar that strongly influenced the thought patterns and cultural practices of its speakers.

After World War II, when both Sapir and Whorf were dead, other anthropologists, linguists, and psychologists tried to devise experiments that would test the influence of language on culture and thought. These researchers advanced what they called the **Sapir-Whorf hypothesis:** the claim that the culture and thought patterns of people were strongly influenced by the language they spoke. Immediately, however, the researchers faced a familiar problem: How do you define "language" and "culture" and "thought" with sufficient rigor so that it becomes possible to measure the degree to which one does or does not influence the other(s)? In practice, "language" was equated with "grammatical code," and tests were devised to measure whether speakers whose grammars possessed (or lacked) certain grammatical structures were correspondingly forced to perceive (or prevented from perceiving) those structures when they looked at the world around them. For example, does an absence of grammatical marking on verbs for past, present, and future tense mean that speakers of that language cannot perceive the passage of time? Or, if a language has only three terms for basic colors (e.g., *black, white,* and *red*), does this mean that speakers of that language cannot tell the difference between the colors an English speaker identifies as *green* and *blue*?

Actual research showed that questions posed in this fashion were far too simplistic, both about grammars and about human perception. Any language is always a part of some culture—that is, it is learned, not innate, and it is intimately interrelated with all cultural practices in which its speakers engage—and thinking cannot easily be distinguished from the linguistic and cultural activity in which it is regularly involved. Thus, it is virtually impossible to tease language, culture, and thought apart, let alone to figure out the direction of the causal arrows that supposedly link them to one another. By the early 1960s, most anthropological linguists had concluded that there was no solid evidence that grammatical features of particular languages *determined* thought patterns or cultural practices. The fact that many people throughout the world were bi- or multilingual, successfully communicating with speakers of languages with sometimes very different grammatical codes (e.g., Hopi and English), called into question the supposition that people typically were monolingual—that is, they knew or spoke fluently only one language from birth to death.

In the 1950s and 1960s, a number of anthropologists developed a research program known as **ethnosemantics** or **ethnoscience** that aimed for greater accuracy and sophistication. As the labels suggest, their goal was to discover the systems of linguistic meaning and classification developed by people in their own languages and used in their own cultures. Borrowing the linguistic contrast between phonetic and phonemic studies of the sounds of language, ethnoscientists explicitly contrasted **etic** categories devised by outside researchers and **emic** categories devised by native speaker-informants. Their goal was to describe as faithfully as possible the emic categories used by informants in their own language, and so they encouraged a rigorous set of research practices involving substitution frames in order to protect their data from etic contamination.

For all their achievements, however, ethnoscientists continued to work with a theoretical model of language and culture in which researchers and informants were understood to belong to mutually exclusive monolingual and monocultural worlds. It was not that anthropologists failed to recognize the inaccuracy of the model. Fieldwork and study had made many of them bi- or multilingual and bi- or multicultural, and a history of colonial conquest followed by linguistic and cultural imperialism had often made many of their informants bi- or multicultural and bi- or multilingual as well.

3.4 Language and Society

The necessity of taking this bi- and multilingualism/culturalism into theoretical account prompted Hymes to urge his colleagues to move beyond the study of individual languages to the study of speech communities. A **speech community** is any concrete community of individuals who regularly interact verbally with one another. It might be a village or a neighborhood or a city; today it might include "virtual communities" created by Internet chat rooms or e-mail. Hymes pointed out that if you delimit a speech community and then do an inventory of all the different kinds of language used by members of that community, you will quickly discover not merely one version of one language in use, but rather a variety of forms of one language (and sometimes more than one language) in use. Some varieties will be **regional dialects:** versions of a particular language associated with particular geographical settings, such as the Appalachian versus Texan versus New England dialects of North American English. Some will be **social dialects:** versions of a particular language associated with particular social groups, such as the "Cockney" working-class dialect of London as contrasted with the "BBC English" of the educated British upper middle class. Still others will be social **registers:** versions of a particular language associated with particular social settings, such as a court of law or an elementary school playground or a house of religious worship. Every member of the speech community may not be able to converse fluently in all the varieties represented in the community, but all members will ordinarily have control of several varieties, each of which will be called for in a different set of circumstances.

This approach developed in anthropological linguistics by Hymes was supported by similar approaches developed in sociolinguistics by sociologists such as John Gumperz. **Sociolinguistics** is usually defined as the study of the relationship between language and society. Traditionally, it has been interested in correlations between social variation (e.g., class or ethnic stratification) and linguistic variation (e.g., in the form of regional or social dialects), as well as correlations between particular social settings and linguistic registers. Together, Gumperz and Hymes developed analytic concepts that meshed in interesting ways. For example, if every speech community is characterized by a number of different language varieties, then every member of that speech community can be described in terms of her or his **verbal repertoire:** the sum total of verbal varieties a particular individual has mastered.

Gumperz and others were able to show that the number and nature of the varieties within an individual's verbal repertoire not only offer a good set of indicators as to that individual's social identity and status but also are a good predictor of that individual's probable success in interacting verbally with speakers of different identities and statuses. Gumperz described verbal repertoires as sets of weapons that one could deploy in verbal (and social) struggles with others. Like soldiers with a range of weapons, people with more varieties in their repertoires could attain objectives in a range of social situations. They could switch from one variety (or code) to another as the situation demanded, a phenomenon called

code-switching. Some sociolinguists have described speech communities in which everyone was fluent in two codes (either two dialects of a single language or two different languages), a phenomenon described as **diglossia.** Where diglossia occurs, speakers generally use each code in mutually exclusive settings (e.g., one at home and the other at school), switching back and forth between codes as the situation demands. One insight provided by studies of verbal repertoires is that speakers with fewer codes at their command are both socially and verbally limited in their interactions with others.

Hymes's suggestion that anthropological linguistics should focus on how people develop communicative competence in speech communities characterized by multiple codes stimulated research in a number of related areas. One was the comparative study of childhood acquisition of communicative competence, which involved mastering not only grammatical rules but also rules for appropriate use. Another was the study of classifications of forms of talk in specific cultures and examination of the various contexts in which these forms were used. A third was the study of culture-specific verbal performances like storytelling, in which the codes known by the storyteller and her or his listeners were resources upon which the storyteller could draw in exercising individual artistic agency.

Studies of verbal performance emphasized all those features of language that formal linguists ignored, such as figurative language, wordplay, deliberate rule-breaking and code-switching to achieve certain rhetorical effects. Anthropological linguists carrying out cross-cultural research on verbal performance were able to show that, however central the rules of grammar remain for effective linguistic communication, in real life, when people struggle to defend their interests using whatever tools are available, rules of grammar and rules of use can be bent or broken to achieve other communicative effects. And if rules can be broken, perhaps they are as much a product of other social and cultural communication as they are shapers of that communication.

The focus on multiple linguistic varieties present in all speech communities and on rules for their appropriate use inevitably drew attention to the fact that not all varieties were accorded equal respect and that most linguists who talk about "the" grammar of language X ordinarily had in mind only one high-prestige variety of language X. If they were, like Chomsky, educated linguists studying their own native language, the grammar in question was likely to be that language's literary standard, such as Standard English. And since native-speaker linguists were told to trust their own intuitions in deciding whether certain usages were "grammatical," it became increasingly clear that, in practice, "linguistic competence" meant competence in the standard variety. Despite linguists' assertions that their work was descriptive, not prescriptive, nonstandard varieties inevitably appeared ungrammatical with respect to the standard, making those varieties (and, by extension, their speakers) look defective.

3.5 Discourse

Such judgments looked suspiciously like the old-fashioned opinions of prescriptive grammarians. From the point of view of linguistic anthropologists, they reflected sociocultural evaluations of speakers associated with those linguistic varieties, evaluations that inevitably reflected the unequal power relations between evaluators and those being evaluated. Linguistic anthropologists began to focus explicitly on the way linguistic usage and evaluations of linguistic usage were shaped by power struggles between various subgroups within a society. They emphasized that rules of "grammaticality" or "cultural acceptability" often are based on linguistic forms preferred by powerful groups in society. As a result, disadvantaged groups may choose to express resistance against a given power structure by refusing to use the linguistic forms endorsed by the powerful. Some linguistic anthropologists have shown how this takes place in the course of public and private performances of different culturally recognized forms of **discourse** (talk), such as storytelling, oratory, popular theater, and traditional forms of poetic expression (e.g., funeral laments). Such work made very clear that those who engage in particular forms of discourse are not forced by rules of grammar or culture to say some things rather than others. Quite the opposite: they struggle to use the rules of grammar and culture as *resources* to convey their own, often subversive, messages to their audiences.

The focus of scholars like Hymes and Gumperz on speech communities whose members each possessed verbal repertoires consisting of multiple language varieties often was seen as a way of displaying the complexity and coordination of cultural and linguistic variation within a society. It also highlighted the sophistication with which people regularly matched appropriate forms of discourse to appropriate audiences or settings. Following the rise of postmodern critique in anthropology in the 1980s, however, attention began to shift to the prisonlike rules that aimed to constrain people's behavior and speech within particular limits and to the struggles in which people engaged to resist such limitation. In linguistic anthropology, this reorientation was assisted by the adoption of the concepts and approach of a group of Russian literary and linguistic scholars associated with Mikhail Bakhtin, whose key texts had recently been translated into English. Hymes and Gumperz's image of speech communities whose members made use of multiple varieties of languages was echoed in Bakhtin's concept of *heteroglossia*, or "many-voicedness," among speakers in a society. The emphasis of Bakhtin's discussion, however, was on how different groups of speakers, each rooted in their own particular (and unequal) positions within society, struggle for control of public discourse.

Linguistic anthropologists influenced by Bakhtin were particularly interested in the discourse of low-status groups that could not safely challenge those who dominated them in an open fashion. Bakhtin's concept of *double-voiced discourse* proved very useful, for it emphasized that the "same" words or expressions can mean different things to different speakers who use them in different contexts. Bakhtin was especially interested in the ironic use of language, in which listeners understand that words mean the opposite of what they ordinarily signify because of the context in which they are uttered, and in parodic language, in which officially acceptable language is exaggerated or mimicked with the intention of poking fun. Such forms of double-voiced discourse allow speakers to keep their actual words within acceptable grammatical and cultural boundaries, while elements of the context within which the words are spoken imparts to them a meaning quite different from their formal denotations. Officially, order is upheld, but unofficially, it is held up to ridicule or critique.

To focus on subversive forms of talk like double-voiced discourse is to emphasize the way in which language in cultural contexts of use twists and manipulates the supposedly unvarying and stable elements of formal grammar. The demonstration was so powerful that even formal linguists, working in the Chomskian tradition, had to take notice of language in use. They began to include a **pragmatics** component in their formal grammars, which purported to catalogue universal rules of use obeyed by all speakers of all languages who wanted to communicate successfully with others. Linguistic anthropologists quickly pointed out, however, that the kinds of rules proposed by formal pragmatics betrayed the linguists' assumption that the primary purpose of linguistic communication was to convey faithfully from speaker to hearer factual information about the world. This communication, moreover, was assumed to take place in a conversational setting between disinterested parties of equal social status. (Table 3.1 lists the components of formal linguistic analysis.)

Communication sometimes does involve the transmission of information between equals. Linguistic anthropologists were able to show, however, that such communication is only a small, and highly idealized, part of what normally goes on when real people with differential linguistic and cultural knowledge, living in real societies characterized by social inequality, try to communicate

TABLE 3.1 Components of Formal Linguistic Analysis

COMPONENT	APPLIES TO
Phonology	Phonemes/sound patterns
Morphology	Morphemes/word formation
Syntax	Sentence structure
Semantics	Meaning
Pragmatics	Language in use

with one another. As a result, linguistic anthropologists argue that every analysis of language use in cultural context must include information from ethnopragmatics. **Ethnopragmatics** is the study of the culturally and politically inflected rules of use that shape particular acts of speech communication among particular speakers and audiences, in the specific cultural settings in which they regularly occur. Put another way, the "universal" rules of formal pragmatics turn out to be so idealized and culture-bound that they are of little help when we try to understand what is going on in most verbal interactions in most cultural settings in most societies.

3.6 Language Contact and Change

Considering linguistic interaction within a context of struggle among speakers with unequal access to valued resources in a society has also refreshed our understanding of languages called pidgins and creoles. A **pidgin** language traditionally has been defined as a reduced language with a simplified grammar and vocabulary that develops when speakers of mutually unintelligible languages come into regular contact and so are forced to communicate with one another. Those who speak pidgins are native speakers of other, fully developed languages and use pidgins only in restricted settings with those who do not speak their native language; for this reason, pidgins are said to have no native speakers. However, when pidgins persist over two or more generations, they often begin to change. Specifically, their grammar sometimes becomes more complex, their vocabularies increase, they are used in a wider variety of social settings, and children learn them as first languages. When this happens, according to the traditional view, the pidgin has developed into a **creole** and functions just like any other natural human language.

For a long time, it was thought that the evolution from pidgin to creole was regular and inevitable, but it has become increasingly clear that pidgins and creoles can persist indefinitely along with other language varieties in the speech communities in which they are found. That is, speakers of pidgins also live in speech communities where different linguistic varieties have specialized uses. Moreover, such communities are regularly shaped by unequal power relations, which means that different varieties enjoy different levels of prestige and that those with more prestigious varieties in their verbal repertoires enjoy decided political and social advantages. Linguistic anthropologists and sociolinguists have pointed out that the most recent wave of pidginization followed European colonization throughout the world. They note further that pidgins and creoles developed under colonial (and postcolonial) political regimes in which mastery of the written language of the colonizer (e.g., English, French, or Dutch) has been a prerequisite for economic and social mobility. Thus, groups in the society that have been deprived of the opportunity to become literate in the colonizer's (or nation-state's) official "standard" language variety are also deprived of access to most of the wealth, power, and prestige in society.

Such a situation helps explain the sometimes violent struggles that occur in contemporary nation-states, especially in those that were once European colonies, about which language or languages will be the "official" language of schooling and of government. If people live in a society whose members speak a number of different languages and language varieties and if access to the most highly valued resources in society depends on fluency or literacy in only one official language, then it is easy to see that speakers of each language group will want their own language to be the official language.

Debates over "official" languages illustrate the operation of **language ideology:** the beliefs and practices about language that are linked to struggles between social groups with different interests, and which are regularly revealed in what people say and how they say it. The study of language ideology by linguistic anthropologists is central in settings with a history of colonization. Yet even when most members of a society are fluent or literate in the official language, they may be vigilant in policing the "purity" of that language, trying to eliminate linguistic borrowing from other languages. For example, when capitalist business practices and technology, originally developed in European languages, are imported into societies whose members do not speak a European language, the temptation is strong simply to borrow the European vocabulary and expressions for these practices and objects, rather than inventing new terms in the local language. The temptation is even stronger if printed instructional materials in the European language are also imported, for few poor countries on the periphery of the capitalist global economy have the resources to translate these materials into the languages of the local population. However, the influx of imported vocabulary may well be seen as a form of linguistic colonization. And like political colonization in the past, it is often resisted by **linguistic nationalism:** official, sometimes militant, efforts to proscribe the use of foreign terms and to promote the creation of alternatives in the local language.

Linguistic nationalism is hardly limited to former colonies of European powers. Citizens of European countries like France have periodically displayed linguistic nationalism when they protest the growing popularity among French speakers of expressions borrowed from American English. Like the citizens of former colonies, these French people fear that the influx of American English symbolizes a serious blow to the power and prestige of their own language and the nation to which its speakers belong.

For Further Reading

FORMAL LINGUISTICS

Akmajian et al. 2001

LINGUISTIC ANTHROPOLOGY

Agar 1994; Bonvillain 1993; Duranti 1997; Salzmann 1998

READINGS IN ANTHROPOLOGICAL LINGUISTICS/LINGUISTIC ANTHROPOLOGY

Blount 1995; Brenneis and Macaulay 1996; Duranti 2001

DISCOURSE

Hill and Irvine 1992; Schultz 1990

LANGUAGE IDEOLOGY

Morgan 2002; Schieffelin, Woolard, and Kroskrity 1998

4

Culture and the Individual

The key terms and concepts covered in this chapter, in the order in which they appear:

agency

cultural configurations

personality
culture-and-personality research
basic personality structure
modal personality
projective test

enculturation
child-rearing practices

ethnic psychoses

self
self-awareness
self-actualizing
independence training

dependence training
cognition

ethnoscience

schemas
prototypes

cognitive capacities
cognitive styles
global style
field-dependent
articulated style
field-independent

emotion

subjectivity
trauma
structural violence

Some fifty years ago, American anthropologist Clyde Kluckhohn (1905–68) famously observed that, in some ways, every individual is like *all other* human beings, like *some other* human beings, and like *no other* human beings. Those attributes we share with *all* other human beings we share by virtue of being members of the same biological species, with the same anatomy, physiology, and range of physical and mental capacities, including the capacity for symbolic language and culture. Those attributes we share with *some* other human beings are *cultural* similarities. The great insight of social sciences like anthropology has been that individuals do *not* reinvent for themselves from scratch totally new cultural practices based on personal preference alone. Rather, we all begin by acquiring the shared ways of speaking, acting, and interpreting experience in use among the particular group of people among whom we grow up. At the same time, even human beings who have lived their entire lives immersed in the cultural practices of the same society are never simply cookie-cutter replicas of one another. Individual members of the same family or kinship group or ethnic group are very different from one another, based not only on such factors as gender and age differences but also on personal talents and inclination. Each of us has not only a unique set of genes (identical twins excepted!) but also a unique biography, making each of us, in some ways, like no other person on earth.

4.1 From Individualism to Agency

The Western capitalist societies that produced the first anthropologists were immersed in a culture that placed unusual emphasis on individuals. Unlike most other cultures from other places or times, capitalist culture exalts individuals and encourages (or forces) them to reject ties to other people, such as relatives, that they have not freely chosen. This position, called *individualism,* is based on a view of human nature that sees individuals as the primordial "natural" units in the human world. Individuals are believed to be endowed by nature with the desire to pursue their own personal self-interest above all else. While they might decide to sacrifice some of their natural, individual liberty to create societies in which the weak are protected from the strong, social obligations are always seen as "unnatural" restrictions on "natural" individual liberty. Seventeenth-century English philosopher Thomas Hobbes (1588–1679) imagined the life of early humans in a "state of nature" along these lines, an account that anthropologist Marshall Sahlins called the *origin myth of capitalism* (see Chapter 5 for a discussion of myth).

Individualism was well entrenched in the cultures to which the first social scientists belonged, but evidence from their reading and research caused many of them to question its universality. Within the bounds of a single society or cultural group, the differences between individuals are indeed striking. However, cross-cultural comparison immediately highlights all the attributes that those same individuals have in common, when contrasted with the members of another cultural group. Indeed, the value placed on individualism in the United States or Europe is recognized as a cultural matter as soon as capitalist culture is contrasted with non-capitalist cultures from elsewhere in the world (or even from earlier periods of European history). Therefore, social scientists in capitalist societies generally have been engaged in an ongoing debate concerning the degree to which the consciousness of individual human beings is or is not dominated by the beliefs and practices they acquire as members of particular societies.

Some anthropologists have used ethnographic evidence showing the ways individuals are molded by social, cultural, and historical forces in order to criticize extreme defenses of individualism used by Western elites to justify capitalist cultural practices. North American cultural anthropologists active early in the twentieth century, like Kluckhohn, seemed caught in the middle. Fully aware of the extent to which people's desires, values, and actions are molded by cultural forces, they nevertheless felt compelled to demonstrate the ways in which individuals might rise above cultural conditioning to assert their individuality. By the end of the twentieth century, anthropologists had mostly rejected the old-fashioned, extreme contrasts between "individual free will" and social, cultural, or historical "determinism." While they remain critical of defenses of individualism that ignore culture and history, they nevertheless now widely agree that individuals are not robots programmed by their cultures to think and behave only in prescribed ways. Contemporary anthropologists use the term **agency** to refer to individuals' abilities to reflect systematically on taken-for-granted cultural practices, to imagine alternatives, and to take independent action to pursue goals of their own choosing. Unlike deterministic accounts, this view recognizes degrees of individual freedom; but unlike discussions of "free will," it accepts that people's ideas are always embedded in the cultural practices of their own time and place, which restricts in some ways both the alternatives they are able to imagine and their abilities to act freely in pursuit of those alternatives.

4.2 Culture and Personality

How did anthropological ideas about the relationship between culture and the individual develop? In North America, the earliest efforts arose as Boasian anthropologists sought a persuasive way to characterize differences between cultures. A key move was made by Ruth Benedict (1887–1948) who, in her 1934 book *Patterns of Culture*, urged her readers to think of the integrated patterns of a particular culture, or **cultural configurations**, as if they were the integrated patterns of an individual personality. This metaphor—that cultures were essentially individual personalities "writ large"—was perhaps an inevitable development in a society that exalted individualism. Indeed, Boas and his students were persuaded that psychology—the study of individual minds—held important clues for the understanding of culture.

As a result, cultural anthropologists began to look at individual personality for evidence that would reveal the unique configurations of the culture to which an individual belonged. In general, **personality** refers to ways of thinking, feeling, and acting that are unique to a specific individual and that might explain that individual's consistency of behavior over time and across a variety of social settings. Anthropologists who offered hypotheses about the factors responsible for the development, structure, and function of individual personalities shared a number of concerns with psychologists. But whereas psychologists typically studied these matters only among members of their own society, anthropologists explicitly used cross-cultural ethnographic information to assess the degree to which distinct personality configurations were regularly associated with particular cultures. In the middle decades of the twentieth century, this became known as **culture-and-personality research.**

Anthropologists of the culture-and-personality school have investigated a range of issues concerning the relationship between individuals and culture. For example, if a culture could be understood as an individual personality writ large, did this mean that the individual personalities of all those who belonged to the culture were the same? One psychological anthropologist, Abraham Kardiner, proposed that all members of a society did come to acquire what he called a **basic personality structure** in the course of individual development, as they adapted to what he called the *primary institutions* of their society. Primary institutions include established ways that members of the society organize family life (including child care and sexual expression) and economic life (how they make a living). Basic personality structures would be similar throughout a society if all members had to adapt to the same primary institutions. Kardiner also spoke, however, of *secondary institutions:* established religious or ritual practices that help individuals cope with the challenges presented by primary institutions—for example, when subsistence horticulturalists develop elaborate rainmaking rituals, which they observe every planting season, to reduce their anxieties about the disaster that would ensue if the rains failed and their crops died. Basic personality structure would change, Kardiner argued, if a people's primary institutions changed. And he predicted that larger societies with a more complex division of labor would generate a wider range of personality types than would smaller societies with more homogenous institutions.

Many critics of culture-and-personality research found even these specifications to be vague and difficult to demonstrate. Later studies attempted to gather a much richer body of data on personality traits from a wide range of sources and to use statistical analysis to interpret the results. Such studies preferred to speak not of basic personality but of **modal personality,** a "typical" personality for members of a particular society, which was revealed as the central tendency of a frequency distribution.

Debates about basic versus modal personalities highlight one of the persistent challenges of culture-and-personality research: how to gather valid information about personality characteristics. One way anthropologists tried to meet this challenge involves supplementing the usual range of anthropological fieldwork techniques with testing methods borrowed from psychology.

One technique that has been widely used in culture-and-personality research is the **projective test.** For example, the anthropologist may present informants with a series of ambiguous images or sketchy drawings and ask them to describe what they think the images or drawings represent. Because the images and drawings are deliberately vague and open to a wide variety of possible interpretations, anthropologists assume that subjects will *project* their own personalities into the images; that is, they will interpret the images in a way that reveals their own personality traits and psychological preoccupations. If culture truly is a prime shaper of individual personality, then subjects from the same culture should produce very similar results on the same projective test. Unfortunately, experience has shown that responses to projective tests, like the images used in the tests, are not always easy to interpret. Making sense of them requires considerable additional information about the culture of the subjects and about the subjects themselves, including their understanding of the purpose of the test-taking situation.

4.3 Enculturation

Some anthropologists doing culture-and-personality research have asked questions about how individual personalities develop as children mature into adults. Unlike most conventional psychologists, however, anthropologists do not automatically assume that personality development is identical in all human societies. For example, Margaret Mead, another student of Boas, explicitly addressed this issue in her first important book, *Coming of Age in Samoa,* published in 1928. Mead's work in Samoa focused on **enculturation:** the social processes through which children come to adopt the ways of thinking, feeling, and behaving considered appropriate for adults in their culture. Mead argued that the stressful period of adolescence experienced by maturing children in Western industrial societies was neither universal nor inevitable. She used ethnographic data to show that children growing up in Samoan culture developed a different set of personality traits and experienced little or no adolescent stress.

A generation of cultural anthropologists in North America followed Mead's example, carrying out research on enculturation processes in a wide range of different societies. Their work was given a strengthened theoretical framework when some anthropologists, including Mead herself, began to consider the ideas of Sigmund Freud (1856–1939). Freud offered a framework of psychological stages of development (somewhat different for males and for females) through which every child supposedly passed on the way to adulthood. He further argued that children's success or failure in passing through these stages would determine their degree of mental health in adulthood, explaining a variety of adult psychological disturbances in terms of an individual's lack of success at one or another stage. The resulting psychological damage ranged from fairly mild *neuroses* to extremely serious *psychoses,* which were so debilitating that individuals appeared to lose touch with reality and were unable to establish satisfying lives with others in society.

Freud's emphasis on the importance of individual experience in early childhood for the formation of adult personality suggested new ways to conceptualize enculturation. Anthropologists who adopted a Freudian orientation focused, as he did, on the shaping of children's emotional development as they negotiated relationships with their parents in the first three years of life. But they also tested the claims of Freudian psychology against ethnographic evidence in a wide range of cultures. After all, Freud's theories were based on his experiences with late-nineteenth-century middle-class Viennese patients with psychological disturbances of one kind or another. Anthropologists wanted to determine how much of Freudian psychology was culture-bound and how much might be universally valid in all human societies.

Because Freud stressed the importance of young children's experiences in their families, psychological anthropologists began to pay attention to **child-rearing practices:** the ways in which adults (especially parents) in a particular culture tried to shape children's behavior to bring it in line with culture-specific ideals of appropriateness. They would study, for example, the way in which infants were handled: Were they allowed to move their arms and legs freely, or were they tightly swaddled for several months? Could such treatment be shown to have consequences for the child's later personality development? Like Freud, these psychological anthropologists focused on key events such as the weaning of nursing babies from the breast or the teaching of bowel and bladder control (i.e., toilet training). Freud considered emotionally fraught power struggles in these areas to be inevitable and frequently traumatic for children. Thus, anthropologists were interested in what the personality consequences for children might be in cultures that, for example, allowed children to nurse until 3 or 4 years of age or in which indoor toilets and Western sanitation practices were absent.

Cross-cultural child-rearing studies produced a wealth of information about the different ways in which children were enculturated to become successful adults in different cultures. This information convinced many anthropologists that Freud's ideas were indeed heavily influenced by the middle-class, patriarchal, Viennese culture in which they had been formed. Many anthropologists concluded that the repressive values and practices of that culture (particularly its restrictions on females) did more to explain the neuroses and psychoses Freud identified than did his supposedly universal series of developmental stages. Not only were such maladjustments absent in cultures with different values and practices, but sometimes the "maladjusted" behavior was viewed positively. For example, individuals who would be labeled psychotic by a Freudian because they claimed to hear the voices of invisible beings or to converse with the dead have been given high status in many societies as *shamans,* a particular kind of religious practitioner and curer (see Chapter 5 for details on shamans). In addition, ethnographers have encountered forms of beliefs and behavior in many non-Western societies that are considered "abnormal" by members of those societies but are found in no other societies and often do not appear on the diagnostic lists of medically recognized psychological disorders that have been developed by Western psychology and psychiatry. These culture-bound syndromes have been called **ethnic psychoses:** mental and emotional behaviors and experiences that are viewed as unusual and disturbing to the members of particular ethnic groups. Examples include such disorders as the so-called arctic hysterias recognized by a number of peoples living in circumpolar latitudes and anorexia nervosa, the eating disorder restricted to Western industrial societies in which individuals (mostly young women) believe they are too fat, refuse to eat, and sometimes die as a result.

Among other things, this focus on child-rearing practices promised to shed light on larger cultural issues related to the particular role accorded individualism in Western capitalist societies. The prototype of successful individuals in these societies is the *entrepreneur;* those individuals who are particularly adept in finding ways to pursue their own individual self-interest. Such entrepreneurs are admired for their ability to break with tradition, especially when they generate new ideas and new wealth by means of capitalist business practices. Many people, both in Western societies and elsewhere, believed that all societies that wanted to prosper and become "modern" would have to produce similar kinds of individuals, but such personality types were far more common in the West. Anthropologists and others wondered if there was something about the way children were enculturated in the United States and Europe that imparted to them the skills and motivation to become entrepreneurs.

4.4 The Self

Strong individualists, for example, seemed to regard themselves as distinct and unique objects, separate from other things and individuals in their society. This has been called a person's sense of **self.** Successful individualists, however, also possess a high degree of **self-awareness.** That is, they can realistically assess their likes, dislikes, strengths, and weaknesses, as well as the degree to which their goals do or do not mesh with those of other people and institutions. They are able and willing to pursue personal goals that correspond to their unique talents and opportunities, even in the face of social opposition. To use the expression popularized by Abraham Kardiner, a key figure in culture-and-personality research around the years of World War II, such individuals are **self-actualizing.** For many observers, self-actualizing individuals, each seeking to develop as fully as possible a unique set of gifts in pursuit of unique personal goals, had made Western nations rich and powerful. Did Western child-rearing practices hold the key?

Comparative work by a number of anthropologists suggested that, indeed, the way children were reared affected their willingness and ability to self-actualize. Anthropologists came to distinguish two broad kinds of child-rearing practices. One kind, sometimes called **independence training,** engages adults with children in ways that promote the children's ability to rely on themselves, rather than others, to achieve personal goals. Such training is the rule in middle-class North American households, for example. These parents encourage babies to sleep alone in their own beds, in their own rooms; they reward young children for accomplishing simple tasks without assistance; they expect older children to perform household chores alone; and they may encourage teenagers to earn the money for fashionable clothes, a car, or college expenses. By the time they reach adulthood, these children will have the expectation that their future well-being is in their own hands and that nobody else, often including their parents, can or should help them define or achieve their goals. They are, in other words, primed to self-actualize, possessing all the basic skills and experiences needed by a capitalist entrepreneur.

Most societies of the world, however, do not traditionally rear their children to become independent and self-reliant; quite the contrary, their enculturation practices have been described as a form of **dependence training.** Most societies, in most times and places, have very strong group structures—kinship groups, religious or ethnic groups, regional groups, classes, or castes. Culture in these societies regularly teaches that each group member's first duty is to act in such a way as to promote the well-being of the group, because only if the group is strong will the individual be strong. Children are not encouraged to strike out on their own but instead are encouraged to conform to adults' wishes and to rely on them to protect their interests. Regardless of personal inclinations, for example, children would be likely to allow elders to arrange their marriages, having come to accept, however grudgingly, that their individual welfare cannot be separated from the welfare of the group and that group leaders know best.

Although culture-and-personality research brought to light much important cross-cultural evidence, it was increasingly criticized for drawing sweeping conclusions on the basis of equivocal or incomplete evidence. To the extent that these researchers relied on Freudian psychology to justify their claims, their conclusions were questioned when Freud's ideas eventually came under fire. Feminists, for example, argued that his theories were so deeply rooted in Western European patriarchal biases that they could offer little insight. Other works by non-Western scholars and clinicians raised similar criticisms, based on the difficulties they encountered in applying Freud's work to their own societies. In addition, a revolution in psychology, which focused on the psychological roots of rational thinking, came to supplant the Freudian models of human emotional development. A key figure in this transformation was the Swiss psychologist Jean Piaget (1896–1980), who offered his own developmental scheme. Piaget described four stages in the development of rational thinking in children, from their earliest explorations of the world around them to mastery of the highest levels of abstract calculation in higher mathematics.

4.5 Cognition and Cognitive Anthropology

Anthropologists inspired by Piaget abandoned the culture-and-personality orientation of their predecessors and began to emphasize cross-cultural studies of **cognition**: the mental processes by means of which individual human beings make sense of and incorporate information about the world. Rather than focusing on individual emotional and sexual development in the context of family relationships, cognitive anthropologists were interested in the effect culture might have on perception, reason, logic, and the way people classified objects and experiences in the world. This change in orientation first became well known in the work of anthropologists in the 1950s and 1960s who came to be known as ethnoscientists (see Chapter 3). **Ethnoscience** as a school of thought was interested in the ways people in different cultures categorized their experiences and classified objects and events in the wider world. Working in the native language of their informants, they made great efforts to expunge the influence of their own Western scientific (or etic) categories and to faithfully elicit their informants' indigenous (or emic) systems of classification (see Chapter 3 for further details). Cognitive anthropologists who studied non-Western classification systems discovered that, although there was considerable overlap between, for example, indigenous classifications of plants and animals and biological classifications offered by Western scientists, usually there were also significant differences. Often, these differences had to do with the functional or symbolic significance of certain plants or animals or other objects found in everyday life. Objects or events might be classified as "the same," for example, because they were all associated with the same daily activity or jointly figured in a key ritual.

These segments of culturally significant activity were understood as key cognitive units, or **schemas,** whose overall configuration overshadowed the parts of which they were composed. This meant that objects or events took their central meanings from the role they played in schemas of high cultural salience, not because they all possessed the same set of abstract attributes. Put another way, people classify objects in terms of **prototypes:** typical instances of objects or events they are familiar with and know most about. English speakers living in the temperate United States, for example, are likely to think of robins as prototypical birds because of their high level of experiential and cultural significance; that is, we associate robins with the return of spring and renewed natural growth. Other living things will then be classified as "birds" based on the degree to which they resemble robins; for example, small songbirds like cardinals will be much closer to the bird prototype than will large flightless birds like ostriches.

Prototypes and schemas clearly are related to each other. Together, they provide groups of people with distinctive, shared cognitive tools they can use to make sense not only of the regularities of everyday life but also of new, unexpected objects or experiences that challenge those regularities. Some cognitive anthropologists have specialized in schema theory, which focuses on the ways in which preexisting cultural schemas and prototypes shape expectations, encouraging us to interpret new experiences in ways that conform to past experience and even to reconfigure our memories of past experiences to bring them into line with present understandings.

Some of the questions asked by cognitive anthropologists parallel the questions asked by culture-and-personality theorists: Do different cultures shape individuals with different kinds of cognitive skills? Are the cognitive skills required for success in the world of Western capitalism themselves products of capitalist culture? Anthropologists generally agree that all members of the human species share the same general range of **cognitive capacities:** innate abilities to classify, compare, draw inferences, and so forth. If adults in different cultures perform differently when asked to complete the same cognitive tasks, therefore, does this mean that their culture has somehow molded their cognitive capacities in a particular direction? Cognitive anthropologists carried out cross-cultural tests designed to provide answers. Many used tests borrowed from psychologists, such as cards showing objects of different shapes and colors, which research subjects were then asked to classify and reclassify as many times as they could.

As with projective tests used by culture-and-personality researchers, the results of the tests used by cognitive anthropologists often were ambiguous and difficult to interpret, and for many of the same reasons. Specifically, it was not always clear that the subjects understood the purpose of the test the way the anthropologists did, and subjects frequently drew upon local cultural understandings of which the researchers were initially unaware, in order to make sense of the test.

4.6 Cognitive Styles

Nevertheless, this research did yield interesting information concerning what have been called **cognitive styles:** typical ways that individuals (or members of the same group) tackle a particular task. Anthropologists were struck by the fact that many non-Western subjects who had never been to a Western-type school typically used what was called a **global style;** that is, they first focused their attention on the situation as a whole, before paying attention to the detailed elements that made it up. Global style was said to be **field-dependent;** that is, subjects required knowledge of the broader context in which the elements were embedded in order to make sense of the elements themselves. This contrasted with the **articulated style** regularly used by educated Western subjects. In this style, they first paid attention to the detailed elements that make up the situation and only later looked for the relationships these elements might have with one another. Articulated style was said to be **field-independent;** that is, subjects could consider individual elements in themselves, without paying attention to the context in which they were embedded. (Table 4.1 summarizes the key features of cognitive styles.)

The field-independent, articulated style that required people to ignore context looked as though it might be the outcome of independence training, in which self-actualizing individuals are taught

---

TABLE 4.1   Cognitive Styles

GLOBAL	ARTICULATED
Field-Dependent	*Field-Independent*
Attention to wider context first; then focus on internal elements	Attention to individual elements first; then focus on wider context

to ignore contextual relationships that might restrict them. Similarly, the field-dependent global style looked as though it might be the result of dependence training, in which individuals are urged to embed or submerge their personal identity into the wider contextual identity of the group. In fact, as cognitive anthropologists did more detailed work in both Western and non-Western cultures, they showed that *all* people in *all* cultures are able to make use of global and articulated styles; the main differences have to do with which cognitive styles are considered appropriate for which tasks. Because both rules of appropriateness and kinds of tasks vary considerably from culture to culture, there is a high likelihood that people from different cultures will interpret the "same" task in different ways and will choose different cognitive strategies to cope with it. However, one big difference does seem to hold universally: those individuals, regardless of cultural background, who have experienced Western-style schooling consistently perform like educated people from Western cultures on cognitive tests.

4.7 Emotion

In recent years, some cognitive anthropologists have returned to a study of **emotion,** but their emphasis is quite different from that of the culture-and-personality theorists. Rather than emphasizing emotion as rooted in the body or sexuality, cognitive anthropologists view emotions as categories of feeling or patterns of affect. These anthropologists build on work by social psychologists who have argued that what English speakers call "emotion" actually combines a fairly undifferentiated physical arousal with specific meanings that give the arousal its particular "emotional" quality. Anthropologists focus on the meanings used to distinguish emotional experiences, arguing that different cultures create distinct categories of feeling associated with specific cultural meanings. One consequence of this approach is the conclusion that "emotions" are not "the same" everywhere but are heavily influenced by local cultural categories of feeling. Indeed, some anthropologists argue that without culturally created categories of feeling to help them, people do not know what they feel! That is, people's emotional experiences are often ambiguous, and anthropologists study how cultural beliefs about feeling help resolve such ambiguities by specifying which kinds of persons are entitled to feel which kinds of culturally specific emotions in which culturally defined contexts.

Questions of entitlement point to questions of power, and differences in power, that are enjoyed by different subgroups or individuals within particular social settings. In recent years, anthropologists have tried to incorporate the effects of political inequality into their understandings of individual psychological functioning. This has led them to speak not only of individual personality or individual self, but of individual **subjectivity:** interior experiences of persons that are shaped by their locations in a particular field of power relations. To focus on subjectivity in our analysis is to acknowledge the way in which individuals are to some extent the initiating subjects, or agents, of their own actions. However, subjects are never absolutely free to act as they choose. Our action is circumscribed by various forms of social, economic, and political inequality we encounter in the societies in which we live. That is, we occupy various subject positions in society, and are subject to the institutional forms of power in which those subject positions are embedded

Predictable institutional relationships enculturate, or socialize, individuals into forms of subjectivity that reflect established forms of political power. But social and cultural patterns are sometimes overturned by unpredictable experiences that leave enduring marks on the subjectivities of individuals who live through them. Unfortunately, such experiences are increasingly common in the early twenty-first century, as societies in many parts of the world experience violent conflicts. Armed conflict and war regularly produce **trauma,** severe suffering caused by forces and agents beyond the control of the individual. Large-scale violence aims to destroy not just individuals but the social order. Both individual and cultural factors contribute to the trauma, and are equally implicated in recovery from trauma. Anthropologists have also drawn attention to less dramatic forms of violence that cause considerable human suffering. **Structural violence,** for example, results from the way that political and economic forces structure risk differently for different subgroups within a population, such that some groups are more vulnerable to infectious disease, or domestic violence, than are other groups.

For Further Reading

GENERAL OVERVIEWS

Bock 1994

CULTURE AND PERSONALITY APPROACHES

Barnouw 1985

CROSS-CULTURAL PSYCHOANALYTIC APPROACHES

Doi 1985; Kakar 1981

CULTURE AND COGNITION

Cole and Scribner 1974; Lave 1988

PSYCHOLOGICAL ANTHROPOLOGY APPROACHES

Ingham 1996; Schwartz, White, and Lutz 1992

CULTURE AND EMOTION

Lutz 1988

SOCIAL SUFFERING

Kleinman, Das, and Lock 1997

5

Religion, Worldview, and Art

The key terms and concepts covered in this chapter, in the order in which they appear:

worldview

religion
animism
ancestor cult
gods
polytheistic religions
mana
oracle
dogma
orthodoxy

myths
origin myths
ritual
religious rituals
prayer
sacrifice
congregation
orthopraxy

rite of passage
liminal period
communitas
magic

witchcraft

shamans
priests

conversion
syncretism
revitalization

art
aesthetic
art by intention
art by appropriation
ethnomusicology

Human beings in all cultures try to make sense of their experience in ways that link them meaningfully to the wider world. Anthropologists use the term **worldview** to refer to the result of such interpretive efforts: an encompassing picture of reality based on a set of shared assumptions about how the world works. Anthropologists have long been interested in how worldviews are constructed and how people use them to make sense of their experiences. Worldviews establish symbolic frameworks that highlight certain significant domains of social experience while downplaying others. Multiple worldviews may coexist in a single society, or a single worldview may dominate.

5.1 Religion

As they began to compare cultures, anthropologists repeatedly encountered worldviews that reminded them of the religions they knew from Euro-American societies. Over the years, they have tried with mixed success to craft definitions of religion that took these diverse beliefs and practices into account. Most definitions that are currently in use do seem to agree that a **religion** is a worldview in which people personify cosmic forces and devise ways to deal with them that resemble the ways they deal with powerful human beings in their society. In practice, this means that people with religious worldviews conceive of the universe as populated by powerful forces that may understand human language and take an active interest in human affairs. Although their presence ordinarily may not be detectable by the human senses, they are never very far away. They may monitor human behavior and send punishments to those who violate moral rules, but if human beings approach them in the proper manner, they may use their power to confer benefits. Such personified beings have been variously called gods, goddesses, spirits, ancestors, ghosts, or souls.

While some anthropologists continue to use the term *super-natural* to refer to such beings or the realm they inhabit, most contemporary anthropological writing on religion avoids this term because it imposes on other societies a distinction between "natural" and "supernatural" worlds that those societies often do not recognize. Similar problems affect many other terms that Western observers, anthropologists included, have used to describe and analyze different religions. For this reason, some influential definitions of religion do not mention beings of any kind but focus on symbols and the ways in which people use symbols to bring meaning and coherence to the interpretation of their experiences.

Anthropologists have suggested a variety of reasons why religion seems to be so important in human societies: it is a way for people to deal with uncertainty that they cannot otherwise control, it is a way to provide meaning for people's lives, it explains the otherwise unexplainable (suffering, death, the mysterious in everyday life), and it helps to create social solidarity among those who adhere to it.

Confronted with enormous diversity in the religious traditions of the world, anthropologists proceeded to classify them according to type. For example, some religions propose that objects like trees or stones or rivers may have souls or spirits associated with them who may interact with people for good or for ill. The nineteenth-century English anthropologist E. B. Tylor (1832–1917) used the term **animism** to describe religions based on belief in the existence of such souls or spirit beings (*anima* is the Latin word for "soul"). Although most contemporary anthropologists no longer use this term because of the disparaging connotations it has acquired over the years, it may still be found in discussions in the field of comparative religion in which "world religions" like Christianity or Islam are contrasted with "animist religions" in which the only personified forces that are recognized are souls or spirits associated with features of the local landscape. The set of beliefs and practices associated with these souls and spirits are certainly real in some societies in the world today—traditional Inuit and Australian Aboriginal societies, for example—but many scholars prefer to use terms like "traditional religion" to avoid the persisting implication that animism is something that "more advanced" societies have evolved away from.

In societies where the connections of kinship do not end with physical death, religion may take the form of what is called an **ancestor cult** (for more about kinship see Chapter 9). In these systems, the ancestors are believed to maintain a strong interest in the lives of their descendents and are believed to act to maintain social order by sending sickness or other misfortune when the rules by which people are supposed to live are violated. In these societies, it is often the most senior people who gain great power from the ancestor cult, since they are closest to becoming ancestors.

Other societies recognize the existence of sentient and personified forces that are less local and more powerful. The entities may be called **gods,** and traditions in which there are many such beings are sometimes called **polytheistic religions.** The gods in polytheistic religions may have many of the personal attributes of human beings, including gender, and they may produce children with one another or with human beings, as did the gods in the religion of ancient Greece. But in some societies, the cosmic force or forces recognized are barely personalized at all. This is true in the case of **mana,** a Melanesian term introduced into anthropology in the nineteenth century to designate a cosmic force whose only human-like attribute is the ability to respond to human beings who use the correct symbolic formulas when they want to harness or channel this force for their own purposes. Another minimally personified cosmic force is an **oracle,** an invisible force capable of understanding questions addressed to it in human language and willing to respond truthfully using symbolic means that human beings with the proper cultural knowledge can interpret.

The beliefs people have regarding the nature of the world and the beings that inhabit it form one part of a religious worldview. But societies differ in how systematically they have organized this knowledge and in how much leeway they allow their members to offer alternative interpretations. In some societies, religious knowledge of this kind is highly detailed, carefully organized, and formally passed on from generation to generation. When the truths it is believed to contain may not be questioned, such knowledge is sometimes called **dogma** or **orthodoxy** (correct belief). In other societies, however, religious beliefs are not systematized, and no great emphasis is placed on orthodoxy, with the result that different adherents to the tradition may offer varied or conflicting interpretations of it.

5.2 Myth

Important components of religious traditions are **myths**: stories whose truth seems self-evident because they do such a good job of integrating personal experiences with a wider set of assumptions about the way society, or the world in general, must operate. Those myths that explain the creation of the world or of particular features of the landscape or of human beings are often called **origin myths.** Other myths may recount the adventures of the gods, the consequences of their interactions with human beings, or what will happen when the world ends. Although enduring religious myths are believed to embody important insights into life's purposes, they are more than morality tales. They are usually a highly developed verbal art form as well, recited for purposes of both entertainment and instruction, and the occasion of their telling offers verbal artists the opportunity to demonstrate their creative, aesthetic skills. Frequently, the "official" myth tellers are the most powerful or respected groups in society, such as the elders or political leaders or religious specialists. Myths have a social importance because, if they are taken literally, they tell people where they have come from and where they are going and, therefore, how they should live right now.

The study of myth has always been important in anthropology. Over time, two major approaches to the study of myth have had a lasting impact on the field. The first approach comes from Bronislaw Malinowski, who argued that myths are charters for social action; that is, the beings and places who figure in the myths can be referred to by living people in order to justify present-day social arrangements. For example, an origin myth about a particular kinship group may describe where members of the group first appeared on the land and the places they subsequently visited. This myth can be used by living members of that kinship group to defend their claims to land in the territories that their ancestors visited and to negate claims to the same land made by other members of the society. In short, to understand why myths have the content they do and how that content changes over time, one must understand the social beliefs and practices of the people who tell them.

The second approach to myth comes from the French anthropologist Claude Lévi-Strauss (1908–). While not denying Malinowski's observations about the practical uses to which myths could be put, Lévi-Strauss showed that the very structures of mythic narratives are meaningful and worth studying in their own right. In this sense, myths are cognitive tools for resolving logical contradictions in human social experience that cannot otherwise be overcome in the world that human beings know. In particular, myths are attempts to deal with oppositions of continuing concern to members of a particular society, such as the opposition between men and women, nature and culture, or life and death, or opposing styles of postmarital residence (postmarital residence is discussed in Chapter 10). Although these oppositions may be irresolvable in everyday life, myths offer an imaginative realm in which alternative possibilities and their (frequently undesirable) consequences can be explored.

Many scholars, including Malinowski and Lévi-Strauss, have assumed that the people who believe in myths typically are unaware how their myths are structured or how they use myths to defend their interests. Recent anthropological work, however, acknowledges that ordinary members of a society often *are* aware of how their myths structure meaning. And it is precisely this awareness that permits them to manipulate the way myths are told or interpreted in order to gain support for the version or interpretation that furthers their goals.

5.3 Ritual

Anthropologists use the term **ritual** to identify certain repetitive social practices, many of which have nothing to do with religion. A ritual is composed of a sequence of symbolic activities, set off from the social routines of everyday life, recognizable by members of the society as a ritual, and closely connected to a specific set of ideas that are often encoded in myth. What gives rituals their power is that participants assert that the authorization for the ritual comes from outside themselves—from the state, society, God, the ancestors, or "tradition." For example, in a courtroom, when people rise as the judge enters or refer to the judge as "your honor," they are not doing so because they feel like it or because the individual judge insists on it but because of the authority of the state and the Constitution. Thus, by responding in court, "Not guilty, your honor," one is accepting the authority of not just the judge but also of the court, the justice system, and the Constitution. (Indeed, this is the difference between a wedding rehearsal and a wedding.) Even when rituals are invented or transformed, those involved with them attempt to connect the innovations to external sources of authority. For example, at our university's graduation ceremony, the graduates are asked to applaud the parents, relatives, and friends who have helped them achieve that moment. While this part of the ritual was proposed by a former president, his justification for the innovation was that it took account of something profoundly important in the social world that the institution needed to acknowledge, and it was in keeping with the other elements of the graduation ceremony.

Much work in recent years in anthropology has explored the relationship between ritual and power, and much of this work has concentrated on rituals that are not religious. But the role of ritual in religious contexts remains an important area of study. If the universe is indeed populated by powerful personified beings that take an interest in human affairs, then it is to the very great benefit of human beings to devise ways of dealing with them. All religious worldviews assume that communication between personified cosmic forces is possible and potentially beneficial, but it can take place only if carried out in the correct way. Most religious traditions have developed specialized social routines for communication with the gods that, if performed correctly, should ensure successful communication. As a consequence, **religious rituals** are distinctive in that they regularly involve attempts to influence or gain the sympathy of a particular personified cosmic being. One kind of religious ritual involves addressing these personified forces in human speech, often out loud, while holding the body in a conventional posture of respect; this is called **prayer.** Another kind of religious ritual involves offering something of value (goods, services, money, or an appropriately slaughtered animal) to the invisible forces or their agents; this is called **sacrifice.** Prayer and sacrifice frequently are performed when members of a religious tradition come together in processions, meetings, or convocations; this is called **congregation.**

Members of some religious traditions insist that correct ritual behavior is essential at times of prayer or sacrifice and that any deviation will nullify the ritual. Indeed, some religious traditions aim to ritualize virtually every waking act adherents perform, a style of religious practice called **orthopraxy** (correct practice). Not all religious traditions that value ritual are orthoprax, however; many entertain a range of opinion regarding correct practice, and individual people or independent religious practitioners are free to develop their own rituals or variants of more broadly recognized rituals.

One particular kind of ritual has drawn considerable attention from anthropologists: the **rite of passage,** which occurs when one or more members of a society are ritually transformed from one kind of social person into another. Rites of passage often are initiations into adulthood, when girls are made women or boys made men, but they may also mark marriages (when single people become a married couple), the birth of children (when a new life enters the world), or funerals (when living kin become ancestors). These and other so-called life-cycle transitions frequently are marked by rituals that connect participants to ancestors or gods or other cosmic forces. Anthropologists point out that rites of passage regularly follow a three-part sequence. First, the ritual passengers (i.e., the persons who are changing their social position) are *separated* from their previous, everyday existence. Next, they pass through a *transitional* state, in which they are neither in the old position nor yet in the new one. Finally, with their new status, they are *reaggregated,* or brought back, into the everyday social world. The second, transitional stage of the ritual was particularly significant for anthropologist Victor Turner (1920–83), who referred to it as the **liminal period** (from the Latin word *limen,* meaning "threshold"). Turner noted that when people are on the threshold, they are "betwixt and between," neither in nor out. In rites of passage, the symbolism associated with the transitional period often expresses that ambiguity: it is described as being in the womb, being invisible, being in the wilderness, or as death. Ritual passengers in the liminal stage tend to develop an intense comradeship with one another; social distinctions that separated them before the ritual and will separate them again afterward become irrelevant. Turner called this liminal social relationship **communitas,** which is best understood as an unstructured or minimally structured community of equal individuals. In rites of passage concerned with initiation, for example, the liminal period is a time in which those being initiated are tutored in knowledge and skills that their elders believe they must master if they are to be successful in the stage of life they are about to enter.

5.4 Magic and Witchcraft

Anthropologists have also paid much attention to another form of ritual called **magic.** The persistence of definitions of magic that include the term *supernatural* is another indication of the difficulty of using one culture's definitions to describe practices in other cultures. Generally, magic refers to ritual practices that do not have technically or scientifically apparent effects but are believed by the actors to have an influence on the outcome of practical matters. People may believe that the correct performance of such rituals can result in healing, the growth of plants, the recovery of lost or stolen objects, getting a hit in baseball, or safely sailing an outrigger canoe in the Pacific Ocean. The classic anthropological explanation of magic comes from the research of Bronislaw Malinowski in the Trobriand Islands early in the twentieth century. Malinowski suggested that all living societies have developed effective knowledge and practical techniques for dealing with the world. At the same time, however, they also realize that their practical control over the world has limits. Where their techniques and knowledge are sufficient for accomplishing their goals, magic is not used. But when the outcome is uncertain, regardless of the skill and insight people may have, they are likely to resort to magical practices. The use of magic in such situations, Malinowski argued, has the practical function of reducing anxiety, thereby allowing people to concentrate on what they are able to control. He observed, for example, that Trobriand Islanders he knew used outrigger canoes to go fishing both in the protected lagoons around the islands and also in the Pacific Ocean. When they fished in the lagoons, which were safe and secure, they put their canoes into the water and got straight to work. But when they were going past the lagoons into the open ocean, which was unpredictable and dangerous, they recited spells and used other techniques throughout the voyage.

Traditional anthropological discussions of magic have emphasized that most magical practices seem to be based on one of two underlying ideas: like affects like, and things that at one time have been in contact continue to affect each other even when they are separated. Practices based on the idea that like affects like have been called *imitative magic*. A familiar example is the so-called voodoo doll: a pin stuck in the back of the doll will supposedly cause a stabbing pain in the back of the victim the doll represents. Today, anthropologists suggest that *analogy* is a more accurate description of the underlying principle behind such a practice than is *imitation*. This is because the symbolic relations between the ritual objects (i.e., the doll and the pin) and their magical "world" is extended, by analogy, to the target of the magic (i.e., the enemy) and its "world." In other words, the ritual sticking of a pin into the back of a doll is analogous to the sticking of a (magical) knife into the back of a human enemy. The causal connections believed to operate in the world of the ritual objects (dolls, pins, herbs, etc.) and the invisible forces that link the two worlds together are the result of particular cultural understandings not shared by all human observers.

Ritual practices based on the idea that things that have once been in contact continue to affect each other even when they are separated have been called *contagious magic*. For example, hair or nail clippings were once part of a person's body, and a personal garment has had sustained contact with the body of the person who wears it. Many societies have the belief that if one can secure a few strands of hair or nail clippings from an individual, or a piece of clothing that the person has worn, and work a spell over these things, the spell will affect that person. Because wholes always remain connected to their parts, even when the parts are no longer in contact with the whole, acting on the part (e.g., the shirt) will continue to affect the whole (i.e., the person who wore it).

In the late nineteenth century, when unilineal evolutionary schemes were popular in anthropology (see Chapter 12 for details), many anthropologists proposed that magic and religion were separate stages in the progressive evolution of human thought that culminated in science. But subsequent ethnographic research, especially work done in the past few decades, has made it clear that magic, religion, and science may coexist in the same society and may even be used by the same people, who resort to different ways of coping with the world in different social contexts. In some cases, people in search of a solution to a serious problem, such as infertility, may be unwilling to dismiss any beliefs or practices that offer a solution, alternatively consulting medical doctors, praying in church, and consulting practitioners of alternative therapies that some might argue are based on magic.

It is important to stress that interest in identifying and defining the true nature of magic was historically of greatest concern to two categories of Western critics: missionaries eager to demonstrate the superiority of their version of "religion" over what they considered to be the superstitious "magical" practices of "primitive peoples," and defenders of science, who wanted to demonstrate its superiority over both magic and religion. The more science was stressed as the embodiment of rationality, the more necessary it became to stress the "irrational" features of religion and magic.

Anthropologists committed to cultural relativism in the early twentieth century were more interested in stressing the sensible side of seemingly exotic beliefs and practices like magic and witchcraft. Malinowski, as we have seen, focused on the positive practical side effects of belief in the efficacy of magic spells. E. E. Evans-Pritchard

(1902–73), in his classic monograph *Witchcraft, Oracles, and Magic among the Azande* (first published in 1937), demonstrated that the beliefs and practices associated with all three phenomena were perfectly logical, if one accepted certain basic assumptions about the world.

Among the Azande, **witchcraft** involves the performance of evil by human beings believed to possess an innate, nonhuman "witchcraft substance" that can be activated without the individual's awareness. (Other anthropologists, using Azande witchcraft as their prototype, have applied the term to similar beliefs and practices found in other societies.*) For the Azande, witchcraft tends to explain misfortune when other possibilities have been discounted. For example, if a good potter carefully prepares his pots and fires them as he always does, but they still break, he will attribute his misfortune to witchcraft, and his neighbors will probably believe him. But if a careless potter is sloppy when firing his pots, and they break, he may claim that witchcraft was the cause, but no one who knows him will believe it.

Evans-Pritchard showed that the entire system of Azande beliefs and practices concerning witchcraft, oracles, and magic was perfectly rational if one assumed that unseen forces exist in the world and that nothing happens to people by accident. For example, when someone falls very ill or dies, the Azande assume that the person has been bewitched. But the Azande are not helpless, because they know they can consult oracles who will help them pinpoint the witch responsible. Once the oracle has identified the witch, they can send a ritual message to the accused witch, who can offer a ritual reply that will stop the witchcraft, if indeed he (it is usually a man) has been the cause of it. If the bewitched person dies, however, the next step is to obtain vengeance magic, which can be used to seek out the witch responsible and kill him.

The Azande do not collapse in fear in the presence of witchcraft because they know how to deal with it. Moreover, they

---

*This technical use of the term should not be confused with everyday uses of the word in contemporary Western societies, still less with the practices of followers of movements like Wicca, which are very different.

make an accusation of witchcraft only after cross-checking the oracle's pronouncements carefully. Because all the steps in the process are carried out in great secrecy, who has accused whom and who has killed whom with vengeance magic is not open to public scrutiny, so that contradictions in the system are rarely exposed. This, Evans-Pritchard suggested, is how all complex belief systems operate, even in the so-called scientific West. After all, the "scientific method" at its most stringent is hardly followed regularly by ordinary citizens, or even scientists once they are outside the laboratory. Evans-Pritchard's work has inspired many subsequent studies that debunk ethnocentric Western notions about the supposed irrationality of magic and religion.

Beliefs and practices bearing a resemblance to Azande witchcraft are found in many societies, in Africa and elsewhere. Comparative studies of these phenomena revealed interesting variation in the patterns of witchcraft accusations in a given society. Patterns of accusation fall into two basic types: witches are evil outsiders, or witches are internal enemies, either members of a rival faction or dangerous deviants.

These different patterns of accusation have different effects on the structure of the society in which they are made. If the witch is an evil outsider, witchcraft accusations can strengthen in-group ties as the group unites in opposition to the witch. If the witch is an internal enemy, however, accusations of witchcraft can weaken in-group ties, perhaps to the point at which one or more factions in a community might leave and build a new village; then the entire social structure may have to be rebuilt. This, anthropologists argued, was not really a bad thing, since what had prompted the accusations of witchcraft in the first place was a community that had grown too large for the prevailing political organization to maintain order. The witchcraft accusations provided a relatively nondestructive way to restore the community to the proper size for a kinship-based political system. If, on the other hand, the witch is a dangerous internal deviant, to accuse that person of witchcraft might be an attempt to control the deviant in defense of the wider values of the community.

5.5 Religious Practitioners

Anthropologists also have devoted attention to the organization of religion as a social and cultural institution. Virtually without exception, anthropologists have stressed that complex sets of religious beliefs and practices are not merely the by-products of idiosyncratic individual invention. Rather, they are the products of collective cultural construction, performing social and cultural tasks that involve far more than tending to the spiritual needs of supporters.

The contrast between different kinds of religious institutions in different societies can be illustrated with reference to the existence and role of specialized religious practitioners. In many small-scale societies, specialized ritual knowledge or practice may simply belong to elders who perform required rituals for their kin. Other societies, however, do accord a special status to religious specialists, and anthropologists have classified them in two broad categories: shamans and priests. **Shamans** are part-time religious specialists commonly found in small-scale egalitarian societies. The term *shaman* itself comes from Siberia, and Siberian shamans constitute the prototype that anthropologists have used to classify similar religious specialists in many other societies. They are believed to have the power to contact powerful cosmic beings directly on behalf of others, sometimes by traveling to the cosmic realm to communicate with them. They often plead with those beings to help their people— by curing them, for example—and they may also bring back messages for them. In other cases, the shaman enters an altered state of consciousness to seek and remove the cause of an illness that is afflicting a person who has come for healing. In many societies, the training that a shaman receives is long and demanding and may involve the use of powerful psychotropic substances. The position of shaman may be dangerous. The effects of entering altered states of consciousness can be long-lasting. The power to contact cosmic beings or to heal is itself perceived as ambiguous in many societies: the person who can intervene for good can also intervene for ill, and shamans are sometimes feared as well as admired.

Priests, by contrast, are skilled in the practice of religious rituals, which are carried out for the benefit of the group or individuals within the group. Priests frequently are full-time, formally trained specialists. They are found in hierarchical societies in which status differences between rulers and subjects are paralleled in the unequal relationship between priest and laity. Priests do not necessarily have direct contact with cosmic forces; rather, their major role is to mediate that contact successfully for their people by ensuring that the required rituals have been properly performed.

5.6 Change in Religious Systems

Much ethnographic work has sought to describe and explain the details of particular religious systems, but the way change affects religious belief and practice has also been of great interest. When the members of a society are faced with drastic changes in their experiences—because of conquest, natural disaster, or radical dislocation (e.g., by migration)—they frequently seek new interpretations that will help them cope with the changes. In some cases, the individuals or groups in question will adopt an entirely new worldview, frequently a religious system, in the process of **conversion**. But in other cases, the result is a creative synthesis of old religious practices and new ones introduced from the outside, often by force, in a process called **syncretism**. Recently, some anthropologists have pointed out that most studies of religious syncretism have not paid sufficient attention to the unequal relationships between the parties that are syncretizing. Many have assumed that the worldview that changes most is the one belonging to the group with the least power. In some cases, syncretistic practices may indeed be introduced from above by powerful outsiders trying to ease tensions by deliberately making room for local beliefs. In other cases, however, syncretism can be seen as a way of resisting new ideas imposed from outside and above, masking old practices under the labels of the new imported ones.

Sometimes social groups struggling with change defend or refashion their own way of life in a process that anthropologists call **revitalization:** a deliberate, organized attempt by some members of a society to create a more satisfying culture. Revitalization movements arise in times of crisis, most often among groups facing oppression and radical transformation, usually at the hands of outsiders (e.g., colonizing powers). Revitalization may take a syncretistic form, but syncretism also may be rejected in favor of *nativism*, a return to the old ways. Some nativistic movements anticipate a messiah or prophet who will bring back a lost golden age of peace, prosperity, and harmony, a process often called *revivalism, millenarianism,* or *messianism.*

In recent years, anthropologists have examined not only the power relations involved in syncretism and revitalization but also the way different worldviews are related to the creation and maintenance of power relations within societies. For example, power differences may be sustained by differential knowledge, as when some groups of people within a society have access to important knowledge that is not available to everyone or when a limited number of individuals exercise control over key symbols and ritual practices. In many cases, those with power in the society seem to have successfully made use of the self-evident truths embodied in their worldview to continue to control others.

5.7 Art

In Western societies, the term **art** includes sculpture, drawing, painting, dance, theater, music, and literature, and such similar processes and products such as film, photography, mime, mass media productions, oral narrative, festivals, and national celebrations. When anthropologists talk about art in non-Western societies, they begin by focusing on activities or products that resemble art in the West. Whether non-Western peoples refer to such activities or products as "art," the activities and products themselves are universal. They seem rooted in playful creativity, a birthright of all human beings, but differ from free play because they are circumscribed by rules. Artistic rules direct particular attention to, and provide standards for evaluating, the *form* of the activities or objects that artists produce. One anthropological definition of art is that it consists of "culturally significant meaning, skillfully encoded in an affecting, sensuous medium" (Anderson 2004, 277). The term *sensuous* refers to the senses, so a sensuous medium is one that can be perceived by one or more of the human senses. The media through which culturally significant meaning can be encoded are vast, and include painting on various surfaces; carving wood, bone, antler, and stone; singing and chanting; creating and playing musical instruments; story-telling; dancing; tattooing; and a theoretically infinite range of other media. These media, and the kinds of skills required to work with them, are culturally recognized and characterized. For example, the Baule of the Ivory Coast make a number of different kinds of sculptures out of wood, some of which are portrait masks that are supposed to resemble their subjects (Vogel 1997). Others are representations of powerful, dangerous spirits which are not understood as portraits at all.

Art is often said to have an aesthetic element to it. The term **aesthetic** can be used to refer to theories about the nature and value of art, but can also be usefully defined as "appreciative of, or responsive to, form in art or nature" (Alland 1977, xii). Something that is aesthetically successful generates a positive or negative response for the artist, and perhaps for anyone else who experiences it ("I like this," "I hate this"). Indifference is the sign of something that is aesthetically unsuccessful. It is probably the case that the aesthetic response is a universal feature in all cultures and, as with play, may be part of the human condition. This does not mean that everyone in all places and at all times responds in the same way to a given work of art—quite the contrary, there is ample evidence that aesthetic response varies from place to place. Nevertheless, as part of one of anthropology's projects over the years, anthropologists have been eager to undermine the complacent Western assumption of cultural and social superiority, and emphasizing the presence of "art" in non-Western societies, even when people in a particular society do not recognize a similar term, has contributed to this project.

In recent years, it has become increasingly the case that a very wide range of products of human activity are considered to be art by people in Western societies, and it is equally clear that many of those products were not produced to be "art." Western art museums present furniture, religious or devotional objects, jewelry designed for personal adornment, technology, arms and armor, and much more from Western history as art, and they do the same for objects from non-Western societies as well. Anthropologist

Shelly Errington (1998) usefully distinguishes between **art by intention** and **art by appropriation.** Art by intention includes objects that were made to be art, such as Impressionist paintings. Art by appropriation, however, consists of all the other objects that "became art" because at a certain moment certain people (they could be local artists, or museum curators, art dealers, art collectors, interior designers) decided that they belonged to the category of art. Because museums, art dealers, and art collectors are found everywhere in the world today, so too it is now the case that potentially any material object crafted by human hands can be appropriated by these institutions as "art." It is also the case that people whose products have been appropriated as art can also begin to produce art by intention. Australian Aboriginal peoples began to produce acrylic paintings to be sold in the art market in the 1970s, based on ancient techniques and styles that were originally of profound religious and spiritual significance.

The development of a global art market has been paralleled in popular music, where there has been a tremendous amount of cross-fertilization as well as the development of local traditions that meld rock-and-roll styles from several different parts of the world into creative and satisfying musics. The sharing of "mp3s" via the Internet has led to an extraordinary globalization of musical taste, such that heavy metal bands from Finland find eager listeners in Chile.

The study of the musics of the world, particularly the relationship of music to society and cultural ideas and practices, is the field of **ethnomusicology.** Ethnomusicology can include the study of music and social, cultural, or gender identity; the role of music and musicians in a society; the effect of music on social life; and the study of sound as a form of communication. Recent advances in recording technology have made it possible for ethnomusicologists to include CDs of the music they have studied in the books they publish, which has enormously expanded the impact of their work.

As with music, so too with dance. Anthropologists who have studied dance in different human societies have demonstrated how dance is connected with the expression of gender; how it is connected with the expression of emotion; how it is connected with sculpture, masking, and religious practice; and how it is a form of self-expression.

For Further Reading

GENERAL ANTHROPOLOGICAL WORKS ON RELIGION

Bowen 1998a; Child and Child 1993; Klass 1995; Wallace 1966

READINGS ON RELIGION

Bowen 1998b; Hicks 1999; Lambek 2002; Lehman and Myers 1996

ART

Alland 1977; Errington 1998; Myers 2003; Vogel 1997

6

The Dimensions of Social Organization

The key terms and concepts covered in this chapter, in the order in which they appear:

society
status
role
ascribed status
achieved status
social structure
institutions
social organization
functionalism
mechanical solidarity
organic solidarity

egalitarian societies
stratified societies
rank societies
sodalities
age set
age grades
secret societies
caste

social mobility
class
bourgeoisie
proletariat
clientage
patron-client relationships
compadrazgo
fictive kin
state
bureaucracy

race
ethnic group
ethnocide
genocide

sex
gender
postmodernism
berdache

ONE OF THE BASIC CLAIMS of anthropology is that human beings are a social species; that is, we have evolved to live with, and depend upon, others of our own species. Biological anthropologists have demonstrated, for example, that human infants are born earlier in the gestational process than are infants of apes and monkeys and that our young are dependent on other members of the group for far longer (fifteen to twenty years and more) before they are capable of establishing themselves as mature adults. Human interdependence means that we cannot survive as lone individuals but need to live with others; that is, we must live in society. When anthropologists speak of human society, at minimum they mean a group of human beings living together whose interactions with one another are patterned in regular ways. Such organized groups might also be identified by the particular geographical territory they inhabit, by the particular language they speak, or by the particular customs they follow—any or all of these features might distinguish them from other, neighboring societies. Such distinctive features, in turn, are mostly cultural, which is why anthropologists developed the habit of speaking as if each identifiable society came equipped with its own culture, and vice versa. Still, anthropologists recognize that no culture is monolithic, that cultural patterns may be borrowed or shared by people in different societies, and that a single society may contain within it representatives of different cultural traditions.

6.1 What Is Social Organization?

Anthropologists, together with other social scientists, have developed a set of analytic concepts that help describe and explain the orderly interdependence of human life in society. In particular, they have noted that people who interact in society do so not as unique individuals but as incumbents of publicly recognized social positions. Each such social position is called a **status,** and all individuals come to occupy a range of different statuses in the course of their lives as they take part in a variety of social interactions.

People know what to do in such interactions because each status is associated with a corresponding **role:** a bundle of rights and obligations appropriate for occupants of the status in question. Thus, for example, the kinship status of *parent* might include, among other things, the right to discipline one's children and the obligation to feed them and send them to school. Violation of the role requirements associated with a particular social status generally brings about disapproval from other members of society.

Social scientists also distinguish two basic kinds of social statuses found in all societies: ascribed and achieved. An **ascribed status** is a status over which you have little control: you are born into it or grow into it. Anthropologists often use examples from human kinship systems to illustrate ascribed status. When you are born, you are automatically your parent's child, son or daughter; when you have children of your own, you automatically become a parent, mother or father. Such ascribed statuses ordinarily cannot be discarded, and any person who qualifies will be expected to fulfill the role obligations that go with the status. Very different, however, is an **achieved status,** one that you may not assume until or unless you meet certain criteria through your own (or others') efforts. For instance, being a college graduate is an achieved status, and achieving that status ordinarily requires both hard work and financial resources. Each member of a society occupies a mix of ascribed and achieved statuses.

Statuses and their accompanying roles are not isolated but are often linked to one another in complementary pairs or sets. For example, the statuses of parents and children (or mother and daughter, father and son, mother and son, or father and daughter) are reciprocal relationships. Thus, the right of parents to discipline their children matches the obligation of children to obey their parents (in theory, at least). To describe such a cluster of statuses with complementary roles is to begin to identify key enduring social relationships that provide a foundation for regularized, patterned social interaction, or **social structure.** But social structure is not simply a matter of interlinked and complementary statuses and roles attached to individuals. Most societies regularly associate particular sets of statuses with particular social groups defined in such terms as gender, family, lineage, clan, occupation, and political or religious affiliation. The relationships that link members of these various social groups may also be highly structured, often around a common task or cultural focus. The clusters of social statuses and groups that share such a common focus usually are called **institutions.** Thus, we speak of educational institutions that unite individuals and groups whose social statuses focus on educational issues or of political institutions that bring together individuals and groups whose statuses focus on the allocation of power in the society. Sometimes social structure refers only to the arrangement of status positions and groups with respect to each other. By contrast, **social organization** refers to the interlocking role relationships that are activated when statuses have incumbents and groups have members, all of whom are going about the daily business of living.

All this terminology is associated with the school of social scientific thought called **functionalism** (for more about functionalism, see Chapter 12). Functionalism was at its most influential in the early twentieth century and has since been much criticized, but many anthropologists and sociologists continue to find its terminology useful for describing basic social relations, even when they do not accept some of its more elaborate assumptions.

6.2 Dimensions of Social Organization

One issue of great interest in the early years of anthropology and sociology was the contrast between large and powerful European nation-states, with industrial technology and a complex division of labor, and small-scale societies, with little or no social stratification, whose members used simple tools to make a living and who were socially organized almost entirely on the basis of kinship. The contrast was sometimes phrased as an opposition between so-called civilized and so-called primitive societies. Sociologists were supposed to explain how "civilized" societies worked, and anthropologists were supposed to explain how "primitive" societies worked.

One widely influential model was proposed by Emile Durkheim (1858–1917), a French sociologist considered a founder of both modern sociology and modern anthropology. Durkheim was interested in what held a society together, contrasting societies held together by mechanical solidarity with those held together by organic solidarity. Mechanical solidarity characterized small-scale, kinship-based societies, in which all the tasks necessary for survival were carried out on a family level and families stayed together because they shared the same language and customs.

However, because kin groups were more-or-less self-sufficient in terms of meeting their survival needs, they could split off from one another relatively easily. Thus, mechanical solidarity could not bind together large numbers of people over long periods of time. Organic solidarity, by contrast, characterized large-scale societies, such as nation-states. In such societies, the tasks necessary for survival became specialties of different subgroups in a complex division of labor. For example, because those who specialized in pot making or metalworking might not have had the time or resources to produce their own food or clothing, they became dependent on other specialists—food producers or tailors—for these goods and services. Such interdependence meant that any single occupational grouping could not easily break away from the larger social whole, since it was not self-sufficient. Like the organ systems of a living body, specialized subgroups of complex societies clung together and depended on one another to survive, thereby preserving the overall health and strength of the whole. Thus, organic solidarity could hold much larger societies together far more securely than could mechanical solidarity.

Anthropologists incorporated concepts like these into their own analytic toolkit as they attempted to make sense of the variety of forms that different human societies assumed in different times and places. They also introduced new concepts to highlight further distinctions revealed by ethnographic research. One of the most basic is the fourfold classification of societies on the basis of their form of political organization: band, tribe, chiefdom, and state (discussed at greater length in Chapter 7). Another is the very similar fourfold classification of societies on the basis of their form of economic organization: foragers, herders, extensive agriculturalists, and intensive agriculturalists (discussed at greater length in Chapter 8). The correlations between these different classifications highlight the connections between the ways people make a living and the ways they organize themselves politically.

The correlation is not perfect, however, and this is highlighted by another pair of concepts that crosscuts the earlier classifications. That is, anthropologists distinguish between **egalitarian societies,** in which all members (or component groups) enjoy roughly the same degree of wealth, power, and prestige, and **stratified societies,** in which some members (or component groups) have greater (and often permanent) access to some or all of these three valued resources. But the history of the transition from egalitarian societies (bands and tribes, in the current classification) to stratified societies (chiefdoms and states) is not fully understood. Some anthropologists pay particular attention to societies known through ethnography or history or archaeology in which egalitarian relations have begun to erode but in which permanent, inherited patterns of social stratification have not yet been established. Such societies, like those of the indigenous peoples of the northwest coast of North America or the Trobriand Islanders of Papua New Guinea, depended on foraging or extensive agriculture for subsistence, just as many egalitarian societies do. But they also have social structures that elevate certain individuals and their families above everyone else, allowing them privileged access to a limited number of high-status positions. Anthropologist Morton Fried called these **rank societies,** some of whose members ranked above others in social honor but did not have disproportionate access to wealth or power. The consensus is that fully stratified societies probably developed out of rank societies, but the exact mechanisms for the transition have been much debated and may well have been somewhat different in each case.

Ethnographic evidence supported Durkheim's observation that small-scale societies tend to be organized primarily on the basis of kinship. As we discuss in Chapter 9, kinship systems must be fairly elaborate to carry out this task, and anthropology traditionally has sought to understand and compare the many different kinship systems that human beings have devised. However, even egalitarian societies whose social organization centered on kinship often invented additional forms of social organization that crosscut kinship groups and bound their members together at a more inclusive level; anthropologists often refer to such groups as **sodalities.**

Sodalities can take many forms. Among the best known ethnographically are the age-set systems from eastern Africa and the secret societies from western Africa. Found in such societies as the Nyakyusa living in present-day Tanzania, an **age set** is made up of a group of young men born within a specific time span, such as five years; thus, a new age set is formed regularly every five years. Age sets typically progress through a sequence of statuses, or **age grades,** as their members grow older. There might be three age grades through which every age set must pass—for example, a junior, senior, and elder grade. Promotion from one age grade to the next typically is marked by rituals. Many societies with age-set systems devote particular attention to the *initiation* ritual that transforms boys into adult men, but societies differ in the degree of ritual elaboration with which they surround the passage of different sets from one grade to the next. Age-set systems have played different roles in different societies as well. Those sets belonging to junior age grades frequently have been characterized as *warriors,* but it is important to recognize that their activities as fighters or raiders often were subject to the control of men in senior age grades. Moreover, members of societies with age sets and age grades frequently use the age-grade structure as a way of thinking about time and attempting to regulate its passage by ritual means.

The Mende, Sherbro, Kpelle, and other neighboring peoples who today live in the western African nation-states of Sierra Leone, Ivory Coast, Liberia, and Guinea developed **secret societies** as forms of social organization that crosscut kinship groupings. Some secret societies admit only men as members, others admit only women, and at least one admits both men and women. Only adults may belong to secret societies, and children must undergo initiation rituals in order to achieve that status and gain admittance; some anthropologists have undergone initiation as part of their research. The "secret" part of secret societies refers to the special knowledge revealed only to initiates, which they are not allowed to share with outsiders. Initiates may also progress to higher positions within the society to which they belong, but they must pay fees and receive special instruction to do so. In addition to these internal activities, secret societies also carry out specific tasks in public. Social relations between men and women tend to be highly egalitarian in cultures with secret societies; for example, the male Poro society and female Sande society of a village might jointly be responsible for supervising public behavior and sanctioning those who violate expected rules of conduct.

Forms of social organization, such as kinship and sodalities, can still be found in societies that are socially stratified, but their scope and importance is modified by new features of social structure that sustain the inequalities on which social stratification is based. That is, stratified societies are internally divided into a number of groups that are arranged in a hierarchy. The two most important such hierarchical structures studied by anthropologists have been caste and class.

6.3 Caste and Class

Anthropologists traditionally describe **caste** societies as stratified societies in which membership in a particular ranked subgroup is ascribed at birth and in which **social mobility,** or movement by individuals out of the subgroup in which they were born, is not allowed. Although the original prototype for caste societies comes from India, anthropologists have used the term to describe similar social arrangements in other societies.

In India and elsewhere in South Asia, each caste traditionally is defined not only as the endogamous group within which members must choose mates (see Chapter 10 for a definition of endogamy) but also in terms of a traditional occupation with which the caste is identified (salt maker, farmer, warrior, priest, etc.). Each occupation, and the caste associated with it, is ranked on a scale of purity and pollution, with higher-ranked castes subject to various dietary and other taboos required to maintain caste purity. Highest on the purity scale are the *Brahmins*, the vegetarian priestly caste, and lowest are the out-castes or untouchables, who eat meat and whose occupations (leatherworker, street sweeper) regularly bring them into contact with polluting substances such as dead animals and excrement. Recent studies of caste societies have demonstrated that the high ritual status of the Brahmin caste does not mean that Brahmins dominate the caste system; rather, these studies emphasize the centrality of the king and his warrior caste, the *Ksatriya*. Kings could determine the relative rank of local castes, for example, and from the king's perspective, the function of these other castes, including the Brahmins, was to protect him from pollution. By the end of the twentieth century, caste relations had undergone significant modification in urban India: castes close in rank sometimes came together in political alliances, and members of the same caste but from different regions of the country (e.g., Brahmins) came together to build solidarity on a national level. Unfortunately, Indian cities have also been the site of caste violence in recent years, when members of more favorably situated castes clash with those struggling to escape from a permanent position at the bottom of the caste hierarchy.

Social **class,** by contrast, is the term anthropologists use to describe ranked subgroups in a stratified society whose members are differentiated from one another primarily in economic terms, either on the basis of income level or, as Karl Marx (1818–83) proposed, on the basis of the kind of property owned by members of different classes. In an industrial capitalist society, for example, Marx argued that class divisions had formed between the **bourgeoisie,** or capitalist class, which owned the means of production (tools, knowledge, raw materials), and the **proletariat,** or working class, which owned only their labor power, which they sold to bourgeois factory owners in exchange for cash wages (see Chapters 8 and 11 for further discussion of these terms). Either way, members of some social classes are seen to have privileged access to material resources, while the access of members of other classes to these resources is more or less severely restricted.

Moreover, ruling classes use their privileged situation to dominate less powerful classes.

Traditionally, anthropologists have distinguished class from caste on the grounds that social classes are not closed and social mobility from one class into another is not forbidden. An emphasis on class mobility tends to highlight exceptional, successful individuals who have moved from lower to higher classes, while overlooking the enduring rigidity of class boundaries for most people in many societies (Great Britain, for example) as well as cases of downward class mobility. At the same time, emphasizing the inability of individuals in a caste system to move from a lower-ranked to a higher-ranked caste overlooks the ways in which permanent members of different castes sometimes collectively succeed in elevating the relative position of their caste within the overall caste system.

The members of ranked subgroups in stratified societies do not always accept the position they are supposed to occupy in a class or caste hierarchy, and struggles between such groups do occur. Marx, in particular, emphasized the class antagonism between bourgeoisie and proletariat, which he predicted ultimately would produce class warfare in which the workers would overthrow the capitalist order and establish socialism. Anthropologists working in India have challenged the view that people occupying the lowest ranks in the caste system necessarily accept their low status as right and proper. Indeed, the caste violence that has occasionally erupted in Indian cities in recent decades testifies to the unwillingness of those at the bottom of the system to accept such a position. At the same time, interactions between individuals from different levels of a hierarchical social system is not regularly characterized by such violence, and members of different ranked groups find nonviolent ways to establish relationships with one another. If different groups are associated with different occupations, their members may have only impersonal contact with one another when they need one another's services—for example, in the workplace. But many societies have developed institutionalized cross-hierarchy connections that allow individuals belonging to differently ranked groups to create a more personalized relationship. Anthropologists often call such connections **clientage** or **patron-client relationships,** since they normally involve a member of a high-ranking group (the patron) and a member of a low-ranking group (the client). A well-documented example of clientage is the Latin American institution of *compadrazgo,* or coparenthood. Such a relationship may be created when a low-ranking married couple (the clients) asks a high-ranking individual (the patron) to serve as their child's *compadre,* or godparent, at the child's baptism. If the patron agrees and participates in the baptism ritual, then that individual and the child's parents will have a new relationship. They will call each other by the kin terms *compadre* or *comadre,* and their relationship will become less formal and more friendly. Because they are now *compadres,* the child's parents will feel freer to approach their patron *(compadre/comadre)* when they are in trouble, and he or she will be morally obliged to help them out. Conversely, if their patron needs supporters (e.g., in politics), they ordinarily will feel obligated to supply that support. Because clientage institutions like *compadrazgo* frequently remake the relationship of unrelated individuals on the model of formal kinship, anthropologists sometimes describe *compadres* as **fictive kin.**

Stratified societies with large populations and a complex division of labor ordinarily are associated with the political form called the **state** (discussed in more detail in Chapter 7). The organic solidarity of state societies is maintained by a new kind of institution neither present nor needed in small-scale, egalitarian societies: bureaucracy. A **bureaucracy** is a hierarchically organized set of formal statuses, each of which is associated with a highly specific role and all of which are designed to work together to ensure the smooth functioning of complex organizations such as state governments or business corporations. Ideally, bureaucrats defend the avowed purposes of the organizations they serve, and much of their work involves following proper procedures in performing the particular tasks for which they are responsible. Complex organizations could not function without bureaucracies, but the formality and complexity of bureaucratic procedures often frustrates outsiders and may tempt bureaucrats to manipulate their positions for their own personal benefit.

Descriptions in terms of caste or class may be useful in tracing the gross outlines of the structure of complex stratified societies, but they are rarely sufficient to characterize all the significant dimensions of social organization found in such societies. Anthropologists recognize the importance of additional categories used by members of these societies that may be embedded within or may crosscut caste or class structures. With this in mind, they also have long paid attention to the category of race and have grown increasingly interested in distinctions framed in terms of ethnic identity, gender, and sexual preference.

6.4 Race

The concept of **race** was deeply intertwined with the very origin of anthropology as a discipline (see discussion in Chapter 2). Although some late-nineteenth-century physical anthropologists hoped to demonstrate a causal connection between the physical attributes of a group and their language and customs, early-twentieth-century anthropologists worked hard to expose the flaws in such attempts. The modern concept of culture was developed to explain how individuals could learn *any* language or culture, regardless of their biological origins, and to argue against schemes that tried to classify the world's peoples into mutually exclusive races and to rank them hierarchically.

At the same time, the absence of any biological basis for racial categories has never prevented people in some societies from inventing *cultural* categories based on a group's supposed origins or physical appearance and then using such categories as building blocks for their social institutions. Precisely because racial categories are culturally constructed on the basis of superficial appearances, however, different societies may draw the boundaries around racially defined social groups in different ways.

For example, as the twenty-first century dawns, people living in the United States tend to classify people into several different racial categories, but the great divide remains between two major racial categories, black and white. The enslavement of Africans by Europeans in the United States and the continued oppression of their descendants even after emancipation in the nineteenth century have created a social reality for residents of the United States in which the divide between black and white appears so obvious as to be beyond question. To be sure, continued world domination by societies whose ruling groups trace their origins to Europe has sustained a global hierarchy in which light skin is valued over dark skin. And yet, outside the United States, in the Caribbean or in Brazil, where Africans also suffered under European slavery, race is understood in different ways. Rather than an unchanging identity that people carry around with them everywhere they go, the racial identity one claims, or is accorded by others, may vary from situation to situation, depending on who else is present. That is, in any particular social setting, those with the lightest skin may claim, and be accorded, the identity of "white," but when they move into a different setting and interact with others whose skin is lighter than theirs, they may have to accept being assigned to one of a variety of lower-status, nonwhite categories. Some anthropologists use the term *colorism* to describe this pattern of racial classification, in contrast to the once-and-for-all pattern of racial classification found in the United States.

Moreover, social mobility and the cultural changes that accompany it—learning the dominant language, getting an education, finding gainful employment, adopting new customs in diet and dress—may be interpreted as movement from one racial group into another. Thus, in some parts of Latin America, indigenous people who cut their hair, speak Spanish, wear European clothing, get an education, and find Western-style occupations may be classified by other members of their society as "white" or "mixed" rather than "indigenous," even though their outward biological features have not altered. Anthropologists sometimes use the term *social race* to describe these cases, in which so-called racial labels are used to refer to cultural rather than physical differences between groups.

6.5 Ethnicity

The distinction between classifications based on biology and on culture is thus not clear-cut. This highlights the ways that people can emphasize or downplay any of a wide range of physical and cultural attributes, either to define an identity for themselves or to assign an identity to others. This ambiguity appears when we consider another important social category investigated by anthropologists, that of the **ethnic group.** Ethnic groups usually are distinguished from other kinds of social groups based on attributes defining group membership that are cultural in nature: shared language, shared religion, shared customs, shared history. However, because all this cultural sharing could never have occurred if group members did not regularly interact, and even intermarry, ethnic identity is often thought, by both group members and outsiders, to be rooted in some common biological origin. Indeed, some anthropologists think of racial identity as being no different from ethnic identity, except that racial identity supposedly is biological in origin while ethnic identity has a cultural origin. And in practice, the concepts of both race and ethnic group often overlap with the concept of nation (discussed in more detail in Chapter 7).

All such cultural identities—whether understood in terms of kinship or race or ethnic identity—develop in opposition to other, similar identities in a complex social setting. Thus, the boundaries that eventually come to be recognized between races or ethnic groups are a product of both internal self-definition and external definition by others. Of course, a sense of group belonging, and the ability to distinguish one's own group from neighboring groups, stretches far back into the human past. What makes the study of racial or ethnic or national identity so important today, however, is the new role such groups take on within the boundaries of contemporary nation-states.

As discussed in Chapter 7, nation-states are relatively new forms of political organization, first developing in late-eighteenth-century and nineteenth-century Europe and the Americas and later spreading throughout the globe following the dissolution of Western colonial empires. Before the French Revolution, European states were ruled by kings and emperors whose access to the throne was officially believed to have been ordained by God. After the French Revolution, which thoroughly discredited the divine right of kings and proclaimed the "Rights of Man," a new basis for legitimate state authority had to be found. Over the course of the nineteenth century, the notion developed that rulers were legitimate only if they ruled over other members of the nation to which they themselves belonged.

When legitimacy began to depend on the perfect overlap of nation and state, on a recognized bond of cultural or linguistic or religious—that is, national—identity between ruler and ruled, the persistence of groups with different forms of identity within the boundaries of the nation-state became problematic. If such groups successfully resisted assimilation into the nation that the state was supposed to represent, their existence called into question the legitimacy of the state and its rulers. Indeed, if their numbers were sufficient, they might well claim that they were a separate nation, entitled to a state of their own! This situation describes much contemporary political life at the turn of the twenty-first century, when ruling regimes in more and more nation-states, fearful of losing stability and legitimacy in the eyes of the world, engaged in violence against all citizens who challenged their right to rule. **Ethnocide** (the destruction of a culture) and **genocide** (the physical extermination of an entire people) have often been the result, generating movements of refugee and immigrant populations whose social and political status is often anomalous and ambiguous in a world of nation-states.

In recent years, anthropologists have paid particular attention to the ways in which oppressed racial and ethnic groups, whether resident or immigrant, have struggled to mobilize their members to resist oppression. This has occurred in countries all over the world, including those of Europe and North America. As forces of globalization have weakened nation-states and promoted the flow of large numbers of people of various backgrounds into societies different from their own, new ethnic contacts and ethnic frictions have developed.

6.6 Gender

These global ethnic phenomena are a striking illustration of the way in which contemporary cultural developments have led anthropologists to rethink many long-held assumptions. But some anthropologists might argue that even further reaching has been the continuing impact of feminism on social science scholarship. In the early decades of the twentieth century, most ethnographies, including those written by women, were based primarily on the views of male informants, even concerning matters pertaining to women. Thus, most discussions of "the culture" of a group in fact portrayed culture from the viewpoint of men (often high-status men). When women were discussed at all, it was usually in the context of marriage and the family, and the assumption seemed to be that women's cultural roles as wives and mothers followed "naturally" from the biological facts of pregnancy and lactation. Margaret Mead's demonstration in the 1930s of the lack of correlation between biological sex and culturally expected behaviors of males and females in society was a well-known exception to this pattern.

Beginning in the 1960s, however, feminist anthropologists forced a serious reexamination of traditional assumptions about the roles of women and men in human society. Their first success was to present overwhelming ethnographic evidence showing that the cultural roles of women and men in any society could not be predicted from or reduced to their biological anatomy. It has thus become commonplace in cultural anthropology to use the term **sex** to refer to the physical characteristics that distinguish males from females (e.g., body shape, distribution of body hair, reproductive organs, sex chromosomes). By contrast, **gender** is used to refer to the culturally constructed roles assigned to males or females, and these vary considerably from society to society. Early feminist anthropology emphasized, as Mead had done, that gender and biological sex did not correlate.

As feminist anthropologists began examining past ethnographies for gender bias, they also encouraged new ways of doing research and writing ethnography that explored women and their activities in *all* areas of life, not merely marriage and family. Anthropologists now commonly acknowledge that "the culture" of any particular group may well look different to women than it does to men, and they bring this awareness to their own fieldwork and ethnographic writing.

The thoroughgoing reconsideration of traditional anthropological concepts promoted by feminists, ethnic minorities, indigenous peoples, and others in recent years can be placed within the context of the larger intellectual critique of modernity, including modern scientific rationality, that has been called **postmodernism** (discussed in Chapters 1 and 12). Much postmodern criticism has been directed at concepts that are presumed to capture the universal essences of objects, relationships, or processes in the world. Thus, feminist anthropologists have struggled to debunk the supposed universal "truths" about women, showing that "women" was itself a problematic category that flattened out all the many different ways in which human persons with a female reproductive anatomy might live their lives. Women of different races and classes and ethnic groups, it has been shown, often lead very different lives within the same "culture." The categories of "race" and "class" and "ethnic group" can also be seen as problematic, since the experiences of, for example, men and women belonging to the same race, class, or ethnic group are also very different from one another. Moreover, the relevance of one's ethnic identity, as well as one's willingness to acknowledge it, has been shown to differ in different social settings.

6.7 Sexual Preference.

In recent years, one of the most important attempts to pick apart the supposed essence of a cultural category has been made by anthropologists and other social scientists exploring the highly controversial topic of sexual preference. Same-sex sexual practices have become an accepted topic for research in anthropology. One result has been that the traditionally unquestioned "normality" of heterosexual sexual practices has been called into question, and the culturally variable links between biological anatomy, gender identity, and sexual preference have been explored in a variety of ethnographic contexts. In a manner parallel to the development of feminist anthropology, legitimation of "homosexuality" as a practice and as a topic of study was followed by critiques highlighting the Western male bias tacitly attached to the term. As a result, the varieties of "homosexual" experience in Western societies have been scrutinized, allowing the recognition of important differences in the experiences of gay, lesbian, bisexual, and transgendered individuals. These studies have been supplemented not only by ethnographic research on similar topics in other cultures but also by a reexamination of older ethnographic writings about societies in which nonheterosexual practices have been institutionalized. In this regard, anthropologists have given particular attention to research and writing on the cultural and sexual practices of the so-called berdache.

The term **berdache** traditionally has been used in anthropology to refer to indigenous (especially Native American) social roles in which men (and sometimes women) were allowed to take on the activities, and sometimes the dress, of members of the opposite sex. Sometimes berdache is defined as "male transvestite," but this definition is inadequate because it ignores the fact that a man who took on other aspects of a woman's role might also, as women did, establish sexual relationships with men. Indeed, the term meant "male prostitute" to the early French explorers in the Americas who first used it to describe the men they observed engaging in such behavior.

Today, many gay and lesbian anthropologists refuse to use the term, as do many contemporary members of indigenous societies who view themselves as modern embodiments of these alternative-gender roles. Some have proposed using terms like *third gender* or *two spirit* instead, although no consensus has yet been achieved. As ethnographic research on alternative-gender roles and sexual practices in a wide variety of societies accumulates, a more adequate set of analytic concepts is likely to be developed. At present, this research continues to generate controversy, not only in societies whose members condemn nonheterosexual intercourse but also among anthropologists whose theoretical and personal views on sexuality are not easily reconciled.

For Further Reading

GENDER/SEXUALITY

Blackwood and Wieringa 1999; Bonvillain 1995; Di Leonardo 1991; Gutmann 1997; Herdt 1994; Miller 1993; Stone 1997; Suggs and Miracle 1993; Weston 1993

SOCIAL ORGANIZATION

Fried 1967; Graburn 1971

ETHNICITY

Williams 1989

COLONIALISM

Pels 1997

RACE

Smedley 1999

GENOCIDE AND ETHNOCIDE

Messer 1993; Nagengast 1994

7

Political Anthropology

The key terms and concepts covered in this chapter, in the order in which they appear:

state
political anthropologists
politics

coercive power
power
persuasive power

political ecology
ecological
    anthropology
political economy

raiding
feuding
mediator
negotiation
bloodwealth
warfare

egalitarian
band

tribes
chiefdoms

social stratification
caste
class
slaves
sumptuary
wealth
prestige

complex societies
acephalous
consensus

headman
big man

statuses
roles
authority
bureaucracy

formalization
sanctions
law
substantive law
procedural law
civil law
criminal law
law codes
courts
adjudicate
crime

nationalism
nation
nation-states
imagined
    community

domination
hegemony
ideology
hidden transcripts

WHEN NINETEENTH-CENTURY ethnologists from Europe and North America began to compare societies across space and over time, they noticed not only that members of different societies made a living in different ways but also that daily life in all these varied societies seemed to unfold in an orderly and predictable manner. The presence of apparent social order in societies of different sizes, organized according to a variety of diverse social principles, puzzled some observers because of their own assumptions about what made social order possible. These ethnologists lived in societies whose leaders assumed that individual human beings were naturally selfish and competitive, and thus could live peaceably together only if they were compelled to do so by threat of physical force. That is, they believed that social order was not natural but could result only from the external imposition of power.

7.1 Power

Power often has been understood first and foremost in terms of physical coercion, especially by European philosophers and social scientists, who traditionally define power in terms of one individual's ability to compel others to do what he or she wants them to do. This view of power seemed natural in societies like those of Europe and America that were organized into states. Anthropologists agree that states were not invented in Europe but first appeared several thousand years ago in half a dozen different regions of the world. Anthropologists group these states together, ancient and modern, because they appear to share certain prototypical features. That is, for anthropologists, a **state** is an independent political entity that controls a geographical territory with clear boundaries and that defends itself from external threats with an army and from internal disorder with police.

States have specialized institutions to raise revenue by collecting taxes and to carry out other public duties, such as maintaining roads and markets. All of these tasks become possible because the state monopolizes the legitimate use of physical force.

Certainly, European history, following the religious wars of the sixteenth and seventeenth centuries and the revolutions of the late eighteenth and nineteenth centuries, seemed to prove that nothing less than deadly force in the hands of a strong state will keep people in line. Without the state, according to seventeenth-century philosopher Thomas Hobbes, life was supposed to be "nasty, brutish, and short." And yet, historical and ethnographic materials suggested strongly that, elsewhere in the world, many societies not organized into states had long been able to conduct their external and internal affairs in an orderly fashion. Could it be that power was successfully institutionalized in these societies in forms other than the state?

These kinds of questions have traditionally been asked by **political anthropologists.** These scholars share with political philosophers and political scientists an interest in **politics:** the ways in which power relations (particularly unequal power relations) affect human social affairs. Political anthropologists have paid particular attention to how members of different societies go about making public decisions that affect the society as a whole. They also are interested in why people either accept these decisions as right and proper or criticize them as wrong and improper. Political anthropologists compare how leadership is understood and exercised, how competition between rivals is regulated, and how disputes are settled. In all these areas, people's cultural beliefs and practices clearly play a large role. In recent years, increasing attention has been focused on the ways in which larger regional and global power relations shape opportunities for the exercise of power by local groups (see additional discussion of global issues in Chapter 11).

To study all these dimensions of power requires a view of power that does not limit it merely to **coercive power,** or the use of physical force. For many anthropologists, a more useful definition of **power** would be a generalized capacity to transform. From this point of view, coercion is only one kind of power, and attention must be paid to all those other forms of influence that transform people's practical activities or their ideas about the world *without* relying on physical force. Forms of **persuasive power** range from the charisma of a religious prophet, to the formally proscribed but ubiquitous ability of weaker members of society to manipulate social rules to promote their own well-being, to the outright refusal of compliance shown by factory workers who go on strike.

7.2 Political Ecology and Political Economy

As the latter example suggests, for anthropologists, political issues do not develop in a vacuum but are intimately related to other dimensions of collective life, especially economic matters. The intersection of politics and economics has been approached in two main directions by anthropologists. **Political ecology** pays attention to the ways in which human groups struggle with one another for control of (usually local) material resources. This approach fits within the broader orientation of **ecological anthropology,** which focuses on the relationships linking particular human populations and the immediate ecological settings to which they must adapt to survive (see additional discussion of populations and environments in Chapter 8). Although some political ecologists emphasize the way in which ecological factors shape the political struggle for resource control, others emphasize the way in which the outcome of political struggles determines which groups will have access to how much of which resources.

By contrast, other political anthropologists see their work as falling within the purview of what has been called **political economy;** that is, the focus is on the political creation (and consequences) of the division of labor in society. Political anthropologists studying non-Western societies that have been subject to colonial domination often find a focus on political economy useful. This perspective offers a framework for describing and explaining how capitalist colonialism disrupted indigenous pre-capitalist political and economic arrangements, reorganized relations of production, expropriated local wealth and power, and promoted the formation of new social classes.

7.3 Disputes and Dispute Resolution

One important focus of political anthropology has been on how the members of different societies, living within different kinds of economic and social institutions, handle their relations with their neighbors. Recall that a key task of the state as a political institution was to defend itself from external attack and from internal subversion. Anthropologists were curious about how societies not organized as states handled these matters. The ethnographic record shows that a variety of mechanisms, formal and informal, have been developed in different times and places. As they often have done when confronted with ethnographic variety, anthropologists invented classifications to sort out the patterns of dispute (and dispute resolution) about which they had information.

Scale is always important when considering these various mechanisms. Consider, for example, the issue of warfare. At the turn of the twenty-first century, when those of us who live in industrialized nation-states think about "warfare," we typically think of a conflict like World War I or World War II, in which the professional armies of two or more nation-states clash using modern weapons (machine guns, tanks, bombs, etc.). The war ends when one side concedes defeat, lays down its weapons, and agrees to formal, written terms of surrender. But such a model of warfare has almost nothing in common with the kinds of violent clashes more typically found in smaller-scale, nonindustrial societies without states. To make the differences plain, ethnologists worked out a set of categories that could distinguish modern warfare from these other kinds of conflict.

For example, violent conflicts can be distinguished from one another in terms of how long they last and what goals they are expected to achieve. **Raiding**, for instance, is defined as a short-term use of force with a limited goal, such as stealing a few head of cattle or other material goods, usually from a neighboring group. Pastoral peoples commonly resort to raiding to recover animals they believe are owed them or simply to increase the size of their own herds at the expense of a nearby group of herders. Raiding can be contrasted with **feuding,** which describes ongoing, chronic hostilities between groups of neighbors or kin. Feuds are politically destabilizing because they are potentially endless. Often a feud begins when a member of one kin group takes the life of a member of a neighboring kin group. Relatives of the dead person feel obliged to avenge the death of their kinsman or kinswoman and so vow to take the equivalent of "an eye for an eye, and a tooth for a tooth." In this way, feuding can be seen as a form of negative reciprocity (defined in Chapter 8). Feuding groups do not feel obliged to take the life of the specific individual who killed their relative; the death of any member of the group to which the killer belongs will restore the balance. But the group responsible for the first death will then feel obligated to avenge the death visited on them as repayment for the first death, and so on.

Peoples who engage in feuding are quite aware that this form of retaliation can escalate into a bloodbath. Therefore, some groups have invented cultural institutions that feuding groups can call upon to achieve settlement, such as a **mediator:** a formally recognized, neutral third party to whom the disputing parties can appeal to settle their differences. Mediators have no coercive power of their own but instead rely on the persuasive power of **negotiation**—that is, of verbal argument and compromise—to induce the hostile parties to come to a mutually acceptable resolution of their dispute. Mediators play an exceedingly important role when the parties to a feud are close neighbors who must somehow find a way to coexist despite their mutual grievances. Often mediators appeal to traditional practices designed to mollify the aggrieved party, such as an offer by the offending party of a given amount of material wealth (e.g., in livestock or other valuables), a payment frequently referred to as **bloodwealth.** Some anthropologists view the invention of bloodwealth as a major cultural achievement that for millennia has managed to short-circuit feuds and restrain their destructive capacity.

Warfare, by contrast, involves violent conflict on a significantly larger scale. Entire societies mobilize against each other, trying to kill as many members of the other society as possible until one side surrenders to the other. Warfare occurs when persuasive means of dispute resolution, such as diplomacy, either do not exist or have failed or are ignored, and physical combat becomes the only avenue open to settle differences. Of course, none of these classificatory labels is airtight; all of them are designed to highlight what appear to be salient similarities and differences from a political point of view. Real-life cases are always more complex and ambiguous than the labels themselves might suggest. For example, feuding carried out on a grand-enough scale begins to look a lot like warfare.

7.4 Forms of Political Organization

The contrast between feuding and warfare draws our attention back to an issue that has preoccupied so many political anthropologists: societies that engage in warfare typically have some form of centralized political organization, whereas societies that engage in feuding typically do not. Prehistorians and political anthropologists have compared the different political systems known from archaeology, history, and ethnography. Like the nineteenth-century evolutionists, they recognize four broad types of political systems that appear to have developed over the 200,000 or so years our species has existed and that correlate broadly with other cultural attributes, such as subsistence strategies and types of kinship organization (for discussion of subsistence strategies see Chapter 8; for kinship organization see Chapter 9). In the mid-twentieth century, anthropologists like Elman Service and Morton Fried offered new interpretations of cultural evolution that incorporated critiques of nineteenth-century schemes. Their work has influenced most subsequent anthropological discussions of comparative political systems.

The earliest political forms appear to have been **egalitarian;** that is, all (adult) members of the society had roughly equal access to valued resources, both material and social. The oldest human societies we know about archaeologically depended on foraging, and the egalitarian political form associated with this mode of subsistence has been called the **band.** Foraging societies are small in scale; historically and prehistorically, they were few in number and widely scattered across the land. Bands of foragers typically number no more than fifty individuals coresident at the same time. Tasks are assigned on the basis of gender and age, but the division is not rigid. Kinship systems are generally bilateral (defined in Chapter 9), and bands create alliances with one another through marriage. Relations of economic exchange are organized on the basis of reciprocity (defined in Chapter 8).

The domestication of plants and animals marked a major shift in the subsistence strategy, supporting somewhat larger egalitarian social groups that anthropologists call **tribes.** The major social change associated with those who took up *horticulture* (extensive agriculture) or those who began to herd animals is seen in the appearance of unilineal kinship groups (defined in Chapter 9) that became the joint owners of property in the form of farmland or herds. New cultural forms such as age grades (defined in Chapter 6) may create social links that crosscut kinship groups. Kin groups may compete with one another for resources, but they are not ranked hierarchically; indeed, within each kin group, the access of adults to communal resources remains broadly equal.

The first evidence of the erosion of egalitarian political forms is found in those societies organized as **chiefdoms.** Chiefdoms make use of the same forms of subsistence and kinship as tribes, but new social arrangements show the emergence of distinctions among lineages in terms of status or ranking. In particular, one lineage is elevated above the rest, and its leader (the chief) becomes a key political figure whose higher status often derives from his role in redistributive economic exchanges (defined in Chapter 8). The chief's higher rank (and that of the lineage to which he belongs) gives him an increased opportunity to favor his kin and his supporters with material or social benefits, but he has very limited coercive power. Significant power remains in the hands of lineages, who continue to control their own communal wealth in land or herds.

The social differentiation, ranking, and centralization that are incipient in chiefdoms are fully realized with the appearance of states. The state organization described previously (with its territory, army, police, tax collectors, and so forth) did not appear until well after the invention of intensive agriculture approximately 10,000 years ago, which generated surpluses that could be used to support full-time occupational specialists such as potters, weavers, metalworkers, priests, and kings.

7.5 Social Stratification

As well as monopolizing physical force, state organization enforces **social stratification;** a permanent, inherited inequality between the various component groups of which the society is composed. (Table 7.1 lists the basic forms of political organization.) Anthropologists frequently distinguish between **caste** societies, in which the members of distinct stratified groups are not allowed to move out of the stratum in which they were born, and **class** societies, in which some social mobility up or down the class hierarchy may occur (see Chapter 6 for details). At the very bottom of a class or caste hierarchy may be found a social category whose access to valued resources is so restricted that members do not even control their own labor. Anthropologists often describe these individuals as **slaves.**

Stratification means that some groups have disproportionate access to valued resources. For example, high-ranking groups may have **sumptuary** privileges; that is, they may be the only members

TABLE 7.1   Forms of Political Organization

Band

Tribe

Chiefdom

State

of society entitled to wear certain fabrics or eat certain foods. In stratified societies, moreover, valued resources include not just material **wealth** (e.g., land or herds) or cultural **prestige** (e.g., esteem or respect) but also power itself. That is, those who rule the state are able to use their monopoly on coercive power to keep the lion's share of wealth and prestige and to perpetuate this inequality from one generation to the next. Because of the elaborate division of labor and its hierarchical organization in stratified castes or classes, state societies often are called **complex societies,** especially by archaeologists and prehistorians, who contrast them with the less elaborate and more egalitarian bands and tribes that preceded them chronologically.

Those political anthropologists interested in the evolution of the state frequently have speculated on the forces that could have been responsible for transforming egalitarian political relations that had endured for thousands of years into unequal political relations. Many different single, unique causes, or *prime movers,* have been proposed to account for the emergence of political inequality and centralized hierarchy (e.g., population pressure, dependency on irrigation, conquest by neighbors, and environmental circumscription, to name but a few). The consensus among contemporary prehistorians seems to be that no single factor can explain all cases in which inequality and centralization emerged from egalitarian political arrangements. For example, archaeologists have uncovered the remains of many early societies organized as chiefdoms that never developed into states. It seems clear that while certain underlying factors must have been present, contingent historical factors also played an important role.

Some anthropologists are further concerned that preoccupation with explaining the "rise of the state" smuggles back into the analysis assumptions of unilineal evolutionism that had supposedly been expunged long ago. Such a preoccupation can make a drive toward social complexity from band, to tribe, to chiefdom, to state seem inevitable and irresistible, even if the paths to complexity are varied and have not always been taken and even though human history is littered with the fall of states and the disintegration of empires. To the extent that states and empires and other encompassing forms of social complexity are seen as powerful generators of inequality and oppression, moreover, the rise of state control will not necessarily be viewed as progressive, and the disintegration of an empire may be viewed as liberating. Overall, the open-ended unpredictability of future sociopolitical changes can then be openly acknowledged, and more attention can be paid to the ways in which societies organized with different degrees of complexity can coexist with and reshape one another.

7.6 Forms of Political Activity

The classification of political systems as bands, tribes, chiefdoms, and states can be useful even if one is not interested in their possible evolutionary relationships. Many political anthropologists have used these categories as prototypes for distinct forms of political life and have been more interested in exploring how these forms actually work. Such anthropologists have been intrigued by the striking contrast between egalitarianism and inequality, between diffuseness of power in egalitarian societies and centralized monopoly of power in stratified societies. As Meyer Fortes and E. E. Evans-Pritchard put it more than fifty years ago, centralized societies like chiefdoms or states have *heads* (e.g., chiefs or kings or presidents), whereas uncentralized societies do not; that is, they are **acephalous** (without heads). As Fortes and Evans-Pritchard noted, acephalous societies were not politically chaotic, but political order in such societies clearly seemed to be the result of cultural mechanisms rather different from the mechanisms upon which centralized societies relied. Many anthropologists set about trying to identify just what those mechanisms were. To describe a band or tribe as "stateless" or "acephalous" is to describe it in terms of what it lacks: a state, or a head of state. As indicated previously, however, some anthropologists prefer to describe bands and tribes in terms of what they possess, which is a high degree of political equality accorded to all adults (or, sometimes, to all adult males). People in the

United States or Europe tend to equate political equality with forms of electoral democracy. But to do so is misleading, because our forms of electoral democracy occur within the framework of a state, whereas the political equality found in egalitarian societies exists apart from the state.

To be sure, we find in bands and tribes many characteristics that might be justly described as "democratic"; for example, political decisions that affect the society as a whole must involve the consent of all the adults (or adult males) in the society. But members of egalitarian societies typically do not go to the polls to vote formally for or against a particular policy, with the understanding that whichever position gains the most votes wins. Instead, informal discussion and negotiation about alternatives take place among all adults who will be affected, a process that is feasible when the group is small, as is typical in most band and tribal societies. Eventually, a decision that all adult members of the society accept emerges from this process, a result known as **consensus.** This does not mean that consensus is easy to achieve. Precisely because no adult in an egalitarian society can force any other adult to do anything, negotiations require enormous verbal skill. Successful negotiators often employ a range of techniques, ranging from indirectly suggesting, to cajoling, to shaming, to predicting dire consequences for failure to comply. In all cases, we are referring here to the exercise of persuasive, not coercive, power.

Not surprisingly, some individuals in egalitarian societies are more skilled, imaginative, and successful negotiators than others, and their achievements do not go unrecognized. Indeed, their achievements lead other members of their society to accord them great prestige. Individuals in bands or tribes who enjoy such prestige may be asked for advice or deferred to when decisions must be made, because their past achievements, as hunters or ritual specialists, or fighters or diplomats, give their opinions greater weight than those of ordinary folk. Anthropologists have used the term **headman** to identify such individuals, who may be the ones chosen by their fellows to deal with outsiders in ambiguous or threatening situations. In fact, outsiders (such as representatives of a colonial power) often have assumed that members of indigenous groups who mediated between their own group and the colonial administration were leaders with coercive power. As we have seen, however, this assumption was incorrect when applied to headmen in bands or tribes, who have no capacity to force others to do their will. When colonial officials tried to incorporate "headmen" into their chain of command, expecting them to enforce compliance on the local level, they regularly discovered that, despite their prestige, headmen had no power to issue orders or force people to obey them. With the passage of time, under continued colonial rule, headmen often found themselves caught in an untenable position: expected by members of their own tribe to defend tribal interests against the colonial administration and expected by the colonial administration to extract compliance with colonial edicts from fellow tribesmen.

Another well-known anthropological example illustrating the exercise of persuasive power in egalitarian societies is that of the **big man.** Big men are "big" because of their ability to use their personal persuasive skills to arrange complex regional public events that involve kin and neighbors. In New Guinea, for example, big men gain personal prestige by organizing elaborate exchanges of valuables between their own and neighboring tribes. Such exchanges often begin as a kind of bloodwealth exchange: An end to hostilities is negotiated when the aggressors promise to present the aggrieved tribe with a quantity of wealth in the form of pigs, shells, money, and other valuables. Big men compete with one another to organize the collection and presentation of these goods, which is a major achievement, given that they have no coercive means to compel other members of their tribe to participate. Moreover, the initial exchange that marks the end of hostilities is rarely the last one. If the tribe that has received wealth wants to maintain or enhance its own prestige, it must eventually reciprocate with a return gift. It falls to big men in the receiving tribe to plan and carry out the reciprocal exchange, and they always aim to return more than they received, in order to enhance both their personal reputations and the reputation of their group.

7.7 Status and Role

The shift from egalitarian to stratified and from uncentralized to centralized political organization is also ordinarily a shift from largely informal sources of persuasive power to formally recognized social positions, or **statuses,** to which specific activities, or **roles,** are attached (see other references in Chapter 6). Persons occupying formal political statuses in a state (e.g., tax collectors) need not rely purely on their personal persuasive ability to get others to do what they want. Instead, they possess **authority:** the ability to exert influence and even limited coercive power because they legitimately occupy a formal political office. The powers exercised by tax collectors are ordinarily strictly delimited; if they tried, say, to use the authority of their office to gain control of property to which they were not entitled, they probably would be punished. Still, as long as they stayed within their prescribed sphere, tax collectors would probably (if grudgingly) be recognized as within their rights to demand appropriate sums from properly identified citizens, and the citizens, more often than not, would comply.

7.8 Social Control and Law

State societies function successfully because all the complex activities that take place within them are monitored by a more or less complex army of hierarchically organized public functionaries, each occupying a separate formal office with its own proper responsibilities and coercive powers. This form of public administration, or **bureaucracy,** illustrates another distinctive feature of states as forms of political organization: the **formalization** of a wide range of tasks (see also Chapter 6). To formalize a bureaucratic or political office means to specify, explicitly and publicly, the rights and responsibilities of the officeholder. State societies formalize a wide range of tasks that are carried out by informal or barely formalized means in bands, tribes, and chiefdoms. For example, gossip is a very effective way to enforce conformity in small-scale societies without a police force. By contrast, state societies formalize not only leadership positions but also occupational qualifications and the public social rules that members of the society are expected to obey. Perhaps even more significantly, states formalize the **sanctions,** or penalties, to be meted out if social rules are broken.

Most anthropologists agree that, in societies without states, including chiefdoms, proper social conduct is enforced largely by local groups using informal means. When, however, a centralized government publicly sets forth both explicit formal definitions of right conduct and explicit penalties for failure to observe such standards and backs these definitions with its monopoly on coercive power, anthropologists generally agree that it is appropriate to speak of **law.** In particular, they have been interested in comparing the ways in which law has developed or is administered in noncapitalist state societies.

The appearance of formal law in a state does not mean that informal means of social control disappear. Rather, formal law is ordinarily used to sanction only the most serious crimes, such as theft, murder, or treason. Formal laws usually aim to be universal in scope, applying to all members of a society who possess certain attributes, and they usually focus on compliance (or lack thereof) with specific obligations (rights and duties) that all such individuals are expected to honor. Such a system of law is known as **substantive law,** and it is often the most interesting ethnographically, since it encodes notions of right conduct that show much cross-cultural variation. Substantive law contrasts with **procedural law,** which describes how those accused of breaking the law are to be treated. Anthropologists who compare legal systems cross-culturally also often distinguish between **civil law,** the breaking of which affects only one or a few individuals, and **criminal law,** which regulates attacks against society or the state. Modern industrial states have developed complex **law codes,** in which explicit rules covering many areas of social, economic, and political life are articulated, together with the penalties incurred for breaking them.

Of course, members of any society, when accused of breaking the law (informal or formal), often deny that they have done so. As we saw, egalitarian societies have developed their own informal ways of resolving such disputes, including mediation, feuding, and wealth exchange. In state societies, by contrast, formal laws and penalties are accompanied by formal legal institutions, such as **courts,** for resolving disputes. Informal dispute resolution remains in the hands of the affected parties: Recall that feuding kin groups, together with a mediator, must work out *a* resolution of their differences that satisfies the groups. Different disputants, however, might work out their differences in entirely different ways. It is this lack of uniformity in dispute resolution that a state tries to overcome in two ways. First, the state removes resolution of the dispute from the hands of the parties involved and puts it into the hands of a formal institution, the court; second, it evaluates the disputants' claims against the universal rights and responsibilities encoded in laws with uniform penalties. Because the court is supposed to be an impartial forum, care must be taken to ensure that the truth is told. Thus, all court systems develop rituals designed to achieve that end, such as the administration of oaths or ordeals to those who give evidence. In the end, the formal officers who preside in a court of law (i.e., judges) **adjudicate** the case before them; that is, based on the law code, they decide how a dispute will be settled.

Clearly, this entire apparatus can exist only in complex state societies producing sufficient surplus wealth to support the specialized formal court system, with its law code, lawyers, judges, and punishments. In other words, a formal system of laws requires a formal system of punishments, or penal code, without which a full-fledged court system cannot function. Indeed, this system defines, for the society in which it is found, what formally counts as **crime** and what does not. New laws can be promulgated that turn formerly tolerated behavior (e.g., public begging) into a crime or that decriminalize formerly illegal behavior (e.g., when taxes are abolished, not paying one's taxes is no longer illegal). Documenting changes in a legal system can offer important insights into the changing values and practices of the society to which the legal system belongs.

7.9 Nationalism and Hegemony

Much of the ethnographic data on which the previous discussions are based were gathered in societies that once enjoyed political autonomy but at some time in the last 500 years came under the economic or political control of Western colonial powers. To be sure, capitalist colonialism did not affect all areas of the world at the same time or to the same degree, and many precolonial political institutions and practices survived, albeit under changed circumstances, well into the twentieth century. But the last two decades of the twentieth century exhibited an intensified push of capitalist practices into those areas of the globe that previously had been buffered from some of their most disruptive effects. And many political anthropologists in recent years have become less interested in local political particularities and more interested in global forces that increasingly shape the opportunities for local political expression.

Such anthropologists pay attention to political processes that began with the spread of European colonial empires. Political conquest and incorporation within one or another European empire destroyed many indigenous political institutions. However, colonial political practices stimulated colonized peoples to rethink and rework their understanding of who they were and how they should do politics. Much current anthropological investigation focuses on the paradoxical consequences of political independence in former European colonies.

The issues are complex and varied, but many anthropologists have been interested in the phenomenon of **nationalism.** Traditionally, anthropologists used the term **nation** as a synonym for ethnic group or tribe—that is, to identify a social group whose members saw themselves as a single people, because of shared ancestry, culture, language, or history. Such nations/tribes/ethnic groups did not necessarily have any connection to political systems we call states until the late eighteenth century, and especially the nineteenth century, in Europe. By the end of the nineteenth century, many Europeans believed that the political boundaries of states should correspond with cultural and linguistic boundaries—that is, that states and nations should coincide and become **nation-states.** In the latter half of the twentieth century, newly independent postcolonial states tried to realize the nation-state ideal by attempting to build a shared sense of national identity among their citizens, most of whom belonged to groups that shared few or no political or cultural ties in pre-colonial times.

At the same time, many groups that claim a common "national" identity on the basis of culture or history or language find themselves encapsulated within a larger state or, worse, scattered across the territorial boundaries of more than one state. Following the nation-state logic, many of these groups see themselves as legitimate nations entitled to their own states. As the twenty-first century unfolds, the explosive potential built into these situations has created difficult political challenges for millions of people across the globe and seems to cry out for anthropological analysis.

Many anthropologists have borrowed Benedict Anderson's concept of the nation as an **imagined community** (also discussed in Chapter 2), whose members' knowledge of one another does not come from regular face-to-face interactions but instead is based on their shared experiences with national institutions, such as schools or government bureaucracies, and the bonds created from reading the same newspapers and books. The often violent postcolonial histories of aspiring nation-states, involving coups d'état and civil strife, has demonstrated to participants and observers alike that national identity cannot be imposed by coercion alone. Persuasive power must also be used, which is why anthropologists have drawn on the work of Antonio Gramsci (1891–1937). Reflecting on the reasons the Italian nation-state was so much less successful in becoming unified than its European neighbors, Gramsci emphasized a contrast between the role of authoritarian domination (or coercive power) and hegemony (or persuasive power) that many contemporary social scientists have found useful. **Domination** can put a regime in power, but domination alone will not keep it in power. For one thing, it is expensive to keep soldiers and police on constant alert against resistance; for another, the people come to resent continued military surveillance, which turns them against the regime. This is why long-term stability requires rulers to use persuasive means to win the support of their subjects, thereby making a constant public show of force unnecessary. Gramsci used the term **hegemony** to describe control achieved by such persuasive means.

A variety of tactics can be used to build hegemony, including neutralizing opposition from powerful groups by granting them special privileges, and articulating an explicit **ideology** that explains the rulers' right to rule and justifies inequality. If the ideology is widely promulgated throughout the society (e.g., in schools, through media) and if rulers make occasional public gestures that benefit large sections of the population, they may forestall rebellion and even win the loyalty of those whom they dominate. Because hegemony depends on persuasive power, however, it is vulnerable to the critical attention of the powerless, whose reflections on their own experiences may lead them to question the ruling ideology. They may even develop interpretations of their political situation that challenge the official ideology. Sometimes the term **hidden transcripts** is used to describe these alternative (or *counterhegemonic*) understandings, since they are frequently too dangerous to be openly proclaimed. Because hidden transcripts offer an alternative, however, they offer openings to more sustained critiques of the status quo that eventually could lead to open rebellion.

Many anthropologists find the concept of hegemony to be useful because it offers a way of showing that oppressed groups that do not rise up in open revolt against their oppressors have *not* necessarily been brainwashed by the hegemonic ideology. Rather, such groups possess sufficient agency to create counterhegemonic interpretations of their own oppression. If they do not take up arms, therefore, this is probably because they have accurately concluded that rebellion would not succeed under current conditions. The concepts of hegemony and hidden transcripts help anthropologists to demonstrate that political concepts such as "freedom," "justice," and "democracy" do not have fixed meanings but may be the focus of cultural and political struggle between powerful and powerless groups in a society.

For Further Reading

POWER

Arens and Karp 1989; Wolf 1999

POLITICAL ANTHROPOLOGY

Fried 1967; Lewellen 1992; Service 1962, 1975

LAW

Harris 1997; Nader 1997; Pospisil 1971

NATIONALISM

Anderson 1983; Hughey 1998; Tambiah 1997

HEGEMONY AND HIDDEN TRANSCRIPTS

Scott 1987, 1992

8

Economic

Anthropology

The key terms and concepts covered in this chapter, in the order in which they appear:

domestic groups

subsistence strategies
domestication
foragers
food producers
transhumance
slash-and-burn
swidden
shifting cultivation
extensive agriculture
intensive agriculture
mechanized
industrial
agriculture
surpluses

capitalism

formalists

economy
scarcity

substantivists
original affluent
  society
modes of exchange
reciprocity
redistribution
potlatch
leveling mechanisms

proletariat
bourgeoisie

labor
means of production
consumers
alienation
mode of production
classes
relations of
  production

peasant
cash crops

production for use
production for
  exchange

formal economy
informal economy
articulating modes
  of production

consumption
basic human needs

ecological
  anthropologists
human ecologists
behavioral ecological
  anthropologists
culture inheritance
  theorists

conspicuous
  consumption

S INCE ITS FORMATIVE YEARS as a discipline, anthropology has been interested in the many and varied ways in which human beings in different societies make a living. In the late nineteenth century, anthropologists devoted much attention to the tools and techniques developed by various peoples to secure their material survival and well-being in a range of climates and habitats. Indeed, the objects people made for these purposes—spears, snares, fishnets, bows, arrows, hoes, plows, baskets, and the like—formed the collections of early ethnological museums in Europe and North America. Early anthropological theorists paid particular attention to the activities in which these objects figured, called the "arts of subsistence" by Lewis Henry Morgan (1818–81).

8.1 The "Arts of Subsistence"

Morgan focused on large-scale variation in patterns of the arts of subsistence in different human societies when he constructed his great unilineal scheme of cultural evolution (a discussion of this approach is found in Chapter 12). His key criterion for ranking subsistence patterns was technological complexity: the simpler the toolkit, the more "primitive" the society's arts of subsistence. Morgan's final scheme encompassed three great "ethnical periods"—Savagery, Barbarism, and Civilization—through which, he claimed, every human society either had passed or would pass as it evolved.

Morgan assumed that the society in which he lived had evolved further and faster than others on the globe and that, consequently, the arts of subsistence characteristic of those other societies could accurately be described in terms not only of what they possessed but also of what they lacked. Thus, "savages" were all those peoples who had never domesticated plants or animals for their subsistence. Morgan subdivided them into lower, middle, and upper categories based on the complexity of the tools and skills they had devised for living off nature's bounty; "upper savages," for example, not only controlled fire and fished but had mastered the bow and arrow. The invention of pottery signaled for them the beginning of Barbarism. "Barbarians" herded animals and/or cultivated plants, and they also invented new subsistence tools and techniques, such as iron implements and irrigated fields. All these advances were incorporated into the next ethnical period, that of "Civilization," which Morgan believed could be identified as soon as writing appeared.

Anthropologists have long since removed terms like *savage* and *barbarian* from their professional analytic vocabulary. They are well aware of how evolutionary schemes like Morgan's can be (and have been) used to rationalize the domination of the world by so-called civilized societies. But one does not have to accept these aspects of Morgan's analysis to recognize the importance of his classification of different arts of subsistence. He had collected information about a wide range of societies. He had hypothesized that variation in their arts of subsistence was systematic, showing up, for example, in correlations between particular technological developments and particular forms of social organization (especially kinship organization) in **domestic groups** (i.e., those whose members live in the same household). Karl Marx and Friedrich Engels (1820–95) read Morgan and were persuaded that his ethnical periods documented changes in precapitalist modes of production. But again, one does not have to be a Marxist to be both impressed and puzzled by the patterns of subsistence to which Morgan drew attention.

8.2 Subsistence Strategies

In early-twentieth-century North America, Franz Boas and his students, having roundly rejected unilineal schemes of cultural evolution, were suspicious of grand explanations and unwilling to make far-reaching claims (for more on the Boasians, see Chapter 12). But they were interested in documenting with great care how particular peoples went about making their living. As a result, throughout much of the first half of the twentieth century, anthropologists hesitated to do more than offer a loose categorization of the various subsistence strategies adopted by the peoples of the earth. The **subsistence strategies** identified—hunting and gathering (foraging), pastoralism, horticulture, and agriculture—reiterated the distinctions that Morgan had recognized.

The key feature distinguishing these strategies is **domestication:** regular human interference with the reproduction of other species in ways that makes them beneficial to ourselves. Hunter-gatherers—now usually called **foragers** or food collectors—are those who do not rely on domesticated plants or animals but instead subsist on a variety of wild foodstuffs. Their knowledge of their habitats is encyclopedic, and they manage to live quite well by roaming over large tracts of land in search of particular seasonal plant foods, water sources, or game. By contrast, practitioners of the other three subsistence strategies depend on domesticated species and so are sometimes referred to as **food producers** rather than food collectors. Pastoralists rely on herds of domesticated animals, such as cattle, camels, sheep, or goats, and regularly move these herds, sometimes over great distances, as water and forage in one area are used up. In many parts of the world, these movements are patterned in yearly cycles of **transhumance,** as herders move from dry-season pastures to wet-season pastures and back again.

Horticulturalists cultivate domesticated plants by using human labor and simple tools and techniques to modify local vegetation or soil texture before planting their crops. In **slash-and-burn** or **swidden** cultivation, for example, hand tools are used to cut down all vegetation except large trees from an area to be planted. The vegetation is then burned, and the ash serves to fertilize the crops. But swidden farmers can use a particular field for only a few growing seasons before the soil is exhausted and must be left fallow for several years to regenerate. As a result, swidden farmers must move on to clear new fields every few years, which is why their practices are sometimes also referred to as **shifting cultivation.** Shifting cultivation is highly productive and energy efficient, but it functions well only when farmers have access to enough land to live on while old fields lie fallow long enough (often from seven to ten years or more) to regenerate.

Shifting cultivation is thus sometimes also called **extensive agriculture** because so much land is required to support so few people.

Only with **intensive agriculture** do we find societies exploiting the strength of domestic animals, by harnessing them to more complex tools like plows and growing and harvesting crops with the help of irrigation and fertilizers. Intensive agriculturalists first appeared some 10,000 years ago in Southwest Asia. Their farming practices are intensive because the techniques they employ allow them to produce more than shifting cultivators could produce on the same amount of land, while keeping their fields in continuous use. Contemporary intensive farming practices, often called **mechanized industrial agriculture,** rely on industrial technology for machinery, fertilizers, pesticides, and herbicides. This form of agriculture uses vastly more energy than does shifting cultivation, but it enables a few farmers to produce enormous amounts of food on vast expanses of land, their "factories in the field." (Table 8.1 lists the major subsistence strategies.)

Intensive agriculture marked an important break from forms of extensive agriculture because it allowed farmers to produce **surpluses** beyond what they required to survive from harvest to harvest and still save enough seed for the next year's crop. Agricultural surpluses supported the first ancient civilizations by making possible new and complex forms of social organization, involving a specialized division of labor that promoted technical developments in all areas of material life. Writing and its analogues

TABLE 8.1 Major Subsistence Strategies

Foraging

Herding

Extensive agriculture (also known as horticulture, slash-and-burn, swidden)

Intensive agriculture

Industrialized food production

(such as the *quipu* in Andean civilizations) did not drive these changes, but they were extremely useful for various kinds of political, economic, and social record-keeping.

8.3 Explaining the Material Life Processes of Society

In general, fieldworking cultural anthropologists have left investigation of the origin of subsistence strategies and the rise of ancient civilizations to archaeologists and prehistorians. Given the pernicious use to which extreme and exaggerated unilineal evolutionary claims had been put in the nineteenth century, early-twentieth-century ethnographers preferred to document the enormous amount of diversity still to be found in the material life of living societies. But this pursuit of cultural documentation, apparently for its own sake, struck later generations of anthropologists as unwarranted and pernicious in its own way. They sensed there were patterns to be detected and explained, and this required a professional willingness to develop theories that could generalize across particular cases.

One attempt to reintroduce theory into the anthropological study of material life was made by Melville Herskovits (1895–1963) around the time of World War II. Herskovits urged anthropologists to borrow concepts and theories from neoclassical economics, the scholarly discipline rooted in Adam Smith's efforts in the eighteenth century to make sense of the new Western economic system later known as **capitalism.** Herskovits was persuaded that the concepts and theories of neoclassical economies had been refined to such a degree of scientific objectivity and formal precision that they could be applied to economies very different from the one they originally were invented to explain. Those anthropologists who decided to follow Herskovits's suggestion came to be known as formal economic anthropologists, or **formalists.**

Formalists took concepts like *supply, demand, price,* and *money,* which had successfully been used to analyze economic activity in capitalist market economies, and searched for their analogues in non-Western, noncapitalist societies. They realized, of

course, that many such societies had no system of coinage performing all the functions Western money performed. But they
noted that objects like iron bars or lengths of cloth or shells often
seemed to be used much the way people in capitalist societies used
money, as a medium of exchange or measure of value. And so formalists tried to use the ideas neoclassical economists had developed about money to make sense of, say, the way people in society
X used shells. Or formalists might analyze customs in which a
groom's family offered material valuables to the family of a bride
to solemnize a marriage. This transaction looked very much like a
"purchase," with something other than money being offered in
exchange for a highly valued "good," the bride. Formalists thus
tried to explain how much it "cost" to "pay for" a bride in the
society. Adopting the assumptions of neoclassical theory, formalists assumed that each party to a marriage transaction would try
to get as much as possible out of the transaction while giving as
little as possible in return. Therefore, the number of cattle actually
accepted in exchange for a bride would be subject to the forces of
supply and demand, and the parties would agree on a "bride
price" whereby supply and demand balanced.

Formalists did not view themselves as ethnocentric when they
analyzed non-Western, noncapitalist economic activities in this way.
They thought that any culture-bound features of the concepts and
theories they were using had long since been eliminated. But other
anthropologists disagreed. These critics believed that, despite its
sophistication, neoclassical economic theory still bore many traces
of its origins in Western capitalist society. Perhaps the most obvious
trace could be seen in the neoclassical understanding of just what
economy meant: buying cheap and selling dear in order to maximize one's individual utility (or satisfaction).

Critics pointed out that neoclassical economics, like capitalist
society itself, subscribes to a particular view of human nature that
sees isolated individuals as the only genuine human reality. That
is, human beings are viewed as creatures who are by nature self-
interested egoists who always act in ways that will increase their
own individual well-being. Moreover, human beings all live under
conditions of **scarcity**; that is, there will never be enough of all the

material goods they desire to go around. As a result, the basic human condition consists of isolated individuals competing with one another, under conditions of scarcity, to obtain as much of what they want for as little as possible. Society might view such behavior negatively as selfish or greedy, but according to the neoclassical view, human society is artificial, secondary, and legitimate only to the extent that social rules do not interfere with each individual's pursuit of his or her own self-interest. That is, in a world of isolated individuals competing for access to scarce goods, looking out for Number One turns out to be a good thing—indeed, the *rational* thing to do—because putting others' needs first might interfere with maximizing one's own happiness.

Still, Adam Smith and others believed that when competition was carried out among individuals of more or less equal wealth and power, private vice could lead to public virtue. For instance, if you tried to cheat your customers, word would get around, and they would buy from other producers, causing you to lose money. Thus, you end up happier if you make your customers happy as well. Indeed, the price on which the two of you decide ideally ought to provide the best possible value either party might hope to obtain.

Only if such a view of human nature is accepted does neoclassical economic theory make sense. But anthropological critics were convinced that such a view of universal "human nature" could *not* make sense of the economic practices ethnographers had discovered in the *particular* non-Western, noncapitalist societies where they had done fieldwork. They pointed out that many non-Western economic systems were built on the assumption that human beings were, first and foremost, social creatures with legitimate obligations to other members of the societies in which they lived. Indeed, economic arrangements in such societies were shaped to the contours of other religious or political or kinship institutions in the society. That is, economic activities were *embedded* in the noneconomic institutions that made the society as a whole function properly. Rather than a measure of how individuals universally allocated scarce resources among alternative (presumably universal) ends, these anthropologists preferred to think of an economy as the concrete (and particular) way in which material goods and services were made available to members of a given society. Capitalism might allow individuals the freedom to pursue their own self-interest apart from the interests of others, but such an economic system was a recent and unusual addition to the ethnographic and historical record. Those anthropologists who defined economic systems in terms of their substantive institutional arrangements for provisioning their members came to be called **substantivists.** Substantivists argued that describing noncapitalist economic systems using neoclassical economic theory could only distort and misrepresent what was actually going on in those economies.

American anthropologist Marshall Sahlins, a leading substantivist, set about debunking what he viewed as formalist misrepresentation of economic life in non-Western, noncapitalist societies. After surveying a substantial ethnographic literature that described how foragers made a living, for example, Sahlins asked Westerners to reconsider how people might come to obtain more than enough of whatever they wanted—that is, become "affluent." Since the rise of industrial capitalism, many people assumed that the only path to affluence was by producing much, but Sahlins argued that a second "Zen road" to affluence consisted in desiring little. Foragers had very few material desires, and the habitats in which they lived were more than able to satisfy these needs. Thus, Sahlins concluded, the **original affluent society** was not industrial capitalism, but foraging.

8.4 Modes of Exchange

Sahlins also drew upon the work of economic historian Karl Polanyi, whose work also showed just how misleading it was to suppose that all human economies, in all times and places, had been based on capitalist principles, given that the key components of market capitalism had come together only within the past few centuries in western Europe. Polanyi distinguished among different **modes of exchange**—the patterns according to which distribution takes place—and argued that the capitalist mode of market exchange followed principles quite different from the principles that governed exchange in pre- or noncapitalist societies. He emphasized two particular noncapitalist modes of exchange: reciprocity and redistribution.

Sahlins borrowed Polanyi's classification of modes of exchange and tested them against a wide range of ethnographic data. He found that **reciprocity** governed exchange in small, face-to-face societies, especially those whose members lived by foraging. He also distinguished different forms of reciprocity. *Generalized* reciprocity involved no record-keeping, and parties assumed that exchanges would balance out in the long run. *Balanced* reciprocity required both that a gift be repaid within a set time limit and that goods exchanged be of roughly the same value. *Negative* reciprocity involved parties who repeatedly tried to get something for nothing from one another in a relationship that might continue over time, each trying to get the better of the other.

Redistribution as a mode of exchange requires the presence in a society of some central person or institution. Goods flow toward this central point and are then redistributed among members of the society according to their cultural norms of what is appropriate. (Table 8.2 lists the basic modes of exchange.) Varieties of redistribution range from such non-Western institutions as the **potlatch** practiced by the indigenous inhabitants of the northwest coast of North America to the income tax and social welfare institutions of modern nation-states. To the degree that they exist, modes of redistribution act as **leveling mechanisms;** that is, they

TABLE 8.2 Modes of Exchange

Reciprocity
  Generalized
  Balanced
  Negative
Redistribution
Market exchange

shrink gaps between rich and poor. In noncapitalist societies integrated by redistribution, the person responsible for amassing and then redistributing goods earned great prestige for his generosity, but he was often materially worse off afterward than most other members of the group. Polanyi pointed out that both reciprocity and redistribution may persist in societies organized along capitalist lines. In the United States, for example, exchange relations between parents and children ordinarily are governed by generalized reciprocity, and the collection of income taxes and the dispersal of government subsidies to citizens involves redistribution; but most goods and services are produced and exchanged by means of capitalist market mechanisms.

Similar ideas were developed by French anthropologist Marcel Mauss (1872–1950), one of Emile Durkheim's colleagues, who contrasted *gift* economies of small-scale non-Western societies (based on reciprocity and laden with culturally significant noncommercial values) with *commodity* exchanges (in which a good's value is mediated by the capitalist market). A number of contemporary European anthropologists have developed Mauss's ideas to mount their own critique of market-centered analyses of noncapitalist economies.

8.5 Production, Distribution, and Consumption

The debate between the formalists and the substantivists about the proper way to do economic anthropology became quite bitter in the late 1950s and early 1960s, with no resolution. Hindsight reveals that the divide between them was sharpened by the Cold War. In the Cold War years (which stretched from the late 1940s to 1989, when the Soviet Union broke apart), the ideological opposition between the Western "free market" (the First World) and Soviet "communism" (the Second World) was so strong that anyone in the United States who questioned neoclassical economic theory ran the risk of being labeled a "communist sympathizer," which was virtually synonymous with "traitor." Especially after the Cuban Communist Revolution in 1959, views of economic life in non-Western societies that validated the assumptions of neoclassical theory were encouraged by members of the political elite in the United States. They hoped that, by showing a free-market route to economic prosperity, they could keep nations newly freed from colonial control (soon to be known as the Third World) from following Cuba's example.

But the late 1960s and 1970s brought a new dynamic to the Cold War. Citizens in Western countries began to question publicly the official Cold War rhetoric they had been taught. In those unsettled years, some economic anthropologists began to study texts by Marx and his followers. Marxian economic analysis, which offered its own set of formal concepts and theories, appealed to these anthropologists, and they tried to use Marxian analysis to make sense of their ethnographic data on non-Western economic life.

Although the debates among economic anthropologists can sometimes still become bitter, dialogue remains viable because all of them, regardless of perspective, largely agree that economic life can be divided into three phases: production, distribution, and consumption. Where they disagree concerns what motivates human beings to engage in economic activity in the first place and which (if any) of the three phases of economic life is the most important in any economic system. Neoclassical economic theorists, dazzled by the power of modern capitalist markets, saw *distribution* to be key. After all, prices are set in the market when suppliers of goods and buyers of goods reach agreement about how much to offer for what. Historically, capitalist markets developed under circumstances in late-medieval European cities in which certain kinds of people—merchants, artisans—engaged in economic transactions free of the feudal obligations that controlled exchange between lords and peasants in rural areas. This freedom from obligations to others—the freedom to take one's chances buying and selling in the market—seemed to validate a view of human nature that eventually justified neoclassical economic theory in a society in which capitalism had triumphed. And it was a theory written primarily from the point of view of those who had engaged in free-market transactions and prospered.

Marx and his followers, however, paid attention to those whose participation in free capitalist markets kept them mired in poverty. These were the **proletariat,** the workers who toiled for wages in factories owned by the **bourgeoisie,** capitalists who sold for profit the commodities the workers produced. The very different positions of capitalists and workers was due to the fact that capitalists owned or controlled the means of production, whereas the workers owned nothing but their own labor power, which they were forced to sell to the capitalist at whatever price he was willing to pay, in order to survive. The transformation of once communally shared, productive property into the private property of individuals was viewed by Marx as the historical change that, together with industrial technology, produced the capitalist mode of production. The unequal relationship between workers and owners under capitalism meant that, when both met in the market to buy and sell, some of them (the capitalist owners) had considerably greater economic power than did others (the workers). The origins of that inequality required that attention be paid to the *production* phase of economic life.

Although not sentimental about precapitalist economic relations, Marxists pointed out that the "freedom" of free enterprise is double-edged. Noncapitalist economic relations were regularly hedged about with rights and obligations, as the substantivists and Mauss had stressed, and while these certainly constrained the ability of any individual to put his own selfish needs first, they also protected individuals from destitution. Even feudal peasants had economic rights their lords were obliged to respect. But both the protections and the constraints disappeared once labor became "free" in a capitalist system.

Labor is a central concept for a Marxian analysis of economic production, especially social labor in which people work together to transform the material world into forms they can use. In noncapitalist economic systems, people ordinarily work with others to produce goods for their own use, using tools and materials that belong to them. Under industrial capitalism, all this changes. For example, workers might produce shoes in a factory, but shoes, along with the tools, technology, and materials used to make them—what Marx called the **means of production**—belong to the factory owner, not to the workers. Instead, workers receive money wages in exchange for their labor. With these wages, they are supposed to purchase in the market food, clothing, and other goods to meet their subsistence needs; that is, they become **consumers.** Because workers compete with one another for scarce wage work, they must put their individual self-interest first if they are to survive; thus, they come to view their fellows as rivals rather than comrades.

In all these ways, Marx argued, life under capitalism separates workers from the means of production, from the goods they produce, and from other human beings, a situation he called **alienation.** For Marxists, therefore, the isolated individual who is the hero of the capitalist version of "human nature" is actually an alienated social being forced into existence under the historically recent economic conditions of Western capitalism. Marx and most of his followers were interested in understanding how these socioeconomic conditions had developed in Western European societies. Like Marx, many also found the situation intolerable and believed that the point was not to understand society but to change it.

Marxian ideas exerted a powerful influence in anthropology in the latter third of the twentieth century, and economic anthropologists have drawn from them in a variety of ways. It is important to emphasize, however, that even those anthropologists with strong commitments to leftist politics feel quite free to criticize and to reject specific Marxian assumptions or concepts as they see fit. Among those Marxian concepts that have been the most important in economic anthropology, we will emphasize here only one: the mode of production.

8.6 Mode of Production

Marx characterized European capitalism as a mode of production, and he contrasted it with the feudal mode of production that preceded it. A **mode of production** refers generally to the way the production of material goods in a society is carried out. Not only does it involve the tools, knowledge, and skills needed for production (i.e., the means of production), but it also depends on a particular division of social labor in terms of which different groups, or **classes,** of people are responsible for various productive activities, or the **relations of production.** In the feudal and capitalist modes of production, the central division of labor was between rulers and ruled: lords and peasants in feudalism, and owners and workers in capitalism.

A key element in the Marxian analysis of modes of production concerns the nature of the relationship linking classes to one another in a particular society. Marx's point was that, although both classes had to work together for production to succeed, their economic interests were nevertheless contradictory because of their different relations to the means of production. For example, workers want the profits from their labor to go into higher wages, whereas the owners would prefer to keep wages low and keep as much profit as they can for themselves. The potential for class conflict was therefore built into any mode of production. Eventually, Marx predicted, these class contradictions would undermine the mode of production, leading to a revolution that would bring forth a new and improved mode of production.

Anthropologists studying economic conditions in different societies do not necessarily accept Marx's prophecies about revolution. But they have wondered whether the noncapitalist economic patterns revealed by fieldwork might usefully be understood as different modes of production. Some anthropologists working in Africa, for example, thought that the economic arrangements they observed among people who organized their societies (and their economic activities) on the basis of kinship might be framed as a *lineage mode of production*. That is, the opposed "classes" were elder and younger groups within particular lineages that owned important economic resources like agricultural land and implements (the *means* or *forces of production*). Like owners and workers under capitalism, the economic interests of elders and juniors were opposed and might lead to conflict: elders wanted to maintain their control over the forces of production, while juniors wanted to take it away.

8.7 Peasants

Other anthropologists have talked about a *peasant mode of production* observable in many contemporary Latin American societies. These societies are seen to be divided into classes, with peasants dominated by a ruling class of landowners and merchants. Anthropologists use the word **peasant** to refer to small-scale farmers in state societies who own their own means of production (simple tools, seed, and so forth) and who produce enough to feed themselves and to pay rent to their landlords and taxes to the government. Anthropologists have wondered how much autonomy peasants might have in particular societies and under what circumstances that autonomy might be undermined by changing political and economic conditions. For example, what happens to peasants who are forced to deal with the increasing penetration of capitalist market relations?

Many of the world's peasants were first introduced to capitalism as a result of European colonization. Colonized peasants continued to grow subsistence crops for their own consumption, but European colonizers regularly encouraged them to grow other crops that they could sell for cash. Sometimes these **cash crops** had been produced traditionally; in northern Cameroon in Africa, for example, peanuts were a traditional crop that local farmers began to sell on the market during the colonial period. Other times, cash crops were introduced from outside; in northern Cameroon, French colonial authorities introduced the variety of cotton now grown by local farmers and sold for cash. In this way, peasant **production for use** was pushed by colonial authorities in the direction of capitalist **production for exchange** in the capitalist market.

This form of agriculture (i.e., producing crops to be sold for cash rather than to be consumed at home) has had far-reaching effects on the economic life of peasants. To begin with, peasant farmers could continue to produce much of what they consumed, using the money they received for their cash crops to purchase imported goods or to pay taxes and school fees. Unfortunately, by using some of their land to plant cash crops, less was left to plant subsistence crops. In many cases, this led over time to increasing dependence on the money from cash cropping to buy necessities that could no longer be produced, or produced in sufficient quantity, to keep a peasant household going. Indeed, many ethnographers have documented situations in which members of ostensibly "peasant" households regularly leave the farm to perform wage work on plantations or in factories. Without this additional income, many peasant households would collapse.

And this situation, in which members of the same household are alternately farmers and wage workers, has led anthropologists to wonder exactly how to describe and analyze what they are seeing. Are these peasants no longer truly peasants? Does their increasing reliance on wage work for survival mean that they have been "captured" by an expanding capitalist mode of production? Have they been transformed from peasants into a rural proletariat? Some anthropologists have argued that this is indeed the case, and some ethnographic materials support their arguments. In other cases, however, the situation is more complicated. Although members of peasant households rely on wage work to keep their families going, they continue to farm, producing much of the food needed for household subsistence. Some anthropologists refer to these peasants-who-are-also-wage-workers as members of an emerging *peasantariat*.

From the perspective of neoclassical economic theory, members of this Third World peasantariat were understood to be "in transition" from "traditional" to "modern" (i.e., capitalist) economic practices. Neoclassical theory argued that capitalist economic institutions (those that paid taxes, obeyed government regulations, and otherwise adhered to rules set down by the state) belonged to sectors of the modern, national, **formal economy**, into which other, so-called backward sectors of the **informal economy** eventually would be absorbed. In former colonies that had recently become independent states, the formal sector was often quite small, whereas the informal economy was very important, especially in urban areas. Many migrants supported themselves and their families by engaging in all sorts of unregulated, untaxed, and even illegal economic activities, from smuggling, to peddling, to selling cooked food. They also might move from a period of employment within the formal sector to a period in the informal sector and then back again. Moreover, anthropological fieldwork showed that many people active in the formal or informal economy of a city might also have ties to relatives in rural areas who engaged in agriculture and with whom they pooled economic resources.

TABLE 8.3   Modes of Production

Kin-ordered

Tributary

Capitalist

Articulating

Anthropologists working in many so-called Third World societies documented the seeming resilience of precapitalist economic arrangements confronted by more recent capitalist institutions. Such arrangements seemed to be delaying indefinitely the promised transition from "tradition" to capitalist "modernity." Anthropologists of a neoclassical bent might argue that the transition was still inevitable but would simply take longer than they originally predicted. But others of a Marxian bent might suggest that the situation could be best described as a social formation composed of two or more **articulating modes of production.** That is, in settings such as former European colonies in Africa, precapitalist modes of production and the capitalist mode of production, each organized according to different relations of production, apparently have adapted to each other's presence. Under such circumstances, individuals and groups could participate in the pre-colonial relations of production when participation in the capitalist relations of production was too costly or did not suit them for other reasons. Some anthropologists have argued that, in this way, people were able to defend themselves against the potentially destructive effects of the capitalist market. (Table 8.3 lists some basic modes of production.)

8.8 Consumption

The final phase of economic activity is **consumption,** when the goods or services produced in a society are distributed to those who use them up, or consume them. Most economists, whether of neoclassical or Marxian persuasion, traditionally have had little to say about why it is that *these* goods and *these* services (as opposed to other goods and services) get produced and distributed. Either consumption preferences are reduced to the idiosyncratic, unpredictable, and inexplicable choices of individuals (as in neoclassical economics), or they are reduced to basic biological needs (as when Marx stated that human beings need first to eat and drink before they can make history). Some anthropologists have made similar arguments. Bronislaw Malinowski, for example, wanted to show that "primitive" peoples were, in fact, no less human than their "civilized" counterparts. He argued that, although all viable societies must satisfy their members' universal **basic human needs** for food, shelter, companionship, and so forth, each society has invented its own cultural way of meeting those needs. Malinowski's approach, however, failed to address the question of *why*, for example, Trobriand Islanders satisfied their need for food with yams and pork rather than with, say, sorghum and beef.

One way to answer such a question is to point out that yams and pork are locally available for consumption in the ecological setting to which Trobriand Islanders have become adapted. Answers of this form to questions about consumption were developed by ecological anthropologists beginning in the 1950s. **Ecological anthropologists** seek to understand a particular human group as but one population of living things, coexisting with other living populations in a particular environment. They share the same focus as other scholars who call themselves **human ecologists.** The approach of ecological anthropologists differs somewhat from that of other ecologists interested in humans, primarily because anthropologists have always been interested in how human dependence on culture mediates human adaptation to the environment. In any case, ecologically oriented anthropologists also disagree with one another about the importance of culture in human evolution and ecological adaptation. **Behavioral ecological anthropologists,** for example, have been heavily influenced by the ideas of sociobiology, a school of evolutionary thought that assigns culture little or no role in human adaptation but instead argues that genetically driven and/or environmentally driven necessity keep(s) culture "on a short leash." Other anthropologists, such as **culture inheritance theorists,** find sociobiological accounts

TABLE 8.4 Approaches to Consumption

Basic human needs (Malinowski)
Ecological
   Behavioral ecological anthropology
   Cultural ecology/cultural inheritance theory
Cultural/arbitrary

inadequate. They argue that symbolic culture has played a key mediating role in human evolution and that it continues to exert powerful influences on contemporary human ecological adaptations. (Table 8.4 lists some basic approaches to consumption.)

Culture appears to play an important role in consumption patterns for at least two reasons. First, consumption preferences often are more closely linked to membership in particular social groups than to the ecological setting in which one lives. Second, the consumption preferences people share often involve goods and services that are not easily explained with reference to basic human biological needs. A good illustration is the pattern found in capitalist societies that sociologist and economist Thorstein Veblen (1857–1929) labeled conspicuous consumption. **Conspicuous consumption** involves the purchase and public display of goods known to be costly and unnecessary for basic survival. For example, many people who live in the suburban United States find it necessary to own an automobile for transportation. Getting from home to work to the supermarket to the shopping mall in no way requires the extra speed and power of a sports car, but many suburban residents nevertheless spend tens of thousands of dollars for sports cars. Veblen suggested, and cultural anthropologists agree, that people who drive these cars do so more for symbolic than for practical reasons. That is, they want to show other people (especially those whom they want to impress) that they are so prosperous that they are not limited to purchasing goods for purely practical reasons; rather, they can "waste" cash on non-necessities, on luxurious, ostentatious extras.

Even though our continued existence requires a minimal level of food, water, shelter, and human companionship, ethnographic research has powerfully demonstrated that it is virtually impossible to separate peoples' indispensable *needs* from their discretionary *wants*. This is because all human groups attach cultural meanings to the goods and services they consume. For this reason, Veblen's pattern of conspicuous consumption within the capitalist mode of production constitutes only one end of the continuum of consumption practices documented for different societies with different modes of production. In all cases, what people consume makes a statement about who they are, what they value, and where their loyalties lie.

The anthropological study of consumption has contributed greatly to a critique of approaches to consumption that would reduce it to biological necessity or individual idiosyncrasy. Anthropologists have shown how consumption patterns associated with such seemingly unproblematic foods as meat or sugar have been shaped by cultural beliefs and practices in different times and places. In particular, they have shown what happens when consumption goods are turned into commodities under a capitalist mode of production. This process has been under way now for several centuries and continues to affect the consumption choices of people throughout the world. For example, "fast food" becomes highly valued when a capitalist mode of production draws into the paid workforce those household members who previously had the time, energy, and resources to prepare meals from scratch. And the particular kind of fast food people come to prefer increasingly is shaped by expensive media campaigns designed to persuade consumers using the same tactics Veblen described a century ago.

Many anthropologists have begun to examine the way consumption practices in non-Western societies are changing as a result of these processes, however, and they have been able to show that non-Western consumers of Western-made products are not simply the dupes of advertisers and marketers. Daniel Miller, in particular, has been able to help redirect the focus of studies of commodity consumption by anthropologists. Under conditions of globalization, Miller argues, mass-produced commodities are on offer to people everywhere, and anthropologists should not automatically assume that choosing to consume such commodities signifies the triumph of Western imperialism or the loss of cultural authenticity. Rather, the members of many societies in the world have selected some Western material goods and rejected others based on how well they think those goods will enhance or enrich their own traditions. Thus, Otavalan weavers in Ecuador purchase television sets to entertain weavers producing traditional textiles in locally owned shops, with the result that production increases, enabling Otavalan merchants to more successfully compete in an international market for indigenous products. Under such circumstances, the consumption of television strengthens, rather than diminishes, Otavalan tradition. Indeed, the recent successful participation in the institutions of international capitalism by non-Western peoples, from Otavalan textile producers to Japanese, Chinese, and Korean businessmen, suggests that there is perhaps nothing intrinsically "western" about capitalism or consumption. These cases suggest that consumption of goods sold in capitalist markets need not mean that consumers are being obediently programmed to replace their own traditions with Western consumerism; instead, they are *indigenizing* and *domesticating* capitalist practices and consumer goods as they create their own alternative versions of modernity.

For Further Reading

ECONOMIC ANTHROPOLOGY

Gudeman 1986; Halperin 1994; Littlefield and Gates 1991; Plattner 1989; Sahlins 1972; Wilk 1996

PEASANTS

Kearney 1996; Netting 1993; Wolf 1962, 1982

CONSUMPTION

Coe and Coe 1996; Colloredo-Mansfeld 1999; Fiddis 1991; Miller 1995, 1998; Mintz 1985, 1996

MONEY

Weatherford 1997

9

Kinship and Descent

The key terms and concepts covered in this chapter, in the order in which they appear:

relatedness
kinship
new reproductive technologies
descent
consanguineal kin
adoption

bilateral descent
cognatic descent
bilateral kindred

unilineal descent
patrilineal
agnatic
matrilineal
uterine
unilineal descent groups
patrilineage
matrilineage
lineage
clan

kinship terminologies
fictive kin
generation
gender
affinity
collaterality
bifurcation
relative age
sex of linking relative
parallel cousins
cross cousins

Hawaiian
Eskimo
Iroquois
bifurcate merging
Crow
Omaha
Sudanese

PEOPLE IN ALL SOCIETIES live in worlds of social ties. They consider themselves to be connected to other people in a variety of different ways, and also consider that there are some people to whom they are not connected at all. Some anthropologists refer to these socially recognized connections as **relatedness**. There are many forms of relatedness that may be recognized in a given society, based on such categories as friendship, marriage, adoption, procreation, descent from a common ancestor, common labor, co-residence, sharing food, and sharing some kind of substance (blood, spirit, or nationality, for example). One of the most important forms of relatedness that has interested anthropologists since the birth of the field in the late nineteenth century has been **kinship**: the various systems of social organization that societies have constructed on principles derived from the universal human experiences of mating, birth, and nurturance. Members of Western societies influenced by the sciences of biology and genetics frequently believe that kinship relationships are (or should be) a direct reflection of the biology and genetics of human reproduction. Nevertheless, they are aware that, even in their own societies, kinship is not the same thing as biology.

9.1 Kinship vs. Biology

Europeans and North Americans know that in their societies mating is not the same as marriage, although a valid marriage encourages mating between the partners. Similarly, all births do not constitute valid links of descent; in some societies, children whose parents have not been married according to accepted legal or religious specifications do not fit the cultural logic of descent, and many societies offer no positions that they can properly fill. Finally, not all acts of nurturance are recognized as adoption. Consider, for example, the status of foster parents in the United

States, whose custody of the children they care for is officially temporary and can terminate if someone else clears the hurdles necessary to adopt those children legally.

Thus, mating, birth, and nurturance are ambiguous human experiences, and culturally constructed systems of kinship try to remove some of that ambiguity by paying selective attention to some aspects of these phenomena while downplaying or ignoring others. For example, one society may emphasize the female's role in childbearing and base its kinship system on this, paying little formal attention to the male's role in conception. Another society may trace connections through men, emphasizing the paternal role in conception and reducing the maternal role to that of passive incubator for the male seed. A third society may encourage its members to adopt not only children to rear but adult siblings for themselves, thus blurring the link between biological reproduction and family creation. Even though they contradict one another, all three understandings can be justified with reference to the panhuman experiences of mating, birth, and nurturance.

Every kinship system, therefore, emphasizes certain aspects of human reproductive experience and culturally constructs its own theory of human nature, defining how people develop from infants into mature social beings. Put another way, kinship is an *idiom*: a selective interpretation of the common human experiences of mating, birth, and nurturance. The result is a set of coherent principles that allow people to assign one another membership in particular groups. These principles normally cover several significant issues: how to carry out the reproduction of legitimate group members (marriage or adoption), where group members should live after marriage (residence rules), how to establish links between generations (descent or adoption), and how to pass on social positions (succession) or material goods (inheritance). Collectively, kinship principles define social groups, locate people within those groups, and position the people and groups in relation to one another both in space and over time. While this set of principles may be coherent, it is also open to modification, negotiation, and even legal challenge, as is shown by the ambiguities and questions raised by the consequences of **new reproductive**

technologies—technologically mediated reproductive practices such as in vitro fertilization, surrogate parenthood, and sperm banks.

9.2 Descent

Discussions in anthropology tend to specialize in different aspects of kinship. Culturally defined connections based on mating are usually called *marriage* and are often referred to as *affinal* relationships (the term is based on *affinity*, which means "personal attraction"). These relationships, which link a person to the kin of his or her spouse, will be discussed in the next chapter. In this chapter, we will consider culturally defined relationships based on birth and nurturance, which anthropologists traditionally call **descent**. People related to one another by descent are what English speakers often refer to as "blood" relations and are socially relevant connections based on either parent-child relationships or sibling relationships. Anthropologists use the term **consanguineal kin** to refer to all those people who are linked to one another by birth as blood relations (the word comes from the Latin *sanguineus*, meaning "of blood"). In addition, however, a consanguineal kinship group may include individuals whose membership in the group was established not by birth but by means of culturally specific rituals of incorporation that resemble what Euro-Americans call **adoption**. Incorporation via adoption often is seen to function in a way that parallels consanguinity, because it makes adopted persons and those who adopt them of the "same flesh." The transformation that incorporates adoptees frequently is explained in terms of *nurturance:* feeding, clothing, sheltering, and otherwise attending to the physical and emotional well-being of an individual for an extended period.

Ethnographers have shown repeatedly that kinship bonds established by adoption can be just as strong as bonds established through birth. An interesting recent example comes from research among groups of gay and lesbian North Americans who established enduring "families by choice" that include individuals who are not sexual partners and who are unrelated by birth or marriage. Given that these chosen family ties are rooted in ongoing material and emotional support over extended periods of time, one might reasonably suggest that the people involved have based their relationships on nurturance and have "adopted" one another.

Because they are based on parent-child links that connect the generations, relations of descent have a time depth. In establishing patterns of descent, the cultures of the world rely on one of two basic strategies: either people are connected to one another through *both* their mothers and fathers, or they are connected by links traced *either* through the mother *or* the father, but not both.

9.3 Bilateral Descent

When people believe themselves to be just as related to their father's side of the family as to their mother's side, the term that is used is **bilateral descent** (this is sometimes also referred to as **cognatic descent**). Anthropologists have identified two different kinds of kinship groups based on bilateral descent. One is the *bilateral descent group,* an unusual form that consists of a set of people who claim to be related to one another through descent from a common ancestor, some through their mother's side and some through their father's; the other is the *bilateral kindred,* a much more common form that consists of all the relatives, related through males or females, of one person or group of siblings.

The **bilateral kindred** is the kinship group that most Europeans and North Americans know. A bilateral kindred forms around particular individuals and includes all the people linked to that individual through kin of both sexes—people usually called *relatives* in English. These people form a group only because of their connection to the central person, known in the terminology of kinship as *Ego.* In North American society, bilateral kindreds assemble at events associated with Ego: when he or she is baptized, confirmed, bar or bat mitzvahed, married, or buried. Each person within Ego's bilateral kindred has his or her own separate kindred. For example, Ego's father's sister's daughter has a kindred that includes people related to her through her father and her father's siblings—people to whom Ego is not related. This is simultaneously the major strength and major weakness of bilateral kindreds. That is, they have overlapping memberships, and they do not endure beyond the lifetime of an individual Ego. But they are widely extended, and they can form broad networks of people who are somehow related to one another. (Figure 9.2, Eskimo kinship terminology, also illustrates a bilateral kindred. See page 166.)

Kinship systems create social relationships by defining sets of interlocking statuses and roles (defined in Chapter 6). Thus, a man is to behave in the same way to all his "uncles" and in another way to his "father," and they are to behave to him as "nephew" and "son." (Perhaps he owes labor to anyone he calls "uncle" and is owed protection and support in return.) In anthropology, these are referred to as the *rights and obligations of kinship*. In a bilateral kindred, the "broad networks of people who are somehow related to one another" means that no matter where a person may be, if he or she finds kin there, the person and the kin have a basis for social interaction. This basis for interaction is different from the possible social interactions that the person might have with strangers (in this case, nonkin).

Organization in bilateral kindreds is advantageous when members of social groups need flexible ways of establishing ties to kin who do not live in one place. They are also useful when valued resources, such as farmland, are limited and every generation must be distributed across available plots in an efficient and flexible manner. Bilateral kindreds become problematic, however, in at least four kinds of social circumstances: when clear-cut membership in a particular social group must be determined, when social action requires the formation of groups that are larger than individual families, when conflicting claims to land and labor must be resolved, and when people are concerned with perpetuating a specific social order over time. In societies that face these dilemmas, unilineal descent groups usually are formed.

9.4 Unilineal Descent

The second major descent strategy, **unilineal descent,** is based on the principle that the most significant kin relationships must be traced through *either* the mother *or* the father but not both. Unilineal descent groups are found in more societies today than are any other kind. Those unilineal groups that are based on links traced through a person's father (or male kin) are called **patrilineal** (or **agnatic**); those traced through a mother (or female kin) are called **matrilineal** (or **uterine**). (Note that lineages are institutions—people do not choose whether they'd like to be patrilineal or matrilineal; these are the standardized long-established social forms through which they learn about individuals and groups to whom they are related and how to interact with them.)

Unilineal descent groups are found all over the world. They are all based on the principle that significant relationships are created via links through one parent rather than the other. Membership in a unilineal descent group is based on the membership of the appropriate parent in the group. In a patrilineal system, an individual belongs to a group formed by links through males, the lineage of his or her father. In a matrilineal system, an individual belongs to a group formed by links through females, the lineage of his or her mother. "Patrilineal" and "matrilineal" do not mean that only men belong to one and only women to the other; rather, the terms refer to the principle by which membership is conferred. In a patrilineal society, women and men belong to a **patrilineage** formed by father-child links; similarly, in a matrilineal society, men and women belong to a **matrilineage** formed by mother-child connections. In other words, membership in the group is, in principle, unambiguous: an individual belongs to only one lineage. This is in contrast to a bilateral kindred, in which an individual belongs to overlapping groups. (Figure 9.4, Crow kinship terminology, page 169, also illustrates a matrilineage; Figure 9.5, Omaha kinship terminology, page 170, also illustrates a patrilineage.)

Talk of patrilineal or matrilineal descent focuses attention on the kind of social group created by this pattern of descent: the lineage. A **lineage** is composed of all those people who believe they can specify the parent-child links that connect them to one another through a common ancestor. Typically, lineages vary in size from twenty or thirty members to several hundred or more.

Many anthropologists have argued that the most important feature of lineages is that they are corporate in organization. That is, a lineage has a single legal identity such that, to outsiders, all members of the lineage are equal in law to all others. In the case of a blood feud, for example, the death of any opposing lineage member avenges the death of the lineage member who began the feud; the death of the actual murderer is not required (feuding is defined in Chapter 7). Lineages are also corporate in that they control property, such as land or herds, as a unit.

Finally, lineages are the main political associations in the societies that have them. Individuals have no political or legal status in such societies except through lineage membership. They have relatives who are outside the lineage, but their own political and legal status derives from the lineage to which they belong.

Because membership in a lineage is determined through a direct line from father or mother to child, lineages can endure over time and in a sense have an independent existence. As long as people can remember their common ancestor, the group of people descended from that common ancestor can endure. Most lineage-based societies have a time depth that covers about five generations: grandparents, parents, Ego, children, and grandchildren.

When members of a descent group believe that they are in some way connected but cannot specify the precise genealogical links, they compose what anthropologists call a **clan.** Usually, a clan is made up of lineages that the larger society's members believe to be related to one another through links that go back to mythical times. Sometimes the common ancestor is said to be an animal that lived at the beginning of time. The important point to remember in distinguishing lineages and clans is that lineage members can specify the precise genealogical links back to their common ancestor ("Your mother was Eileen, her mother was Miriam, her sister was Rachel, her daughter was Ruth, and I am Ruth's son"), whereas clan members ordinarily cannot ("Our foremother was Turtle who came out of the sea when this land was settled. Turtle's children were many and for many generations raised sweet peas on our land. So it was that Violet, mother of Miriam and Rachel, was born of the line of the Turtle..."). The clan is thus larger than any lineage and also more diffuse in terms of both membership and the hold it has over individuals.

Because people are born into them, lineages endure over time in societies in which no other form of organization lasts, and therefore, the system of lineages becomes the foundation of social life in the society. Although lineages might be the foundation of social life, however, this does not mean that they are immovable and inflexible. People can use lineage and clan membership to pursue their interests. Because lineage depth frequently extends to about five generations, the exact circumstances of lineage origins can be hazy and open to negotiation. Perhaps "Miriam" and "Rachel" from the preceding example have another sister whom everyone "forgot about" until someone appears who claims lineage membership as a descendant of the forgotten sister. If there are good reasons for including this descendant in the lineage, this claim might well be accepted.

By far the most common form of lineage organization is the patrilineage, which consists of all the people (male and female) who believe themselves to be related to one another because they are related to a common male ancestor by links through men. The prototypical kernel of a patrilineage is the father-son pair. Female members of patrilineages normally leave the lineage to marry, but in most patrilineal societies, women do not give up their membership in their own lineages. In a number of societies, women play an active role in the affairs of their own patrilineages for many years—usually until their interest in their own children directs their attention toward the children's lineage (which is, of course, the lineage of their father, the woman's husband).

By contrast, in a matrilineal society, descent is traced through women rather than through men. Superficially, a matrilineage is a mirror image of a patrilineage, but certain features make it distinct. First, the prototypical kernel of a matrilineage is the sister-brother pair—a matrilineage may be thought of as a group of brothers and sisters connected through links made by women. Brothers marry out and often live with the families of their wives, but they maintain an active interest in the affairs of their own lineage. Second, the most important man in a boy's life is not his father (who is not in his lineage) but his mother's brother, from whom he will receive his lineage inheritance. Third, the amount of power women exercise in matrilineages is still being hotly debated in anthropology. A matrilineage is not the same thing as a *matriarchy* (a society in which women rule); brothers often retain what appears to be a controlling interest in the lineage. Some anthropologists claim that the male members of a matrilineage are supposed to run the lineage, even though there is more autonomy for women in matrilineal societies than in patrilineal ones; they suggest that the day-to-day exercise of power tends to be carried out by the brothers or sometimes the husbands. A number of studies, however, have questioned the validity of these generalizations. Trying to say something about matrilineal societies in general is difficult, since they vary a great deal. The ethnographic evidence suggests that matrilineages must be examined on a case-by-case basis.

9.5 Kinship Terminologies

People everywhere use special terms to address and refer to people they recognize as kin; anthropologists call these **kinship terminologies.** Consider the North American kinship term *aunt*. This term seems to refer to a woman who occupies a unique biological position, but in fact, it refers to a woman who may be related to a person in one of four different ways: as father's sister, mother's sister, father's brother's wife, or mother's brother's wife. From the perspective of North American kinship, all those women have something in common, and they are all placed into the same kinship category and called by the same kin term. Prototypically, one's aunts are women one generation older than oneself and are sisters or sisters-in-law of one's parents. However, North Americans may also refer to their mother's best friend as "aunt." By doing so, they recognize the strength of this system of classification by extending it to include **fictive kin** (also discussed in Chapter 6).

Despite the variety of kinship systems in the world, anthropologists have identified six major patterns of kinship terminology based on how people categorize their cousins. The six patterns reflect common solutions to structural problems faced by societies organized in terms of kinship. They provide clues concerning how the vast and undifferentiated world of potential kin may be organized. Kinship terminologies suggest both the external boundaries and the internal divisions of the kinship groups, and they outline the structure of rights and obligations assigned to different members of the society.

The major criteria that are used for building kinship terminologies are listed here, from the most common to the least common:

- *Generation.* Kin terms distinguish relatives according to the **generation** to which the relatives belong. In English, the term *cousin* conventionally refers to someone of the same generation as Ego.

- *Gender.* The **gender** of the individual is used to differentiate kin. In Spanish, *primo* refers to a male cousin, and *prima* to a female cousin. In English, cousins are not distinguished on the basis of gender, but *uncle* and *aunt* are distinguished on the basis of both generation and gender.

- *Affinity.* A distinction is made on the basis of connection through marriage, or **affinity.** This criterion is used in Spanish when *suegra* (Ego's spouse's mother) is distinguished from *madre* (Ego's mother). In matrilineal societies, Ego's mother's sister and father's sister are distinguished from each other on the basis of affinity. The mother's sister is a direct, lineal relative, and the father's sister is an affine; they are called by different terms.

- *Collaterality.* A distinction is made between kin who are believed to be in a direct line and those who are "off to one side," linked to Ego through a lineal relative. In English, the distinction of **collaterality** can be seen in the distinction between mother and aunt or between father and uncle.

- *Bifurcation.* **Bifurcation** distinguishes the mother's side of the family from the father's side. The Swedish kin terms *morbror* and *farbror* are bifurcating terms, one referring to the mother's brother and the other to the father's brother.

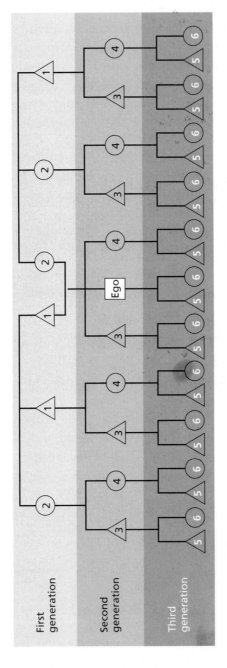

Figure 9.1 Hawaiian kinship terminology. Numbers represent kin terms. Ego uses the same kin term to refer to all those assigned the same number.

♦ *Relative age.* Relatives of the same category may be distinguished on the basis of **relative age**—that is, whether they are older or younger than Ego. Among the Ju/'hoansi of southern Africa, for example, speakers must separate "older brother" *(!ko)* from "younger brother" *(tsin).*

♦ *Sex of linking relative.* This criterion is related to collaterality. The **sex of linking relative** distinguishes cross relatives (usually cousins) from parallel relatives (also usually cousins). Parallel relatives are linked through two brothers or two sisters. **Parallel cousins,** for example, are Ego's father's brother's children or Ego's mother's sister's children. Cross relatives are linked through a brother-sister pair. **Cross cousins** are Ego's mother's brother's children or father's sister's children. The sex of either Ego or the cousins does not matter; the important factor is the sex of the linking relatives.

The six major patterns of kinship terminology that anthropologists have identified in the world are based on how cousins are classified. These patterns were named after the societies that represent the prototypes. The first two patterns discussed here are found in association with bilateral descent systems.

Bilateral Patterns

The **Hawaiian** pattern is based on the application of the first two criteria: generation and gender. The kin group is divided horizontally by generation, and within each generation are only two kinship terms, one for males and one for females (Figure 9.1). In this system, Ego maintains a maximum degree of flexibility in choosing the descent group with which to affiliate. Ego is also forced to look for a spouse in another kin group because Ego may not marry anyone in the same terminological category as a genetic parent, sibling, or offspring.

The **Eskimo** pattern reflects the symmetry of bilateral kindreds. A lineal core—the nuclear family—is distinguished from collateral relatives, who are not identified with the father's or the mother's

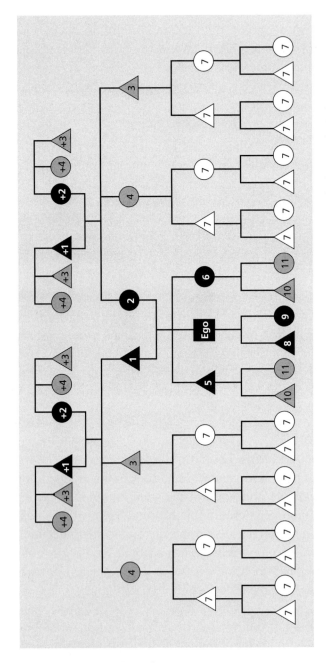

Figure 9.2 Eskimo kinship terminology. All those indicated in black represent Ego's lineal relatives, those in gray represent Ego's collateral relatives, and those in white are cousins. The symbol + equals grand (for example, +1 = grandfather).

side. Once past the immediate collateral line (aunts and uncles, great-aunts and great-uncles, nephews and nieces), generation is ignored. The remaining relatives are all "cousins," sometimes distinguished by *number* (second or third) or by *removal* (generations away from Ego[1]) (Figure 9.2). This is the only terminological system that sets the nuclear family apart from all other kin. If the Hawaiian system is like a cake made up of horizontal layers of kin, this system is like an onion, with layers of kin surrounding a core.

Unilineal Patterns

The **Iroquois** pattern is sometimes known in the literature as **bifurcate merging,** because it merges Ego's mother's and father's parallel siblings with Ego's parents (Figure 9.3). The sex of the linking relatives is important in this system: The parents' parallel siblings are grouped together with the parents, whereas cross siblings are set apart. This is repeated on the level of cousins. In a bilateral system, these distinctions would be meaningless, but in a unilineal system, they mirror the lines of lineage membership. If Ego is a male, he will use one term to refer to all women of his matrilineage who are one generation older than he is. Their children are all referred to by another set of terms, one for males and one for females. Similarly, in his father's matrilineage, all men in the father's generation are referred to by one term. Their children are called by the same set of terms used for the cousins on the mother's side.

The **Crow** pattern is a matrilineal system named after the Crow people of North America, but it is found in many other matrilineal societies. This system distinguishes the two matrilineages that are important to Ego: Ego's own and that of Ego's father (Figure 9.4). As in the Iroquois system, the gender of the linking relative is important, and both parents and their same-sex

---

[1] Ego's "first cousin once removed" can be one generation older or younger than Ego. For example, your cousin Suzanne's daughter is your first cousin once removed, but so is your father's cousin Arnold. Arnold's son, Eric, is your second cousin.

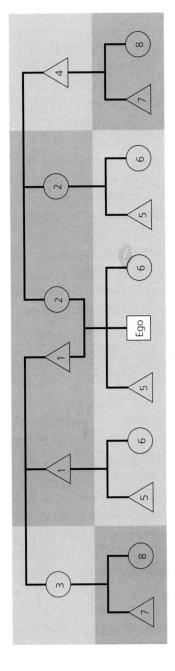

Figure 9.3 Iroquois kinship terminology.

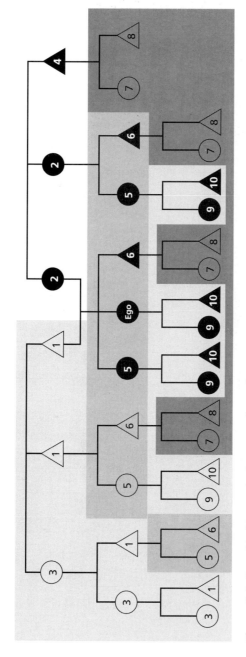

Figure 9.4 Crow kinship terminology. Members of Ego's matriline are represented in black. Note the merging of generations and what follows as a result: All children of 3s are 1s and 3s; all children of 2s are 5s and 6s; all children of 5s are 9s and 10s; and all children of 4s and 6s are 7s and 8s—*regardless of generation.*

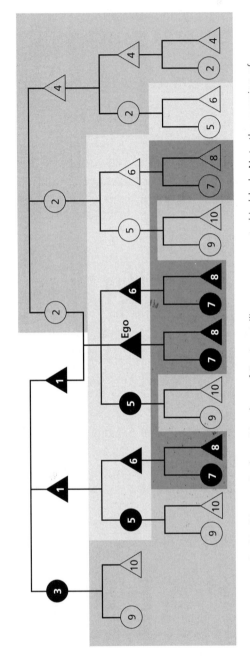

Figure 9.5 Omaha kinship terminology. Members of Ego's patriline are represented in black. Note the merging of generations and what follows as a result: All children of 4s are 2s and 4s; all children of 1s are 5s and 6s; all children of 6s are 7s and 8s; and all children of 3s and 5s are 9s and 10s—*regardless of generation.*

siblings are grouped together. Their children—Ego's parallel cousins—are in the same category as Ego's siblings. The terms for cross cousins follow lineage membership, which is more important than generation. In Ego's own matrilineage, all the children of males are referred to by the same term regardless of their generation; their fathers are in Ego's matrilineage, but *they* are not. On the side of Ego's father's matrilineage, all male members are distinguished by one term, and all female members by another, regardless of generational relationship to Ego.

The system known as **Omaha,** found among some patrilineal peoples, is the mirror image of the Crow system. All the members of Ego's mother's patrilineage are distinguished only by gender, and all the children of women in Ego's patrilineage are referred to by the same term, one for males and one for females (Figure 9.5). Lineage membership again is more important than generation, a principle that often is hard for people living in bilateral kindreds to grasp.

Finally, in the **Sudanese** pattern, each related person is referred to by a separate term (Figure 9.6). While this was originally seen as a relatively rare terminological pattern found in patrilineal societies, especially in northern Africa, it is also a very common pattern in South Asia and Southwest Asia, where it is found among speakers of Turkish, Arabic, Urdu, and Hindi, as well as other northern Indian languages. (Table 9.1 lists the basic patterns of kinship terminology.)

TABLE 9.1 Patterns of Kinship Terminology

BILATERAL DESCENT	UNILINEAL DESCENT
Hawaiian	Iroquois
Eskimo	Crow
	Omaha
	Sudanese

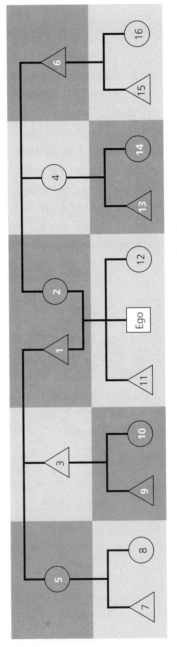

Figure 9.6 Sudanese kinship terminology. Each person related to Ego is referred to by a separate term.

172

For Further Reading

KINSHIP

Carsten 2000, 2003; Collier and Yanigasako 1987; Graburn 1971; Parkin 1997; Peletz 1995; Schneider 1968, 1984; Stone 1997, 2001

ADOPTION

Weismantel 1998

NEW REPRODUCTIVE TECHNOLOGIES

Icahn 2000; Strathern 1992

REPRODUCTION AND POWER

Ginsburg and Rapp 1995

10

Marriage and Family

The key terms and concepts covered in this chapter, in the order in which they appear:

marriage

exogamy

endogamy

neolocal

bilocal

patrilocal

virilocal

matrilocal

uxorilocal

avunculocal

ambilocal

monogamy

polygamy

plural marriage

polygyny

polyandry

bride service

bridewealth

dowry

hypergamy

sororate

levirate

family

conjugal family

nonconjugal family

nuclear family

polygynous family

extended families

joint families

blended family

family by choice

divorce

ANTHROPOLOGICAL DISCUSSIONS of marriage and the family complement discussions of descent and round out our study of kinship. As we saw in Chapter 9, the complexities and ambiguities of descent are many. The study of marriage and the family offers just as many complications, the first of which is how to define these terms.

10.1 What Is Marriage?

If we take what Euro-Americans call *marriage* as a prototype of a particular kind of social relationship, we discover in all societies institutions that resemble what people in the United States would call marriage. At the same time, the range of beliefs and practices associated with these institutions is broad, and the degree of overlap is not great. Nevertheless, we tend to classify all these institutions as *marriage* because of the key elements they do have in common. On these grounds, a prototypical **marriage** involves a man and a woman, transforms the status of the man and the woman, and stipulates the degree of sexual access the married partners may have to each other, ranging from exclusive to preferential. Marriage also establishes the legitimacy of children born to the wife and creates relationships between the kin of the wife and the kin of the husband.

We stress the prototypical nature of our definition because, although some societies are quite strict about allowing females to marry only males, and vice versa, other societies are not. The ethnographic literature contains many examples of marriage or marriagelike relationships that resemble the prototype in every respect except that the partners may be two men or two women (as defined according to biological sex criteria) or a living woman and the ghost of a deceased male. Sometimes these marriages involve a sexual relationship between the partners; sometimes they do not. Apparently, the institution we are calling *marriage* has been viewed by members of many societies as so useful and valuable that they allow it to include partners of many different kinds—even though in all cases the prototype people have in mind seems to be a union between a man and a woman.

Examining the definition of marriage just offered, we note that marriage is a rite of passage: The parties go from the social status of single to the social status of married. In every society, this transformation of status is accompanied by adoption of new roles, but the rights and obligations associated with these roles vary enormously from culture to culture. Prototypically, among the rights and obligations of spouses are socially sanctioned sexual relations with each other. But, again, the nature and exclusivity of these sexual relations vary from culture to culture: some cultures insist that the partners may have sex only with each other; some view sexual encounters outside marriage less seriously for one partner (usually the husband) than for the other partner; and at least one culture allowed the husband and wife to have sexual intercourse if they wish, but after spending one night together, they need never see each other again.

In most cultures, it is assumed that the married partners will have children, and the institution of marriage provides the children with a legitimate ascribed social status, based on who their parents are. In some cases, it is as if the father's and the mother's statuses were plotted on a graph, allowing the status of their child to be placed precisely in the social space where the x- and y-axes intersect; in other cases, the child's status depends solely on the position of one or the other parent. In addition, in most cultures, marriage creates formal relationships between the kin of the husband and the kin of the wife. By contrast, while mating may produce grandparents, it cannot produce in-laws or a formal relationship between the parents of the father and the parents of the mother. This aspect of marriage also has important social consequences.

10.2 Whom to Marry and Where to Live

Societies use kinship systems to exercise control over the marriages contracted by their members. When marriage rules specify that a person is to marry outside a defined social group—extended family,

lineage, clan, class, ethnic group, or religious sect, for example—
anthropologists say that the society in question practices **exogamy**
(or *out-marriage*). The opposite situation—in which a person is
expected to marry *within* a defined social group—is called
endogamy. These patterns may be obligatory (i.e., strictly enforced)
or merely preferred.

Once married, the spouses must live somewhere. Anthropologists
have identified six patterns of postmarital residence. **Neolocal** residence, in which the new partners set up an independent household at a place of their own choosing, should be familiar to people
who have grown up in the United States, Canada, and most of
Europe. Neolocal residence tends to be found in societies that are
more or less individualistic in their social organization, especially
those in which bilateral kindreds also are found. Neolocal residence exists throughout the world but is most common in nation-
states and in societies bordering the Mediterranean Sea. Some
societies with bilateral kindreds have **bilocal** residence patterns, in
which married partners live with (or near) either the wife's or the
husband's parents. Despite this flexibility in allowing married
partners to make decisions regarding where they might live, very
few societies with bilocal residence have been described in the
anthropological literature.

The most common residence pattern in the world, in terms of
the number of societies in which it is practiced, is **patrilocal** residence, in which the partners in a marriage live with (or near) the
husband's father. (In older anthropological writing, the term
virilocal is sometimes used to distinguish residing with the husband's kin from residing specifically with the husband's father, for
which the term *patrilocal* was reserved.) Patrilocal residence is
strongly associated with patrilineal descent systems—about 85
percent of societies in which postmarital residence is patrilocal are
also patrilineal. If children are born into a patrilineage and inherit
from the father or other patrilineage members, then there are
advantages to rearing them among the members of the lineage.

When the partners in a marriage live with (or near) the wife's
mother, anthropologists use the term **matrilocal** residence.
(Again, in older anthropological writing, the term **uxorilocal** is

sometimes used to refer to residence with the wife's kin, as distinct from living with the wife's mother.) Matrilocal residence is found exclusively in matrilineal societies (some matrilineal societies are patrilocal). Anthropologists who study matrilineal societies have observed that sometimes the married partners live with the husband's mother's brother. This is based on the logic of matrilineal descent, in which the socially significant older male in a man's life is his mother's brother, because he is a member of the man's matrilineage while his own father is not. In these cases, anthropologists use the term **avunculocal** residence, building on the word *avuncular,* meaning "of uncles." As might be expected, avunculocal residence is found only in matrilineal societies, and, in contrast to matrilocal residence, it emphasizes the inheritance and labor patterns linking men in a matrilineage. A rare pattern called **ambilocal** residence is associated with ambilineal descent, in which the married partners may live with either the husband's or wife's group. This term is sometimes used interchangeably with the term *bilocal* and can be used to distinguish this pattern in unilineal societies from the pattern in bilateral societies.

10.3 How Many Spouses?

You may have noticed that we use the phrase married partners rather than the more common married couple. This is because the number of people who may be married to one another at the same time also varies across cultures. The major distinction is between societies that permit more than one spouse to a person and those that do not. A marriage pattern that permits a person to be married to only one spouse at a time is called **monogamy.** The term can also be used to refer to any marriage in which one person has only one spouse.

The term **polygamy** is used to refer to marriage patterns in which a person may have more than one spouse, a practice also sometimes called **plural marriage.** Polygamy has two major forms: polygyny and polyandry. **Polygyny** is a marriage pattern in which a man may be married to more than one woman at a time. It is the most common of all marriage patterns in the world in terms of number of societies in which it is permitted. Polygyny enables a lineage, especially one with male children, to establish alliances with many other lineages through marriage.

In polygynous societies, it should be noted, not every man has more than one wife. In Islamic societies, for example, a man is permitted to have as many as four wives, but only on the condition that he can support them all equally well. Today, some Muslim authorities argue that "equal support" must be emotional as well as material. Furthermore, convinced that no man can feel exactly the same toward each of his wives, they have concluded that monogamy must be the rule. Other polygynous societies set no limit on the number of wives a man can marry. However, regardless of any limitations on the number of wives, polygynous societies are faced with a real demographic problem: because the number of men and women in any society is approximately equal, for every man with two wives, there is one man without a wife. To help solve this problem, men may be obliged to wait until they are older to marry, and women may be pressed to marry at a very young age; but even these practices do not completely eliminate the imbalance. As a result, polygyny is regularly connected with power in societies that practice it. That is, those men who are rich and powerful have multiple wives; those men who are poor and powerless either cannot marry, marry very late, have relationships outside of marriage, or marry women who are equally dispossessed.

Polyandry, a pattern in which a woman is married to more than one man at a time, is the rarest of the three marriage patterns. In some polyandrous societies, a woman may marry several brothers. In others, she may marry men who are not related to one another and who all will live together in a single household. The tendency in polyandrous societies—especially in those in which a woman marries a set of brothers—is to intensify the connections between lineages and to limit the number of potential heirs in the next generation, because no matter how many husbands a woman has, there is a limit to the number of offspring she can bear. (Table 10.1 lists basic marriage patterns.)

TABLE 10.1 Marriage Patterns	
MONOGAMY	POLYGAMY
Monogamy	Polygyny Polyandry

10.4 Marriage as Alliance

In most societies, a marriage is an alliance between two families or lineages, not merely between two individuals, and it frequently requires traditional exchanges of wealth to legitimize it. These are usually characterized as bride service, bridewealth (or bride price), and dowry. In some societies, the prospective groom must work for the family of the bride for a predetermined length of time before they may marry, a practice called **bride service**. Other societies solemnize marriages with an exchange of **bridewealth**: certain symbolically important goods that are transferred from the immediate family of the groom (or his lineage) to the family of the bride (or her lineage) on the occasion of their marriage. *Symbolically important goods* include those things that are considered to be appropriate for exchange at a marriage in a specific society—for example, cattle, cash, shell ornaments, cotton cloth, or bird feathers. Bridewealth exchange is most common in patrilineal societies that combine agriculture, pastoralism, and patrilocal postmarital residence. Through their research in societies that exchange bridewealth, anthropologists have found that it is fundamentally incorrect to think of bridewealth as "buying" a wife. Rather, anthropologists view bridewealth as a way of compensating the bride's relatives for the loss of her labor and childbearing capacities. That is, when the bride goes to live with her husband and his lineage, she will be working and producing children for his people, not her own.

Bridewealth transactions create affinal relations between the relatives of the wife and those of the husband. The wife's relatives, in turn, use the bridewealth they receive for her to find a bride for her brother in yet another kinship group. In many societies in eastern and southern Africa, a woman gains power and influence over her brother because the cattle that her marriage brings allow him to marry and continue their lineage.

Dowry, by contrast, is typically a transfer of family wealth, usually from parents to their daughter, at the time of her marriage. It is found primarily in the agricultural societies of Europe and Asia, but it has been brought to some parts of Africa with the arrival of religions like Islam that support the practice. In societies in which both men and women are seen as heirs to family wealth, dowry is sometimes regarded as the way women receive their inheritance. Dowries often are considered the wife's contribution to the establishment of a new household, to which the husband may bring other forms of wealth or prestige. In stratified societies, the size of a woman's dowry frequently ensures that when she marries, she will continue to enjoy her accustomed style of life. In some stratified societies, an individual of lower status sometimes marries an individual of higher status, a situation in which the children will take on the higher status. This practice is called **hypergamy,** and it is usually one in which the lower status person is the wife and the dowry is seen (sometimes explicitly) as an exchange for the higher social position that the husband confers.

The ties that link kinship groups through marriage are sometimes so strong that they endure beyond the death of one of the partners. In some matrilineal and some patrilineal societies, if a wife dies young, the husband's line will ask the deceased wife's line for a substitute, often her sister. This practice, called the **sororate** (from the Latin *soror,* "sister"), is connected with both alliance strength and bridewealth. That is, both lines—that of the widower and that of the deceased wife—wish to maintain the alliance formed (and frequently continued) by the marriage. At the same time, if a man marries the sister of his deceased wife, the bridewealth that his line gave to the line of the first wife will not have to be returned, so the disruption caused by the wife's death will be lessened. In many societies, if the husband dies the wife may (and in rare cases be obligated to) marry one of his brothers.

This practice, called the **levirate** (from the Latin *levir,* "husband's brother"), is intended, like the sororate, to maintain the alliance between descent groups. In some societies, it also functions as a kind of social security system for widows, who might otherwise be destitute after the death of their husbands.

10.5 Family

Marriage frequently is understood, both by scholars and by the people who marry, as creating families. *Family* is another term that seeks to label a practice that is apparently universal but so variable as to make definition difficult. One minimal definition of a **family** would be that it consists of a woman and her dependent children. Some anthropologists prefer to distinguish the **conjugal family,** which is a family based on marriage—at its minimum, a husband and wife (a spousal pair) and their children—from the **nonconjugal family,** which consists of a woman and her children. In a nonconjugal family, the husband/father may be occasionally present or completely absent. Anthropologists note that nonconjugal families are never the only form of family organization in a society and, in fact, are usually rather infrequent. However, in some large-scale industrial societies, including the United States, nonconjugal families have become increasingly common. In most societies, the conjugal family is coresident—that is, spouses live in the same dwelling, along with their children—but in some matrilineal societies, the husband lives with his matrilineage, the wife and children live with theirs, and the husband visits his wife and children.

Families can be characterized according to their structure. The neolocal, monogamous family is called the **nuclear family** and is composed of two generations, the parents and their unmarried children. In the nuclear family, each member has a series of evolving relationships with every other member: husband and wife, parents and children, and children with one another. These are the principal lines along which jealousy, controversy, and affection develop in neolocal monogamous families.

The **polygynous family** is composed of the husband, his cowives, and their children. The polygynous family adds complexity in the older generation not found in the nuclear family—the relationships among the cowives, and the relationship of the group of wives with the single husband. Additional complexity arises in the younger generation, as children have connections to half-siblings (the same father but a different mother) and full siblings (the same father and same mother), as well as an additional set of adults in their lives—their mother's cowives. These differences make the internal dynamics of polygynous families different from those of nuclear families.

The two family structures discussed so far are similar in that they are two generations in depth and involve one set of spouses (a man and a woman in the nuclear family, a man and his wives in a polygynous one). When families include a third generation—parents, married children, and grandchildren—anthropologists speak about **extended families.** When families maintain a two-generation depth but expand outward so that a set of siblings and their spouses and children lives together, anthropologists talk about **joint families.** Simply put, a joint family is composed of several brothers and their wives and children, or several sisters and their husbands and children. In societies in which they are found, extended and joint families are ideal patterns, which means that although people might want to live that way, not everyone is able to.

In recent years in the United States, anthropologists have observed the emergence of new family types. The **blended family** occurs when previously divorced people marry, bringing with them children from their previous marriages. The internal dynamics of the new family—which can come to include his children, her children, and their children—may sometimes have some similarities to the dynamics of polygynous families. Specifically, the relations among the children and their relations to each parent may be complex and negotiated over time. (Table 10.2 summarizes the basic family types.)

A second new form is the **family by choice,** a term used by some GLBT (Gay, Lesbian, Bisexual, Transgender) people to refer to families that are not the product of heterosexual marriage. Derived from a model that resembles kinship based on nurturance (defined in Chapter 9), some North American GLBT people argue that "whatever endures is real." As a result, the group of people

TABLE 10.2 Types of Families

NONCONJUGAL FAMILIES	CONJUGAL FAMILIES	FAMILIES BY CHOICE
Mother and children	Nuclear	Enduring ties that are
	Polygynous	not the product of
	Extended	heterosexual marriage
	Joint	
	Blended	

that endures—which may include some or all of the kin of each member of the couple, their close friends, and children of either member or children who may be adopted—forms a family. GLBT activists have used this model as a resource in their struggle to obtain for long-standing families of choice some of the same legal rights enjoyed by traditional heterosexual families, such as hospital visiting privileges, partner insurance coverage, joint adoption, and property rights.

Marriages do not always last forever, and almost all societies make it possible for married couples to **divorce**—that is, to dissolve the marriage in a socially recognized way, regulating the status of those who were involved with the marriage and any offspring of the marriage. In some societies, it is not merely the people who were married who are involved in the divorce; it may also include other family or lineage members of the divorcing parties whose relationships are also changed by the divorce. In societies in which bridewealth is part of the marriage ceremony, for example, divorce may cause difficulties if the bridewealth must be returned. In such societies, a man who divorces a wife or whose wife leaves him expects her family to return to him some of the bridewealth he offered in exchange for her. But the wife's family may well have exchanged the bridewealth they received when she married to obtain wives for her brothers. As a result, her brothers' marriages may have to be broken up in order to recoup enough bridewealth from their in-laws to repay their sister's ex-husband or his line. Sometimes a new husband will repay the bridewealth to the former husband's line, thus letting the bride's relatives off the hook.

Grounds for divorce vary from society to society, as does which party may initiate divorce. Common grounds for divorce often include nagging, quarreling, cruelty, violence, stinginess, and adultery. Cross-culturally, a frequent ground for divorce is childlessness.

Families break apart and new households form in other ways besides divorce. In joint families, for example, the pressures that build up among coresident brothers or sisters often increase dramatically on the death of the father. In theory, the eldest son inherits the position of head of household from his father, but his younger brothers may not accept his authority as readily as they did the father's. Some younger brothers may decide to establish their own households, and so the joint family gradually splits. Each brother whose household splits off from the joint stem usually hopes to start his own joint family; eventually, his sons will bring their wives into the household, and a new joint family emerges out of the ashes of an old one.

For Further Reading

Many of the readings for Chapter 9 also deal with marriage and family. Here are some readings specific to these topics:

MARRIAGE

Goody and Tambiah 1973; Levine 1988; Sacks 1979; Schuler 1987

FAMILY

Netting, Wilk, and Arnould 1984; Weston 1991

11

Globalization and the Culture of Capitalism

The key terms and concepts covered in this chapter, in the order in which they appear:

colonialism
neocolonialism

corvee

cultural imperialism
westernization
internal colonialism

subaltern
nationalism

modernization
  theory
revolutionary
  movements
alienation
proletarianization

dependency theory
neoliberalism

international political
  economy
world system theory
core
periphery
semiperiphery
deterritorialization
reterritorialization
diaspora

globalization
cyberculture

postmodern
  condition
identity politics
cultural pluralism
accommodation
multiculturalism

acculturation
syncretism
cargo cults
assimilate

cultural
  hybridization
long-distance
  nationalism
transborder state
transborder
  citizenship

human rights
cultural rights
ethnocide
genocide

cosmopolitanism

ANTHROPOLOGISTS HAVE SPECIALIZED in taking seriously the ways of life of people in "remote" parts of the world— remote, that is, from the activities and concerns of most people in the Western capitalist nations from which the anthropologists traditionally came. Until very recently, limitations rooted in the technologies of transportation and communication meant that, even when political or economic ties linked territories at some distance from one another, the movement of people or goods or ideas from one place to another was slow and cumbersome. By 5000 years ago, the growth of states and their expansion into empires drew peoples in several regions of the world into intensified contact with one another. At the beginning of the twenty-first century, however, economic or political events whose consequences used to be felt only within restricted geographical regions regularly affected people living in regions of the world that used to be considered remote from one another. It was only a little over five centuries ago that European explorers began to make contact, and then to conquer, indigenous groups on all continents, eventually establishing far-flung colonial empires that lasted until the middle of the twentieth century. The relationships established by European colonial domination created the conditions for the emergence, by the end of the twentieth century, of a fully integrated global economy.

11.1 The Cultural Legacy of Colonialism

Europeans did not invent **colonialism**, which can be defined as political conquest of one society by another, followed by social domination and forced cultural change. Since the rise of the first states in antiquity, regions of varying sizes have been brought together in different parts of the world as a result of imperial expansion, and what is today Western Europe was marginal to most of them. None of those earlier empires, however, ever attained the scope of the European colonial empires, especially during their period of greatest expansion, which stretched roughly from the end of the nineteenth century until shortly after World War II, when European colonies began to gain their independence. At that time, many observers hoped that the relationships of subjugation between colonizer and colonized would dissolve. They hoped that different geographical regions of former empires would regain the kind of autonomy that had so often followed the breakup of empires in the past. Such hopes were dashed, however, when the ties between former colonies and their former imperial rulers not only did not disappear after independence, but instead often reappeared in the form of "consultancies" to the new governments. These persisting relationships in the absence of imperial political domination have often been called **neocolonialism,** and social scientists have struggled to explain why they are so resilient.

Many scholars, anthropologists included, decided that neocolonial ties were basically economic in nature, and that their strength came from an international division of labor which colonialism itself had established. Once certain geographical regions within an empire became specialized in specific economic tasks within the imperial economy, the argument went, those relationships became very difficult, if not impossible, to dislodge, even when the empire itself no longer existed. Much evidence was collected to document the forced social and cultural change wrought on the economic, social, and cultural lives of colonized peoples in order to create this international division of labor during the period of European colonial rule.

The European empires of the last two centuries were, by and large, not made up of settler colonies. Except for select areas like southern or eastern Africa for the British, or Morocco and Algeria for the French, European soldiers and administrators were always relatively limited in number; the colonizers relied on superior military technology, rather than sheer numbers, to impose their will. They were neither able nor, in most cases, interested in remaking colonized societies from top to bottom, but they did institute certain changes that would make it easier for them to achieve the economic goals that were their primary motivation. Thus, large tracts of land were regularly appropriated from colonized peoples for the purpose of resource extraction (mining, for example) or for growing cash crops valued in Europe (see Chapter 8 for further discussion of cash crops), displacing indigenous farmers and herders from their lands and turning them into wage-workers forced to seek employment on plantations, in mines, or in the growing cities. Economic efficiency further required the building of infrastructure (roads, ports, etc.) by which cash crops or minerals could be transported out of colonies and back to Europe. Colonists regularly relied on the labor of colonized peoples to build such infrastructure, sometimes resorting to the use of **corvee,** or forced labor, in which laborers were required to work a given number of days on a given project or risk fines or imprisonment.

As colonial economic control increased, colonized peoples became familiar with European economic practices such as the use of money to purchase commodities or the production of goods for exchange. Adopting wage work and purchasing goods to meet subsistence needs increasingly became a necessity, as people were deprived of the land on which they formerly had grown subsistence crops or as their traditional artisanal production of pots or cloth or farm implements was supplanted by manufactured items produced in and imported from Europe. Over time, indigenous peoples had to come to terms with these cultural practices, and the way they did so has varied from time to time and place to place. They were coping with what many scholars have called **cultural imperialism,** a situation in which the ideas and practices of one culture are imposed upon other cultures, which may be modified or eliminated as a result. Western colonialism appeared to produce a distinctive kind of cultural imperialism, frequently called **westernization,** in which the ideas and practices of Western European (or North American) culture eventually displaced many of the ideas and practices of the indigenous cultures of the colonies. In places where European settler colonies eventually broke from Europe, as in North, Central, and South America, anthropologists often speak of **internal colonialism** imposed on indigenous peoples within the borders of independent states.

11.2 Analyzing Sociocultural Change in the Postcolonial World

The contradiction inherent in most colonial policies urging cultural assimilation however, was that even the most highly "assimilated" members of colonized societies could never hope to be treated as equals by their colonial masters. This realization by growing numbers of educated members of **subaltern** (lower-ranked) groups helped fuel the movement for independence from colonial control, which gained momentum after World War II. By virtue of their shared colonial history and their shared rejection of domination, independence leaders argued that they and their followers had developed a distinct sense of themselves as "a people" or "nation," an orientation that came to be called **nationalism.** Nationalist leaders in colonies claimed that colonized peoples, like other "nations" of the world, had a right to political self-determination; that is, they were entitled to become independent nation-states.

In the postcolonial world of the 1950s and early 1960s, the leaders of many newly independent nation-states were hopeful that their countries could escape the impoverished status they had occupied under colonial rule. Although such leaders rejected the notion that their citizens needed to become "civilized," they were committed to the idea that their societies needed "development" and "modernization." Many economists in Western nations agreed with them. In a manner reminiscent of Lewis Henry Morgan, these economists subscribed to a unilineal theory of economic development, often referred to as **modernization theory.** They studied the economic histories of the first nations in the world to "develop" or to "modernize"—that is, to create economies based on industrial production and capitalist business practices. Some economists believed that they had discovered a universal recipe for modernization that would guarantee economic development in any new nation that followed their advice.

Modernization theory did not view industrial capitalism as a distinctive cultural system, but rather as the most highly developed economic system yet produced on the face of the earth. It assumed that "nations" were units that passed naturally through stages of economic growth at different rates and that the more "mature" nations ought to assist the "young" nations to attain maturity. However, economists from Western industrial nations insisted that the leaders of new nations carefully follow their recipe for development. Like parents dealing with sometimes unruly adolescent children, they worried that young nations eager to modernize might resist disciplined evolution through the stages of economic growth and look for a shortcut to economic prosperity.

During the Cold War years, when modernization theory developed, the tempting shortcut was seen as socialist revolution. The twentieth century has been marked by a series of revolutions all over the globe, the best known being those in Mexico, Russia, China, Vietnam, Algeria, Cuba, and Nicaragua. In 1969, anthropologist Eric Wolf characterized all but the Nicaraguan revolution (which would take place ten years later) as wars waged by peasants to defend themselves from the disruptions caused in their societies by capitalist market penetration. Following the Russian Revolution, opponents of the capitalist system elsewhere in the world also formed **revolutionary movements** whose explicit aim was to throw capitalists out of the country by force. Although many rank-and-file members of the revolutionary movements had modest dreams of return to a more prosperous status quo ante, their leaders often hoped to replace capitalism with some locally appropriate form of socialist society. After the successful Cuban Revolution in 1959, when Fidel Castro and his supporters openly committed themselves to socialism and allied with the Soviet Union, modernization theory became the foreign-policy option of choice in the United States, a potentially powerful approach to economic development that might woo potential revolutionaries elsewhere away from the Marxist threat (see Chapter 8).

The Marxist threat was real because Marxists argued that the factor responsible for the impoverished economies of postcolonial states was precisely what the modernization theorists were offering as a cure, namely, capitalism (see Chapter 8 for a detailed discussion). A key feature of capitalism is the way it creates separation, or **alienation,** of workers from the tools, raw materials, and technical knowledge required to produce goods. When, for example, peasants are pushed off the land and forced to work for wages in mines or on commercial farms, they are caught up in a process sometimes called **proletarianization:** a process of class formation that transforms people deprived of subsistence resources into workers at the bottom of the capitalist political economy.

Once these transformed relations of production are well entrenched, political independence alone will not make them go away. For example, successful commercial plantations will not automatically be dismantled so that peasants can reclaim lands to farm, because the landlords (whether outsiders or locals) will be unwilling to give up the wealth that can be accumulated by using wage laborers to produce cash crops for the international capitalist market. This, it is argued, is why political independence brought neocolonialism rather than economic independence to so many parts of the world. The economies and cultures of colonized peoples had been so thoroughly remade under capitalist colonialism that cutting off all ties to former masters would have resulted in economic catastrophe.

In the 1960s, Latin American economists and sociologists were trying to understand why their nations, free of official colonial domination for over a century, were no better off than the newly independent states of Africa. Articulating an analytic framework that came to be called **dependency theory,** they argued that poverty and "underdevelopment" were a *consequence* of capitalist colonial intervention in otherwise thriving independent societies, and not some original lowly state in which colonized territories had been languishing until the colonizers arrived. Capitalist colonialism *reduced* colonies to a state of underdevelopment in which their economies came to depend on decisions made outside their borders by colonial rulers who were promoting their own interests, not the interests of the colonies. Indeed, they argued, the "development" of rich countries depended on the deliberate impoverishment of other parts of the world. From this perspective, capitalist recipes for economic "development" could hardly be the solution to "underdevelopment," for capitalism had created the underdevelopment in the first place.

Modernization theory and dependency theory both see "development" as a natural process that is a natural part of all social life, but they differ in their understanding of the forces that encourage it or block it. Modernization theory not only views capitalist entrepreneurship as the key to self-sustaining economic growth but also personifies nation-states as primordial sociocultural units, each of which is individually responsible for its own successful modernization. In recent years, the individualism at the center of modernization theory has reappeared in the guise of **neoliberalism,** in which international institutions like the World Bank and the International Monetary Fund urge individual nation-states to pursue their own economic self-interest in competition with one another. Neoliberalism replaces the goal of achieving prosperous national self-sufficiency with the goal of finding a niche in the global capitalist market. State bureaucrats have had to divert funds away from state institutions that subsidized poor citizens, in order to invest in economic enterprises that would earn income in the market.

Dependency theory, by contrast, rejects the individualistic analysis along with its conclusions. Nation-states are *not* primordial entities, but are historical creations; and some nations of the world were able to become powerful and rich only because they forced other societies into weakness and poverty. The fates of a rich country and its poor colonies (or neocolonies) are thus intimately interrelated. Social-scientific perspectives that take this observation as their starting point usually are said to pay attention to an **international political economy** (see Chapter 7). In recent years, many anthropologists interested in the international political economy have become sharp critics of neoliberalism.

An ongoing struggle between anthropologists favorable to modernization theory and those critical of it was a feature of the Cold War years of the 1950s and 1960s. By the 1970s, critics of modernization theory were active in anthropology, many of them influenced by dependency theory. By the 1980s, however, many anthropologists agreed that dependency theory was too simplistic to account for the complexities of the postcolonial world. Many anthropologists thus adopted the broader perspective of **world system theory,** an analytical framework first suggested in the 1970s by sociologist Immanuel Wallerstein.

World system theory expanded upon and strengthened the Marxist critique of capitalist colonialism inherent in dependency theory. Wallerstein's most original idea was to apply a functionalist analytic framework (see Chapter 12) to the capitalist world system, which was, in his opinion, the only social system that came close to being self-contained and self-regulating in the structural-functionalist manner. Wallerstein stressed that capitalism was a *world* system, not because it included the entire world, but because the system incorporated territories scattered across the globe in order to maintain itself and to grow. Unlike empires, which in the past had united far-flung territories under a single political authority, the capitalist world system united far-flung territories *by economic means alone,* through the capitalist market.

Modernization theorists, as we noted, conceive of nation-states as autonomous actors ranked in various positions along a continuum from "backward"/"underdeveloped"/"less-developed" and so on to "developed" industrial economies. By contrast, analysts who adopted a world system perspective use a different terminology, classifying nation-states and other political entities in terms of the role they play within the world system's international division of labor. Thus, those countries that are fully industrialized, monopolize technological expertise and innovation, control financial decision-making for the system as a whole, and pay relatively high wages to skilled workers are said to belong to the **core** of the world system. Core nations today include the former European colonial powers, the United States, and Japan. By contrast, those countries whose main contributions to capitalism are raw materials for industries in the core and expanding markets for manufactured goods are said to belong to the **periphery** of the world system. The ranks of peripheral nations are dominated by former colonies. Finally, some countries are said to belong in the **semiperiphery;**

these nations either were once part of the core or look as though they might someday be able to move into the core. In recent years, China, India, Brazil, and Indonesia often have been considered semiperipheral by world system theorists.

World system theory has established itself within anthropology as a powerful analytic framework for making sense of recent historical developments in the global political economy and their effects on the local communities in which anthropologists have traditionally carried out fieldwork. Thinking in terms of world systems, rather than empires, has also changed the way historians and social scientists approach world history outside Europe prior to the rise of capitalism. Geographer Janet Abu-Lughod, for example, has made a persuasive case for the existence of a thirteenth-century world system centered in India that organized trade by land and sea from Southeast Asia to Western Europe and from China to East Africa. Some anthropologists have been inspired by Abu-Lughod's work, not only because it provides a fuller historical context for understanding the development of cultures they study in the lands that formerly belonged to this world system, but also because it shows that the capitalist world system is not the only world system ever to exist, and that Western cultural hegemony is not inevitable.

Following the end of the Cold War in 1989, cultural anthropologists were among the social scientists who observed a series of far-reaching and intensifying global changes. From one point of view, it looked as though the fall of socialism in the former Soviet Union and the adoption of capitalist economic practices in China was making it possible for the capitalist world system to swallow up the entire world. From another point of view, however, the forces that were responsible for these new interconnections appeared to be so powerful that they were undermining key features of the world system.

For example, world system theory rests on the assumption of an international division of labor in which people in different geographical regions specialize in different economic tasks. This makes it both possible and meaningful to distinguish core from semiperipheral from peripheral nations. However, the vast improvements in transportation and communication technologies in recent decades has permitted a breakdown in the link between economic role and territory. Anthropologists have described a massive **deterritorialization** of both peoples and activities from their former exclusive locations in one or another region of the world system, together with complex processes of **reterritorialization** of those migrants and those activities elsewhere in the world. Anthropologists often face the challenge of carrying out fieldwork among people whose ancestors may have been rooted in a single territory but who themselves may be living in a **diaspora** of migrant populations located in many different places.

In the past, such movements of peoples encountered many barriers, but today demand for certain kinds of workers in core countries has promoted migration, both legal and illegal, of people from periphery, to core. At the same time, technology-dependent manufacturing activities that used to take place exclusively in the core have been relocated in peripheral nations to take advantage of low wage rates. Wage work in manufacturing formerly enabled citizens of core nations with little formal education to earn middle-class incomes; the cost and inconvenience of moving factories out of the core meant that workers could bargain for higher wages and greater benefits with some success. Today's cutting-edge manufacturing plants, however, can be shipped to peripheral countries and quickly set up. They can also be quickly dismantled, in order to move them elsewhere in the periphery where labor costs are lower. Increasingly, jobs that require knowledge of computerized technology are also reterritorializing to peripheral or semiperipheral locations: workers' salaries can be lowered with no decrease in work efficiency, thanks to modes of high-tech electronic communication such as the Internet. Although the manufacturing jobs that have been deterritorialized out of the core are welcome in poor peripheral countries, the loss of such jobs in core countries has caused severe hardship and dislocation for the newly unemployed.

11.3 Globalization

The intensifying flow of capital, goods, people (tourists as well as immigrants and refugees), images, and ideas around the world has come to be called **globalization**. People need not ever leave their homes, however, to be buffeted by the forces of globalization. The explosive development of computer technology, e-mail communication, and the Internet has not been confined to the kind of economic restructuring described above. It has also enabled many other kinds of links among people who have never seen one another, creating global networks, or *virtual communities,* that reach beyond the boundaries of nation-states. Many anthropologists have become interested in the growth of **cyberculture:** the distinct beliefs and practices developing in connection with the growth of computer-mediated communication. The cultural possibilities that might be produced by unbridled cyberexchanges on a global level remain limited, however, because access to computer-mediated communication is still largely the preserve of middle-class users with mastery of computer technology and literacy in English. In addition, various national governments continue to try to restrict their citizens' access to cybercommunication, with varying degrees of success.

The forces of globalization have little respect for the kinds of social, cultural, religious, political, and geographical boundaries that are used to discipline and routinize contacts between vastly different categories of ideas, images, practices, and peoples. Thus, globalization and its consequences—especially the way it appears to have overcome traditional limits of time and space—are an excellent illustration of what many anthropologists and other scholars describe as the **postmodern condition.** This term refers to the situation in which human beings find themselves at the dawn of the twenty-first century: time is compressed, distances are annihilated. Under these conditions, the supposed benefits of "rational scientific modernity"—prosperity, equality, peace—appear more elusive today than ever, and have increasingly been called into question (see Chapter 1).

After 1989, for example, the certainties of the Cold War years gave way to bewilderment for many citizens of the United States: Who were our enemies? Who were our friends? Indeed, who are "we" and who are "they"?

Since a terrorist attack destroyed the World Trade Center in New York City on September 11, 2001, many Americans have been persuaded that "terrorists" have stepped into the slot that used to be occupied by "communists." But this has hardly led to unanimity in the United States regarding how "terrorists" are to be identified or how they should be fought. Some terrorist groups might be international, but both the United States and Europe have experienced attacks by terrorist groups that were home-grown.

The struggle to manage situations of uncertainty and insecurity of this kind has given rise to a phenomenon sometimes called **identity politics:** struggles by groups to create and sustain exclusionary political alliances defined more narrowly than, and often in opposition to, a common identity as citizens of a nation-state. Although neither the nation-state nor citizenship has disappeared, many groups and individuals clearly refuse to accept them as overriding standards beneath which all other communities and identities should be subordinated or eliminated. Put another way, the hegemony of the nation-state and citizenship has been challenged.

The postmodern challenge of identity politics exposes the fact that societies and cultures that have been portrayed, either by their members or by outsiders, as homogenous and harmonious, are more often characterized by **cultural pluralism.** That is, they are made up of a multiplicity of heterogenous subgroups whose ways of thinking and living vary, whose interests may be opposed, and whose cooperation is not automatic. Although coercion by ruling elites may give the appearance of cultural uniformity, pluralism emerges when coercion weakens. It becomes apparent that some members of a society have serious reservations about the values and practices they have been pressured to accept. That is, rather than having willingly adopted, or *assimilated to*, the dominant majority culture, they may view their relationship to that culture as one of simple **accommodation.**

Cultural heterogeneity becomes even more complex in societies that have experienced recent immigration, producing a situation that is often called **multiculturalism.** The nation-states of western Europe, for example, have all received large numbers of new immigrants from all over the world in recent decades. Citizens who already have differences with one another are challenged to make room for various groups of new arrivals, while each set of migrants is faced with constructing a place for itself among a variety of other contending groups with different cultural backgrounds. Living permanently surrounded by cultural heterogeneity regularly produces struggles over pressures to assimilate and disputes about how much the members of each group ought to accommodate to each other or to the norms of the wider society.

11.4 The Cultural Effects of Contact

Anthropologists probably have always been aware that the non-Western societies in which they were doing fieldwork had been heavily affected by imperialist forces of one kind or another. This awareness was surely responsible at least in part for the relativistic defense of bounded, internally harmonious "cultures" so important in the early twentieth century. Anthropologists like Margaret Mead (1901–1978) and Bronislaw Malinowski (1884–1942), for example, regularly drew attention to what they saw as the misguided and pernicious effects of colonizers and missionaries on indigenous cultures. Shortly before his death, Malinowski wrote about the enormous changes taking place in indigenous cultures as a result of colonialism, and American anthropologists like Melville Herskovits (1895–1963) were drawing attention to the processes of cultural change that colonial encounters (external and internal) had set in motion. It was only after World War II, however, and especially after the achievement of political independence by former European colonies, that the colonial situation itself became an explicit focus of ethnographic study.

When anthropologists began to address the consequences of cultural contact, they invented a new vocabulary to try to describe the processes that seemed to be at work. In the United States, Herskovits and his colleagues spoke of **acculturation:** a process by which cultures in contact borrow ideas and practices from one another, thereby modifying or replacing traditional ideas and practices. The study of cultural borrowing had always been important in North American anthropology, and anthropologists pointed out that the process often involved reshaping the borrowed item in order to make it fit into preexisting cultural arrangements. When viewed by an outside observer, the result often was described as **syncretism:** a mixing of elements from two or more traditions. For example, a syncretistic religion emerges when missionary Christianity and a traditional indigenous religious system both contribute to new shared spiritual practices that are neither wholly "Christian" nor wholly "traditional" (see Chapter 5).

Frequently cited examples of religious syncretism are the so-called **cargo cults** that developed in Melanesia and New Guinea in the decades after colonial conquest, many of them stimulated by contact with the United States military during World War II. The "cargo" refers, in general, to the abundant manufactured goods brought to the islands by Western missionaries, traders, and soldiers. Although cargo cults differed in many specifics of belief and practice, they had in common the mixture of Christian religious doctrine and traditional indigenous beliefs about ancestors. A key feature was the belief that the ancestors would return on ships or planes, bringing for their kin the cargo that Europeans possessed in such abundance. In some places, members of the cargo cult even constructed models of airplanes or control towers that had the ritual function of enticing the ancestors and their cargo.

Acculturation theorists realized that processes of cultural borrowing and modification might be mutual—with the partners involved taking from and giving to one another on an equal, unconstrained basis—or that they could be skewed in one direction only, as a result of unequal power relations. The latter situation could often be found under colonial rule. For example, children in colonies frequently were taken from their home villages and taught the colonizer's language and culture in boarding schools deliberately designed to cut children off from the influence of their families' traditional way of life. In such cases, the goal was often explicitly to "civilize" the children, which in the circumstances meant to replace the children's culture with that of the colonizer. That is, the colonizers wanted these children to **assimilate** to colonial society and culture, to cut off identification with their culture of origin and become totally absorbed in the ways of Europeans. Pressure to assimilate is not unique to colonial situations; it is commonly encountered by refugee or immigrant groups moving into societies dominated by cultural traditions very different from their own. In both cases, however, the goal of assimilation is the same: the disappearance of distinctive cultural features that set the lower-ranking and less influential subaltern groups apart from those privileged and powerful groups who dominate them.

Struggles over multiculturalism at home and charges of cultural imperialism abroad forced anthropologists to reexamine the processes that ensue when people of different cultural backgrounds come into contact. Their field research showed that the realities of cultural exchange were much more complex than the struggles of identity politics or the worries about cultural imperialism would lead one to imagine. Their efforts were complemented by the actions of individual members of different subaltern groups who refused to assimilate to a hegemonic culture, asserted their right to pick and choose from global culture the customs they wanted to follow, and resisted attempts by other members of the groups to which they belonged to police their beliefs and behavior (see Chapter 2).

The charge of Western cultural imperialism—that Western cultures were dominating and destroying other cultures, producing global cultural homogenization—did not hold up to scrutiny. The notion of cultural imperialism denies agency to non-Western people who make use of Western cultural forms. It also ignores the fact that many non-Western cultural forms have been adopted by members of Western societies (sushi, for example). Finally, it ignores the fact that cultural forms sometimes bypass the West entirely as they move from one part of the world to another (movies from India, for example, that have been popular in Africa for decades). These are all examples of the active reconciliation of cultural practices from elsewhere with local practices, in order to serve local purposes: that is, they are examples of indigenization—sometimes also called *domestication* or *customization* (see Chapter 2).

The rate of cultural borrowing followed by indigenization has speeded up enormously under conditions of globalization. This has led many social scientists to describe the process as **cultural hybridization**. The emphasis in discussions of cultural hybridization is on forms of cultural borrowing that produce something completely new from the fusing of elements of donor and recipient cultures. Rather than speaking of dependency and cultural loss, this discourse emphasizes creativity and cultural gain. It acknowledges the agency of those who borrow, and helps discredit the notion that "authentic" cultural traditions never change. This approach offers a new angle from which to consider such phenomena as cargo cults. Rather than being viewed simply as curious products of culture contact, cargo cults began to look like creative attempts by colonized groups deprived of the promised benefits of capitalist colonialism to make sense of their deprivation and to overcome it by innovative religious means.

But the concept of cultural hybridization is not without problems. Cultural hybridity implies the mixture of two or more non-hybridized, "pure" cultures, which are not supposed to exist. Furthermore, hybrid identities are not always liberating if they are not freely adopted. Indeed, anthropologists have been able to show that cultural hybridization is experienced differently by those with power and those without power. Those with power are the ones more able to pick and choose as they please from the offerings of global culture. Indeed, cultural hybridity has been commodified, on display and for sale at international music festivals and ethnic art markets. Those who can consume these multicultural offerings on their own terms experience cultural hybridity very differently from those who have hybridity thrust upon them. These latter are often members of poor and marginal migrant groups who feel unable to protect themselves from forms of cultural hybridization they have not chosen and which threaten their own fragile survival structures. When cultural hybridity becomes fashionable, the experience of hybridized elites is highlighted, and the class exploitation and racial oppression that hybridized non-elites continue to experience often disappears from view. To ignore these alternative ways of experiencing hybridity is misleading and dangerous.

11.5 Globalization, Citizenship, and Human Rights

Identity politics practiced in a context of globalization has led to the development of a variety of new understandings about the nature of the nation-state and citizenship that anthropologists have begun to study. For example, in the contemporary world migrants from one part of the world to another regularly keep in touch with those they left behind, and this can lead to their continuing support of nationalist struggles in their homeland, a phenomenon called **long-distance nationalism.** Sometimes, those left behind in the homeland try to create a **transborder state,** by reaching out to those who have migrated elsewhere, claiming them as citizens of their nation of origin even if they are also citizens of the state to which they have migrated. Such **transborder citizenship** may be written into laws granting dual nationality or extending voting rights in the country of origin to migrants who are citizens elsewhere.

The emergence of transborder states exposes the fact that some formally-recognized nation-states in fact cannot meet the needs of all their citizens, some of whom they must send abroad as migrants. The emergence of transborder citizens calls into question traditional beliefs about citizenship in a nation-state. It becomes clear that *legal citizenship,* granted by the state, is often at odds with the *substantive citizenship* in which migrants engage in their new homelands, as they take action to build better lives for themselves and their families. Indeed, given the unparalleled opportunities for mobility that globalization offers those with the right connections and resources, the very idea of citizenship in a single nation-state is undermined. For example, elite overseas Chinese families with business interests all over the world have created a kind of *flexible citizenship* which allows them, with multiple passports and ample funds, to move from one nation-state to the next, or to settle family members in different nation-states, depending on which regime serves their family interests best. Cultivating the ability to reap the advantages, or to circumvent the obligations, connected with citizenship in any particular nation-state, these elite Chinese have developed a *postnational ethos* in which the very concept of nationalism has lost meaning.

In a globalized world, in which people in many peripheral countries have become familiar with the ideology of individual **human rights** developed in powerful core cultures, local groups may claim that they have been deprived of their natural rights to life, liberty, or property. They often find allies in core nations who support their demands that their human rights as individuals be respected. Such claims frequently have been made by citizens of nations whose leaders signed the United Nations Declaration on Human Rights but who find their own rights being violated by those same leaders.

When minority groups are subject to coercive attempts at cultural assimilation, they may resist and demand that the wider society respect not only their individual human rights but also the shared **cultural rights** of the group to which they belong. The argument has been made in recent years, in national and international legal forums, that cultural groups have rights of their own, distinct from the rights of their individual members. Such cultural rights usually include whatever is seen as necessary to keep the group's culture viable, such as adequate economic and political resources to preserve their values and practices, including their language, and pass them on to future generations. Indeed, international debates over human rights—individual versus group rights, political and civil rights versus socioeconomic rights, rights as defined by nation-states versus the right of self-determination by indigenous and other minority groups within their borders— show that defining human rights is an ongoing multicultural project of global proportions.

This has led some anthropologists to suggest that a culture of human rights has emerged under globalization, in which individuals and groups of many different kinds, in many different parts of the world, resort to courts of law to receive redress when they believe their human rights have been violated. One of the most striking consequences of this development has been the ways in which filing a human rights claim makes it necessary for plaintiffs to craft their case using the categories that human rights law recognizes. If these legal categories are at odds with categories that are meaningful to the plaintiffs, plaintiffs often have no choice but to tailor their case to match the categories that the law recognizes. Plaintiffs may be forced to portray themselves or their culture in ways that contradict their own self-understandings, or else give up the opportunity to have their day in court. Even if they win their case—perhaps especially if they win—these experiences are bound to affect their views of themselves and their culture, in ways they may not have intended but cannot easily reverse. At the beginning of the twenty-first century, there is probably no place on earth where the discourse of human rights has not penetrated, while global networks established by human rights treaties and courts of law make it possible for a local case to gain international attention with great rapidity.

That claims for cultural rights, as well as individual rights, are taken seriously at the beginning of the twenty-first century often is seen as evidence for the postmodern circumstances in which we live. Sociopolitical entities like nation-states, however, depend for their legitimacy on their being run by representatives of the "nation." The pressures to assimilate recalcitrant minorities may range from **ethnocide,** or the deliberate destruction of a cultural tradition, to **genocide,** or the mass murder of an entire social or cultural group whose presence is seen as threatening to those who run a state, as has been documented in Nazi Germany, Rwanda, the former Yugoslavia, and elsewhere. In the face of such intergroup violence, anthropologists and other social scientists have struggled to define ways of dealing with the differences that divide cultural and political groups that cannot avoid having to deal with one another. Is it possible to imagine a way of managing cultural or political differences in ways that do not lead to violent conflicts, that do not require complete assimilation, but that allow people of different backgrounds to live comfortably with the differences of others?

One recent suggestion has been that the contemporary multicultural challenges may be met if we find a way to promote among all the value of **cosmopolitanism.** Cosmopolitanism refers to being at ease in more than one cultural setting. It was promoted by the Stoic philosophers of ancient Rome, and revived by the philosopher Emmanuel Kant during the Enlightenment. For Kant, to be a cosmopolitan meant to be experienced in the ways of western Europe, and it was applied to elites only. Those who would promote cosmopolitanism today, however, want to extend the concept to include the alternative "cosmopolitanisms" of non-elites such as poor migrants who manage to deal gracefully with the culturally hybrid experiences they encounter, and the multiple perspectives they must juggle whenever they find themselves answerable to different groups of people with different values and practices.

To cultivate this kind of cosmopolitan awareness is often difficult. For one thing, it requires more than simply being open to, or inclusive of, other cultures. Many anthropologists would argue that it also requires acknowledging the legacy of inequality bequeathed on many of the world's people by colonialism. In addition, it requires recognition that the cosmopolitanism of the future must involve active input from individuals and groups whose views have not been acknowledged in the past. For example, it may well be that a Western concept like "human rights" will become widely accepted, but a cosmopolitan understanding of human rights will need to pay attention to the understandings of human rights that grow out of struggles by non-Western peoples who have indigenized the concept to make it better reflect their own experiences. In the best of circumstances, both Western and non-Western contributors to cosmopolitan projects may be able to offer each other the tools they need to achieve less polarized ways of living simultaneously in multiple worlds. This is a form of cultural hybridization that many anthropologists, and those among whom they work, would very much endorse.

For Further Reading

OVERVIEW

Kearney 1995; Robbins 1999

COLONIALISM

Pels 1997

REFUGEES, GENOCIDE, AND HUMAN RIGHTS

Daniel and Knudsen 1995; Malkki 1995; Messer 1993;
Nagengast 1994

GLOBALIZATION

Abu-Lughod 1989; Appadurai 1996; Featherstone 1990;
Hannerz 1996

DEPENDENCY AND DEVELOPMENT
Lewellen 1995

MIGRATION AND LONG-DISTANCE NATIONALISM
Schiller and Fouron 2002

COSMOPOLITANISM
Breckenridge, Pollock, Bhabha, and Chakrabarty 2002

12

Theory in Cultural Anthropology

The key terms and concepts covered in this chapter, in the order in which they appear:

material phenomena
theory
empirical
fact

unilineal cultural
    evolutionism

biological determinism
races

diffusion
culture traits
historical particularism
culture areas

functionalism
structural functionalism

social determinism
cultural determinism
superorganic

configurations of entire
    cultures
culture-and-personality
    school

ethnoscience
emic
etic

structuralism
French structuralism
bricolage
agency

symbolic anthropology
ecological
    anthropology
cultural ecology
multilineal
    evolutionism
behavioral ecology

cultural materialism
utilitarian

historical materialism

positivism
postmodernism
stopping points
standpoint

ORIGINALLY, ANTHROPOLOGY AIMED to be a science of culture. Its early practitioners modeled themselves on the most successful scientists of their day—the physicists, chemists, and especially the biologists. As much as possible, they aimed to adopt the methodology of science and described their activities using scientific terminology. Thus, important late-nineteenth-century scholars like Lewis Henry Morgan and Herbert Spencer were most explicit about the fact that their work involved a search for the laws of society and culture and that discovering such laws would permit them to describe the relationships of material cause and effect that underlay social and cultural phenomena.

Since their day, the applicability of the scientific method to the study of human social and cultural life has been questioned. Although some cultural anthropologists maintain that the scientific method is appropriate to anthropology, many of their colleagues have concluded either that human cultural life is not an appropriate subject matter for "scientific" analysis or that, if it is, science itself must be reconfigured and its methodology revised in order to provide accounts of human cultural life that are not distorted beyond all recognition (also discussed in Chapter 1).

12.1 Anthropology as Science

Why did early anthropologists think that culture could be studied scientifically? If we believe E. B. Tylor, it was because culture was patterned, orderly, *lawlike*. As Tylor famously said, if law is anywhere it is everywhere. Like physical scientists and social scientists such as Herbert Spencer (1820–1903) and Emile Durkheim, Tylor and other early anthropologists believed that the phenomena of culture—languages, customs, techniques, rituals, and so forth—were **material phenomena,** phenomena that existed in the world and were tangible and measurable and could be registered by the senses. The current shape of these phenomena was the effect of other material causes at work in human society, not of metaphysical or spiritual causes. Durkheim echoed this when he later argued that social facts could be explained only by other social facts. Much of culture seemed resistant to rapid change, but when it did change, it did so in a patterned and lawlike manner. Thus, Tylor, Spencer, and Lewis Henry Morgan described culture as evolving, rather than changing unpredictably or randomly with the passage of time.

In anthropology, as in science, a **theory** is a formal description of some part of the world that explains how, in terms of cause and effect, that part of the world works. Anthropology followed the lead of scientific theorizing in other fields, in which the aim was to explain a complex phenomenon by *reducing* it to a set of simpler elements whose interactions were both necessary and sufficient to produce the phenomenon in question. Because human culture in general and individual cultural traditions in particular are enormously complex phenomena, anthropologists hoped that they might discover those simpler elements and laws that *determined* the direction of cultural evolution.

Early scientists, and anthropologists who wanted to imitate their method, argued that the plausibility of any theory depended on the evidence used to defend it, and they were universal in urging that only solid empirical evidence be allowed. To be **empirical** means that the evidence used to support a theory is the product of hands-on experience and can be inspected and evaluated by observers other than the original researcher. Only evidence that could meet this standard could be considered scientific **fact.** Scientific investigation has always stressed the importance of empirical research, arguing that the evidence of one's senses is a surer foundation for reliable knowledge than speculation unsupported by direct experience and that the objectivity of one's evidence must be tested against the critical observations of others before it is granted.

12.2 Nineteenth-Century Approaches

Nineteenth-century **unilineal cultural evolutionism** is generally regarded as the first theoretical perspective to take root in the discipline of anthropology. Evolutionary thought in nineteenth-century biology is ordinarily associated with Charles Darwin

(1809–82), but cultural evolutionary thought actually predated Darwin's 1859 publication of *On the Origin of Species* and was already well developed in the work of Darwin's contemporary Herbert Spencer. Spencer thought that human societies could usefully be compared to living organisms and stressed that, over time, like living organisms, societies increased in both size and internal complexity. Spencer's ideas had parallels with the work of his contemporary, Lewis Henry Morgan. Morgan is best remembered for two key contributions to the development of anthropological theory: his emphasis on patterned variation in kinship terminologies, which led him to speculate about the different forms human families might assume in different societies, and his attempt to connect these patterns of family organization to patterns of subsistence in a universal evolutionary sequence. The sequence he proposed drew together many contemporary ideas about the evolution of culture, including the idea that all cultures everywhere either had evolved or would evolve through the same sequence of stages: Savagery, Barbarism, and Civilization (also discussed in Chapter 8).

Morgan recognized that his scheme was tentative in places and required more evidence to sustain certain claims. Nevertheless, like other cultural evolutionists in this period, he was convinced that he had discovered underlying laws of cultural change and that better empirical evidence collected by future researchers would refine the patterns he had exposed.

In a scientific world where researchers hope to reduce complex effects to simple causes, theories of cultural evolution were challenged by other theories that claimed to explain the diversity of human social life in different ways. One of the strongest competitors in the late nineteenth century was the argument that biological differences between different human populations explained their different ways of life or, put another way, that a group's way of life was determined by its distinct, innate biological makeup. This approach, called **biological determinism,** is also known as *scientific racism*, for it claimed to have empirical evidence that supported both the existence of biologically distinct human populations, or **races,** and the relative rankings of these races on a scale of superiority and inferiority. Not surprisingly, this Eurocentric framework assumed that light-skinned European races were superior to darker-skinned African or Asian or Native American races, since the latter had been conquered and dominated by the former.

Late-nineteenth-century evolutionary anthropologists never fully separated themselves from the biological determinists. Even though their defense of a universal set of cultural evolutionary stages presupposed a common humanity and common destiny shared by all the peoples of the world (which they sometimes described as the *psychic unity of mankind*), they believed that this common potentiality had not been equally developed in all living human populations and that its actual degree of realization was indicated by the stage of cultural evolution a particular society had achieved. Thus, although the descendants of people whose way of life was classified as "savage" might one day achieve the same level of sophistication as a contemporary people classified as "barbarian," there was no question of considering them equal at the present time. People living at a more highly evolved level of culture were simply viewed as more highly evolved *people* than those living at lower levels. Not until the twentieth century and the work of North American anthropologists like Franz Boas and his students would scientific racism be rejected as an explanation of human cultural diversity (also discussed in Chapter 2).

12.3 Early-Twentieth-Century Approaches

Although unilineal evolutionary schemes were built on valid observations about changes in human subsistence strategies and incorporated empirical evidence about kinship that has proved reliable over time, these schemes also included (as all scientific theories do) considerable speculation. As the twentieth century began, German anthropologists were offering a very different universal theory of culture change, based on the supposedly regular spread of various cultural items from group to group by **diffusion,** or borrowing. Some proponents of both views were becoming increasingly extreme in their claims. In the face of this extremism, Boas in the United States denounced both theories. In the best scientific fashion, he used empirical ethnographic and historical evidence to expose the inadequacies of both forms of reductionism. Boas agreed that cultures changed over time, but such change could not be confined to passage through a single sequence of progressive evolutionary stages. Rather, historical evidence showed that cultures sometimes simplified over time, instead of becoming more complex, and in any case could easily skip stages by borrowing advanced cultural inventions from their neighbors. Similarly, although cultures are full of cultural items or activities, called **culture traits,** borrowed from neighboring societies, anthropologists go too far if they assume that most human groups are incapable of inventing anything on their own and must await the innovations that spread from a few favored sites of cultural creativity. Boas pointed out that some social problems—how to organize kinship, for example—have only a few possible solutions and are likely to be independently discovered again and again by widely separated peoples.

Boas and his students rejected both extreme evolutionary schemes and extreme diffusion schemes, preferring to focus on the distinct histories of change in particular human societies, an approach that came to be called **historical particularism.** By comparing the culture histories of neighboring peoples, they were able to trace the limits of diffusion of many cultural traits, eventually producing maps of **culture areas** far smaller and more complex than the vast maps of the German diffusionists.

The theoretical extremism that Boas rejected was also rejected in England and France at about the same time. Although not ruling out the possibility of one day being able to construct a theory of cultural evolution, anthropologists like Bronislaw Malinowski and A. R. Radcliffe-Brown (1881–1955) in England and sociologist/ anthropologist Emile Durkheim and his colleagues in France declared a moratorium on speculations about cultural evolution unsupported by empirical evidence. All urged that research focus instead on living societies in order to collect precisely the kind of detailed empirical evidence that might one day enable the construction of a plausible theory of cultural evolution.

Malinowski set an example with his own field research in the Trobriand Islands. Not only was he a pioneer in modern participant-observation field methods, but he also set standards for the collection of ethnographic data that had a lasting influence on subsequent generations of anthropologists. His approach was to classify the customs and beliefs he learned about in the field in terms of the function each one performed in the satisfaction of what he called *basic human needs* (also discussed in Chapter 8). For this reason, his research program became known as **functionalism.** Malinowski's main goal in much of his ethnographic writing was to debunk contemporary stereotypes of "savage" peoples as irrational, compulsive slaves to their passions, and so he emphasized repeatedly how orderly and well organized Trobriand life was and how customs that appeared irrational to ignorant outsiders could actually be shown to play important functions in meeting the Trobriand Islanders' basic human needs.

The theoretical response of other British and French anthropologists was to focus not on the function of particular customs in meeting the needs of individual human beings but rather on their function in preserving the structure of the society itself. Hence, this school of thought came to be called **structural functionalism.** Heavily influenced by the writings of Durkheim, Radcliffe-Brown was its most tireless promoter in Britain. Structural-functionalists were concerned with what kept societies from falling apart (discussed in Chapter 7), and they were able to demonstrate that a variety of social practices described by ethnographers—witchcraft accusations, kinship organization, myths, and the like—performed this function.

In the mid-twentieth century, an antagonism developed between structural-functionalist British social anthropologists (as they called themselves) and North American cultural anthropologists. In retrospect, the antagonism seems rather trivial, but for many anthropologists at the time, the issue was whether anthropology would be taken seriously as a science. As we have seen, British social anthropologists, via Radcliffe-Brown, who was influenced by Durkheim, took *society* as their defining concept. To them, human bodies arranged in space in particular configurations constituted the unquestionable reality that must be shaped by material laws of cause and effect operating in the social realm.

North American anthropologists, however, focused on the concept of *culture*—the ideas, beliefs, values, and meanings that different groups of people developed to express their understanding of their lives and themselves.

For a British social anthropologist, nothing could be less material, and thus possess less causal power, than ideas, beliefs, and values. For the most outspoken of them, culture was a by-product, or a rationalization of material social arrangements that had nothing to do with culture but were instead the inevitable outcome of the operation of universal social laws (the necessity of maintaining social solidarity so that the social group endures over time) that automatically forced living human organisms into particular social configurations in particular circumstances. But North American cultural anthropologists countered such arguments by emphasizing the power of culture to shape all aspects of peoples' lives, including the ways they organized their societies.

To counter the **social determinism** advocated by some structural-functionalists, some cultural anthropologists proposed a form of **cultural determinism**. For example, A. L. Kroeber (1876–1960), one of Boas's students, argued that culture was a **superorganic** phenomenon (to be contrasted with inorganic matter and organic life). That is, although culture was carried by organic human beings, it existed in an impersonal realm apart from them, evolving according to its own internal laws, unaffected by laws governing nonliving matter or the evolution of living organisms, and essentially beyond the control of human beings whom it molded and on whom, in a sense, it was parasitic.

The views of social determinists and cultural determinists were so extreme, in part because they completely rejected any explanation of society or culture that would locate its origins either outside human individuals in some unseen, immaterial, personalized force like God or within human individuals in the psychological structure of their minds. Durkheim, Radcliffe-Brown, and Kroeber, each in his own way, struggled to defend the view that sociocultural beliefs and practices constituted a distinct scientific subject matter that had to be explained in its own terms by specialists who understood how it operated—that is, by social (or cultural) scientists like themselves.

In North America, cultural anthropologists developed a series of theoretical perspectives based on their conviction that culture shaped human behavior, including the construction of particular forms of social structure. In the early twentieth century, inspired by the work of Ruth Benedict, they turned to psychology and attempted to apply what was understood about the configuration of individual human personalities to the **configurations of entire cultures.** Attempts to explain why adults from different cultures held different values and engaged in different practices promoted attention on child-rearing practices, leading to the development of the **culture-and-personality school,** to which Margaret Mead was a major contributor (also discussed in Chapter 4).

12.4 Mid-Twentieth-Century Approaches

Developments in the study of language inspired other cultural anthropologists to borrow insights from linguistics in attempting to explain how culture worked. One outcome of this was the development of **ethnoscience,** a movement in cultural anthropology that involved borrowing the techniques perfected by descriptive linguists to elicit information about culturally relevant domains of meaning by studying how the members of a particular group classified objects and events in their environments. Ethnoscientists were extremely concerned that the taxonomies they elicited not be contaminated by the imposition of their own cultural perspectives. Therefore, they went to great pains to preserve the boundary between the culturally relevant categories of their informants, called **emic** categories, and the categories that were the product of anthropological theory, called **etic** categories (also discussed in Chapter 3).

Another rather different attempt to apply insights from linguistics to cultural analysis was developed by French anthropologist Claude Lévi-Strauss. Inspired by the so-called structural linguistics of Swiss scholar Ferdinand de Saussure (1857–1913, see Chapter 3), particularly its analysis of phonemic structures, Lévi-Strauss tried to see whether the same kinds of structural patterns might be found in other domains of culture. Lévi-Strauss first applied his structural analysis—later called **structuralism** or **French structuralism**—to the study of kinship systems, but he gained an international reputation both inside and outside anthropology for his structural studies of myth (myth is discussed in Chapter 5).

Lévi-Strauss collected multiple variants of numerous myths from indigenous societies in the Americas and appeared to be, on the surface at least, as interested in explaining cultural diversity as other contemporary cultural anthropologists. But he parted company with those anthropologists, such as ethnoscientists, who used linguistic methods to produce more detailed and accurate descriptions of culture but who still thought of culture as a historically contingent set of learned beliefs and practices. Instead, Lévi-Strauss saw surface diversity as the by-product of much simpler underlying processes of thought rooted in the structure of the human mind itself. Lévi-Strauss argued that, because all human beings were members of the same species, they possessed the same innate mental structures. The most obvious of these structures, he asserted, was the tendency to classify phenomena in terms of binary oppositions, like male-female, night-day, up-down, or mind-body. Lévi-Strauss argued that the diversity of cultural phenomena around the world was a surface diversity, the output produced by people with identical mental structures who were working with different kinds of natural and cultural resources. All people thus were engaged in a kind of cultural tinkering, what he called **bricolage,** in which they combined and contrasted elements of their experience in complex constructions rooted in a universal set of human mental structures.

Structuralism was immensely influential inside as well as outside anthropology. Literary critics, in particular, seized upon structuralism as a theoretical toolkit that could help them dissect the structure of literary or artistic work. But Lévi-Strauss and other structuralists also had their critics. Early criticism mostly concerned the validity of particular structural analyses of myths or other cultural phenomena. Different analysts, using what they thought were the same structuralist methods, frequently produced different analyses of the same cultural materials, leading critics to raise the question of just how "scientific" structural analysis actually was and how much it depended on the analysts' own interpretive style.

Later criticisms, which fed into postmodernism, pointed out that structuralists (not unlike the Chomskyan linguists mentioned in Chapter 3) assume that cultures are monolithic and that cultural products, like myths, can have only a single "correct" reading. Structuralists wanted their readings accepted as objectively valid, like scientific discoveries, but their critics argued that the attempt to reduce all the variants of a myth to a single underlying structure ignored the possibility that the variants themselves contained important information about the social, political, or historical self-understanding of the myth-tellers. Rather than simply being the vehicles through which myths worked themselves out across time and space, perhaps the members of each society who recounted the myth were agents attempting to use the resources of myth to make sense of specific concrete social experiences. By reducing all cultural forms to the innate structures of the human mind, structuralism appeared to some observers to be merely a new kind of biological determinism.

Structuralism is only one of a series of theoretical perspectives in contemporary cultural anthropology that have come under fire because of their apparent denial of human **agency** (defined in Chapter 4). An ongoing struggle in anthropology concerns the relationship of culture to the individual (discussed in Chapter 4). While most contemporary parties to the struggle agree that culture is learned, they disagree concerning how much is learned, how important it is for human survival, and how far individuals can go in modifying or rejecting aspects of their cultural heritage.

A different and very influential approach to human action developed in anthropology in the 1960s. This is referred to as **symbolic anthropology,** or sometimes *interpretive anthropology,* because of its emphasis on systems of meanings rather than on innate structures of mind or on the material dimensions of human life. For symbolic anthropologists, human culture is a system of symbols and meanings that human beings create themselves and then use to direct, organize, and give coherence to their lives. The most prominent symbolic anthropologists of the last part of the twentieth century were Mary Douglas, Victor Turner, and Clifford Geertz.

The work of Mary Douglas (1921–) combines a commitment to Durkheimian functionalism with an emphasis on the ways in which cultural symbols both reflect and shore up particular social orders. In her most famous book, *Purity and Danger* (1966), she explored widespread beliefs about purity and pollution in different societies, arguing that pollution was best understood as "matter out of place" within a particular symbolic order. Douglas drew attention to the ways in which a particular society's ideas about purity and pollution were regularly based on a metaphoric connection between the human body and society. She argued, for example, that symbolic practices that appeared to be concerned with protecting vulnerable human bodies from pollution were actually concerned with keeping vulnerable social structures from falling apart. Social vulnerabilities were symbolically represented as bodily vulnerabilities, as when the orifices of the body were seen to stand for points of entry into or exit from the body politic. Thus, food taboos designed to protect individual bodies from ingesting polluting substances could be understood as a symbolic way of protecting a vulnerable social order from dangerous outside forces. Douglas's work focuses on forms of symbolism that appear to be universal in human cultures, an emphasis that sets her apart from both Turner and Geertz, who both paid far more attention to the particular symbolic practices of specific societies.

Victor Turner (1920–83) was trained as a structural functionalist in England but became dissatisfied with examining abstract social structure. Rather than emphasizing people's unthinking conformity to the underlying principles that ordered their society, Turner's work emphasized practice and performance. His work came to focus on *social dramas:* people's concrete interactions and conflicts in everyday social life. Turner showed how social dramas not only offered anthropologists insight into the structure of a given society but also revealed how people in that society made sense of their lives. Turner's interest in social dramas led him into studies of ritual (see Chapter 5), pilgrimage, and theater. In all of these studies, he was concerned with how the symbols of a particular group of people—those "things that stand for other things"— were used as stores of meaning and as resources for social action.

For Turner, what mattered were not the symbols themselves but what they meant to specific people and how they led to action in specific social situations.

Like Turner, Clifford Geertz (1926–) has also been interested in symbols and their interpretation. For Geertz, culture is a system of symbols and meanings that are publicly displayed in objects and actions. Drawing on literary theory more than on drama theory, Geertz came to see cultures as made up of *texts*, "stories that people tell themselves about themselves." In his view, the anthropologist's job is to learn to read those texts, not the way natives did, since it was impossible to get inside the natives' heads, but from within the same cultural context. Geertz proposed the phrase *thick description* for this process of finding the local meanings of cultural texts and in so doing drew attention to the fact that written texts were the typical product of ethnographic fieldwork. Beginning in the early 1970s, many anthropologists increasingly came to see that their task was to *write about* other societies, not merely to collect and analyze data, and that their ethnographies should be understood as texts to be read alongside the natives' own texts.

Both Geertz and Turner were influential outside of anthropology as well, in such branches of the humanities as religious studies and literary theory. Indeed, a common complaint about Geertz's work was that by relying so heavily on the interpretive skills of the anthropologist, it made the field more like literary criticism than social science.

The mid-twentieth century also saw a revival of evolutionary thinking in North American cultural anthropology. The new evolutionary anthropology rejected biological determinism, together with the racist evolutionary scheme that went with it. At the same time, evolutionary anthropologists accepted current biological theories of evolution by natural selection and argued that human biological evolution, like the biological evolution of all organisms, involved adaptation to the environment. If varying modes of human adaptation were not the outcome of variations in human biology, some anthropologists reasoned, then perhaps the environments themselves were responsible for human cultural diversity.

Anthropologists who ask such questions today usually are described as doing one or another kind of **ecological anthropology** (see Chapter 8).

Ecologists and ecologically inclined anthropologists generally analyze particular human populations as parts of *ecosystems;* that is, they are one group of living organisms that, together with other organisms, make their living within a given environmental setting. This setting is called a *system* because it exhibits a balance in terms of the variety and size of different populations and the resources they depend upon to survive and reproduce. This balance is usually described in terms of a patterned flow and exchange of energy. Stable ecosystems are ones in which each population occupies its own *niche;* that is, all coresident populations make their livings in different ways and do not compete with one another.

An important founder of ecological approaches in cultural anthropology was Julian Steward (1902–72). His analytic framework, which is called **cultural ecology,** studied the ways in which specific human cultures interacted with their environment. Steward was an evolutionary thinker: He argued that cultural change over time was conditioned by the specific kinds of cultural developments, particularly in subsistence technology, available in a given society and the ways in which members of that culture used their technology to obtain what they needed to survive from the particular environment in which they lived. As cultural systems changed the way they interacted with their environments, thus changing their adaptations, they evolved to new levels of sociocultural integration.

Steward did not believe in the universal stages of cultural evolution supported by his contemporary Leslie White (1900–75). For White, cultural evolution was a general process encompassing all the cultures of humanity. White recast the major stages of cultural evolution proposed by nineteenth-century anthropologists (and by Karl Marx) in terms of how much energy per capita per year was captured by particular cultural systems. For White, cultures evolved as they captured more energy or as their technologies improved, or both. Using these criteria, White identified three major evolutionary turning points: (1) the domestication of plants and animals (the agricultural revolution of antiquity), (2) the beginnings of mechanization (linked to the "fuel revolution" at the beginning of the nineteenth century), and (3) the technological harnessing of atomic energy in the mid-twentieth century. Steward's approach to cultural evolution, by contrast, has been described as **multilineal evolutionism.** Steward focused not on global evolutionary trends but rather on particular sequences of culture change, showing how local, evolutionary trajectories in similar societies could go in different directions, depending on the society's overall culture, its technology, and the particular environment to which each society was adapting. Today, those evolutionary anthropologists who assign symbolic culture a key role in their explanations of human adaptations to their environments (e.g., cultural inheritance theorists) are sometimes said to be continuing the practices of cultural ecology and multilineal evolutionism pioneered by Steward.

Research in ecological anthropology addresses debates about human agency because some ecological anthropologists argue that human adaptations are heavily circumscribed by environmental restrictions. In common with sociobiology, for example, **behavioral ecology** applies to human societies the same analytic principles that have been used to study the social behavior of animals, especially the social insects (e.g., ants). Indeed, sociobiology-inspired behavioral ecological anthropologists claim that, over the millennia, natural selection operating on individuals in particular environments not only has selected for genes responsible for the physical and behavioral traits of *individuals* but also has operated to increase the frequency in individuals of genes that control our *social* behavior.

Behavioral ecologists thus argue that we have been programmed to respond to others in stereotypical (but individually adaptive) ways that neither cultural conditioning nor individual willpower can modify. Put another way, behavioral ecology stresses that natural selection has produced human beings programmed to automatically find ways of maximizing their own individual self-interest, which in evolutionary terms means getting as many of one's genes into the next generation as possible (see Chapter 8). Behavioral ecology has little or no role for symbolic culture in its accounts of human adaptation, because acting in terms of arbitrary symbol systems could potentially mislead individuals into acting in ways that go against their own self-interest, such as taking risks for others with no obvious gain for oneself (or one's genes). If such evolutionary programming is as extensive as some behavioral ecological anthropologists claim, it would appear to restrict human agency just as much as the kinds of biological programming claimed by the biological determinists.

By drawing attention to ecological factors that affect cultural adaptations, ecological anthropologists have attempted to show the inadequacies of cultural theories that take no account of the material conditions of human life. Two other theoretical movements in the latter half of the twentieth century, each rather different from the ecological approaches described previously, also tried to argue for theories of culture that take the material world into account.

One such attempt has been the **cultural materialism** of Marvin Harris (1927–2001), a theoretical perspective rooted in Harris's idiosyncratic readings of Marx, Engels, White, and Steward. He tries to tame what he sees as the extravagant claims of cultural determinists by pointing out the material constraints with which any cultural adaptation must come to terms. He attempts to show that particular customs that shock or disgust us today, such as warfare, cannibalism, or infanticide, were invented to ensure human survival in some past habitat. Although these are cultural inventions, their inventors are no more conscious of why they are doing what they do than are the human beings described by behavioral ecologists. In both cases, moreover, the same kinds of self-interest calculations are said to govern the selection of particular practices. Indeed, both behavioral ecology and cultural materialism take an essentially **utilitarian** approach to the explanation of the evolution of cultural diversity: in any given case, behaviors are selected because they confer the greatest good, either for a particular individual (behavioral ecology) or for the group (cultural materialism).

The other brand of materialism that has been influential in recent cultural anthropology is the **historical materialism** based on the writings of Karl Marx and his followers. The main feature distinguishing Harris's cultural materialism from Marxian historical materialism is the role of the material forces of history. Whereas Harris's approach explains cultural adaptation or evolution in terms of local conditions, the Marxian approach explains cultural evolution in world-historical terms; after all, Marx was another nineteenth-century unilineal evolutionist. But the ways in which he differed from other unilineal evolutionists made him an inspiration for anthropologists dissatisfied with accounts of culture change that did not take into account social and political conflict, domination, and inequality (discussed in Chapters 7, 8, and 11). Marx attributed large-scale sociocultural change to the working out of material contradictions within the organization of society (its relations of production). Ecological constraints are less important than the social constraints and contradictions generated by a particular, culturally constructed mode of production (e.g., between landowners and the people who own no land and so must rent from the owner). Marxian ideas were also attractive because, in at least some of his writings, Marx suggested that human beings could exercise agency— could "make history"—albeit not under conditions of their own choosing. The material constraints of history limited the action they could take, limited even the alternatives they could imagine to the present order, but did not necessarily turn them into puppets unable to affect their cultural surroundings. Although the political hopes inspired by historical materialism have dimmed considerably with the end of the Cold War, Marx's crucial insights into the workings of capitalism and the mechanisms of domination continue to offer theoretical inspiration to some anthropologists.

12.5 Contemporary Debates

At the beginning of the twentieth century, cultural anthropologists wanted to create a science of culture. At the beginning of the twenty-first century, cultural anthropology has split into two camps divided not only over whether a science of culture is possible but also over whether science itself, as traditionally conceived, is possible. One camp consists of those who defend the traditional understanding of science, which many call **positivism** (see Chapter 1). They are committed to the view that universal, objective truth can be discovered by rational methods, that scientific explanations involve reducing complex effects to their simpler determining causes, and that these procedures ultimately will unify knowledge from all domains of experience in one grand "theory of everything."

The other camp takes very seriously the critique of modern science embodied in **postmodernism.** Its members regard the universalizing, reductionist approach of positivist science as inadequate and distorting when applied to the study of culture. For them, taking symbolic culture seriously requires a reflexive, interpretive approach in which the details of specific cultural realities are not eliminated, in which people's individual voices and their unique understandings are not silenced by generalizations. They call into question the supposed universal truths of "scientific anthropology." (Table 12.1 lists the key theoretical positions in anthropology.)

Since the late 1980s and early 1990s, many anthropologists have realized that, for all their political attractiveness, extremist positions are unsatisfactory. The issues are complex, however, because some kinds of progressive politics, such as the condemnation of genocide, seem to rest squarely on the assumption that all human beings everywhere are bearers of universal human rights that *nobody* can be permitted to ignore. It is precisely in the area of human rights that the critics of interpretivism have made their most powerful argument. If all action is culturally relative, they argue, then one has no grounds for international condemnation of leaders of nation-states who persecute their own citizens. If postmodernists have their way, they conclude, and all forms of culture are assumed to be equally valuable, then the grounds for moral outrage at genocide evaporate. Indeed, the leaders of genocide campaigns frequently attempt to silence international critics by defending their actions as culturally appropriate for their societies, and they accuse their critics of ethnocentrism or imperialism. Some

TABLE 12.1   Key Theoretical Positions in Anthropology

LATE NINETEENTH CENTURY	FIRST HALF OF TWENTIETH CENTURY	MID- TWENTIETH CENTURY	LATE TWENTIETH CENTURY
Unilineal evolution	Historical particularism	Ethnoscience	Symbolic anthropology
Diffusion	Functionalism	Structuralism	Behavioral ecology
	Structural functionalism	Ecological anthropology	Cultural materialism
	Cultural determinism	Cultural ecology	Postmodernism
	Culture-and-personality approach	Multilineal evolutionism	

cultural anthropologists are quite open about what have been called the **stopping points** beyond which their analysis cannot go. For those of a traditional positivist bent, it may be deterministic theories that attempt to construct scientific bases for racism or sexism or other forms of social inequality. For those of an interpretivist bent, it may be forms of relativism that would explain away, say, poverty or violence against women.

The most courageous and interesting work is being done by those who try to walk a very fine line between the extremes of determinism (whether biological, cultural, ecological, or historical) and the extremes of relativism. Because there are no clear guidelines for how to do this successfully, at present one encounters a variety of experiments in fieldwork, in theory, and in the work of combining them in written ethnography. One of the most exciting of these developments involves the attempt to reexamine the ways in which knowledge is produced in different scholarly disciplines, including anthropology, and by different kinds of researchers, be they "positivists" or "interpretivists" or something in between.

One of the reasons why many contemporary anthropologists insist on walking the narrow line between positivism and interpretivism is that they realize that there is no simple relation between a particular set of knowledge claims and a particular political agenda. Claiming that women are "natural peacemakers," for example, might be a justification for placing women in high political office but has more often been used (at least in the West) as a justification for keeping women outside of politics because of their supposed incapacity to make war.

Responsible scholarship (as well as responsible politics) thus requires paying more attention to what Donna Haraway calls the "situated knowledges" produced by differently oriented observers engaged in different forms of knowledge production. Taking the orientation of observers into account also makes for better theory. For example, recent work on the history of anthropology has brought to light the significance of intellectual precursors whose work has been overlooked in past histories of the field, but whose contributions to the ongoing development of anthropology have been vital. They range from Karl Marx and Max Weber to W. E. B. Du Bois and Zora Neale Hurston.

Attention to the position of an observer—his or her **standpoint**—builds on the insights that emerged when cultural anthropologists began to pay attention to the reflexive dimension of fieldwork and recognized that making clear the historical, social, cultural, political, and economic contexts within which scholarly research is conducted can actually *increase,* rather than decrease, our ability to recognize where a particular set of knowledge claims are strongest and where they are weakest. Thus, Ethnographer A's observations about the culture of the X people may be an extremely accurate reflection not of the views of all members of the society but only of elite males, since young people and women did not talk to Ethnographer A. Similarly, claims about the causes for patterned social behavior in a termite nest may be very strong in the context of research on social insects but very weak in its attempt to invoke the same causes to explain patterned social behavior in human societies. It is not necessary to dismiss either Ethnographer A or biological science as totally false simply because some of the knowledge claims made by some scholars fail to explain crucial features of human social and cultural life.

This same approach has also led anthropologists to question the assumption that anthropological categories—ritual or kinship, for example—are timeless, universal structures that are not dependent on historical contingencies for the ways in which they are expressed among specific groups of people. The strengths of much recent work in cultural anthropology lie in continuing commitment to ethnographic particularities that frequently resist assimilation into predictable theoretical categories. Much contemporary ethnography relates macro processes of globalization with the micro level of specific people's everyday life. This work, cultural anthropologists often discover, calls into question both positivist and postmodern positions because it focuses on the often unpredictable ways people come to terms with these forces as they construct meanings in the historical and cultural contexts of their own changing lives. This enduring commitment to recognizing the reality of other perspectives and taking them seriously keeps cultural anthropology a vibrant, exciting, and compelling discipline with great potential for allowing human beings to come to know and understand themselves better.

For Further Reading

THEORY

Behar and Gordon 1996; Bernard 2000; Darnell 2001; Geertz 1973; Harrison and Harrison 1999; Knauft 1996; Kuper 1996; McGee and Warms 1996; Moore 1997; Rosaldo 1989

Appendix: Reading Ethnography

As we saw earlier, an ethnography is a scholarly work about a specific way of life. It is based on the author's lived experience with a specific group of people over a period of time, ideally at least a year. Ordinarily, an ethnography is based on knowledge of the other way of life that is both deep and broad—anthropologists try to learn as much as they can about as much of their hosts' way of life as possible. The anthropologist may then write a general description of the way of life or (as is more common today) explore a particular problem of importance in anthropology from the perspective of the people that he or she knows. Ethnography is therefore a kind of *writing*; it is not just a straightforward reporting of "the facts." Some of the same techniques that readers have learned for reading in other genres can be applied to reading ethnography. An ethnography is an exercise in representing a set of beliefs and practices, and this raises issues of ethics, politics, and interpretation. In this appendix, we offer you some suggestions for getting as much as possible from your reading of ethnographies.

The Parts of an Ethnography

How is an ethnography put together? While each ethnography has its own unique characteristics, there are several features that many ethnographies, as a style of writing, share. Ethnographies generally begin with a preface, in which the author may "set the scene," introduce him- or herself, explain how the field research to be reported came about, and thank a set of people for their help. The preface can be useful to a reader even if he or she doesn't recognize any of the names at the end. It can give the reader an idea about the purpose of the ethnography and why the author wrote it. The reader can learn if the ethnography is a revision of the author's doctoral dissertation or a new work, written after the author received his or her Ph.D. It can give the reader an idea of how long ago the author was in the field and perhaps what theoretical directions the author might take.

The preface is usually followed by an introductory chapter that tends to have two major parts: an entrance narrative and the academic context of the work. The entrance narrative dates back to the earliest classic ethnographies in anthropology—both Malinowski's *Argonauts of the Western Pacific* (1922) and Raymond Firth's *We, The Tikopia* (1936), for example, begin with entrance narratives that are well known in anthropology. In the entrance narrative the author invites the reader to join him or her in experiencing the first impressions of the field—what things looked like at the beginning, sounded like, smelled like, what the local people looked like and how the anthropologist was received at first, and how he or she lived. This narrative is useful in several ways: it gives the reader a sense of the author as a person, acquaints the reader with the author's field situation, and orients the reader to the ethnography. At the same time, it also serves as a way for the author to establish a kind of complicity with the readers, to introduce them to the author's legitimacy as a trustworthy source—to convince readers that they can have confidence in what the author will argue in the rest of the book. At the most basic level, this is the equivalent of saying, "I was there. Trust me."

The other part of the introductory chapter can be difficult for nonspecialists to get through. In a sense, what makes an ethnography an ethnography is that it is part of an ongoing debate within anthropology. Ethnographers do not just write about their experiences—their work is ordinarily intended to address current issues within the discipline of anthropology. Writing an ethnography that is not just for classroom use, then, obliges the author to spell out where his or her work fits in cultural anthropology: Who are the other scholars who have influenced him or her? What are the theoretical issues that the author plans to address? These issues are dealt with early in an ethnography, and take the form of a section in which the author reviews the regional and theoretical literature, indicating the strengths and weaknesses of work by other scholars among the same or related people, and the strengths and weaknesses of theorists who have addressed similar issues. This can be challenging for nonspecialists since they usually do not have very much experience with the theoretical issues involved, nor do they recognize any of the names that are being cited by the author (for other anthropologists, this section is very important because it provides hints and clues as to the directions the author will take in the rest of the ethnography). A further difficulty is that the author may choose to use a highly elaborated theoretical language in this section. You need to ask yourself (or your instructor) how much of this section is required reading. At the very least, you might want to try to apply the theoretical approaches discussed in Chapter 12 in order to put the arguments the author is making into a theoretical context. It is not necessary to memorize the names of other scholars that are cited in this part of the text, but it is useful to try to follow the argument that the author is making. This section may be one of the points that your instructor will choose to discuss in lecture to help the class make sense of the key issues to be raised in the ethnography.

The style of most ethnographies now changes abruptly as the author shifts to the presentation of data and interpretation of those data. Here is the heart of the ethnography, as the author presents a set of descriptions and analyses that will simultaneously represent aspects of a way of life and make an argument about their meaning. Here, the author has carefully and intentionally chosen the order and topics of the chapters. A book is always composed—some material included, other material left out—to make the points the author wants made. Part of your job as an intelligent reader is to try to figure out why the author has structured the book in *this* particular way. In some cases, of course, the author tells the readers in the preface or the introduction why the chapters are in the order in which they are found, but sometimes readers have to try to figure out the logic. Sometimes the sequence of chapters is chronological, following a ritual, agricultural, or calendrical cycle, or based on the anthropologist's own acquaintance with the community. More common, perhaps, is a sequence of chapters based on the complexity of the topics to be raised, beginning with the most straightforward and ending with the most complex, or where the topics of later chapters require information that can only be presented in earlier chapters. Another common format is to begin with the environmental setting or history of the community or people who are the subjects of the ethnography, and then once the historical and ecological background is established, the author turns to the social and cultural worlds of the community. In other cases, authors may choose to arrange their chapters by the emotional difficulty or cultural unfamiliarity of the topics presented. Authors may feel that all the details of their arguments must be presented first before getting to material that their readers might find difficult to accept without the necessary background. Alternatively, they may have concluded that their readers need to know and sympathize with their informants before readers are introduced to aspects of informants' lives that might be difficult for readers to understand or accept.

There are many other ways to structure an ethnography, but in all cases that structure is something to which the author has given considerable thought. This doesn't mean that the author is always successful, by the way. Once they have figured out the logic, readers may decide that the author has not presented the material in a way that convinces them, satisfies them ("I wish she had written in greater detail about . . . "), or explains to them what the author wanted them to know ("I still don't understand why the people in the ethnography do . . . "). Sometimes authors may have omitted material that readers consider important. Sometimes there may be too much material that readers find tangential or that becomes overly repetitive. In other cases, readers may have had experiences that differ so much from the ethnographer's interpretation, that they cannot accept either the accuracy of the ethnography or the universality of the claims ("I was in high school at the same time the author was doing his research in a high school. We did things very differently. Maybe what the author found was true in that school because it was not like other high schools.").

Following the body of the ethnography is the conclusion. Here, the style often changes again, as the author attempts to tie up the loose ends, summarize, and connect the body of the work with the theoretical issues that motivated him or her which are set out in the introduction. Sometimes this is also a place where authors may return to a style that resembles the style of the first chapter, as they are concerned to situate their work in the context of other work on similar topics: there may be more discussions of theory, more citations of work by other scholars, and an attempt to make a statement that is more general and abstract than anything in the preceding chapters. Here, your job is to try to figure out where the concluding remarks come from. Do they seem justified, based on what has been presented before, or does the author go too far or not far enough? Does the author connect the ethnographic chapters to the conclusion in a way that makes sense to you? Having finished the book, do you feel that you know something about the world that you had not known before? That you have gotten a sense of "being there"?

The Use of Indigenous and Local Terms

One of the most distinctive stylistic features of ethnographic writing is the use of indigenous or local terms. Readers of ethnography may have been taken aback and perhaps puzzled by this ethnographic usage; they may even find it makes reading the ethnography more difficult. There are several reasons why ethnographers may use many indigenous or local terms. At one level, it is further proof to the readers that authors know what they are talking about—they have learned the language that the local people use and they are able to demonstrate this in their writing. Also, there may be other people who speak that language who read the book. Whether the language in question is the Kiriwinian that Malinowski learned in the Trobriand Islands in 1915–18 or the German that Daphne Berdahl used in the small town of Kella in the 1990s, scholarly professionalism requires that ethnographers record information about the languages of research as accurately as possible, so that other fluent speakers will be able to recognize how the ethnographer has made sense of the language. Such linguistic accuracy is further proof that the authors can be trusted.

In a way, this is the equivalent of "showing your work" in a math class. But more importantly, it is a reflection of one of the fundamental assumptions in anthropology—that other people create through their languages coherent and meaningful ways to look at the world, and that the language used to live those worlds *does not map perfectly onto English*. Using indigenous or local terms becomes a way of signaling dimensions of a way of life that are different from that of the ethnographer. Part of the ethnographer's job, as Bruce Knauft (2004, 18) puts it, is "learning and conveying concepts that are important to other people even when they exceed our initial understanding." For all of these reasons, then, the use of indigenous or local terms can be seen as a characteristic of the style of writing we call ethnographic. So, in reading ethnography, readers should not panic over the many indigenous or local terms that appear—it's unlikely that your instructor expects you to memorize all of them!—but should use the terms as indicators of important points of entry into understanding a way of life that is different from their own.

The Photographs

Many ethnographies are illustrated, usually with photographs. This is also an area that should draw the reader's attention. Photographs have been part of ethnographic writing since the first ethnographies—Malinowski's *Argonauts of the Western Pacific* (1922) contains 66 photographs, and he was following a guide to field photography first published in 1899. It is likely the case that the use of the camera in early ethnography was based on the idea that the camera was a tool of "scientific" recording, and it is certainly the case that Malinowski was very thorough in his use of cameras in the Trobriand Islands (see Young 1998). But it is well worth the reader's time to examine the photographs in any ethnography he or she is reading and think about why they are there and what they contribute to the ethnography. After all, it adds to the expense of publishing a book to include photographs, and so they are not there just because the author thought it would be nice to include a few. First, the photographs are yet another way for the ethnographer to establish credentials—the photographs, especially when taken by the ethnographer or spouse, are a testimony to the fact that the ethnographer was there; often they signify that the author was well accepted by local people (many ethnographies have at least one image of the author interacting with local people). In both cases, the message is "I was there. You can trust what I am telling you."

Second, the photographs can set the scene, moving the reader from imagining the scene to having a picture of the scene. Sometimes even the most vivid writing cannot express the distinctive reality that the ethnographer wishes to convey. The photographs can help by giving the readers a visual reference for the ethnographer's descriptions and analyses. The photographs can also communicate details of the social and physical environment that the ethnographer may have neglected or found excessively complex to describe. Indeed, the photographs can allow readers a kind of complicity with the author by allowing them to check their interpretation of a scene against the author's. Third, the photographs can humanize the people with whom the ethnographer lived. For example, a tightly composed portrait that fills the photographic frame with a face is not a very useful photograph for seeing the social and physical world in which people live, but it is very effective at establishing the common humanity of subject, photographer, and viewer. Finally, from the use of captions and references in the text to the photographs, the ethnographer can create a dialogue between the text and the photographs that will allow the reader to understand better the world the ethnographer is trying to evoke.

It must be said, however, that photographs have sometimes been used to exoticize the people in them. Some ways of drawing attention to costume, facial or body painting, body mutilations, ritual postures, activities, housing, or material objects can portray people as so alien that readers viewing the photos may see them as being socially or culturally abnormal or inferior, or may see only differences, losing sight of the commonalities they may share. For example, a text that only includes photographs of people in "traditional" costume can leave the impression of quaintness or exoticism: that this is how people dress on a daily basis, even when the traditional costume is only worn once a year, or just for photographs. In recent years, anthropologists have critically examined the use of photographs in ethnography, and consider very carefully the photographs they include with their own work. It is important to remember that photographs do not speak for themselves. Photographs are ambiguous, which is why they are given captions or discussed in the text of the ethnography itself.

As you read an ethnography with photographs, you might ask yourself some questions about the way these images are treated. Are there extensive captions? Do the captions refer to the text, and does the text refer to the photographs? Are the photographs of people? Places? Both? How much of the scene is included in the photographs (that is, are most of the photographs close-ups of people, or are the people always surrounded by their environment)? Do the photographs draw you into the society or do they distance you? Are there things in the text that you wish were illustrated with a photograph? Can you figure out why the author chose the photographs that appear in the book? Do the photographs make you want to go where the ethnographer has been? Do you feel that you know the society better having seen the photographs?

Why Are You Reading This Ethnography (and How Should You Read It)?

Even before you open an ethnography, you should ask yourself (and perhaps your instructor, too) why you are reading it, because why you are reading it will affect *how* you read it. The goal of reading an ethnography is not to memorize the multitude of details that are found within it. Frequently, the goal of reading an ethnography is to get a sense of a way of life very different from your own, as well as to learn how the people described in the ethnography make sense out of their lives. The explicit focus of the ethnography might be economic activities or kinship reckoning, but your first goal ought to be to look for overall patterns, rather than to remember details like the term for "Father's-Sister's-Daughter marriage," or the exact sequence of events in spirit possession.

You might be asked to read more than one ethnography in order to compare the ways of life of peoples on different continents, or with different ways of making a living, or in order to find out what has happened to people whose ancestors used to farm, but who now work in a factory in Malaysia or Mexico. You might also be reading an ethnography set in your own world, and the instructor's goal may be to get you to think about the ways in which your way of life, like that of other people elsewhere, is also a social and cultural construction. Even if your instructor has not told you why you are being asked to read this ethnography or specifically what to look for, you can often figure this out if you think about what the instructor has been discussing in class, or where this ethnography is placed on the course syllabus.

In all cases, you should read actively and with paper and pencil handy. As noted above, all writing in anthropology is part of an ongoing dialogue within the field, and you should make yourself part of that dialogue: reading is active, not passive. If you don't understand what the author is saying, make a note, either on paper or in the margin of the book (if it's yours, of course!). If you don't agree with something the author has written, make a note. If you are really impressed with something the author has written, make a note. If you want to know more about something the author has written, make a note. You and the author are in this together, and what you write in (and about) the book becomes part of the text.

Although it is difficult to do, especially when you are just starting out, think about what the author may have omitted, or not discussed. Does the author not write about men? Or women? Does the author talk about globalization, or the effects that nation-building efforts may have had on the people about whom you are reading? Does the author ignore or pay attention to conflicts within the group the ethnography is about? Are there topics that you would like to know more about? Is there anything that would make this book speak more directly to you?

One final set of questions to ask has to do with the ethnographer him- or herself. How does the ethnographer appear in the book? What role does the ethnographer take? Does the ethnographer give the impression of being a detached, outside observer or does the ethnographer take a political position? Was the ethnographer an advocate for the people, or working in an applied way with or for a group of people? Does the ethnographer take a position about any of the issues that are raised? What does the ethnographer reveal about him- or herself? About the purposes of the research? About how it came about? About who paid for it? About the nature of his or her interactions with the people in the study? In some cases, particularly in older ethnographies, the author appears as a character in the entrance narrative and then never makes another entrance. In other cases, the ethnographer is one of the characters in the book, sometimes as an observer, sometimes as a narrator, sometimes as someone whose experiences become part of the data being collected. It will be valuable to you to think about the effect this strategy has on your reading, and on the ethnography more generally.

It has been a long time since ethnographies were taken at face value. Contemporary ethnographers are aware as never before that their texts are not innocent documents—they are not simply objective reports of the heaps of data the ethnographer collected like ripe fruit on the trees of knowledge. They are part of an ongoing debate within the discipline of anthropology; they are based on an unequal, carefully negotiated relationship between the ethnographer and the set of people with whom he or she worked; they are necessarily partial (there were subjects and events that the ethnographer did not or was not allowed to see); and they have political implications. They can be used by governments, by political groups within the society, and by scholars in other fields for purposes not intended by the ethnographer. As a result, ethnographers have become increasingly diligent about positioning themselves and their research in explicit contexts. They make clear who they are, how they were received both personally and politically, who they were able to spend time with, who paid for their research, how it was managed and carried out, and what parts of it may have been used by or objected to by local people of various kinds. They do this so the significance of their data will be neither under- nor overestimated. Knowing who collected the data, how it was collected, from whom, and how it was interpreted makes the significance of ethnography stronger and more precise.

That said, it is important not to lose sight of the fact that a key factor motivating ethnography itself is an undeniable fascination with the varied ways of life people continue to make for themselves in different geographic, historical, political, and cultural settings. Ethnographies reveal the sometimes surprising inventiveness and resilience of people facing challenges of many kinds. Reading ethnography is an excellent pathway into the richness of the human experience. Enjoy!

Bibliography

Abu-Lughod, Janet. *Before European Hegemony: The World System A.D. 1250–1350*. New York: Oxford University Press, 1989.

Agar, Michael. *Language Shock: Understanding the Culture of Conversation*. New York: Morrow, 1994.

———. *The Professional Stranger*. 2d ed. San Diego: Academic Press, 1996.

Akmajian, Adrian et al. *Linguistics: An Introduction to Language and Communication*. 4th ed. Cambridge, MA: MIT Press, 2001.

Alland, Alexander. *The Artistic Animal*. New York: Doubleday Anchor, 1977.

Anderson, Benedict. *Imagined Communities*. London: Verso, 1983.

Anderson, Richard L. *Calliope's Sisters: A Comparative Study of Philosophies of Art*. 2nd ed. Upper Saddle River, NJ: Pearson Prentice Hall, 2004.

Appadurai, Arjun. *Modernity at Large: Cultural Dimensions of Globalization*. Minneapolis: University of Minnesota Press, 1996.

Arens, W., and Ivan Karp. *Creativity of Power: Cosmology and Action in African Societies*. Washington, DC: Smithsonian Institution Press, 1989.

Ashmore, Wendy, and Robert Sharer. *Discovering Our Past: A Brief Introduction to Archaeology*. 3d ed. Mountain View, CA: Mayfield, 2000.

Baer, Hans, Merrill Singer, and Ida Susser, eds. *Medical Anthropology and the World System*. 2d ed. Westport, CT: Praeger, 2003.

Barnouw, Victor. *Culture and Personality*. 4th ed. Homewood, IL: Dorsey, 1985.

Behar, Ruth. *The Vulnerable Observer*. Boston: Beacon Press, 1997.

Behar, Ruth and Deborah Gordon, eds. *Women Writing Culture*. Berkeley: University of California Press, 1996.

Bernard, Alan. *History and Theory in Anthropology*. New York: Cambridge University Press, 2000.

Bernard, H. Russell. *Research Methods in Anthropology*. 2d ed. Thousand Oaks, CA: Sage, 1994.

Blackwood, Evelyn, and Saskia E. Wieringa, eds. *Female Desires: Same-Sex Relations and Transgender Practices across Cultures*. New York: Columbia University Press, 1999.

Blount, Ben G., ed. *Language, Culture, and Society: A Book of Readings*. 2d ed. Prospect Heights, IL: Waveland Press, 1995.

Bock, Philip K., ed. *Psychological Anthropology*. Westport, CT: Praeger, 1994.

Bohannan, Paul. *How Culture Works*. New York: Free Press, 1995.

Bonvillain, Nancy. *Language, Culture, and Communication: The Meaning of Messages*. Englewood Cliffs, NJ: Prentice-Hall, 1993.

———. *Women and Men: Cultural Constructions of Gender*. Englewood Cliffs, NJ: Prentice-Hall, 1995.

Bowen, John, ed. *Religions in Practice: An Approach to the Anthropology of Religion*. Needham Heights, MA: Allyn & Bacon, 1998a.

———. *Religion in Culture and Society*. Needham Heights, MA: Allyn & Bacon, 1998b.

Bradburd, Daniel. *Being There: The Necessity of Fieldwork*. Washington, DC: Smithsonian Institution Press, 1998.

Breckenridge, Carol, Sheldon Pollock, Homi Bhabha, and Dipeesh Chakrabarty, eds. *Cosmopolitanism*. Durham, NC: Duke University Press, 2002.

Brenneis, Donald, and Ronald Macaulay, eds. *The Matrix of Language: Contemporary Linguistic Anthropology*. Boulder, CO: Westview Press, 1996.

Carsten, Janet, ed. *Cultures of Relatedness: New Approaches to the Study of Kinship*. Cambridge: Cambridge University Press, 2000.

———. *After Kinship*. Cambridge: Cambridge University Press, 2003.

Child, Alice B., and Irvin L. Child. *Religion and Magic in the Life of Traditional Peoples*. Englewood Cliffs, NJ: Prentice-Hall, 1993.

Clifford, James. *The Predicament of Culture*. Cambridge, MA: Harvard University Press, 1988.

Coe, Sophie, and Michael Coe. *The True History of Chocolate*. London: Thames & Hudson, 1996.

Cole, Michael, and Sylvia Scribner. *Culture and Thought: A Psychological Introduction.* New York: Wiley, 1974.

Collier, Jane Fishburne, and Sylvia Junko Yanigasako, eds. *Gender and Kinship.* Stanford, CA: Stanford University Press, 1987.

Colloredo-Mansfeld, Rudi. *The Native Leisure Class: Consumption and Cultural Creativity in the Andes.* Chicago: University of Chicago Press, 1999.

Contemporary Issues Forum: Race and Racism. *American Anthropologist* 100(3), 1998.

Daniel, E. Valentine, and John Knudsen, eds. *Mistrusting Refugees.* Berkeley: University of California Press, 1995.

Darnell, Regna. *Invisible Genealogies: A History of Americanist Anthropology.* Lincoln: University of Nebraska Press, 2001.

Di Leonardo, Micaela, ed. *Gender at the Crossroads of Knowledge: Feminist Anthropology in the Postmodern Era.* Berkeley: University of California Press, 1991.

Doi, Takeo. *The Anatomy of Self.* Tokyo: Kodansha International, 1985.

Duranti, Alessandro. *Linguistic Anthropology.* Cambridge: Cambridge University Press, 1997.

———, ed. *Linguistic Anthropology: A Reader.* Malden, MA: Blackwell Publishers, 2001.

Errington, Shelly. *The Death of Authentic Primitive Art and Other Tales of Progress.* Berkeley: University of California Press, 1998.

Featherstone, Mike, ed. *Global Culture: Nationalism, Globalization, and Modernity.* London: Sage, 1990.

Fiddis, Nick. *Meat: A Natural Symbol.* London: Routledge, 1991.

Fox, Richard G., and Barbara J. King, eds. *Anthropology Beyond Culture.* Oxford: Berg, 2002.

Fried, M. H. *The Evolution of Political Society.* New York: Random House, 1967.

Gamst, F. C., and E. Norbeck, eds. *Ideas of Culture.* New York: Holt, Rinehart & Winston, 1976.

Gardner, Katy, and David Lewis. *Anthropology, Development and the Post-Modern Challenge.* London: Pluto Press, 1996.

Geertz, Clifford. *The Interpretation of Cultures.* New York: Basic Books, 1973.

Ginsburg, Faye, and Rayna Rapp. *Conceiving the New World Order: The Global Politics of Reproduction.* Berkeley: University of California Press, 1995.

Goody, Jack, and Stanley Tambiah. *Bridewealth and Dowry.* Cambridge: Cambridge University Press, 1973.

Graburn, Nelson, ed. *Readings in Kinship and Social Structure.* New York: Harper & Row, 1971.

Gudeman, Stephen. *Economics as Culture: Models and Metaphors of Livelihood.* London: Routledge & Kegan Paul, 1986.

Gutmann, Matthew. "Trafficking in Men: The Anthropology of Masculinity." *Annual Review of Anthropology* 26 (1997): 385–409.

Halperin, Rhoda H. *Cultural Economies: Past and Present.* Austin: University of Texas Press, 1994.

Hannerz, Ulf. *Transnational Connections: Culture, People, Places.* London: Routledge, 1996.

Harris, Olivia, ed. *Inside and Outside the Law: Anthropological Studies of Authority and Ambiguity.* New York: Routledge, 1997.

Harrison, Ira, and Faye Harrison, eds. *African-American Pioneers in Anthropology.* Champaign: University of Illinois Press, 1999.

Herdt, Gilbert, ed. *Third Sex, Third Gender: Beyond Sexual Dimorphism in Culture and History.* New York: Zone Books, 1994.

Hicks, David, ed. *Religion and Belief: Readings in the Anthropology of Religion.* New York: McGraw-Hill College, 1999.

Hill, Jane, and Judith Irvine, eds. *Responsibility and Evidence in Oral Discourse.* Cambridge: Cambridge University Press, 1992.

Hughey, Michael. *New Tribalisms: The Resurgence of Race and Ethnicity.* New York: New York University Press, 1998.

Ingham, John M. *Psychological Anthropology Reconsidered.* Cambridge: Cambridge University Press, 1996.

Kahn, Susan Martha. *Reproducing Jews: A Cultural Account of Assisted Conception in Israel.* Durham, NC: Duke University Press, 2000.

Kakar, Sudhir. *The Inner World.* 2d ed. New York: Oxford University Press, 1981.

Kearney, Michael. "The Local and the Global: The Anthropology of Globalization and Transnationalism." *Annual Review of Anthropology* 24 (1995): 547–65.

———. *Reconceptualizing the Peasantry: Anthropology in Global Perspective.* Boulder, CO: Westview Press, 1996.

Klass, Morton. *Ordered Universes: Approaches to the Anthropology of Religion.* Boulder, CO: Westview Press, 1995.

Kleinman, Arthur, Veena Das, and Margaret Lock, eds. *Social Suffering.* Berkeley: University of California Press, 1997.

Knauft, Bruce. *Genealogies for the Present in Cultural Anthropology.* New York: Routledge, 1996.

——— *The Gebusi.* New York: McGraw-Hill, 2004.

Kuper, Adam. *Anthropology and Anthropologists: The Modern British School.* 3d ed. London: Routledge, 1996.

Lambek, Michael, ed. *A Reader in the Anthropology of Religion.* Malden, MA: Blackwell Publishers, 2002.

Lave, Jean. *Cognition in Practice.* Cambridge: Cambridge University Press, 1988.

Lehman, Arthur, and James Myers, eds. *Magic, Witchcraft, and Religion: An Anthropological Study of the Supernatural.* 4th ed. Mountain View, CA: Mayfield, 1996.

Levine, Nancy. *The Dynamics of Polyandry: Kinship, Domesticity, and Population on the Tibetan Border.* Chicago: University of Chicago Press, 1988.

Lewellen, Ted C. *Political Anthropology.* 2d ed. South Hadley, MA: Bergin & Garvey, 1992.

———. *Dependency and Development.* Westport, CT: Bergin & Garvey, 1995.

Littlefield, Alice, and Hill Gates, eds. *Marxist Approaches in Economic Anthropology.* Lanham, MD: University Press of America and Society for Economic Anthropology, 1991.

Lutz, Catherine A. *Unnatural Emotions: Everyday Sentiments on a Micronesian Atoll and Their Challenge to Western Theory.* Cambridge: Cambridge University Press, 1988.

Malkki, Liisa H. "Refugees and Exile: From 'Refugee Status' to the National Order of Things." *Annual Review of Anthropology* 24 (1995): 495–523.

Marcus, George. "Ethnography In/of the World System: The Emergence of Multi-Sited Ethnography." *Annual Review of Anthropology* 24 (1995): 95–117.

Marcus, George, and Michael Fischer. *Anthropology as Cultural Critique: An Experimental Moment in the Human Sciences.* Chicago: University of Chicago Press, 1986.

McElroy, Ann, and Patricia K. Townsend. *Medical Anthropology in Ecological Perspective.* 4th ed. Boulder, Colorado: Westview Press, 2004.

McGee, R. Jon, and Richard Warms. *Anthropological Theory: An Introductory History.* Mountain View, CA: Mayfield, 1996.

Messer, Ellen. "Anthropology and Human Rights." *Annual Review of Anthropology* 22 (1993): 221–49.

Miller, Barbara Diane, ed. *Sex and Gender Hierarchies.* Cambridge: Cambridge University Press, 1993.

Miller, Daniel. "Consumption and Commodities." *Annual Review of Anthropology* 24 (1995): 141–61.

———."Coca-Cola: A Black Sweet Drink from Trinidad." In *Material Cultures: Why Some Things Matter*, ed. Daniel Miller. Chicago: University of Chicago Press, 1998.

Mintz, Sidney W. *Sweetness and Power: The Place of Sugar in Modern History*. New York: Penguin Books, 1985.

———. *Tasting Food, Tasting Freedom: Excursions into Eating, Culture, and the Past*. Boston: Beacon Press, 1996.

Moore, Jerry D. *Visions of Culture: An Introduction to Anthropological Theories and Theorists*. Walnut Creek, CA: AltaMira Press, 1997.

Morgan, Marcyliena. *Language, Discourse, and Power in African American Culture*. Cambridge: Cambridge University Press, 2002.

Myers, Fred. *Painting Culture: The Making of an Aboriginal High Art*. Durham, NC: Duke University Press, 2003.

Nader, Laura. *Law in Culture and Society*. Berkeley: University of California Press, 1997.

Nagengast, Carole. "Violence, Terror, and the Crisis of the State." *Annual Review of Anthropology* 23 (1994): 109–36.

Netting, Robert. *Smallholders, Householders: Farm Families and the Ecology of Intensive, Sustainable Agriculture*. Stanford, CA: Stanford University Press, 1993.

Netting, Robert, Richard Wilk, and E. J. Arnould, eds. *Households: Comparative and Historical Studies of the Domestic Group*. Berkeley: University of California Press, 1984.

Park, Michael. *Biological Anthropology*. 2d ed. Mountain View, CA: Mayfield, 1998.

Parkin, Robert. Kinship: An Introduction to Basic Concepts. Oxford: Blackwell, 1997.

Peletz, Michael. "Kinship Studies in Late Twentieth-Century Anthropology." *Annual Review of Anthropology* 24 (1995): 343–72.

Pels, Peter. "The Anthropology of Colonialism: Culture, History, and the Emergence of Western Governmentality." *Annual Review of Anthropology* 26 (1997): 163–83.

Plattner, Stuart, ed. *Economic Anthropology*. Stanford, CA: Stanford University Press, 1989.

Pospisil, Leonard. *Anthropology of Law: A Comparative Theory*. New York: Harper & Row, 1971.

Rabinow, Paul. *Reflections on Fieldwork in Morocco*. Berkeley, CA: University of California Press, 1977.

Relethford, John. *Fundamentals of Biological Anthropology.* 3d ed. Mountain View, CA: Mayfield, 1996.

Robbins, Richard H. *Global Problems and the Culture of Capitalism.* Needham Heights, MA: Allyn & Bacon, 1999.

Rosaldo, Renato. *Culture and Truth: The Remaking of Social Analysis.* Boston: Beacon Press, 1989.

Sacks, Karen. *Sisters and Wives.* Westport, CT: Greenwood Press, 1979.

Sahlins, Marshall. *Stone Age Economics.* Chicago: Aldine, 1972.

Salzmann, Zdenek. *Language, Culture and Society: An Introduction to Linguistic Anthropology.* 2d ed. Boulder, CO: Westview Press, 1998.

Savage-Rumbaugh, Sue et al. "Spontaneous Symbol Acquisition and Communicative Use by Pygmy Chimpanzees (Pan Paniscus)." *Journal of Experimental Psychology: General* 115 (1986): 211–35.

Schieffelin, Bambi, Kathryn Woolard, and Paul V. Kroskrity, eds. *Language Ideologies: Practice and Theory.* New York: Oxford University Press, 1998.

Schiller, Nina Glick, and Georges Fouron. "Long-Distance Nationalism Defined." In *The Anthropology of Politics*, ed. Joan Vincent. Malden, MA: Blackwell, 2002.

Schneider, David. *American Kinship.* Englewood Cliffs, NJ: Prentice-Hall, 1968.

———. *A Critique of the Study of Kinship.* Ann Arbor: University of Michigan Press, 1984.

Schuler, Sindey Ruth. *The Other Side of Polyandry.* Boulder, CO: Westview Press, 1987.

Schultz, Emily. *Dialogue at the Margins: Whorf, Bakhtin, and Linguistic Relativity.* Madison: University of Wisconsin, 1990.

Schwartz, Theodore, Geoffrey White, and Catherine A. Lutz, eds. *New Directions in Psychological Anthropology.* Cambridge: Cambridge University Press, 1992.

Scott, James. *Weapons of the Weak.* New Haven, CT: Yale University Press, 1987.

———. *Domination and the Arts of Resistance.* New Haven, CT: Yale University Press, 1992.

Service, Elman. *Primitive Social Organization.* New York: Random House, 1962.

———. *Origins of the State and Civilization.* New York: Norton, 1975.

Smedley, Audrey. *Race in North America.* 2d ed. Boulder, CO: Westview, 1999.

Stone, Linda. *Kinship and Gender: An Introduction.* Boulder, CO: Westview Press, 1997.

———, ed. *New Directions in Anthropological Kinship.* Lanham, MD: Rowman & Littlefield Publishers, 2001.

Strathern, Marilyn. *Reproducing the Future: Anthropology, Kinship, and the New Reproductive Technologies.* New York: Routledge, 1992.

Suggs, David, and Andrew Miracle. *Culture and Human Sexuality.* Pacific Grove, CA: Brooks/Cole, 1993.

Tambiah, Stanley. *Leveling Crowds: Nationalist Conflict and Collective Violence in South Asia.* Berkeley: University of California Press, 1997.

Van Willigen, John. *Applied Anthropology.* Rev. ed. Westport, CT: Bergin & Garvey, 1993.

Vogel, Susan M. *Baule: African Art Western Eyes.* New Haven, CT: Yale University Press, 1997.

Wallace, Anthony F. C. *Religion: An Anthropological View.* New York: Random House, 1966.

Weatherford, Jack. *The History of Money.* New York: Crown, 1997.

Weismantel, Mary. *Food, Gender, and Poverty in the Ecuadorian Andes.* Prospect Heights, IL: Waveland Press, 1998.

Weston, Kath. *Families We Choose: Lesbians, Gays, Kinship.* New York: Columbia University Press, 1991.

———. "Lesbian/Gay Studies in the House of Anthropology." *Annual Review of Anthropology* 22 (1993): 339–67.

Wilk, Richard. *Economies and Cultures: Foundations of Economic Anthropology.* Boulder, CO: Westview Press, 1996.

Williams, Brackette. "A Class Act: Anthropology and the Race to Nation across Ethnic Terrain." *Annual Review of Anthropology* 18 (1989): 401–44.

Wolf, Eric. *Peasants.* Englewood Cliffs, NJ: Prentice-Hall, 1962.

———. *Europe and the People without History.* Berkeley: University of California Press, 1982.

———. *Envisioning Power: Ideologies of Dominance and Resistance.* Berkeley: University of California Press, 1999.

Young, Michael W. *Malinowski's Kiriwina: Fieldwork Photography 1915–1918.* Chicago: University of Chicago Press, 1998.

Index

Key terms are defined on boldface page numbers.

Why Do You Need This New Edition?

If you're wondering why you should buy this new edition of *The Curious Researcher*, here are 5 good reasons!

1. **More content on argument** and on the link between inquiry and argument gives you the framework and information you need to write any kind of paper.

2. **Extensively updated information on library databases and online research,** prepared with help from a college library reference specialist, shows you how to find better sources for your paper more easily.

3. **Expanded coverage of crafting research questions** helps you with the task students find most challenging—finding and developing the questions that guide your research.

4. **The most significant revision yet** of this book effectively supports you through the entire research process, with streamlined exercises you can apply and extra attention to key parts of the process such as developing a thesis and an annotated bibliography.

5. **Updated, reorganized coverage of citations** and formats for MLA and APA means that you can cite a wide range of sources—print and electronic—with ease and confidence.

About the Author

Bruce Ballenger, a professor of English at Boise State University, teaches courses in composition, composition theory, the essay tradition, and creative nonfiction. He's the author of seven books, including the three texts in the Curious series: *The Curious Researcher, The Curious Reader,* and *The Curious Writer,* all from Pearson Education. His latest book is *Crafting Truth: Short Studies in Creative Nonfiction* from the same publisher. Ballenger lives with his wife and two children in Boise, Idaho.

The Curious Researcher

A Guide to Writing Research Papers

SEVENTH EDITION

The Curious Researcher

A Guide to Writing Research Papers

Bruce Ballenger

Boise State University

PEARSON

Boston   Columbus   Indianapolis   New York   San Francisco
Upper Saddle River   Amsterdam   Cape Town   Dubai   London   Madrid
Milan   Munich   Paris   Montréal   Toronto   Delhi   Mexico City   São Paulo
Sydney   Hong Kong   Seoul   Singapore   Taipei   Tokyo

For Rebecca, who reminds me to ask, Why?

Publisher: Joseph Opiela
Executive Editor: Suzanne Phelps Chambers
Editorial Assistant: Laney Whitt
Senior Supplements Editor: Donna Campion
Senior Marketing Manager: Sandra McGuire
Production Manager: Jennifer Bossert
Project Coordination, Text Design, and Electronic Page Makeup:
  Integra
Senior Cover Design Manager: Nancy Danahy
Cover Designer: Nancy Sacks
Cover Image: © James McLoughlin/A.G.E. Fotostock
Visual Researcher: Rona Tuccillo
Senior Manufacturing Buyer: Roy Pickering
Printer and Binder: Edwards Brothers
Cover Printer: Lehigh-Phoenix Color

The author and publisher are grateful to the many students who allowed their work to be reprinted here. We would also like to acknowledge the following copyright holders for permission to use their materials in this book:

p. 110—Oliver Lassen/Zefa/Corbis
p. 190—Patrik Giardino/Corbis

Library of Congress Cataloging-in-Publication Data
Ballenger, Bruce P.
  The curious researcher: a guide to writing research papers/
  Bruce Ballenger. — 7th ed.
      p. cm.
  Includes index.
  ISBN-13: 978-0-205-17287-0
  ISBN-10: 0-205-17287-3
      1. Report writing—Handbooks, manuals, etc.   2. Research—Handbooks,
  manuals, etc.   I. Title.
  LB2369.B246 2012
  808'.02—dc22

                                                                2011012939

This book includes 2009 MLA guidelines.

1 2 3 4 5 6 7 8 9 10—EB—14 13 12 11

PEARSON

ISBN 13: 978-0-205-17287-0
ISBN 10:   0-205-17287-3

Contents

Chapter 1
The First Week   23

Chapter 2
The Second Week   51

Chapter 3
The Third Week   101

Chapter 5
The Fifth Week   185

Appendix B
Guide to APA Style   287

Appendix C
Understanding Research Assignments   331

Index   339

Preface

Placing Inquiry at the Heart of the Course

For many of my college writing students, there are two kinds of school writing—"creative" writing and "academic" writing—and the two have very little in common. Creative writing is typically any personal writing assignment—a personal narrative, a reader response, or a freewriting exercise—and academic writing is most anything that involves research. I've spent quite a few years now trying to understand this perceived gap between creative and academic writing, a distinction that I have found troubling because it short-circuits the connection I have been trying to build between the personal and the academic, especially the idea that students' own subjectivities are not only relevant to academic work but an inescapable part of it. I also know from my own experience as an academic that research writing is a very creative enterprise. Why don't my students see that? I've wondered.

The answer, in part, lies with the research paper assignment itself. It seems to encourage a very closed process of inquiry: Come up with a thesis quickly, hunt down evidence to support it, and wrap it up—all the while focusing less on learning something than getting it right: the right number of pages, the right citations, the right margins. This isn't the way academics approach research at all, I've thought. We do research because we believe there is something to discover that we don't already know. How might I help my students understand that? I've concluded that the traditional research paper is unlikely to teach them what I want them most to learn.

I began to see the problem more clearly after I read the Boyer Commission's national report on the state of undergraduate education in America's research universities. The report was sobering. It also reminded me of what I already sensed: For all of our talk about student-centered learning, much of what goes on in undergraduate classrooms is lecture. The aim, above all, is to transmit information, with students as passive recipients of knowledge. But it is mostly the Boyer Commission's call for an inquiry-based curriculum, particularly in students' first and second years, that has changed my thinking. Commission members call for a "radical reconstruction" of undergraduate education. "The ecology of the university," they write, "depends on a deep and abiding understanding that inquiry, investigation, and discovery are the heart of the enterprise.... Everyone at a university should be a discoverer, a learner." The freshman year, in particular, should provide "new stimulation for intellectual growth and a firm grounding in inquiry-based learning."

The Curious Researcher answers that call. The college research paper, probably the most common writing assignment in the university, presents an ideal opportunity to encourage inquiry-based learning and the kinds of thinking it demands. When students wrestle with sources, listening into the ongoing conversation among experts on a topic, the drama of inquiry can unfold for students with questions like these: *What questions does this raise that interest me? How do I decide what's true? What gives me the authority to speak?* Unfortunately, much research paper instruction mostly raises other, less compelling questions: *How many pages does it have to be? How many sources do I have to use? How do you want this structured?* These are all reasonable questions, of course, but they are certainly not the most important ones if we want students to genuinely understand what it means to engage in academic inquiry. While it certainly answers questions about the formal conventions of the research paper like any other research guide, *The Curious Researcher* tries to inspire students to ask those questions that will shape their thinking well after they leave school. But how does it do that?

Teaching the Spirit of Inquiry

Over the years I've refined *The Curious Researcher*'s approach to teaching inquiry, but it still rests on these premises:

1. **Students should have the experience of investigating a topic in an open-ended way, at least initially**. An important first motive to do research is *to find out*, not *to prove*, and the research *essay,* as opposed to the conventional research paper, is more likely to encourage exploration.
2. **There can't be argument without inquiry**. Most research writing in college is argumentative, and that's certainly the approach of most research papers in the disciplines. Yet in most cases, we develop arguments inductively, through inquiry, as well as deductively. We either discover our thesis by exploring the evidence or test our thesis against the evidence, including evidence that is inconvenient or contrary to what we already think.

3. **One of the most useful—and difficult—things to teach and to learn is the power of questions.** Inquiry-based approaches rest on wonder. These investigations often begin with questions of fact—*What is known about the health effects of tanning booths?*—that later flower into a question, say, of policy—*What should be done to minimize the risks of tanning booths?* The power of questions fuels the critical mind and drives the research.

4. **Writing as a way of thinking is a vital tool in discovery and learning.** What students in any discipline can learn in a writing class is how to put language into the service of inquiry. As any composition instructor knows, writing isn't just a means of getting down what you already know. It's much more interesting than that. Writing can help writers *discover* what they think. In an inquiry-based classroom this is invaluable, and we need to teach students how to use writing to not only report the results of their research but to think about what they're discovering *as* they do research.

Ways of Using This Book

Because procrastination ails many student researchers, this book is uniquely designed to move them through the research process, step-by-step and week-by-week, for five weeks—the typical period allotted for the assignment. The structure of the book is flexible, however; students should be encouraged to compress the sequence if their research assignment will take less time or ignore it altogether and use the book to help them solve specific problems as they arise.

Students who follow the five-week sequence usually find that they like the way *The Curious Researcher* doesn't deluge them with information, as do so many other research paper texts. Instead, *The Curious Researcher* doles information out week by week, when it is most needed. I've also been told by instructors who use the book for online classes that the structure of the book is particularly well-suited for teaching research writing in that environment, especially because each chapter contains exercises that help students work on their own to push their projects along.

The Introduction, "Rethinking the Research Paper," challenges students to reconceive the research paper assignment. For many of them, this will amount to a "declaration of independence." During "The First Week," students are encouraged to discover topics they're genuinely curious about and to learn to develop a "working knowledge" of their topics through library and Web research. This working knowledge will guide them as they decide on a tentative focus for their investigations. In "The Second Week," students develop a research strategy, hone their skills in evaluating sources, and then begin working to develop a "focused knowledge" of their topics by systematically searching for information in the library and on the Web. In "The Third Week," students learn notetaking techniques, the dangers of plagiarism, and tips on how to conduct a search that challenges them to dig more deeply for information. During "The Fourth Week," students begin writing their drafts; this chapter also gives tips on integrating sources, structure, voice, and beginnings. In "The Fifth Week," students are guided through the final revision.

Alternatives to the Five-Week Plan

It isn't necessary to follow the five-week plan, of course. You can have students dip into appropriate sections of the book to solve some of the most common problems that arise during the research process. For example, you might begin by introducing students to the techniques of paraphrase and summary in Week Four (Chapter 4), assigning some of the exercises as practice before they begin a research project. You might skip to the material in Week Three (Chapter 3) on evaluating Internet sources and using library databases, to get them acquainted with finding good academic sources. One thing to consider is what idea you'd like to foreground in your course. This would be the idea that would be a central element of every writing assignment. Among the possibilities are the following:

Inquiry	Research Skills	Writing to Learn
Questioning	Evaluating Sources	Notetaking
Essaying	Learning Research Strategies	Reading
Arguing	Understanding Types of Sources	Revising

Each of these would lead you to "frontload" your course with different material from *The Curious Researcher.* An emphasis on research skills, for instance, might suggest you begin with material in Chapters 1 and 2 on strategies for developing working knowledge and focused knowledge on a topic. An emphasis on how to use writing as a tool for discovery might lead you to introduce students to material on double-entry notetaking in Chapter 3 in the first few weeks.

A few other suggestions include the following:

- Research in learning theory suggests that prior beliefs about a subject or task significantly influence learning. Consider always beginning a research writing course in a way that surfaces students' prior beliefs about research writing and the college research paper. Exercise 1 in *The Curious Researcher* is one way to begin this discussion.

- Inquiry-based learning—with the approach that one begins with questions, not answers—is the concept around which the book is built. There is some evidence that one of the things students struggle with most is crafting strong questions. This is the focus of Chapter 1. But the heuristic power of questions is something you can demonstrate in virtually any writing assignment. Consider having students try Exercises 1.1, 1.2, 1.3, and 1.4 early in the course, well before the research paper assignment, to get them thinking not only about possible topics but also about the importance of good questions.

- The distinction between developing working knowledge of a subject and focused knowledge is a major emphasis in Chapters 1 and 2. If assignments in your writing course involve research from the very beginning, you might have students focus on these chapters in the first few weeks of class.

- Finally, another way to proceed is to identify, after one or more assignments, the kinds of problems your students are encountering, and assign relevant exercises and readings from *The Curious Researcher*. The exercises and readings might help students with focusing their papers, smoothly integrating sources into their own writing, understanding plagiarism, and so on. I address these problems in different sections of the book, and you can find them easily in the table of contents and index.

Features of the New Edition

Writing a textbook is like discovering an aunt you never knew you had. She arrives unexpectedly one summer and stands at your door beaming and expectant. Naturally, you welcome her in. How charming she is, and as you get to know your aunt, you get to know yourself. This is her gift to you. At some point, many months later, you see her luggage by the door, and with a certain sadness you send her off. "Come again," you yell as she ambles off. "Come again anytime. I'll miss you!" And you do. Your fondness for this newly discovered relative grows as you learn that other people, who aren't even blood related, like her too.

If a textbook is successful, the aunt returns again and again, of course, and you get to know her well. Though you may wish she wouldn't visit so often, especially in the beginning, after a few weeks there are new conversations and new discoveries. That's the way it has always been for me with *The Curious Researcher*, and it's especially true with this edition. The seventh edition of this book is the most significant revision yet. With each edition, I'm determined to remake the book so that I can confidently recommend to students that it's worth spending their money on the update. I've never been more sure of that than with *The Curious Researcher,* 7e. Here are some of the new features of the book that make me feel that way:

- *Expanded focus on the research question.* I'm really excited about new content that guides students on how to pose and refine questions that will sustain their inquiry projects. There is evidence that this part of the inquiry process—finding good questions—is what students find most challenging. The seventh edition of the book helps students see how questions evolve as they do research, and offers specific suggestions about categories of questions that can help them with this.

- *Updated information on library and online research.* Though I've often asked reference librarians informally for suggestions about how to improve the book, in this edition I worked closely with a reference specialist at my own institution. Her first-hand experience with how students struggle with research and her expertise as a reference specialist helped me focus, simplify, and update much of the material in Chapters 2 through 4 that deal with library databases and academic research on the Web.

- *More on the link between inquiry and argument.* When I speak to writing instructors around the United States on inquiry-based research papers, they frequently wonder about whether urging students to write exploratory essays rather than argumentative ones is problematic. After all, they observe, the argumentative research paper is its most common form. In this edition of *The Curious Researcher,* I've done two things to address this question. First, I've added content on the links between inquiry and argument. They aren't mutually exclusive approaches. On the contrary, inquiry can easily lead to argument; in fact, it often does. I've also added more material on how to write argument-based papers, with more information about structure and developing a thesis.

- *Updated and reorganized chapters on citation.* This book includes, of course, the MLA's 2009 updates and the new conventions from the sixth edition of the APA's *Publication Manual.* But both sections on citation methods, Appendixes A and B, are also reorganized to make them easier to use.

- *The NEW MyCompLab Web site.* The new MyCompLab integrates market-leading instruction, multimedia tutorials, and exercises for writing, grammar, and research—which users have come to identify with the program—with a new online composing space and new assessment tools. The result is a revolutionary application that offers a seamless and flexible teaching and learning environment built specifically for writers. Created after years of extensive research and in partnership with composition faculty and students across the country, the new MyCompLab provides help for writers in the context of their writing, with instructor and peer commenting functionality, proven tutorials and exercises for writing, grammar and research, an e-portfolio, an assignmentbuilder, a bibliography tool, tutoring services, and a gradebook and course management organization created specifically for writing classes. Visit www.mycomplab.com for more information.

I began working on this book back in 1991, and in the many years since then I've been fortunate to have great students who tutored me on what worked and what didn't. In each edition, a few stepped forward to play a more significant role in the writing of the book, contributing their essays as models, sharing their notes, and so on. In this edition of *The Curious Researcher* I want to mention three. First, Andrea Oyarzabal, now a graduate student in our program, reviewed the previous edition and offered great suggestions about how to make it more usable for students. Ashley Carvalho and Patricia Urbick, both students at Boise State, granted me permission to publish their fine research essays in Appendixes A and B, respectively. Thanks to all three students.

I had the great fortune as well to have the advice of Kim Leeder, an associate professor of information resources and library science here at Boise State, who reviewed and commented on the manuscript. Her expertise was invaluable in making sure that this edition was up to date on library databases and search strategies. She reminded me once again how indispensable a reference expert can be to a writer who researches.

The strong support from the Pearson team is key to this book's success. My editor at Pearson, Suzanne Phelps Chambers, is an enthusiastic supporter of the book and always offers wise guidance. My former editor, Joe Opiela, took a risk on *The Curious Researcher* back in the early nineties, and for that I'm grateful. I am particularly appreciative this time around for the outstanding work of Randee Falk. Her editorial guidance on the seventh edition was the key to inspiring me to revise the book in ways I couldn't have imagined alone. Though we both considered taking poison in the midst of editing the section on citations, Randee did not despair and guided me out of the darkness and into the light. I also lucked out when Sarah Burkhart was assigned as project editor for this edition. I've worked with Sarah before, and I've learned to rely on her care and great judgment. Finally, I've met quite a few of the company's sales staff around the country and, without exception, these wonderful and hardworking people treated me with kindness and expressed enthusiasm for the book. Their dedication is key to *The Curious Researcher's* success.

A number of my colleagues at different institutions have been unflagging in their support of *The Curious Researcher* over the years. Among these are Deborah Coxwell-Teague, at Florida State University, and Nancy DeJoy, at Michigan State University. There are many others who I've met traveling to campuses around the country who have been generous in their support and have said very kind things to me about the book. These visits are great learning opportunities for me, and they've been instrumental in an evolution in my thinking about how to teach writing and inquiry to all kinds of students in many different contexts. Thanks to all of you.

Most of all, I'm grateful to my wife, Karen, and my two daughters, Becca and Julia, for always leaving the light on to guide me home.

I would like to thank those individuals who have reviewed my book. Reviewers for the sixth edition included the following: Marilyn Annucci–University of Wisconsin-Whitewater; Garnet Branch–University of Louisiana at Lafayette; George Clark–University of Southern Mississippi; Denise Coulter–Atlantic Cape Community College; Deborah Coxwell-Teague–Florida State University; Tamara Harvey–George Mason University; Lisa R. Neilson–Marist College; Paula Priamos–California State University, San Bernardino; and Amy Randolph—Waynesburg University. I would also like to extend my thanks to the reviewers of this edition: Kathleen J. Cassity–Hawaii Pacific University; Sydney Darby–Chemeketa Community College; Holly DeGrow–Mt. Hood Community College; Tom Hertweck–University of Nevada, Reno; Nels P. Highberg–University of Hartford; Elizabeth Imafuji–Anderson University; Shevaun Watson–University of Wisconsin, Eau Claire.

BRUCE BALLENGER

Rethinking the Research Paper

Unlike most textbooks, this one begins with your writing, not mine. Find a fresh page in your notebook, grab a pen, and spend ten minutes doing the following exercise.

EXERCISE 1

Collecting Golf Balls on Driving Ranges and Other Reflections

Most of us were taught to think before we write, to have it all figured out in our heads before we pick up our pens. This exercise asks you to think *through* writing rather than *before,* letting the words on the page lead you to what you want to say. With practice, that's surprisingly easy using a technique called *fastwriting.* Basically, you just write down whatever comes into your head, not worrying about whether you're being eloquent, grammatically correct, or even very smart. If the writing stalls, write about that; or write about what you've already written until you find a new trail to follow. Just keep your pen moving.

STEP 1: Following is a series of statements about the research paper assignment. Choose one that you believe is true or one you believe is false. Then, in your notebook, write fast for three minutes without stopping about the belief you chose. Why do you think it's true or false? Where did you get these ideas? Is there a logic behind your beliefs? What might that be? Whenever you feel moved to do so, tell a story.

- You have to know your thesis before you start.
- You have to be objective.

■ You can't use the pronoun *I*.
■ You can use your own experiences and observations as evidence.
■ You can use your own writing voice.
■ You're writing mostly for the instructor.
■ You're supposed to use your own opinions.

STEP 2: Now consider the truth of the following statements. These statements have less to do with research papers than with how you see facts, information, and knowledge and how they're created. Choose one of these statements* to launch another three-minute fastwrite. Don't worry if you end up thinking about more than one statement in your writing. Start by writing about whether you agree or disagree with the statement, and then explore why. Continually look for concrete connections between what you think about these statements and what you've seen or experienced in your own life.

■ There is a big difference between facts and opinions.
■ Pretty much everything you read in textbooks is true.
■ People are entitled to their own opinions, and no one opinion is better than another.
■ There's a big difference between a *fact* in the sciences and a *fact* in the humanities.
■ When two experts disagree, one of them has to be wrong.

Very few of us recall the research papers we wrote in high school, and if we do, what we remember is not what we learned about our topics but what a bad experience writing them was. Joe was an exception. "I remember one assignment was to write a research paper on a problem in the world, such as acid rain, and then come up with your own solutions and discuss moral and ethical aspects of your solution, as well. It involved not just research but creativity and problem solving and other stuff."

For the life of me, I can't recall a single research paper I wrote in high school; but, like Joe, I remember the one that I finally enjoyed doing a few years later in college. It was a paper on the whaling industry. What I remember best was the introduction. I spent a lot of time on it, describing in great detail exactly what it was like to stand at the bow of a Japanese whaler, straddling an explosive harpoon gun, taking aim, and blowing a bloody hole in a humpback whale.

*Part of this list is from Marlene Schommer, "Effects of Beliefs About the Nature of Knowledge on Comprehension," *Journal of Educational Psychology* 82 (1990): 498–504.

I obviously felt pretty strongly about the topic.

Unfortunately, many students feel most strongly about getting their research papers over with. So it's not surprising that when I tell my freshman English students that one of their writing assignments will be an eight- to ten-page research paper, there is a collective sigh. They knew it was coming. For years, their high school teachers prepared them for The College Research Paper, and it loomed ahead of them as one of the torturous things everyone must do—a five-week sentence of hard labor in the library or countless hours adrift in the Internet. Not surprisingly, students' eyes roll in disbelief when I add that many of them will end up liking their research papers better than anything they've written before.

I can understand why Joe was among the few in the class inclined to believe me. For many students, the library is an alien place, a wilderness to get lost in, a place to go only when forced. Others carry memories of research paper assignments that mostly involved taking copious notes on index cards, only to transfer pieces of information into the paper, sewn together like patches of a quilt. There seemed little purpose to it. "You weren't expected to learn anything about yourself with the high school research paper," wrote Jenn, now a college freshman. "The best ones seemed to be those with the most information. I always tried to find the most sources, as if somehow that would automatically make my paper better than the rest." For Jenn and others like her, research was a mechanical process and the researcher a lot like those machines that collect golf balls at driving ranges. You venture out to pick up information here and there and then deposit it between the title page and the bibliography for your teacher to take a whack at.

Learning and Unlearning

I have been playing the guitar ever since the Beatles' 1964 American tour. In those days, *everyone* had a guitar and played in a group. Unfortunately, I never took guitar lessons and have learned in recent years that I have much "unlearning" to do. Not long ago, I finally unlearned how to do something as simple as tying my strings to the tuning keys. I'd been doing it wrong (thinking I was doing it right) for about 40 years.

By the time we get to college, most of us have written research papers, beginning as early as the eighth grade. Like anything we think we know pretty well, the research paper, perhaps more than any other school assignment, is laden with largely unexamined assumptions and beliefs. Maybe some of the statements in the first part of Exercise 1 got you thinking about any assumptions you might have about writing academic research papers. Maybe you had a discussion in class about it. From my own research on common beliefs about research writing, I once discovered that one of the most common assumptions first-year college students share is this one: You have to know your thesis before you start a research paper—which obviously implies the belief that discovery is not the point of research.

The second part of Exercise 1 might have gotten you thinking about some beliefs and attitudes you haven't thought much about— what a "fact" is, the nature and value of "opinions," and how you view experts and authorities.

Both sets of assumptions—one about the research paper genre and the other about how we come to know things—have a huge effect on how you approach the assignment. No doubt many beliefs have some truth to them. Other beliefs, however, may need to be *unlearned* if you're going to take your research writing to the next level. Keep these beliefs out in the open where you can see and evaluate them to determine if you have some unlearning to do.

Using This Book

The Exercises

Throughout *The Curious Researcher,* you'll be asked to do exercises that either help you prepare your research paper or actually help you write it. You'll need a research notebook in which you'll do the exercises and perhaps compile your notes for the paper. Any notebook will do, as long as there are sufficient pages and left margins. Your instructor may ask you to hand in the work you do in response to the exercises, so it might be useful to use a notebook with detachable pages. You may also choose to do these exercises on a computer rather than in a notebook. If you do, just make sure that it feels good to write fast and write badly.

Write badly? Well, not on purpose. But if the notebook is going to be useful, it has to be a place where you don't mind lowering your standards, getting writing down even if it's awkward and unfocused. The notebook is where you have conversations with yourself, and what's important is not the beauty of a sentence or airtight reasoning but breathlessly chasing after language that threatens to run away from you. Many of the exercises in this book, including the one that started it, invite you to write badly because in doing so you can use writing to discover what you think.

The Five-Week Plan

If you're excited about writing a research paper, that's great. You probably already know that it can be interesting work. But if you're dreading the work ahead of you, then your instinct might be to procrastinate, to put it off until the week it's due. That would be a mistake, of course. If you try to rush through the research and the writing, you're absolutely guaranteed to hate the experience and add this assignment to the many research papers in the garbage dump of your memory. It's also much more likely that the paper won't be very good. Because procrastination is the enemy, this book was designed to help you budget your time and move through the research and writing process in five weeks. (See the box "Steps to Writing Your Research Essay.")

Steps to Writing Your Research Essay

Week One

- Discover your subject.
- Develop "working knowledge" of your subject.
- Narrow your subject by finding your inquiry question.

Week Two

- Plan a research strategy that balances library and Internet sources.
- Fine-tune search terms.
- Begin developing "focused knowledge" of your subject.
- Plan fieldwork, interviews, or surveys.

Week Three

- Write about your findings.
- Try advanced searching techniques.
- Conduct interviews and surveys.

Week Four

- Write the first draft.
- Re-research.

Week Five

- Clarify your purpose and hone your thesis.
- Revise draft.
- Edit, proofread, and finalize citations.

It may take you a little longer, or you may be able to finish your paper a little more quickly. But at least initially, use the book sequentially, unless your instructor gives you other advice.

Alternatives to the Five-Week Plan

Though *The Curious Researcher* is structured by weeks, you can easily ignore that plan and use the book to solve problems as they arise. Use it when you need to find or narrow a topic, refine a thesis, do advanced searching on the Internet, organize you paper, take useful notes, and so on. The overviews of Modern Language Association (MLA) and American Psychological Association (APA) research paper conventions in Appendixes A and B, respectively, provide complete guides to both formats and make it easier to find answers to your specific technical questions at any point in the process of writing your paper.

The Research Paper Versus the Research Report

In high school, I wrote a research "paper" on existentialism for my philosophy class. I understood the task as skimming a book or two on the topic, reading the entry on "existentialism" in the *Encyclopaedia Britannica,* making some notecards, and writing down everything I learned. That took about six pages. Did I start with a question? No. Was I expressing an opinion of some kind about existentialism? Not really. Did I organize the information with some idea about existentialism that I wanted to relay to readers? Nope. Was I motivated by a question about the philosophy that I hoped to explore? Certainly not. What I wrote was a research *report,* and that is a quite different assignment than most any research paper you'll be asked to write in college.

Discovering Your Purpose

For the paper you're about to write, the information you collect must be used much more *purposefully* than simply reporting what's known about a particular topic. Most likely, you will define what that purpose is and, in an inquiry-based project, it will arise from the question that is driving your investigation. In the beginning, that question may not be very specific. For example, why do dog trainers seem so polarized about the best way to make Spot sit? Later, as you refine the question, you'll get even more guidance about your purpose in the essay. A question like, "What is the evidence that domestic dogs behave like wild animals, and how does this influence theories of training?" might lead you to make an argument or explore some little-known aspect of the issue.

Whatever the purpose of your paper turns out to be, the process usually begins with something you've wondered about, some itchy question about an aspect of the world you'd love to know the answer to. It's the writer's curiosity—not the teacher's—that is at the heart of the college research paper.

In some ways, frankly, *research reports* are easier. You just go out and collect as much stuff as you can, write it down, organize it, and write it down again in the paper. Your job is largely mechanical and often deadening. In the *research paper,* you take a much more active role in *shaping and being shaped by* the information you encounter. That's harder because you must evaluate, judge, interpret, and analyze. But it's also much more satisfying because what you end up with says something about who you are and how you see things.

How Formal Should It Be?

When I got a research paper assignment, it often felt as if I were being asked to change out of blue jeans and a wrinkled oxford shirt and get into a stiff tuxedo. Tuxedos have their place, such as at the junior prom or the Grammy Awards, but they're just not me. When I first started writing research papers, I used to think that I *had* to be formal, that I needed to use big words like *myriad* and *ameliorate* and to use the pronoun *one* instead of *I.* I thought the paper absolutely needed to have an introduction, body, and conclusion—say what I was going to say, say it, and say what I had said. It's no wonder that the first college research paper I had to write—on Plato's *Republic* for another philosophy class—seemed to me as though it were written by someone else. I felt I was at arm's length from the topic I was writing about.

What we're usually talking about when we talk about formality in research writing is trying to locate ourselves in the final product. How is that possible if we can't use first person or can't draw on our personal experiences and observations? If the best research is "objective," aren't we supposed to vacate the building? The simple answer to the last question is "no." Even in the most scientific articles, writers have a presence, though it's often ghostly. They are present in the questions they ask, the things they emphasize, and the words they choose. Academic researchers work within *discourse communities* that may limit their movements somewhat but do not ever bind their feet. "Discourse community" is a term academics use to describe certain identifiable ways in which people with expertise talk to each other, ask questions, or evaluate evidence they consider convincing. We all belong to discourse communities; any time you have a feeling that there are certain things that might be said and certain ways to say them, you're probably thinking of a particular discourse community.

Although you've been going to school for years, you're still fairly new to the academic discourse communities. You don't yet know how they work; that's something you'll learn later as you begin to specialize in your academic major. What's far more important as you begin academic research is developing the habits of mind that will help you know what might be a researchable question and how to see patterns in the information you collect, along with skills like knowing where to find the information you need. Most important of all, you should feel—no matter what you end up writing about—that you're part of an ongoing conversation about your topic: speculating, asking questions, offering opinions, pointing to gaps, making connections. In short, you must not vacate the building but occupy it, and the easiest way to do this, at least at first, is to worry less about the "rules" of the research paper than the process of discovering what you want to say.

The Question Is You

Okay, so how do you have a strong presence in a research paper aside from talking about yourself? More than anything else, you are present by the questions you ask, particularly the inquiry question that is at the heart of your investigation of a topic. An inquiry question both makes you curious about a topic and suggests what might lead to answers in which other people have a stake, too. A good question is a wonderful thing. As kids, my friends and I used to mess with magnets and iron filings. We would scatter iron filings on a steel pot lid and move the magnet around underneath, marveling at the patterns it produced in the filings. Good questions have the same power. They help you to see patterns in information and to organize it in a way that makes scattered information easier to make sense of. Finding the question, particularly the one *key* question about your research topic that most interests you, is how any project becomes *your* project. In an inquiry-based investigation, questions power the process, and learning to ask good ones may be the most essential skill.

Thinking Like an Academic Writer

What does it mean to *think* like an academic writer? These are some habits of mind that are typical:

1. Academic inquiry begins with questions, not answers.
2. Because genuine inquiry must be sustained over time, it's essential that researchers suspend judgment and even tolerate some confusion. You do research not because you know what you think already but because you want to discover what you think.
3. Insight is the result of *conversation* in which the writer assumes at least two seemingly contrary roles: believer and doubter, generator and judge.
4. Writers take responsibility for their ideas, accepting both the credit for and the consequences of putting forth those ideas for dialogue and debate.

A Method of Discovery

If college research assignments don't simply report information on a topic, what do they do? They are organized around what you think—what you believe is important to say about your topic—and there are three ways you can arrive at these ideas:

1. You can know what you think from the start and write a paper that begins with a thesis and provides evidence that proves it.
2. You can have a hunch about what you think and test that hunch against the evidence you collect.
3. You can begin by not knowing what you think—only that you have questions about a topic that really interests you.

Academic inquiry rarely begins with item 1. After all, if you already know the answer, why would you do the research? It's much more likely that what inspires research would be a hunch or a question or both. The motive, as I've said before, is discovery. *The Curious Researcher* promotes a method of discovery that probably isn't familiar to you: essaying.

Essay is a term used so widely to describe school writing that it often doesn't seem to carry much particular meaning. But I have something particular in mind.

The term *essai* was coined by Michel Montaigne, a sixteenth-century Frenchman; in French, it means "to attempt" or "to try." For Montaigne and the essayists who follow his tradition, the essay is less an opportunity to *prove* something than an attempt to *find out.* An essay, at least initially, is often exploratory rather than argumentative, testing the truth of an idea or attempting to discover what might be true. (Montaigne even once had coins minted that said *Que sais-je?*—"What do I know?") The essay is often openly subjective and frequently takes a conversational, even intimate, form.

Now, this probably sounds nothing like any research paper you've ever written. Certainly, the dominant mode of the academic research paper is impersonal and argumentative. But if you consider writing a *research essay* instead of the usual *research paper,* four things might happen:

1. *You'll discover your choice of possible topics suddenly expands.* If you're not limited to arguing a position on a topic, then you can explore any topic that you find puzzling in interesting ways, and you can risk asking questions that might complicate your point of view.
2. *You'll find that you'll approach your topics differently.* You'll be more open to conflicting points of view and perhaps more willing to change your mind about what you think. As one of my students once told me, this is a more honest kind of objectivity.
3. *You'll see a stronger connection between this assignment and the writing you've done all semester.* Research is something all writers do, not a separate activity or genre that exists only on demand. You may discover that research can be a revision strategy for improving essays you wrote earlier in the semester.
4. *You'll find that you can't hide.* The research report often encourages the writer to play a passive role; the research essay doesn't easily tolerate passivity. You'll probably find this both liberating and frustrating. While you may likely welcome the chance to incorporate your opinions, you may find it difficult to add your voice to those of your sources.

As you'll see later in this Introduction, the form a research essay can take may be a bit different from the usual thesis-proof research paper. But even if you write a more conventional (and frankly more common) paper that makes an argument, the method of essaying can help you discover the claims you want to argue.

Firing on Four Cylinders of Information

Whatever the genre, writers write with information. But what kind? There are essentially four sources of information for nonfiction:

1. Memory and experience;
2. Observation;
3. Reading; and
4. Interview.

A particular type of writing may emphasize one source over another. For example, literary analysis obviously leans very heavily on reading. The information largely comes from the text you're studying. A personal essay is often built largely from memory. The research essay, however, is a genre that typically fires on all four cylinders, powered by all four sources of information. For example, for an essay exploring the behavior of sports fans, you may observe the behavior of students at a football game, read critiques of unruly soccer fans at the World Cup or theories about group behavior, and remember your own experience as a fan of the Chicago Cubs (God help you!) when you were growing up.

What makes research writing "authoritative" or convincing is less whether you sound objective than whether you are able to find *varied* and *credible* sources of information to explore your research question. It certainly won't do to write a research essay that, say, only relies on your experiences. This doesn't mean that every good research essay must use all four sources of information, but it certainly should use more than one.

"It's Just My Opinion"

In the end, *you* will become an authority of sorts on your research topic. I know that's hard to believe. One of the things my students often complain about is their struggle to put their opinions in their papers: "I've got all these facts, and sometimes I don't know what to say other than whether I disagree or agree with them." What these students often *seem* to say is that they don't really trust their own authority enough to do much more than state briefly what they feel: "Facts are facts. How can you argue with them?"

Step 2 of Exercise 1, which began this chapter, may have started you thinking about these questions. I hope the research assignment you are about to start keeps you thinking about your beliefs about the nature of knowledge. Are facts unassailable? Or are they simply claims that can be evaluated like any others? Is the struggle to evaluate conflicting claims an obstacle to doing research, or the point of it? Are experts supposed to know all the answers? What makes one opinion more valid than another? What makes *your* opinion valid?

I hope you write a great essay in the next five or so weeks. But I also hope that the process you follow in doing so inspires you to reflect on how you—and perhaps all of us—come to know what seems to be true. I hope you find yourself doing something you may not have done much before: thinking about thinking.

Facts Don't Kill

When my students comment on a reading and say, "It kinda reads like a research paper," everybody knows what that means: It's dry and it's boring. Most of my students believe that the minute you start having to use facts in your writing, the prose wilts and dies like an unwatered begonia. It's an understandable attitude. There are many examples of dry and wooden informational writing, and among them, unfortunately, may be some textbooks you are asked to read.

But factual writing doesn't have to be dull. You may not consider my essay, "Theories of Intelligence" (see the following exercise), a research paper. It may be unlike any research paper you've imagined. It's personal. It tells stories. Its thesis is at the end rather than at the beginning. And yet, it is prompted by a question—Why is it that for so many years I felt dumb despite evidence to the contrary?—and it uses cited research to explore the answers. "Theories of Intelligence" may not be a model for the kind of research essay you will write—your instructor will give you guidelines on that—but I hope it is a useful model for the kind of thinking you can do about any topic when you start with questions rather than answers.

Reflecting on "Theories of Intelligence"

- Read my essay twice. The first time, don't feel compelled to do anything but read it. The second time, however, I want you to read the piece to identify two kinds of content: writing that seems based on outside sources (the kind of material we normally cite in academic writing) and writing that expresses my own thinking and assertions. A great way to visually distinguish these two types of content is to photocopy the essay from the book and mark each type of content with a different color highlighter.

- *What* do you notice about the pattern and the balance between fact and commentary? *Where* do you see each happening in the essay? *How* do your findings about this pattern between the presence of the research and the research either challenge or confirm your previous beliefs about how "research papers" should be written?

Theories of Intelligence
by Bruce Ballenger

At age 55, I've finally decided I'm not as dumb as I thought. This might seem a strange confession from a professor of English, a man who has spent 25 years making his living with his intellect, working all those years in an environment where being "smart" was a quality valued above all others. This revelation—that I'm not as dumb as I thought—is a relief, of course. More and more, I can sit in a meeting of my colleagues and feel okay when I'm unmoved to speak. It pains me less when I can't quite follow someone's argument or sort out the arcane details of a curriculum proposal. Now, more than ever before, I can stand in front of my classes and say, without shame, "That's a good question. I don't really know the answer."

It's quite possible—no, likely—that I'm not nearly as smart as many of the people around me; but I've learned, at last, not to care. Self-acceptance may simply be one of the few blessings of late middle age. I was watching the news the other day and learned of a report on happiness that suggests the midlife crisis is a universal phenomenon. The study, with the straightforward title "Is Well-Being U-Shaped over the Life Cycle?" reviewed data from two million people in 72 countries, and it concluded that American men are most miserable at around age 52, perhaps because they have the sobering realization that life did not unfold the way they hoped it would. Happiness slowly returns when they "adapt to their strengths and weaknesses, and ... quell their infeasible aspirations" (Blanchflower and Oswald 20). It's a great relief for me to know that things should be looking up.

I've considered this idea—that I'm really not that smart but have finally accepted my limitations—but I'm coming around to the belief that I'm probably smarter than I thought I was—that I was *always* smarter than I thought I was. I'm pretty sure this is true for most people and, frankly, the ones who have always known they were really smart—and who behave as if they are quite sure of this—are not the kind of people I usually like very much. Yet even the self-consciously smart people deserve our sympathy because being intelligent really, really matters to most of us. We can live with being unattractive, but no one wants to feel dumb. One of the most popular videos on YouTube is a clip from the Miss Teen USA contest when, during the interview segment of the program, Caitlin Upton, the contestant from South Carolina, was asked this question: "Recent polls have shown that a fifth of Americans can't locate the U.S. on a world map. Why do you think this is?" Her response was, sadly, completely incoherent, and the relentless, often unkind ridicule Upton endured prompted her appearance on the *Today Show* a few days later. "I was overwhelmed," she said. "I made a mistake. Everyone makes mistakes. I'm human" ("Miss Teen on Today"). I'm ashamed to admit that I joined the throngs who gleefully watched the clip and enjoyed Upton's humiliation; at the time, I told myself that my response wasn't personal—it just confirmed my belief that beauty pageants are socially bankrupt. But I know that the real reason I enjoyed it was the relief that it wasn't me up there.

The YouTube clip is now painful for me to watch, not only because the humor in humiliation wears off quickly but also because I recognize in Caitlin Upton a phenomenon I see in myself: We believe that our own intelligence is a script that others author and we cannot revise. Researchers tell us that children typically have one of two theories of intelligence. Some believe that intelligence is an "uncontrollable trait," a thing they are stuck with like eye color or big ears. Others, particularly older children, believe that intelligence is "malleable," something they can alter through effort and hard work (Kinlaw and Kutz-Costes 296). I have never met any of these children, but apparently they're out there.

It is a nearly inescapable fact of American childhood that we are branded as smart or somewhat smart or not too smart or even dumb. For many of us who lack faith in our own intelligence, this branding begins in school, a sad fact that researchers say is especially true of African American kids (Aronson, Fried, and Good 113). I am white, but I can trace my own experience with this by following the scent of old resentments back to memories of school that never lose their bitter taste—even when I try to sweeten them with humor. There was the time in the second grade when I was sent to the back of the room to sit alone in a corner because I couldn't remember all the months of the year. And later, in the eighth grade, I moved from green to orange in the SRA reading packet but never moved again. In those days orangeness was a sign of mediocrity. The shame of never busting through orange to blue, the color Jeff Brickman, Mark Levy, and Betsy Cochran achieved with ease, convinced me that reading and writing were just not my thing, a feeling that was reinforced by my teacher, Mrs. O'Neal, who spattered my essays with red marks. From then on I hated school and, ironically, especially English (a feeling I freely shared on the inside covers of my class yearbooks). I spent my high school days languishing in "Level 3" English and science classes, where I joined the working-class Italian American students from Highwood and the kids from the army base at Fort Sheridan. We found solidarity in hating Shakespeare, lab reports, and the five-paragraph theme. And we pretended to find solidarity in being dumb, though I think most of us were secretly ashamed.

In my junior year, I dated Jan, one of the "smart" kids who moved in a small herd, migrating from one AP class to another. I was awed by her intelligence, and in the twisted logic of an adolescent male, this awe translated into indifference. I pretended I didn't really care about her. Eventually, however, I found Jan's persistent kindness moving and began to write her bad poetry that she copied and bound into a book that she gave me for my birthday. For a time, I entertained the idea that I wasn't unintelligent. Not smart, exactly—not like Jan—but maybe I could hold my own in the AP crowd. Yet what I did not understand back then was that whatever small gains I was making in school could easily be undone at home.

There was never any question that I would go to college. My parents expected it, and so did I. But I knew that I was not destined to go anywhere Jan and her friends were headed—University of Michigan, Brown, Tufts, Beloit, Kalamazoo. I applied to one school, Drake, with rolling admissions, and when I was accepted early, I excused myself from the endless senior chatter about colleges. I pretended I just didn't care. "You're selling yourself short," my father said, disappointed that I wouldn't pursue more schools. My brother—who was two years older—attended my father's alma mater, the University of Rochester, a school with high academic standards. Dad never encouraged me to apply there, confirming what I had already suspected—that I was a dimmer bulb.

My father was an intelligent man, a Rhodes scholar with an interest in British literature who worked for both Chicago and New York newspapers before the booze took him down. Nothing pleased him more than an argument. When I went to college in the early seventies it was an easier time for students to believe in values and ideas without being wounded by the charge that they were being "naïve." My idealism made me an easy target, and when the vodka kicked in, my father would pick up the scent of some belief I held with uninformed fervor and go after it. Even drunk, Dad knew what he was talking about, and with a cold, ruthless logic he would pick apart whatever passion I brought to the dinner table. I felt young, stupid, and hopelessly inadequate. Dad was not a cruel man; what I know now is that his head may have been full, but his heart was empty. His intellect was one of the last things he clung to as drink became the only way to dull some unspeakable pain; in the end, of course, even intellect succumbs.

There were moments after these arguments when I sat seething and my father would turn to me, wagging his finger. "The most important thing you can be, Bruce," he said, "is an intellectual. Live the life of the mind." Oddly enough, I have become an academic, and, had he lived, my father would likely have approved. Yet the ache I feel about Dad these days is that he didn't possess the kind of knowing that might have saved him had he only valued it. One of the things my Dad's alcoholism taught me was how weak-kneed his kind of intelligence could be against the sucker punches of self-loathing. "Your Dad was just too smart for his own good," my mother would say. "Just too smart for his own good."

Theories of intelligence have evolved considerably since I was a child, a time when everyone was taking IQ tests. In the early eighties, Howard Gardener's "multiple intelligences" came as a relief to many of us whose scores on intelligence tests were not worth bragging about. Back then, I never really understood Gardener's theory but seized on the idea that being smart didn't necessarily mean being smart in one way. More recently, in response to his own bad experiences being labeled dumb in school, intelligence expert Robert Sternberg offered a "Triachic Theory of Successful Intelligence." Being smart, he said, isn't just being analytical but being creative and practical, too. Strength in one can compensate for weakness in the other two ("Robert J. Sternberg"). Yet I always sensed that, no matter what Gardener or Sternberg said, there was a kind of intelligence that really counted and that I didn't possess. It was school smarts—the ability to pick apart an argument, to recognize the logical fallacy, and to make an arresting point—all of the things, I see now, that my father could do so well. As an academic, I see these qualities in some of my colleagues, whom I admire and envy. A very few of them, however, use their intelligence to bully people like my father bullied me.

Before I entered the profession, I imagined that many professors were like these intellectual bullies, people who bludgeon others with reason, looking to wound rather than to enlighten. The literary critic Jane Tompkins once wrote that college teachers are often driven by fear, "fear of being shown up for what you are: a fraud, stupid, ignorant, a clod, a dolt, a sap, a weakling, someone who can't cut the mustard" (654), and this is what drives us to do everything we can to prove to our students and others that we're intellectually superior. In rare cases, this fear of being found out turns teachers into intellectual bullies. More often, their anxiety in the classroom leads to what Tompkins calls the "performance model" of instruction: teachers talking at their students, teachers trying desperately to demonstrate how smart they are. It probably is no surprise that this tendency moves easily from the classroom to the department faculty meeting where the stakes feel higher.

I can't recall exactly how things began to change for me, when I started to see that I might revise the script that had governed my life for so long, but I started to notice it in those department meetings. Whether I spoke or not ceased to matter. I didn't decide one day that I was just as smart as my colleagues. I didn't suddenly start believing the strong evidence that I must have some intellectual ability because I enjoyed a successful career as a college professor. There was no sudden epiphany or dramatic moment. I think I just stopped being afraid.

It has helped to know, too, that my own ideas about intelligence don't travel well. In a famous study, developmental psychologist Joseph Glick asked a Liberian Kpelle tribesman to sort 20 items—food, tools, and cooking utensils—in a way that made "sense" to him. He did this quickly enough, pairing a knife with an orange, a potato with a hoe, and other matches that reflected the practical, functional relationships between the items. "This is what a wise man would do," said the tribesman. The researchers then asked, "What would a fool do?" The Liberian then sorted the items in what we would consider "logical" categories, putting food in one pile, cooking utensils in another, tools in another, and so on (Cole, Gay, Glick, and Sharp 84–87). I live a world away, of course, where as I write this my wife, Karen, is putting away the groceries using a logic that a Kpelle tribesman might find curious. The definition of a fool, obviously, depends on who and where you are.

My self-doubts will never go away completely, but I think they have made me a better teacher. I have empathy for my own students in whom I see the same struggle. Just the other night in a graduate seminar, Greg, a particularly bright student, derailed himself in midsentence while interpreting a passage from a Montaigne essay we were reading. "My head just isn't working tonight," he said. "I don't know what's wrong with me." I reassured him that he was making perfect sense, but for the rest of the class Greg was solemn, his hand fixed on his forehead, concealing a brow darkened by frustration. Ironically, Montaigne, a sixteenth-century philosopher and father of the personal essay, constantly questioned his own intelligence, and in the piece we were reading that night Montaigne writes that his "mind is lazy and not keen; it can not pierce the least cloud" (213). And yet, Montaigne's work celebrated his shortcomings as well as his strengths, the very things that make us human. Learning's highest calling, he thought, was to know oneself, and the essay seemed the best vessel into which this self-reflection might be poured, as I have done here.

On the advice of a friend, I recently took up meditation, a practice that often involves visualization. Sometimes as I listen to the slow rhythm of my breathing, there are moments when I meet myself on a beach on Nantucket Island, a place I spent a spring nearly 30 years ago. There are just the two of us there—one young version of myself, with a navy blue beret and his hands thrust in the pockets of his khaki pants, and the other the grayer, bearded man I see in the mirror these days. I am walking with that younger self on the empty beach at sunset, and I have my arm around his shoulders. I am whispering something to him meant to be comforting. I might be saying many things, but lately I imagine it is this: "You're going to be okay." I think that learning to fully believe this will be the smartest thing I'll ever do.

Works Cited

Aronson, Joshua, Carrie B. Fried, and Catherine Good. "Reducing the Effects of Stereotype Threat on African American College Students by Shaping Theories of Intelligence." *Journal of Experimental Psychology* 38.2 (2002): 113–25. Print.

Blanchflower, David G., and Andrew J. Oswald. "Is Well-being U-Shaped over the Life Cycle?" National Bureau of Economic Research Working Paper No. 12935. Cambridge, MA, 2007. Print.

Cole, Michael, John Gay, Joseph A. Glick, and Donald W. Sharp. *The Cultural Context of Learning and Thinking.* New York: Basic Books, 1971. Print.

Kinlaw, Ryan C., and Beth Kutz-Costes. "Children's Theories of Intelligence: Beliefs, Goals, and Motivation in the Elementary Years." *Journal of General Psychology* 34.3 (2007): 295–311. Print.

Montaigne, Michel de. *Essays.* Trans. J. M. Cohen. London: Penguin, 1958. Print.

"Robert J. Sternberg." *Human Intelligence: Historical Influences, Current Controversies, and Teaching Resources.* Indiana U., 7 Oct. 2010. Web. 22 Dec. 2010.

Tompkins, Jane. "Pedagogy of the Distressed." *College English* 52.6 (1990): 653–60. Print.

Creative Research Papers?

Question: How often will I get to write a research paper like "Theories of Intelligence?"

Answer: Not often.

Question: So why should I write one now?

Answer: Because writing a research *essay,* one that also uses some of the conventions of academic writing like citation, is a great introduction to the essentials of academic inquiry. These essentials include the following:

1. In the beginning, at least, the motive behind nearly any kind of research is to answer questions or solve a problem. The research rests on a simple hope: discovery. You write about the doubts about intelligence or the habits of a housefly or the motives of a terrorist because you want to find out something. Formal academic writing shares this motive, too, but it's less apparent in the product, which focuses mostly on the persuasiveness of its conclusions. In the research essay, the process of discovery is often a visible part of the product.

2. The purpose of research writing is not simply to show readers what you know. It is an effort to *extend a conversation about a topic* that is ongoing, a conversation that includes voices of people who have already spoken, often in different contexts and perhaps never together. Research writers begin with their own questions and then find the voices that speak to them. They then write about what others have helped them to understand. This experience of entering into a conversation with sources is much more likely when you are visibly part of it, even if this means using the first person.

3. Normally, when we write conventional research papers we have a very narrow conception of audience: the teacher. In a sense, we tend to write *up* to the instructor because she knows more

Research and Web 2.0

What *form* should your research take? That's easy. You write it up, print it out, and hand it in. In most cases, that's exactly right. But the rise of digital media means there are fresh ways to "publish" researched writing. Web 2.0 is a term used to describe the new wave of online communication that now makes *interactivity* a major feature of online genres. You're not just "pushing" information on users; you are inviting them to respond. As a result, there are new possibilities for reaching people who are interested in your research and even ready to contribute to it. Consider a few of these possibilities:

- *Audio research essays (or podcasts).* Using widely available and easy-to-use audio software, you can turn your research essay into a documentary, integrating not just your voice but also interview clips and even music.
- *Blogged research essays.* Whatever you write doesn't have to simply end up, like most conventional research papers, in a file somewhere, forgotten and ignored. Blogs allow writers to publish their findings *and* get feedback on them.
- *Wikis.* The obvious example of the potential of wikis for collaborative research is Wikipedia. But the wide availability of wiki technology, including on many academic course sites like Blackboard, makes this a promising tool for presenting research that is produced collaboratively.

about the subject than we do. That's actually quite different than most academic writing, which is written to an audience of peers. You should write your research essay to an audience like that; you're trying to make your topic relevant and interesting to people who share in your own "discourse" community. As you advance in college, that community will become more specialized, and so will your writing.

No matter what form your paper takes for this class— whether it's an exploratory research essay or an argumentative one—what happens behind the scenes is similar: If the goal is to engage in genuine inquiry, the kind your professors do, then you begin with this simple question: "What can I learn from this?" From there you begin to listen in to what has already been said by others about your topic; when you know enough, you join the conversation. The process must begin, of course, with figuring out what you want to know. That's the subject of the next chapter.

CHAPTER 1

The First Week

The Importance of Getting Curious

Despite what they say, curiosity is not dead. You know the obituary: At some point around the age of (fill in the blank), we stop wondering about things. We lose that childlike sense that the world is something to explore. Actually, we never stop being curious, especially if we feel like there's a good reason for it. More than ever, we live in an information-rich environment, and the Internet makes information more accessible than ever before. Say you're having a conversation with a friend about deodorant. "I wonder what the first deodorant was?" asks she. "That's the kind of question that the Internet was made for," says you. And within a minute, you report that the first commercial deodorant was a product called "Mum," invented in the 1880s, though noncommercial deodorants were in use 5000 years ago. This kind of short-term curiosity—sometimes called "situational curiosity"—is incredibly common in this Internet age.

On the other hand, genuine research relies on a sustained interest in something. It can begin with situational curiosity. For example, I once wrote an entire books on lobsters, an interest that was initially triggered by childhood memories of eating them during the holidays with my family and, many years later, reading a newspaper article that reported the lobster catch was down 30 percent and some believed the lobster fishery was on the verge of collapse. I wondered, will lobster go the way of caviar and become too expensive for people like me?

That was the question that triggered my research, and it soon led to more questions. What kept me going was my own curiosity. If your research assignment is going to be successful, you need to get curious, too. If you're bored by your research topic, your paper will almost certainly be boring as well, and you'll end up hating writing research papers as much as ever.

Seeing the World with Wonder

Your curiosity must be the driving force behind your research paper. It's the most essential ingredient. The important thing, then, is this: *Choose your research topic carefully. If you lose interest in it, change your topic to one that does interest you, or find a different angle.*

In most cases, instructors give students great latitude in choosing their research topics. (Some instructors narrow the field, asking students to find a focus within some broad, assigned subject. When the subject has been assigned, it may be harder for you to discover what you are curious about, but it won't be impossible, as you'll see.) Some of the best research topics grow out of your own experience (though they certainly don't have to), as mine did when writing about lobster overfishing. Scholars tell us that a good way to sustain your curiosity in a topic is to find something to research that has some personal relevance. Begin searching for a topic by asking yourself this question: *What have I seen or experienced that raises questions that research can help answer?*

Getting the Pot Boiling

A subject might bubble up immediately. For example, I had a student who was having a terrible time adjusting to her parents' divorce. Janabeth started out wanting to know about the impact of divorce on children and later focused her paper on how divorce affects father-daughter relationships.

Kim remembered spending a rainy week on Cape Cod with her father, wandering through old graveyards, looking for the family's ancestors. She noticed patterns on the stones and wondered what they meant. She found her ancestors as well as a great research topic.

Manuel was a divorced father of two, and both of his sons had recently been diagnosed with attention deficit disorder (ADD). The boys' teachers strongly urged Manuel and his ex-wife to arrange drug therapy for their sons, but they wondered whether there might be any alternatives. Manuel wrote a moving and informative research essay about his gradual acceptance of drug treatment as the best solution for his sons.

For years, Wendy loved J. D. Salinger's work but never had the chance to read some of his short stories. She jumped at the opportunity to spend five weeks reading and thinking about her favorite author. She later decided to focus her research paper on Salinger's notion of the misfit hero.

Accidental topics, ideas that you seem to stumble on when you aren't looking, are often successful topics. My research on Maine lobsters was one of those. Sometimes one topic triggers another. Chris, ambling by Thompson Hall, one of the oldest buildings on his school's campus, wondered about its history. After a little initial digging, he found some 1970s news clips from the student newspaper describing a student strike that paralyzed the school. The controversy fascinated him more than the building did, and he pursued the topic. He wrote a great paper.

If you're still drawing a blank, try the following exercise in your notebook.

EXERCISE 1.1

Building an Interest Inventory

STEP 1: From time to time I'll hear a student say, "I'm just not interested in *anything* enough to write a paper about it." I don't believe it. Not for a second. The real problem is that the student simply hasn't taken the time to think about everything he knows and everything he might want to know. Try coaxing those things out of your head and onto paper by creating an "interest inventory."

Start with a blank journal page or word processing document. Define three columns per page with the words below:

PLACES, TRENDS, THINGS, TECHNOLOGIES,
PEOPLE, CONTROVERSIES, HISTORY,
JOBS, HABITS, HOBBIES

Under each title, brainstorm a list of words (or phrases) that come to mind when you think about *what you know and what you might want to know* about the category. For example, for TRENDS, you might be aware of the use of magnets for healing sore muscles, or you might know a lot about extreme sports. Put both down on the list. Don't censor yourself. Just write down whatever comes to mind, even if it makes sense only to you. This list is for your use only. You'll probably find that ideas come to you in waves—you'll jot down a few things and then draw a blank. Wait for the next wave to come and ride it. But if you're seriously becalmed, start a new column with a new word from the list above and brainstorm ideas in that category. Do this at least four times with different words. Feel free to return to any column to add new ideas as they come to you, and don't worry about repeated items. Some things simply straddle more than one category. For an idea of what this might look like, see what Amanda, one of my students, did with this exercise (Figure 1.1).

CONTROVERSIES

Guantanamo Bay
Iraq War
Palestine vs. Israel
Beijing Olympics
Steroids in baseball
Racism/sexism in politics
Gender identity
Homosexual marriage
Death penalty
When is a person created?
Right to euthanasia
Vegetative states
Drinking bottled water
Is organic stuff better?
Does the glass ceiling still exist?
Why are people poor?
Religion in the U.S. government
Sex lives of elected officials
What makes people fat?
Evolution in the school system
Gas vs. ethanol
Sales tax on groceries

TRENDS

Bluetooth headsets
Ipods
Drinking coffee
Crocs shoes
Giant purses
Designer everything
Organic products
Green/eco consciousness
"Some disease" awareness
Celebrity spokespeople
Internet television
Pets as children
Going to prison
Adult-oriented cartoons
Model/actress/singer combo
High-stakes kindergarten
Myspace
Blogs
Cohabiting
White teeth
Specialized TV channels
Hardwood floors
Locavores
Wikipedia
Pink shirts for men
Heated car seats
Splenda
Energy drinks

JOBS

Prison guard
Garbage man
Sewer cleaners
Undertakers
TV anchor
Hotel housekeepers
Rap stars
Child stars
Interior decorators
Manicurists
Tailors
Cobblers
Tour guides

HISTORY

The Holocaust
The Vietnam War
Ancient China
Who built the
    pyramids?
Why did the Aztecs
    die?
When did humans
    leave Africa?
What was President
    Washington like?
The Underground
    Railroad
Feudal Japan
Human sacrifices
Spanish Inquisition
Napoleonic wars
Stonecutter's guilds
Nostradamus
The Gold Rush
Immigrants to the
    U.S. in the 1900s
The Triangle
    Shirtwaist fire
The importance of the
    printing press
Hygiene habits in
    ancient Greece
Gender roles in
    ancient Egypt
Torture chambers
Foot binding
Pre-Christian religions
Canada's freedom from
    Europe

HABITS

Using a toothpick
Fingernail biting
Bouncing a leg
Verbal ticks: "so
    anyway…"
Wringing hands
Eating with mouth open
Chewing gum loudly
Laughing to oneself
Checking locks
Leaving cell phone on
Talking too loud
Nose picking
Hair twirling
Habits vs. superstitions
"God bless you"

FIGURE 1.1   **Amanda's Interest Inventory**

Allot a total of 20 minutes to do this step: 10 minutes to generate lists in four or more categories, a few minutes to walk away from it and think about something else, and the remaining time to return and add items to any column as they occur to you. (The exercise will also work well if you work on it over several days. You'll be amazed at how much information you can generate.)

STEP 2: Review your lists. Look for a single item in any column that seems promising. Ask yourself these questions: Is this something that raises questions that research can help answer? Are they potentially interesting questions? Does this item get at something I've always wondered about? Might it open doors to knowledge I think is important, fascinating, or relevant to my life?

Circle the item.

STEP 3: For the item you circled, generate a list of questions—as many as you can—that you'd love to explore about the subject. Here's what Amanda did with her topic on teeth whitening:

Are tooth whiteners safe?

What makes teeth turn browner over time?

How has society's definition of a perfect smile changed over time?

Are whiter teeth necessarily healthier than darker teeth?

Is it true that drinking coffee stains your teeth?

How much money is spent on advertising tooth whitening products each year?

What percentage of Americans feels bad about the shade of their teeth?

Do dentists ever recommend that people whiten their teeth?

Is there any way to keep your teeth from getting darker over time?

Can teeth get too white?

Why do I feel bad that my teeth aren't perfect?

Do other cultures have the same emphasis on perfectly white teeth as Americans do?

Are there the same standards for men's teeth and women's teeth?

What judgments do we make about people based simply on the color of their teeth?

How does America's dental hygiene compare with that of other countries? Is the "Austin Powers" myth really true?

The kinds of questions she came up with on her tentative topic seem encouraging. Several already seem "researchable." What about you? Do any of your questions give you a hunger to learn more?

Other Ways to Find a Topic

If you're still stumped about a tentative topic for your paper, consider the following:

■ *Surf the Net.* The Internet is like a crowded fair on the medieval village commons. It's filled with a range of characters—from the carnivalesque to the scholarly—all participating in a democratic exchange of ideas and information. There are promising research topics everywhere.

■ *Search a research database.* Visit your library's Web site and check a database in a subject area that interests you. For example, suppose you're a psychology major and would like to find a topic in the field. Try searching PsycINFO, a popular database of psychology articles. Most databases can be searched by author, subject, keyword, and so on. Think of a general area you're interested in—say, bipolar disorder—and do a subject or keyword search. That will produce a long list of articles, some of which may have abstracts or summaries that will pique your interest. Notice the "related subjects" button? Click that and see a long list of other areas in which you might branch off and find a great topic.

■ *Browse Wikipedia.* While the online "free content" encyclopedia isn't a great source for an academic paper, Wikipedia is a warehouse of potential research topic ideas. Start with the main page, and take a look at the featured or newest articles. You can also browse articles by subject or category.

■ *Consider essays you've already written.* Could the topics of any of these essays be further developed as research topics? For example, Diane wrote a personal essay about how she found the funeral of a classmate alienating—especially the wake. Her essay asked what purpose such a ritual could serve—a question, she decided, that would best be answered by research. Other students wrote essays on topics like the difficulty of living with a depressed brother and an alcoholic parent, which yielded wonderful research papers. A class assignment to read Ken Kesey's *One Flew Over the Cuckoo's Nest* inspired Li to research the author.

■ *Pay attention to what you've read recently.* What newspaper articles have sparked your curiosity and raised interesting questions? Rob, a hunter, encountered an article that reported the number of hunters was steadily declining in the United States. He wondered why. Karen read an account of a particularly violent professional hockey game. She decided to research the Boston Bruins, a team with a history of violent play, and examine how violence has affected the sport. Don't limit yourself to the newspaper. What else have you read recently—perhaps magazines or books—or seen on TV that has made you wonder?

■ *Consider practical topics.* Perhaps some questions about your career choice might lead to a promising topic. Maybe you're thinking about teaching but wonder about current trends in teachers' salaries. One student, Anthony, was being recruited by a college to play basketball and researched the tactics coaches use to lure players. What he learned helped prepare him to make a good choice.

■ *Think about issues, ideas, or materials you've encountered in other classes.* Have you come across anything that intrigued you, that you'd like to learn more about?

■ *Look close to home.* An interesting research topic may be right under your nose. Does your hometown (or your campus community) suffer from a particular problem or have an intriguing history that would be worth exploring? Jackson, tired of dragging himself from his dorm room at 3:00 A.M. for fire alarms that always proved false, researched the readiness of the local fire department to respond to such calls. Ellen, whose grandfather worked in the aging woolen mills in her hometown, researched a crippling strike that took place there 60 years ago. Her grandfather was an obvious source for an interview.

■ *Collaborate.* Work together in groups to come up with interesting topics. Try this idea with your instructor's help: Organize the class into small groups of five. Give each group ten minutes to come up with specific questions about one general subject—for example, American families, recreation, media, race or gender, health, food, history of the local area, environment of the local area, education, and so forth. Post these questions on newsprint as each group comes up with them. Then rotate the groups so that each has a shot at generating questions for every subject. At the end of 40 minutes, the class will have generated perhaps 100 questions, some uninspired and some really interesting. You can also try this exercise on the class Web site using the discussion board or group features.

What Is a Good Topic?

A few minutes browsing the Internet convinces most of my students that the universe of good research topics is pretty limited: global warming, abortion rights, legalization of pot, same-sex marriage, and the like. These are usually the topics of the papers you can buy with your Visa card at sites like freeessays.com (yeah, right). These are also often topics with the potential to bore both reader and writer to death because they inspire essays that are so predictable.

But beginning with a good question, rather than a preconceived answer, changes everything. Suddenly subjects are everywhere: What is with our cultural obsession about good teeth? Is it true that lawnmowers are among the most polluting engines around? What's the deal with the devastation of banana crops, and how will that affect prices at Albertson's down the street? Are "green" automobiles really green? Even the old tired topics get new life when you find the right question to ask. For example, what impact will the availability of medical marijuana vending machines in California have on the legal debate in that state?

What's a good topic? Initially, it's all about finding the right question and especially one that you are really interested in (see box below). Later, the challenge will be limiting the number of questions your paper tries to answer. For now, look for a topic that makes you at least a little hungry to learn more.

Where's Waldo and the Organizing Power of Questions

For a long time, I thought school writing assignments were exclusively exercises in deduction. You start by coming up with

What Makes a Question "Researchable"?

- It's not too big or too small.
- It focuses on some aspect of a topic about which something has been said.
- It interests the researcher.
- Some people have a stake in the answer. It has something to do with how we live or might live, what we care about, or what might be important for people to know.
- It implies an approach or various means of answering it.
- It raises more questions. The answer might not be simple.

a thesis and then try to find examples to support it. This kind of writing starts with an idea and supports it with evidence, moving from the general to the specific. There's nothing wrong with this. In a lot of writing situations—say, the essay exam or SAT writing test—this approach makes a great deal of sense. But much academic research, at least initially, works inductively. You look for patterns in information that raise interesting questions, and it is these questions that redirect the researchers' gaze back to the information, this time more selectively and purposefully.

In other words, you start with a lot of data, form a question or hypothesis about the patterns in what you see, and then return to the data again, this time focusing on what is relevant. In this way, you get control of the information by looking at less of it.

The visual puzzles in the *Where's Waldo?* series of children's books is a great example of the power of good questions to manage information. As you know, Waldo, with his red-and-white-striped stocking cap and jersey, is hidden in a picture among hundreds of other people, many of whom look a lot like him. The challenge, quite simply, is to find Waldo in all of this data. Imagine, though, if the game didn't ask "Where's Waldo?" but "Where are the men?" or "Where are the women?" in the picture. Suddenly, much more information is relevant and the search isn't nearly as focused. A better question might be, "Where are the people wearing yellow?" That eliminates some of the data but still leaves a lot to work with. Obviously, "Where's Waldo?" is the best question because you know what you're looking for and what you can ignore.

Similarly, a good inquiry question will focus your investigation of any topic. Starting with an answer—a thesis or main point—before you do any research is efficient; it sets you on a steady march to a destination you already know. But beginning with questions, while sometimes a messier process, is a much more powerful way to see what you don't expect to see. Try the following exercise, and you'll see what I mean.

EXERCISE 1.2

The Myth of the Boring Topic

This exercise requires in-class collaboration. Your instructor will organize you into four or five small groups and give each group a commonplace object; it might be something as simple as a nail, an orange, a pencil, a can of dog food, or a piece of plywood. Whatever the object, it will not strike you as particularly interesting—at least not at first.

STEP 1: Each group's first task is to brainstorm a list of potentially interesting questions about its commonplace object. Choose a recorder who will post the questions as you think of them on a large piece of newsprint taped to the wall. Inevitably, some of these questions will be pretty goofy ("Is it true that no word rhymes with orange?"), but work toward questions that might address the *history* of the object, its *uses,* its possible *impact on people,* or *the processes* that led to its creation in the form in which you now see it.

STEP 2: After 20 minutes, each group will shift to the adjacent group's newsprint and study the object that inspired that group's questions. Spend 5 minutes thinking up more interesting questions about the object that didn't occur to the group before you. Add these to the list on the wall.

STEP 3: Stay where you are or return to your group's original object and questions. Review the list of questions, and choose *one* you find both interesting and most "researchable" (see the box "What Makes a Question 'Researchable'?"). In other words, if you were an editorial team assigned to propose a researched article for a general interest magazine that focuses on this object, what might be the starting question for the investigation? The most interesting question and the most researchable question may or may not be the same.

In Idaho where I live, there are stones called geodes. These are remarkably plain-looking rocks on the outside, but with the rap of a hammer they easily break open to reveal glittering crystals in white and purple hues. The most commonplace subjects and objects are easy to ignore because we suspect there is nothing new to see or know about them. Sometimes it takes the sharp rap of a really good question to crack open even the most familiar subjects, and then suddenly we see that subject in a new light. What I'm saying is this: A good question is the tool that makes the world yield to wonder, and knowing this is the key to being a curious researcher. Any research topic—even if the instructor assigns it—can glitter for you if you discover the questions that make you wonder.

Making the Most of an Assigned Topic

Frequently, you'll be encouraged to choose your own topic for a research essay. But if your instructor either assigns a topic or asks you to choose one within a limited subject, there's still hope. Exercise 1.2, "The Myth of the Boring Topic," suggests that writers can write about nearly any topic—assigned or not—if they can discover good questions. But if all else fails, examine your assigned topic through the following "lenses." One might give you a view of your topic that seems interesting.

■ *People.* Who has been influential in shaping the ideas in your topic area? Is there anyone who has views that are particularly intriguing to you? Could you profile that person and her contributions?

■ *Trends.* What are the recent developments in this topic? Are any significant? Why?

■ *Controversies.* What do experts in the field argue about? What aspect of the topic seems to generate the most heat? Which is most interesting to you? Why?

■ *Places.* Can you ground a larger topic in the particulars of a specific location that is impacted by the issue? For example, controversies over wolf management in the West can find a focus in how the debate plays out in Challis, Idaho, where some of the stakeholders live.

■ *Impact.* What about your topic currently has the most effect on the most people? What may have the most effect in the future? How? Why?

■ *Relationships.* Can you put one thing in relationship to another? If the required subject is Renaissance art, might you ask, "What is the relationship between Renaissance art and the plague?"

Admittedly, it is harder to make an assigned topic your own. But you can still get curious if you approach the topic openly, willing to see the possibilities by finding the questions that bring it to life for you.

Developing a Working Knowledge

If you have a tentative topic that makes you curious, then you're ready to do some preliminary research. At this stage in the process, it's fine to change your mind. As you begin to gently probe your subject, you may discover that there's another topic that interests you more—or perhaps there's a question that hadn't occurred to you. One of the advantages of developing a "working knowledge" of your topic at this stage is that these other possibilities may present themselves.

What's a working knowledge? William Badke, in his great book *Research Strategies*, calls a "working knowledge" of a topic the ability "to talk about it for one minute without repeating yourself." The advantage of developing a working knowledge of your tentative topic at this point is that it will help you find a focus. Aside from giving you something new to talk about when conversation lags at Thanksgiving dinner, a working knowledge helps you to see what *part* of the landscape of your topic you might want to venture into. Here's an example:

Case Study on Developing Working Knowledge: Theories of Dog Training

A few years ago, we took our lab puppy, Stella, to eight weeks of dog training. We thought things went well: She learned a "down stay," she would come when we called, and she wouldn't pull on her leash. Recently, we took our new golden retriever, Ada, to a different trainer and the first thing he said is that the method we used with Stella "simply wouldn't work" with Ada. It was clear that he disapproved of our first trainer's approach. "I don't know how she stays in business," he said. The experience confirmed the feeling I already had that despite advances in the study of animal behavior, there is little agreement on the best way to make Fido sit on command. Dog trainers are a particularly contentious lot.

If I develop a working knowledge on theories of dog training, what might I discover?

1. *Definitions.* I quickly discover that there are competing definitions about things I thought were settled. What, for example, is a "well-behaved" dog? What do trainers mean when they use the term "correction"? What's the difference between "operant" and "classical" conditioning?
2. *Debates.* After just ten minutes of searching online it's obvious that there are fundamental disagreements among dog trainers on a whole range of issues. Should you reward dogs with food or simply with praise? Should disobedient dogs be punished with pain—say, a yank on a prong collar or a jolt from a shock collar—or with removing something they want—a treat or a ball? Should theories of dog training be based on the behavior of wild canines like wolves or based on the belief that there are fundamental differences between them?

3. *People.* It doesn't take much searching on this subject to begin to recognize certain experts or advocates whose names come up again and again in the debates. There is, for example, the "Dog Whisperer" on cable TV, Cesar Milan, who applies some of the principles of the wolf pack to dog training. Then there are behaviorists like Patricia McConnell and Victoria Stilwell, who advocate positive reinforcement.
4. *Contexts.* Before long, I realize that you can understand dog training in more than just the context of debates among trainers. This is a topic that leashes together a whole range of disciplines: animal behavior, social psychology, wildlife biology, and anthropology.

Research Strategies for Developing Working Knowledge

There are many ways to develop a working knowledge of your topic, but generally the research strategy is like many others: Work from more general information to more specialized information. Try these steps:

1. *Begin with a Google search.* Enter as many search terms as you can at one time to narrow the results, with the most important terms first. Save the relevant results (see "Using Zotero to Manage Your Research," page 37).
2. *Search general and subject encyclopedias.* I know that Wikipedia is the first thing that comes to mind, but there are other, better encyclopedias. You'll find bound versions of the venerable *Encyclopaedia Britannica* in your library; your library might also provide free online access. There are online encyclopedias galore, including the *Columbia Encyclopedia* and *Encyclopedia. com.* Subject encyclopedias (see list on page 36) are more focused references, and they are sadly underused by students. There are subject encyclopedias on hundreds of subjects: art history, war, African American literature, nutrition—you name it. (My favorite is the *Encyclopedia of Hell.*) You can find these online at your university library as well as at the Internet Public Library (http://www.ipl.org).
3. *Use the Internet Public Library.* The merger of the Internet Public Library and Librarians' Internet Index created a super site that is a boon to online researchers. This is currently the most successful effort on the Web to bring some order to the chaos that is the Internet. Here you will find specialized encyclopedias, a search portal for finding more reliable sources on your topic, and even special collections.

SUBJECT ENCYCLOPEDIAS

HUMANITIES	SOCIAL SCIENCES
Dictionary of Art	*African-American Encyclopedia*
International Dictionary	*Dictionary of Psychology*
of Films and Filmmakers	*Encyclopedia of Marriage*
Encyclopedia of World Art	*and the Family*
Encyclopedia of Religion	*Encyclopedia of Psychology*
Encyclopedia of Philosophy	*The Blackwell Encyclopedia*
Encyclopedia of African American	*of Social Psychology*
Culture and History	*Encyclopedia of Educational*
Encyclopedia of America	*Research*
Encyclopedia of Sociology	*Encyclopedia of Social Work*
Social History	*Encyclopedia of World Cultures*
	Encyclopedia of the Third World
	Encyclopedia of Democracy
	Guide to American Law:
	Everyone's Legal Encyclopedia

SCIENCE	OTHER
Dictionary of the History	*Encyclopedia of the Modern*
of Science	*Islamic World*
Dictionary of the History	*The Baseball Encyclopedia*
of Medicine	*Encyclopedia of Women*
Encyclopedia of the Environment	*and Sports*
Concise Encyclopedia of Biology	*Encyclopedia of World Sport*
Encyclopedia of Bioethics	*The World Encyclopedia*
Encyclopedia of Science	*of Soccer*
and Technology	*Worldmark Encyclopedia*
Macmillan Encyclopedias	*of the Nations*
of Chemistry and Physics	
Food and Nutrition Encyclopedia	

4. *Try Google Scholar.* Regular Google searches will turn up all kinds of results—mostly commercial sites—but Google Scholar will get you the kind of information that you know you can count on as reliable and authoritative—journal articles and scholarly books. These publications are often "peer-reviewed," so everything that sees print, online or off, passes academic muster.

5. *Start building a bibliography.* Finally, conclude your working knowledge search by collecting the basic bibliographic information on the most useful sources you found. A convenient way to do this is to use a "citation machine," a Web-based program that

automatically prompts you for the bibliographic information and then magically turns it into citations in whatever citation format you want. Don't trust one of these to generate references for your final essay—they can make mistakes—but they're great as a preliminary method for collecting a list of citations. Visit Citation Machine (http://citationmachine.net), bibme (http://www.bibme.org), or another site and enter information about your best sources, choosing APA or MLA format.

Using Zotero to Manage Your Research

It's not hard to quickly accumulate quite a few helpful search results. You can organize these, of course, by using the bookmarking feature in your browser, downloading files to a folder on your computer, or printing them out. But if you use the Firefox browser (available free), consider Zotero as a tool to manage your online research.

Zotero (http://www.zotero.org) is a free application developed by researchers at George Mason University that is integrated into Firefox, and it can save and organize all kinds of Web resources in folders you create that are accessible wherever you have an Internet connection. The program can actually "sense" what kind of online document or image you're looking at and organize the citation information automatically. Not only that: Zotero offers a Word (or Open Office) plug-in that will allow you—while you're writing your paper—to automatically build a bibliography in the right format whenever you cite a source in your text.

Once installed, Zotero will appear as an icon on your browser. Click on it, and your Zotero library will open at the bottom of the browser page. You'll see three columns (see Figure 1.2). On the left will be your library of saved research materials. The middle column will be the open document on your browser, and the right column will be citation information.

The Reference Librarian: A Living Source

There are compelling reasons to visit the library, even at this early stage in your research. First and foremost is that the reference desk is where reference librarians hang out, and these are people you should get to know. They can save you time by guiding you to the very best sources on your topic, and they often give great advice on how to narrow your research question. Reference specialists are invaluable to college researchers; without a doubt, they're the most important resource in the library.

FIGURE 1.2   Zotero

Narrowing the Subject

It never occurred to me that photography and writing had anything in common until I found myself wandering around a lonely beach one March afternoon with a camera around my neck. I had a fresh roll of film (it was that long ago) and, full of ambition, I set out to take beautiful pictures. Three hours later, I had taken only three shots, and I was definitely not having fun. Before quitting in disgust, I spent 20 minutes trying to take a single picture of a lighthouse. I stood there, feet planted in the sand, repeatedly bringing the camera to my face; but each time I looked through the viewfinder, I saw a picture I was sure I'd seen before, immortalized on a postcard in the gift shop down the road. Suddenly, photography lost its appeal.

A few months later, a student sat in my office complaining that he didn't have anything to write about. "I thought about writing an essay on what it was like going home for the first time last weekend," he said. "But I thought that everyone probably writes about that in freshman English." I looked at him and thought about lighthouse pictures.

Circling the Lighthouse

Almost every subject you will choose to write about for this class and for this research paper has been written about before. The challenge is not to find a unique topic (save that for your doctoral dissertation) but to find an angle on a familiar topic that helps readers to see what they probably haven't noticed before. For example, once in a research essay titled "The Bothersome Beauty of Pigeons," I wrote about the most common of subjects—the urban pigeon—and took a close look at its habits and behaviors, finding in them an explanation for my conflicted feelings about "pests" that are inconveniently attractive.

I now know that it was a mistake to give up on the lighthouse. The problem with my lighthouse picture, as well as with my student's proposed essay on going home, was not the subject. It was that neither of us had yet found our own angle. I needed to keep looking, walking around the lighthouse, taking lots of shots until I found one that surprised me, that helped me see the lighthouse in a new way, in *my* way. Instead, I stayed put, stuck on the long shot and the belief that I couldn't do better than a postcard photograph.

It is generally true that when we first look at something, we mostly see its obvious features. That became apparent when I asked my freshman English class one year to go out and take pictures of anything they wanted. Several students came back with single photographs of Thompson Hall, a beautiful brick building on campus. Coincidentally, all were taken from the same angle and distance—straight on and across the street—which is the same shot that appears in the college recruiting catalog. For the next assignment, I asked my students to take multiple shots of a single subject, varying angle and distance. Several students went back to Thompson Hall and discovered a building they'd never seen before, though they walked by it every day. Students took abstract shots of the pattern of brickwork, unsettling shots of the clock tower looming above, and arresting shots of wrought iron fire escapes, clinging in a tangle to the wall.

The closer students got to their subjects, the more they began to see what they had never noticed before. The same is true in writing. As you move in for a closer look at some aspect of a larger subject, you will begin to uncover information that you—and ultimately your readers—are likely to find less familiar and more interesting. One writing phrase for this is *narrowing your subject*. (The photographic equivalent would be *varying distance from the subject*.)

From Landscape Shots to Close-ups

The research reports many of us wrote in high school typically mimicked landscape photography. We tried to cram into one picture as much information as we could. A research report is a long shot. The college research essay is much more of a close-up, which calls for narrowing the boundaries of a topic as much as you can, always working for a more detailed look at some smaller part of the landscape.

You are probably not a photographer, and finding a narrow focus and fresh angle on your research topic is not nearly as simple as it might be if this were a photography exercise. But the idea is the same. You need to see your topic in as many ways as you can, hunting for the angle that most interests you; then go in for a closer look. One way to find your *focus* is to find your *questions*.

Other Ways to Narrow Your Subject

1. **Time.** Limit the time frame of your project. Instead of researching the entire Civil War, limit your search to the month or year when the most decisive battles occurred.
2. **Place.** Anchor a larger subject to a particular location. Instead of exploring "senioritis" at American high schools, research the phenomenon at the local high school.
3. **Person.** Use the particulars of a person to reveal generalities about the group. Instead of writing about the homeless problem, write about a homeless man.
4. **Story.** Ground a larger story in the specifics of a "smaller" one. Don't write about dream interpretation, write about a dream *you* had and use the theories to analyze it.

EXERCISE 1 . 3

Finding the Questions

Although you can do this exercise on your own, your instructor will likely ask that you do it in class this week. That way, students can help one another. (If you do try this on your own, only do Steps 3 and 4 in your research notebook.)

STEP 1: Post a large piece of paper or newsprint on the wall. (In a classroom with computers you can do this exercise in an open Word document.) At the very top of the paper, write the title of your tentative topic (e.g., "Plastics in the Ocean").

STEP 2: Take a few minutes to briefly describe why you chose the topic.

STEP 3: Spend five minutes or so briefly listing what you know about your topic already. This is information you harvested this week from your effort to develop working knowledge on your proposed topic. You might list any surprising facts or statistics, the extent of the problem, important people or institutions involved, key schools of thought, common misconceptions, observations you've made, important trends, major controversies, and so on.

STEP 4: Now spend 15 or 20 minutes brainstorming a list of questions *about your topic* that you'd like to answer through your research. Make this list as long as you can; try to see your topic in as many ways as possible. Push yourself on this; it's the most important step.

STEP 5: As you look around the room, you'll see a gallery of topics and questions on the walls. At this point in the research process, almost everyone will be struggling to find a focus. You can help one another. Move around the room, reviewing the topics and questions other students have generated. For each topic posted on the wall, do two things: Add a question *you* would like answered about that topic that's not on the list, and check the *one* question on the list you find most interesting. (It may or may not be the one you added.)

If you do this exercise in class, note the question about your topic that garnered the most interest. This may not be the one that interests you the most, and you may choose to ignore it altogether. But it is helpful to get some idea of what typical readers might want most to know about your topic.

You also might be surprised by the rich variety of topics other students have tentatively chosen for their research projects. The last time I did this exercise, I had students propose papers on controversial issues such as the use of dolphins in warfare, homelessness, the controversy over abolishment of fraternities, legalization of marijuana, and censorship of music. Other students proposed somewhat more personal issues, such as growing up with an alcoholic father, date rape, women in abusive relationships, and the effects of divorce on children. Still other students wanted to learn about historical subjects, including the role of Emperor Hirohito in World War II, the student movement in the 1960s, and the Lizzie Borden murder case. A few students chose topics that were local. For example, one student recently researched the plight of nineteenth-century

Chinese miners digging for gold in the mountains just outside of Boise. Another did an investigation of skateboard culture in town, a project that involved field observation, interviews, as well as library research.

Crafting Your Opening Inquiry Question

What do you do with the gazillion questions you've generated on your research topic? Throw most of them away. But not yet! If you look carefully at the list of questions you (and your peers) generated in Exercise 1.3, you will likely see patterns. Some of your questions will clump together in more general categories. Perhaps a group of questions is related to the history of your topic, trends, processes, local relevance, and so on. Look for these patterns, and especially questions that might be combined or that inspire new questions.

Your work this week will culminate in the crafting of a tentative inquiry question that will guide your research and writing next week. This question will constantly evolve as you learn more; but for now, create the one question around which you will launch your project. Among the most common types of inquiry questions are sense-making questions, hypothesis-testing questions, and relationship-analyzing questions (see Table 1.1). Don't worry too much about the distinctions between question types; for one thing, they overlap quite a bit. But these categories should help you see some of the kinds of questions you might ask about your topic.

As the name implies, *sense-making questions* arise when we are searching for an explanation (think CSI or Sherlock Holmes). Why

TABLE 1.1 Types of Inquiry Questions

Sense-Making	Hypothesis-Testing	Relationship-Analyzing
Why might this be true or not true?	Is this evidence for or against the idea of _____?	What is the relationship between _____ and _____?
What might explain _____?	Is my assumption about _____ true?	Does _____ cause _____?
	Is it true that _____?	Is _____ similar to _____?

does one dog trainer see "correction" in a way that conflicts with the way another dog trainer sees it?

Frequently, we have hunches about what might be true. *Hypothesis-testing questions* test these assumptions. These are ideas that often emerge when we ask a bunch of sense-making questions; for instance, some preliminary research on the conflicts between dog trainers on the issue of correction suggests that the debate is related to assumptions about whether domestic dogs respond like wild canines— wolves, coyotes, and the like. A hypothesis-testing question might be something like this: Is it true that the often-bitter debates between dog trainers about the best approach to correction is based on assumptions about the links between wild dogs and domestic ones?

Finally, *relationship-analyzing questions* are among the most common types of inquiry questions. Most questions researchers explore have to do with trying to figure out whether one thing causes another thing or whether one thing is like or unlike something else. For example, does painful correction destroy the bond between a dog and its owner?

EXERCISE 1.4

Finding the Inquiry Question

Review the questions you or your class generated in Exercise 1.3, steps 4 and 5, and ask yourself, Which questions on the list am I most interested in that could be the focus of my paper? Remember, you're not committing yourself yet.

Using one or more of the templates suggested in Table 1.1, craft several research questions that seem to capture what most interests you in the topic. For example,

- What might explain the rise of recruiting violations in the NCAA?
- What is the connection between having anorexia and the anorexic's relationship with her father?
- Is it true that the major climate change denial organizations are funded by special interests that oppose cap-and-trade legislation?
- Is risk-based behavior in extreme sports caused by a certain personality type?

Methods for Focusing Your Paper: An Example

A clear, narrow research question is the one thing that will give you the most traction when trying to get your research project moving. It's also one of the hardest steps in the process. Like gulping air after a dive into the deep end of a pool, our natural instinct at the beginning of a research project is to inhale too much of our subject. We go after the big question— why is poverty a problem?—and quickly wonder why we are submerged in information, struggling to find a direction. That's why I've spent so much time on a range of methods to craft a workable research question.

Here's an example of how one student used some of these approaches to satisfy both her general curiosity about the origins of terrorism and her need to write an essay about it that would be interesting, specific, and manageable over a five-week period. Helen used the *time, person, place,* and *story* methods as a means of refining her research question (see "Other Ways to Narrow Your Subject" on page 40). Any one of these questions would be a good starting place for her inquiry into terrorism.

Topic: Terrorism

Opening Question—What is the cause of terrorism by Islamic extremists?

1. *Time as a Focusing Device—What might be the historical roots of Islamic extremism during the first jihad in the seventh century?*

2. *Person as a Focusing Device—Did President Jimmy Carter's policies in the Middle East contribute to the radicalization of some Islamic groups?*

3. *Place as a Focusing Device—Have Islamic religious schools in Pakistan contributed to the extremist thought and the radicalization of Muslim activists?*

4. *Story as a Focusing Device—What might the story of Shehzad Tanweer, one of the men who allegedly participated in the 2005 London bombings, reveal about how young men are radicalized?*

Possible Purposes for a Research Assignment

If you have a decent research question, you're off and running. But your next step should be to pause, look at your question, and think a bit about which of the following purposes are implied by the question you chose. Each of these purposes will profoundly influence the way you read your sources and how you approach writing the first draft. While any essay can use more than one purpose, which would you say is your *main* motive in writing your paper—at least at this moment?

1. *To explore.* You pose the question *because* you're unsure of the answer. This is what draws you to the topic. You're most interested in writing an essay, not a paper; that is, you want to write about what you found out in your research and what you've come to believe is the best or truest answer to the question you pose. Your essay will have a thesis, but it will probably surface toward the end of the paper rather than at the beginning. This is what I would call a *research essay* rather than a research paper, and it's the most open-ended form for academic inquiry. Exploratory essays often begin with sense-making or relationship-analyzing questions.

2. *To argue.* You know you have a lot to learn about your topic, but you have a very strong hunch about what the answer to your research question might be. In other words, you have a hypothesis you want to test by looking at the evidence. Inspired by a hypothesis question ("Is it true that…?"), you report on your investigation. However, you may quickly move from a hunch to a conviction; and then you move immediately into arguing your claim, trying to influence what your readers think and even how they behave. Your thesis is a statement—for example, *Muslim religious schools in Pakistan are not to blame for Islamic extremism*—that you can probably roughly articulate at the beginning of your project. It may very well change as you learn more, but when you write your paper, your purpose is to state a central claim and make it convincing. Frequently, that claim is stated near the beginning of the paper.

EXERCISE 1.5

Research Proposal

This is an important moment in the research process. How well you've crafted your research question will significantly influence the success of your project. You can change your mind later, but for now, jot down a brief proposal that outlines your research plan in your research notebook or to turn in to your instructor. It should include the following:

1. Inquiry question
2. Primary purpose
   - *Explore:* What are additional questions that most interest you and might help you discover the answers to your research question?
   - *Argue:* What theory or hypothesis about your topic are you testing? What is your tentative main claim or thesis?
3. What, if any, prior beliefs, assumptions, preconceptions, ideas, or prejudices do you bring to this project? What personal experiences may have shaped the way you feel? Before you began developing working knowledge on the topic, what were you thinking about it? What are you thinking about it now?

Reading for Research

For this assignment, and many others in your other college classes, you will have to read things that you find difficult. Maybe they seem really boring or full or jargon or hard to follow, or perhaps they seem to be all of those things. Aside from procrastinating, how do you deal with that?

Researchers who study reading say that the best readers are guided by a strong sense of purpose—they know why they are reading something and what they hope to get from it. They also have some knowledge of the *type* of text they're reading. They know where to look for what they need to know. More than anything, though, the strongest readers are those who already have some prior knowledge about the subject. Yet even in situations where you have little prior knowledge of the subject you're reading about, you can still read effectively if you read "rhetorically."

Reading Rhetorically

We all learned to read in school, but we probably never really learned how to read *rhetorically*. Reading rhetorically means selecting particular reading strategies that are most effective in certain situations and for certain purposes and applying them. Actually, you already do this with some texts you encounter every day. For example, there's this:

> u stupid girl, why ru upset & worried? i'm not in a mood or stressed so u shouldn't be + def don't b scared of me-i'm a softy! cu in a bit x

Of course you recognize this kind of text as a familiar genre—the text message—and though you didn't write the message or receive it, you know how to read it. You know the language. You know the social situations that give rise to this kind of message. And you know the writer's purpose.

The sentence that follows is from the first line of a scholarly article titled "The Architecture of the Personal Interactive Homepage: Constructing the Self Through MySpace."

> Structural symbolic interactionism understands the creation of self and identity to occur within existing social structures (Burke, 1980, 2004; Burke and Reitzes, 1981; Burke and Tully, 1977; Cast, 2003; Goffman, 1959; Stets and Burke, 2005; Stryker, 1980).

How are you to read something like this with its unfamiliar references to things like "structural symbolic interactionism" and the list of unfamiliar names in the citation? It's likely that your usual reading strategies will fail you here.

In high school, much of the writing about reading you may have done was in English class, writing critical essays about novels, poems, or short stories. In many ways, reading to write about a novel or a short story is quite different from reading to write research essays. For one thing, there are very basic differences between a literary text and a research article. In a short story, the author's purpose may be *implicit*; you have to "read into" the evidence provided in a narrative to make some interpretation about its meaning. An academic article, on the other hand, is *explicit*. The author states his or her conclusions rather than inviting the reader to make a reasoned interpretation. In addition, academic writing, like the previous example, uses specialized language and conventions—terms, references, evidence, and organizing principles that the people for whom the article was intended (usually other experts in the field) can understand. Stories have their own internal logic and language, but these are usually accessible to most readers even if the meaning is not.

Finally, we usually enjoy the *experience* of reading a story, or at least feel something in response to a good one, but we usually read articles with a much more practical purpose in mind: to acquire information.

Shouldn't the fundamental differences between these types of texts mean that the *way* we read them is also different? I think so. But we rarely think about our reading strategies, pretty much resorting to reading the way we always have in school. Maybe you never highlight, or maybe the pages you've read are fields plowed with yellow rows. Maybe you make marginal notes when you read, or maybe you never write a thing. Maybe you always read everything just once, or maybe you read a text many times to make sure you understand it. Maybe you always read every word, or maybe you skim like a flat rock on smooth water. Whatever your reading practices, becoming aware of them is a first step to reading strategically.

Reading Like an Outsider

Why spend precious time thinking about your reading process? For the same reason this course focuses on the writing process: By becoming aware of *how* you do things that have become habits, you exercise more control over them. In many ways, this book is about challenging old habits and assumptions about research, and this includes approaches to reading when you have to write a research essay. For example, consider what's unique about this situation:

■ In a general sense, you're just reading to collect information. But researchers use what they read in some particular ways: to provide support for their ideas, to create a context for the questions they're asking, and to complicate or extend their thinking.

■ College research often requires students to read the specialized discourses of fields with which they're not familiar. That means they must struggle with jargon and conventions that make reading particularly difficult.

■ Typically, the purpose of the research paper is not to report but to explore or argue. Information is in the service of the writer's own ideas about a topic.

■ In some classes (though probably not this one), the main audience for the research essay is an expert in the subject the writer is exploring.

In a way, the student researcher has to read like an outsider—or, as essayist Scott Russell Sanders put it, "an amateur's raid in a world of specialists." What does this suggest about your reading strategy? First, it makes sense to develop a working knowledge of your topic *before* you tackle the more scholarly stuff. As I noted earlier, research in reading suggests that knowledge of a subject makes a big difference in comprehension and retention of information. Second, your own purposes should firmly guide what you read and how you read it. Mentally juggle at least the three purposes I mentioned earlier—reading for example, for context, and for challenge. Third, anticipate your own resistance to the scholarly writing that seems "boring." It's boring because you're an outsider and haven't broken the code. The more you read in your subject area, the more you'll understand; the learning curve is steep. Fourth, in scholarly writing especially, quickly learn the organizing principles of the articles. For example, in the social sciences, articles often have *abstracts, introductions, methods*, and *discussion* sections. Each provides particular kinds of information that might be useful to you. It often isn't necessary to read an academic article from beginning to end. And, finally, the most important thing: Read with a pen in your hand. In the next chapter, I introduce you to some notetaking strategies that encourage you to use writing to think about what you're reading *as* you're reading it. Write-to-learn activities such as fastwriting can help you take possession of information and help you write a stronger paper.

Reading Strategies for Research Writers

- First develop a working knowledge.
- Let your own purposes guide: example, context, challenge.
- Anticipate your own resistance.
- Learn the organizing principles of articles.
- Read with a pen in your hand.

CHAPTER 2

The Second Week

Developing a Research Strategy

A few years ago, I wanted a pair of good birding binoculars for my birthday. I thought of the local store that seemed to carry the largest selection of binoculars and went there; within 20 minutes or so I had spent about $300 on some Swift binoculars, a brand that is highly regarded by wildlife watchers. Did you ever notice that is often *after* your purchase when you're most motivated to seek out information that reinforces your decision to buy something? Within days of buying the Swifts, I searched the Internet just to make certain that the model I bought was the one recommended by most birders. Sure enough, that seemed to be the case. Then I casually checked the prices on the binoculars, quite certain that I made a fairly good deal on them. To my horror I discovered that I had paid about $100 more than I had to.

Sometimes having no research strategy costs more than time.

A research essay is time consuming, and although you aren't risking money, the quality of your paper will make a big difference in your final grade. Your time and your grade are two reasons that it pays to be thoughtful about *how* you approach gathering and using information. A typical "strategy" is something like this: (1) get the assignment, (2) choose a topic, (3) wait until a few days before the paper is due, (4) madly search the Internet, (5) write the paper the night before you have to hand it in, (6) pray.

This time, you've already approached the paper more strategically than outlined in the typical strategy. In the last chapter, you spent time exploring possible topics, narrowing your focus, and developing research questions that will help guide your search for information. This will make a big difference in the efficiency of your research in the library and on the Web. But what do experienced researchers know that will help you find what you're looking for fast and use what you find effectively? Here's what you will learn this week:

1. How to create a chronology for the searches
2. How to control the language of your searches to get the best results
3. How to perform advanced searches at the library and on the Web, and how to use other sources of information, including surveys and interviews
4. How to evaluate what you find
5. How to take notes that will help you to begin writing your essay even before you begin the draft

Google vs. the Library

Despite all the fat, the carbs, and the empty calories, the convenience of a Big Mac is hard to ignore. Similarly, a few minutes feasting on the information served up by Google is far more convenient than searching an online database at the university library. As one analyst put it recently, "Googling has become synonymous with research." Another called the relentless feast of online information "infobesity."

Should we be wringing our hands about this? The answer is *yes* and *no*. The power and accessibility of Google and other Internet search tools have turned virtually everyone into a researcher. No question is too arcane and no quest is completely hopeless when typing a few words into a search window allows you to lurch through millions of documents in a second. It's really hard to understate the wonder of this. Along with the junk, the results of Internet searches often turn up something useful, even for an academic paper. In fact, at least one study* suggests that when Google searches are matched with searches on library databases, the popular search engine doesn't do too badly. When researchers looked for relevant documents on four test topics, they found a total of 723 sources. Google produced 237 of these, and the library databases turned up 163. Predictably, however, the documents from the library were generally of a much higher quality—they tended to be from more qualified sources: more up-to-date, more balanced, and more accurate. Still, while Google produced more stinkers, researchers concluded that 52 percent of its results were actually pretty good.

Undoubtedly, it's Google's accessibility that makes it so irresistible. In addition to avoiding a hike to the library or sorting through academic

---

*Brophy, Jan, and David Bawden. "Is Google Enough? Comparison of an Internet Search Engine with Academic Library Sources." *Aslib Proceedings: New Information Perspectives* 57 (2005): 498–512. Print.

databases online, Google gives you results you can often find and use immediately. In the Google matchup with the library, 90 percent of the documents produced by the popular search engine were instantly accessible, full-text articles, while the library fared less well—only 65 percent of those results were full text. In some cases, getting an article on a library database required interlibrary loan or a microfilm search.

Yet for all Google's appeal, in academic writing *quality matters.* A lot. You must always try to use accurate sources that are written by people who know what they're talking about. For those kinds of sources, your library is indispensable. The dilemma here is this: Do you value the accessibility of an Internet search above the quality of the library sources? At first, not many of my students struggle with this. Google wins, hands down. But savvy researchers know that's like juggling with one hand—you're making it much harder than it needs to be. In academic research, you need as much relevant, accurate information as you can get. The answer, obviously, is to learn how you can *complement* your Google searches with library searches.

A Complementary Research Strategy

Writers are always better off when they work from abundance. It is far better to have more information than you can use because this allows you to understand your subject more deeply and focus your investigation more narrowly. Attack your research question on multiple fronts—the Internet, the library, and interviews or surveys—and you're much more likely to succeed in finding out what you want to know (see Figure 2.1). This inclusive approach will help you accomplish the three things that make up a sound search strategy:

1. Find *enough* information to fully explore a narrowly focused topic.
2. Find *varied* sources.
3. Find *quality* information.

Find Enough Information by Using the Best Search Terms

Around my house a few years back, the Harry Potter phenomenon had everyone muttering magic words. "Flipendo," said Julia, trying to turn the dog into a gerbil. "Wingardium leviosa," said Becca, who was determined to elevate her little sister six feet off the ground. Chopsticks substituted for magic wands. I knew this because we

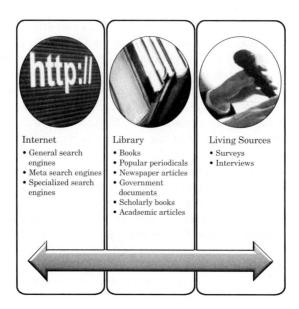

FIGURE 2.1 Maximize coverage of quality sources by investigating on three fronts.

suddenly had too few when the take-out Chinese meal arrived; that was the only part of this magical revival that swept the household that I didn't much like.

Some writers foolishly think that there's magic involved in getting good words to the page when it's really much more simple and not at all mysterious: You have to have your seat in the chair and your fingers on the keyboard or curled around a pen. But there is a kind of magic you can perform as a researcher, and it also involves the right words uttered in the right order. *How* you phrase your search of a library database or the World Wide Web makes an enormous difference in the results. I've come to believe that this ability, almost more than any other, is the researcher's most important skill.

You can harvest more and better results by understanding and effectively using three search tactics:

- *Index searches* deploy the language that librarians use to catalog books and other materials in university libraries.
- *Keyword searches* in library databases use relevant terms with "connectors" like AND, OR, or NOT to produce better results.
- *Keyword searches* on the Web combine a string of terms, along with exact phrases to generate more relevant hits.

Index Searches Using the Library of Congress Subject Headings

An advantage that libraries have over the Web is that information in libraries is more organized. That's the good news. The bad news is that there is so much information to organize that librarians had to develop a special language for searching it. It's not alien language—the words are familiar—but it is a language that requires that certain words be used to reflect the way librarians organize information. These searches, called *index searches,* may therefore initially seem less straightforward than the more familiar *keyword searches.*

More specifically, reference librarians use something called the *Library of Congress Subject Headings (LCSH),* which divides all knowledge into areas. These divisions are the *index terms* that you can use for index searches, which will almost always help you to find more relevant books on your topic. How do you find out these index terms? A couple ways: There is a four-volume book in your library's reference room—sometimes called the "Red Book." These volumes are the standard reference to index terms. You can also go online to search the *LCSH* (http://authorities.loc.gov/). There you can search by subject, name, or title, and the software will tell you what subject headings to use when searching for books in the library. But the easiest method to know what Library of Congress (LOC) terms to use is to go to your library's online book database and do an initial search with terms you *think* might work. When you find relevant books, you'll likely see the relevant LOC terms in your results. For example, I did a keyword search using the term *cyberterrorism* in my library's book database and found a great book: *Cyberterrorism: The Use of the Internet for Terrorist Purposes.* The results page suggested the following index terms as active links that would help me narrow my search:

Cyberterrorism—Prevention

Computer networks—Security measures

Computer security—Law and legislation

Knowing these index terms is a huge help, particularly in the early stages of a research project. Just enter the suggested terms in your library online book index, and you'll be surprised by the quality of the results.

Keyword Searches in Library Databases

Compared to a Google search, library database searches (see a list of some of these databases on pages 79–80) rely much more on coming up with keywords and trying them in different combinations. For example, searching for books using the word "Wildfires" will produce an avalanche that will quickly bury you. Efficient research requires that you maximize the number of relevant results and minimize the number of irrelevant ones. That's where searches that use careful combinations of keywords are so important. Many libraries and Internet search engines use something called "Boolean" connectors to help you when you search databases. (These connectors were invented by George Boole, a British logician, more than 100 years ago.)

The system essentially requires the use of the words AND, OR, and NOT between the search terms or keywords. The word AND, say, between "Animal" and "Rights" will search a database for documents that include *both* of those terms. Just keying in *animal rights* without the AND connector will often get the same results because the AND is implied. If you want to search for *animal rights* as an exact phrase, most library databases ask you to put the phrase in parentheses rather than quotation marks.

The use of the connector OR between search terms, obviously, will produce a list of documents that contain either of the terms. That can be a lot of results. In the early stages of your project, you might want to browse a heap of results; that way you can explore different angles on your topic, see the more common treatments, and discover some alternative search terms. The NOT connector is less frequently used but really can be quite helpful if you want to *exclude* certain documents. Suppose, for example, you were interested in researching the problem of homelessness in Washington State, where you live. To avoid getting information on Washington D.C., where it's also a problem, use the connector NOT.

Homeless AND Washington NOT D.C.

As you can see from the example above, it's possible to use the connectors between a number of terms—not just two. In fact, the art of creating keyword searches is using both the right words (those used by librarians) and using them in the right combinations (those that in combination sufficiently narrow your search and give you the best results).

One final search technique that can be very useful, especially in library database searches, is something called "nesting." This involves the use of parentheses around two or more terms in a phrase. This prompts the computer to look for those terms first. For example, suppose you were searching for articles on the ethics of animal rights, but you were particularly interested in information in two states, Idaho and Montana. You might construct a search phrase like this one:

> **(Montana OR Idaho) AND animal AND rights AND ethics**

Putting the two states in parentheses tells the software to prioritize Montana or Idaho in the results, generating a much more focused list of sources related to animal rights and ethics.

Keyword Searches on the World Wide Web

In the last chapter, you did a subject search on the Web, using popular sites, such as the Internet Public Library (http://ipl.org), that specialize in those kinds of searches. Far more common are searches that use so-called search engines, such as Google. As you probably know, these are remarkable software programs that in a split second "crawl" the Web, searching for documents that contain the keywords you type in. Lately, the magic of these search engines has been tarnished a bit by commercialism, allowing advertisers to purchase priority listings in search engine results and not always making that fact obvious to the searcher. But these search engines are still essential and getting better all the time.

Keyword searches are the most common method of searching the Web, used much than subject searches. Unfortunately, there isn't consistency in search languages. Some permit Boolean searching. Some use a variation on Boolean that involves symbols rather than words.

What Studies Say About How Students Research Online

- Most use a trial-and-error approach to searching.
- They rarely use anything more than basic searches, avoiding advanced searching features.
- Typically, they use only two search terms every session, and these search sessions last an average of 15–19 minutes.
- Only 8 percent use Boolean operators.
- 60 percent admit that they are overwhelmed by the amount of information available to them.
- Nearly three-quarters use the Internet rather than the library.

But Google, the giant of search engines, has made all of this a bit simpler through the search form provided by its Advanced Search option. You can find this on Google's search page. Once in Advanced Search, you can use the boxes provided to perform all the usual Boolean tricks but without having to use the "connector" words like AND, OR, or NOT.

Because of the mind-boggling amount of information on the Web, careful keyword searches are critical. Researchers waste more online time either not finding what they wanted or sifting through layers and layers of irrelevant documents because of thoughtless keyword searches. For example, notice in Figure 2.2 how the search on the relationship between social networks and friendship can be dramatically changed by adding terms. An initial search on Google simply using the keywords *social* and *network* produced a mind-boggling 334 million documents. Just adding *one more* keyword cut the number of hits by 6,000 percent! Finally, when combined with a phrase ("intimacy of friendship"), a search with the two terms *social* and *network* yielded significantly fewer and more focused results.

Find Varied Sources

One of the first things I notice when I'm reading research essay drafts is whether the writer leans too heavily on a single source. Does an author or article reappear again and again on page after page, like a pigeon at a favorite roost? This is not good. It typically means that the writer has too few sources and must keep turning to these few, or one source is especially relevant to the

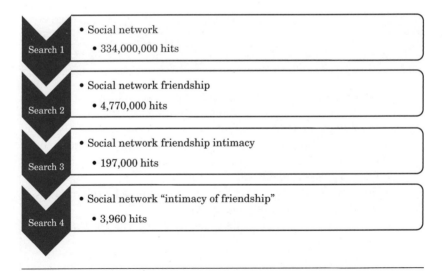

- Social network
  - 334,000,000 hits

Search 1

- Social network friendship
  - 4,770,000 hits

Search 2

- Social network friendship intimacy
  - 197,000 hits

Search 3

- Social network "intimacy of friendship"
  - 3,960 hits

Search 4

FIGURE 2.2   How Multiple Search Terms Narrow Results

topic, and the writer can't resist repeatedly inviting the author to reappear.

Vary your sources. This not only means using a sufficient number so that your essay is informative but also using different *kinds* of sources whenever you can. In part, the kinds of sources you rely on in preparing your paper depend on your topic. Remember my research question on competing theories of dog training? That's a current topic. There's an ongoing debate online and on cable TV about which approach is best. In addition, the topic has a history in the published literature. I'll be checking both newspapers and magazines, along with Web sites, but I'll also search the journals and books at the library. If you're writing about whether the release of secret documents by WikiLeaks endangers U.S. service members in Afghanistan, then much of your information will come from current sources; you're less likely to find books.

There are several ways to think about how sources can be distinguished from each other:

- Are they primary or secondary sources?
- Are they objective or subjective?
- Are they stable or unstable?

Primary vs. Secondary Sources

One way of looking at information is to determine whether it's a *primary* or a *secondary* source. A primary source presents the original words of a writer—his speech, poem, eyewitness account, letter, interview, or autobiography. A secondary source analyzes somebody else's work. Whenever possible, choose a primary source over a secondary one, because the primary source is likely to be more accurate and authoritative.

The subject you research will determine the kinds of primary sources you encounter. For example, if you're writing a paper on a novelist, then his novels, stories, letters, and interviews are primary sources. Research on the engineering of the Chicago River in 1900, a partly historical subject, might lead to a government report on the project or a firsthand account of its construction in a Chicago newspaper. Primary sources for a paper in the sciences might be findings from an experiment or observations. For a paper in business, marketing information or technical studies might be primary sources. A videotape of a theatrical performance is a primary source, while the reviews in the local newspaper are secondary sources.

Objective vs. Subjective

For now, I'm going to sidestep the debate over whether *any* source can be fully objective and simply point out that, generally speaking, we can divide all sources into those that attempt to report facts that have been gathered systematically, minimizing author bias, and those that don't pretend to be anything more than the author's opinion, perhaps supported by evidence gleaned from objective sources. You can probably guess some examples of objective sources: experiments, survey results, carefully designed studies of many kinds. The best of these are "peer reviewed" (see page 62) to double-check their accuracy. As you know, many academics prize these objective sources as the best evidence. Subjective sources are all over the map, from government propaganda to blogs to op-ed essays in the local newspaper. Of course, just because someone is pushing a point of view doesn't make a source useless. It just means that you need to consider how that point of view colors the source and read it more critically.

Stable or Unstable?

When information went digital, a new phenomenon emerged; sometimes information simply disappears. That Web page you cited in your draft, with the great statistics on scooter fatalities, is there one day and gone the next. One of the reasons you cite sources in academic writing is so readers can consult them, making a missing Web page a serious problem. Disappearing Web pages, of course, are hard to predict, but you can make some judgments about the stability of an online source. Has it been around for a long time? Is it routinely updated? Are print versions of an online document available? Is the site associated with a reputable institution? Unstable sources are a shaky foundation for any academic essay. It's best to avoid them.

Find Quality Sources

The aim of your research strategy is not only to find interesting information on your topic but also to find it in *authoritative* sources. What are these? The highest-quality sources are those types found on the bottom of the upside-down pyramid in Figure 2.3. These are works that are most likely to be written by and then reviewed by experts in their field (see "What Does 'Peer Reviewed' Mean?" on p. 62). You find these "peer-reviewed" articles in scholarly journals, some of which are now available online as well as in the library. The downside of dealing with sources at the bottom of the authoritative pyramid is that they may be written in the *discourse* of the field; to you that may make the writing seem jargon-filled and hard to follow. Of course, as a nonspecialist you aren't the intended audience for the work. But the effort to make sense of an academic article really pays off. Your readers know that you're relying on the best information available; beyond that,

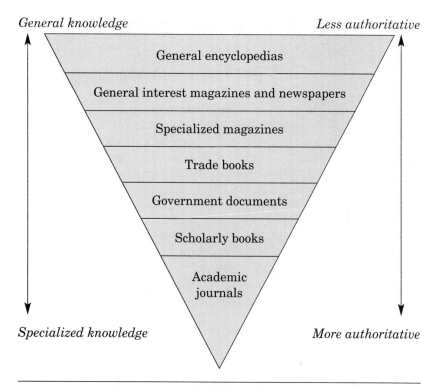

FIGURE 2.3 **Pyramid of Library Sources**

you're more credible because it's clear that you're willing to dig deeply to explore your research question.

When Was It Published?

If you're researching the treatment of slaves in nineteenth-century New Orleans, then currency is obviously less of an issue than it might be if your project were to explore the impact of the Toyota Prius on marketing practices for hybrid vehicles. Generally, in any project related to the social sciences, a recent publication date carries more weight, which is one reason APA citations emphasize date of publication. The currency of Web pages and online documents can also be important. A site that is regularly updated is obviously more likely to have the latest information on the topic.

Why Journal Articles Are Better Than Magazine Articles

If your topic has been covered by academic journal articles, rely heavily on these sources if you can. An article on, say, suicide

What Does "Peer Reviewed" Mean?

Broadly speaking, periodicals, books, Web sites, and magazines are one of two types: scholarly or popular. Popular publications include magazines like *Newsweek* or online sites like *Slate,* which are staff written, usually by nonexperts for a more general audience. Scholarly publications are written and edited by experts for others in their fields, and the best of these are "peer reviewed." This means that before an article is published online or in print, a group of fellow experts read and comment on its validity, argument, factual accuracy, and so on. The article doesn't appear in print until this review is completed and the journal editor is satisfied that the other scholars think the work is respectable.

What does this mean to you? It means that you can count on the authoritative muscle of a peer-reviewed source to help you make a strong point in your paper.

among college students in a magazine like *Time* is less valuable than one in the *American Journal of Psychology.* Granted, the latter may be harder to read, but you're much more likely to learn something from a journal article because it's written by an expert and is usually narrowly focused. Also, because academic articles are carefully documented, you may be able to mine bibliographies for additional sources. And, finally, scholarly work, such as that published in academic journals and books (usually published by university presses), is especially authoritative because it's often subject to peer review. Other authorities in the field have scrutinized the author's evidence, methods, and arguments; the published work has truly passed muster.

Look for Often-Cited Authors

As you make your way through information on your topic, pay attention to names of authors whose works you often encounter or who are frequently mentioned in bibliographies. These individuals are often the best scholars in the field, and it will be useful to become familiar with their work and use it, if possible, in your paper. If an author's name keeps turning up, use it as another term for searching the library databases or Google Scholar. Doing so might yield new sources you wouldn't necessarily encounter in other ways.

Not All Books Are Alike

When writing my high school research reports, I thought that books were always the best sources because, well, books are thick, and anyone who could write that much on any one subject probably knows what she's talking about. Naive, I know.

One of the things college teaches is *critical thinking*—the instinct to pause and consider before rushing to judgment. I've learned not to automatically believe in the validity of what an author is saying (as you shouldn't for me), even if she did write a thick book about it.

If your topic lends itself to using books as sources, then evaluate the authority of each before deciding to use it in your paper. This is especially important if your paper relies heavily on one or two books. Consider the following:

- Is the book written for a general audience or more knowledge-able readers?
- Is the author an acknowledged expert in the field?
- Is there a bibliography? Is the information carefully documented?
- How was the book received by critics? To find out quickly, search the Web using the author's name and title of the book as search terms.

Evaluating Online Sources

Librarians help maintain the order, stability, and quality of information in the library. By comparison, the Internet is anarchy. Everyone knows that you have to be vigilant about trusting the accuracy, balance, and reliability of Web documents. Unfortunately, there's continuing evidence that student researchers still have a hard time assessing the quality of online sources. While the criteria for evaluating sources just mentioned apply to Web documents, Web documents also deserve special attention.

Here are some general guidelines to follow (later I'll suggest a more vigorous approach for evaluating online sources):

- *Always keep your purpose in mind.* For example, if you're exploring the lobbying methods of the National Rifle Association, then you will want to hear, and see, what this organization has to say on its Web site. In looking at the NRA Web pages, you'll know full well that they are not unbiased; however, for your purpose, they are both relevant and authoritative. After all, who knows more about the NRA than the NRA?

- *Favor governmental and educational sources over commercial ones.* There are plenty of exceptions to this, but in general you're wise to rely more heavily on material sponsored by groups without a commercial stake in your topic. How can you tell the institutional affiliation of sources? Sometimes it's obvious. They tell you. But when it's not obvious, the *domain name* provides a clue. The *.com* that follows a server name signifies a commercial site, while *.edu, .org,* or *.gov* usually signals an educational, nonprofit, or governmental entity. The absence of ads also implies a site is noncommercial.

■ *Favor authored documents over those without authors.* There's a simple reason for this: You can check the credentials of an author. You can do this by sending an e-mail message to him or her, a convenience often available as a link on a Web page, or you can do a quick search to see if that author has published other books or articles on your topic. If writers are willing to put their names on a document, they might be more careful about the accuracy and fairness of what they say.

■ *Favor Web pages that have been recently updated over those that haven't been changed in a year or more.* Frequently, at the bottom of a Web page there is a line indicating when the information was posted to the Internet and/or when it was last updated. Look for it.

■ *Favor Web sources that document their claims over those that don't.* Most Web documents won't feature a bibliography. That doesn't mean that they're useless to you, but be suspicious of a Web author who makes factual assertions without supporting evidence.

A Key to Evaluating Internet Sources.   As an undergraduate, I was a botany major. Among other things, I was drawn to plant taxonomy because the step-by-step taxonomic keys for discovering the names of unfamiliar plants gave the vegetative chaos of a Wisconsin meadow or upland forest a beautiful kind of logic and order. The key that follows is modeled after the ones I used in field taxonomy. This one is a modest attempt to make some sense of the chaos on the Web for the academic researcher, particularly when the usual approaches for establishing the authority of traditional scholarship and publications fail—for example, when documents are anonymous, their dates of publication aren't clear, or their authors' affiliations or credentials are not apparent.

If you're not sure whether a particular Web document will give your essay credibility, see Figure 2.4 and work through the following steps:

1. Does the document have an author or authors? If *yes,* go to Step 2. If *no,* go to Step 7.

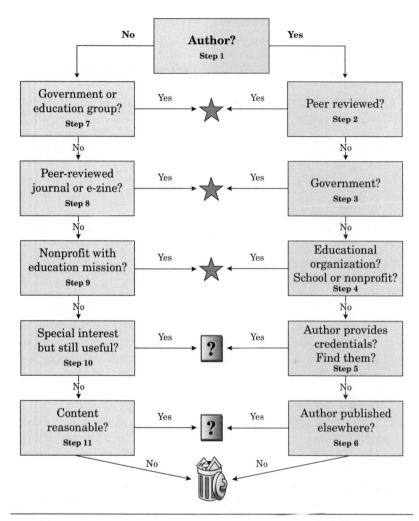

FIGURE 2.4   Follow the flowchart for a rigorous review of a Web document or page, beginning with whether the author is obvious or not. Sites that earn stars are generally more trustworthy. Those with question marks still may be useful, depending on the situation. Be particularly wary of information on commercial or special interest sites.

Authored Documents

2. Does the document appear in an online journal or magazine that is "refereed"? In other words, is there any indication that every article submitted must be reviewed by other scholars

in the field before it is accepted for publication? If *yes*, you've found a good source. If *no* (or you're unsure), go to Step 3.

3. Is the document from a government source? (Online, look for the .gov domain.) If *yes,* then it is likely a good source. If *no*, go to Step 4.

4. Does the document appear in an online publication affiliated with a reputable educational institution (e.g., a university) or nonprofit educational organization (e.g., the American Cancer Society)? (Online, look for the .edu or .org domain.) If *yes*, it's likely to be trustworthy. If *no*, go to Step 5.

5. If the author isn't clearly affiliated with a reputable institution, does he or she offer any credentials that help establish expertise on the topic? (For example, an advanced degree in the relevant discipline is encouraging.) If credentials are missing, can you find an author's credentials by Googling the author's name? Is there an e-mail link to the author so you can inquire about affiliations or credentials? If *no*, go to Step 6.

6. Has the author published elsewhere on the topic in reputable journals or other publications? Check this at the library by searching under the author's name in the catalog or appropriate databases. If *no*, reconsider the value of the source. You could be dealing with a lone ranger who has no expertise on your topic and no relevant affiliations.

Unauthored Documents

7. If the online document has no author, is it from an institutional source like a university (.edu) or the state or federal government (.gov)? If *yes*, then chances are the document is useful. If *no*, go to Step 8.

8. Is the anonymous document published in an online journal or magazine? Is it refereed? (See Step 2.) If *yes*, it's likely a good source. If *no*, go to Step 9.

9. Is the document part of a publication or Web page from a non-government source whose mission is described in the document, and does it suggest that the organization's goals include research and education? Is there a board of directors, and does it include professionals and academics who are respected in the field? If *no*, go to Step 10.

10. Even if the organization offering the information represents a special interest group or business with an axe to grind, the information may be useful as a means of presenting its point of view. Make sure, if you use it, that the information is qualified to make that obvious.

11. Does the site seem reasonable? Try to apply the usual criteria for evaluating a source to this anonymous document. Does it

have a citations page, and do the citations check out? Was it published on the Internet recently? Does the argument the writer is making seem sound? Do the facts check out? If the answer is *no* to all of the above, then don't trust the document. If you can answer *yes* to more than one of these questions, the material might have some marginal value in a college paper.

A good researcher always takes a skeptical view of claims made in print; she should be even more wary of claims made in Internet documents. And while these approaches for evaluating online sources should help, it still can be pretty tricky deciding whom to take seriously in cyberspace. So to sort it all out, always ask yourself these questions: How important is this Internet document to my research? Do I really need it? Might there be a more reliable print version? For an example, see Figure 2.5.

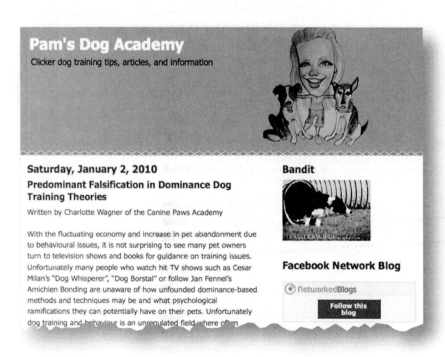

FIGURE 2.5   Evaluating a Web Site: A Case Study. I'm writing about the debates between dog trainers, and I encountered this site. "Pam's Dog Academy" is a blog, and it's got some really interesting information. Overall, how would you evaluate this site as a source for my essay? What exactly do you see that influences your judgment about that? Is there anything about the site that you might want to know? How would you find it?

L et.e~ , ~e~~.~arians, grou...... ...nd a~. ..teu~ ~aine.~ .~ithou~
second thought to the validity of the information being provided to
the reader.

Behaviourist James O'Heare (2003) claims that: "Dominance theory is
probably the most misunderstood commonly used ethological theory
in the dog behaviour field." There are a variety of views on
dominance, including those advocating dominance as a personality
flaw where the dog is trying to take over the owner: "When a dog
growls at the wife or kids in the family, it sees itself as a higher rank
than family members." (Frawley, 2009) and modern establishments
opposing the use of dominance-oriented intimidation techniques:
"Sadly, many techniques used to teach a dog that his owner is leader
of the pack is counter-productive; you won't get a better behaved
dog, but you will either end up with a dog so fearful it has
structure and communication regarding appropriate behaviours, and
one in which their need for mental and physical stimulation is
addressed." B. F. Skinner's operant principles of positive
reinforcement and negative punishment can easily aid in the increase
of desired behaviours and the extinction of undesired traits with the
use of motivation rather than intimidation and suppression through
aversion. There are many associations certifying trainers and
behaviourists which promote the use of learning theory and scientific
methods of understanding and modifying behaviour. Many of these
respected bodies require professionals to either: have a degree
relevant to animal behaviour, further education in training, or
extensive experience with another qualified professional before
accepting applicants to become members. These association include
but are not limited to the: Association of Pet Dog Trainers (APDT),
International Association of Animal Behaviour Consultants (IAABC),
Association of Pet Behaviour Consultants (APBC), Certified Council for
Professional Dog Trainers (CCPDT) and International Positive Dog
Training Association (IPDTA) to name a few.

Written by Charlotte Wagner of the Canine Paws Academy
1 January 2010

RESOURCES

Association of Pet Dog Trainers. (2009) Dominance and Dog Training:
Association of Pet Dog Trainers position statement [www document].
http://www.apdt.com/about/ps/ dominance.aspx (Accessed 7
December 2009)
Coppinger, L. and Coppinger, R. (2004) Dogs: A new understanding
of canine origin, behaviour and evolution. Romford, Essex: Crosskeys
Select.
Dennison, P. (2005) How to Right a Dog Gone Wrong. Loveland:
Alpine.
Donaldson, J. (1996) The Culture Clash. Berkeley: James and
Kenneth.
Fennel, J. (2006) The Practical Dog Listener. London: HarperCollins.
Frawey, E. (2009) Dealing with the Dominant Dog [www document]
http://leerburg.com/ pdf/dealingwithdominantdog.pdf (Accessed 10
December 2009)
Millan, C. and Peltier, M. J. (2006) Cesar's Way. New York: Crown.
O'Heare, J. (2003) Dominance Theory and Dogs. Ottawa: DogPsych.
Science Daily (2009) Using 'Dominance' to Explain Dog Behaviour is
Old Hat [www document] http://www.sciencedaily.com/releases
/2009/05/090521112711.htm (Accessed 7 December 2009)

► **June** (1)
► **May** (3)
► **April** (3)
► **March** (1)
► **February** (5)
▼ **January** (8)

**Both Ends of the Leash: Fear
Reduction**

**Bandit's Puppy Picture Photo
Contest...**

**Training your dog to come
when called, reliability...**

Clicker Mechanics

Why Not Punishment?

**Debunking the Dominance
Myth - Dog Public**

**Pet dogs rival humans for
emotional satisfaction**

**Predominant Falsification in
Dominance Dog Trainin...**

► **2009** (67)

About Me

Pam's Dog Academy
San Diego, CA, United
States

I have been training for
over 5 years. I opened my
dog training business in 2007. I only
train using clicker training and Positive
Reinforcement.

View my complete profile

**Here are some awesome
blogs...**

🅱 **DOGMANTICS**
   1 week ago

FIGURE 2.5   (Continued)

Developing Focused Knowledge

If working knowledge equips you to sustain a 1-minute dinner conversation on your topic, then focused knowledge is enough for you to make a 15- or 20-minute presentation to the rest of the class (for more on presentations, see the box "Working Together: In-Class News Conference"). You'll probably be able to answer all of your classmates' questions. You'll hardly be an expert, but you'll probably know a lot more about your topic than any of your peers.

Focused knowledge is the product of smart research this week and the next, refining your search terms, knowing where to look for the most useful information, and using your time efficiently. As you'll see later in this section, focused knowledge also depends on what you *do* with what you find. Most important, especially at this point, are these two questions:

1. Is this information relevant to my inquiry question?
2. Does it *change* my question?

At its most basic, relevance is simply deciding whether that article or book you found is on topic. Say you're researching the disappearance of the world's frogs, and you find a *Scientific American* article called "Extinction Countdown: World's Frogs Are Disappearing." It obviously couldn't be more relevant. But, as you develop more focused knowledge, you can make more focused judgments. *How* is a source relevant? With some traditional research papers, this question may simply mean, how does it support my point? But genuine academic inquiry is about discovery, and because it begins with questions, information isn't just used to line up ducks in the service of a preconceived point. The relevant sources you encounter online and in the library can help your project in many more ways:

■ *Refine the inquiry question.* Last week your question was, "Why are the world's frog's disappearing?" But you read some articles and browse some books and you realize that a more focused and interesting question is this: "How is climate change influencing the worldwide decline in amphibians?"

■ *Help the literature review.* A very common move in most academic research is establishing what has already been said about the question you're posing. Which scientists have published on frogs and climate change? What do they agree on? What are the disagreements? What don't they know?

Working Together: In-Class News Conference

By the end of this week, you should be ready to make a presentation to your class on your topic. Imagine that it's a press conference similar to the ones shown on television. You will give a 15-minute talk on your topic to your classmates, who will later, like veteran newspaper reporters, follow up with questions. Your presentation will be carefully timed. It shouldn't be any longer than the allotted time limit; any less than the allotted time suggests that you haven't yet developed a focused knowledge of your topic.

Plan your presentation with the following things in mind:

- *Rather than simply report everything you've learned about your topic, try to give your talk some emphasis.* For example, focus on what you've learned so far that most surprised you and why. Or present the most common misconceptions about your topic and why they miss the mark. Or provide some background about why the question you're exploring is important and share some of the answers you've discovered so far. If your topic has a personal dimension, tell the story, and share how your research has helped you understand your experience differently.
- *Don't read a speech.* It's fine to have notes with you—in fact, it's a good idea—but try to avoid reading them. Make your presentation as interesting as you can. After all, this is a chance to discover what other people think about your topic—what interests them about it and what doesn't. This talk is a great chance to try out some approaches to your topic that you may later use to make your essay more compelling.
- *Consider visuals.* PowerPoint or Prezi (see http://prezi.com) presentations are great because they help you organize the talk. Also think about photographs, graphs, charts, and other visual ways to present your information.
- *Begin by stating your focusing question.* Every presentation should start by establishing what question is driving your investigation. You might even put this on the board when you begin.

> While you listen to your peers' presentations, think about what questions they raise that interest you. These might be questions of clarification, questions about an assertion the presenters or one of their sources made, or areas that the speakers didn't cover but that you wonder about. Imagine that you're a hard-nosed reporter anxious to get the story right.

■ *Reveal interesting patterns.* Scholars who study the differences between how experts and novices do research often notice this: Experienced researchers see patterns in data that novices don't notice. Experts *expect* patterns, and you should look for them, too. Does the information you find seem to tell a story? Does the most persuasive information suggest a particular answer to your research question? Are there relationships between facts, theories, or claims that surprise you? Are there any unexpected contradictions, causes, or connections? For example, in Figure 2.6, I've created a "word

FIGURE 2.6 Looking for Patterns

cloud" of the last 320 words you just read. A "word cloud" takes some text and creates an image that represents word frequency in the text. The visually bigger words are repeated more than the smaller ones. Note the pattern of emphasis on certain subjects and relationships— questions and information, relevance and research, change and focus. In a sense, when you develop focused knowledge on your topic, you gather a cloud of information much like this one, except richer and more complicated. Constantly analyze the relationships in what you're finding—what are the most frequent arguments, which ideas seem connected, what facts stick out?

What About a Thesis?

Ultimately, you must have a thesis, something you are saying about your research question. But when should you know what that is?

Are You Suspending Judgment?

Should you have a thesis at this point? That depends on the purpose of your project. If it's exploratory, if your motive is to discover what you think, then it's too early to make any bold statements that answer the question you're researching. It might even be counterproductive. Inquiry-based investigations depend on your willingness to *suspend judgment* long enough to discover what you think.

Are You Testing Assumptions?

If, however, you feel that you have developed some ideas about what you want to say, now might be an excellent time to make a list of your theories, assumptions, or beliefs about your topic. They will be invaluable guides for your research this week because you can examine these beliefs against the evidence and potentially break through to new understandings about your research question.

What Are You Arguing?

In some cases, you know what you think is the best answer to your research question even before you've done much investigation of the topic, and your motive is to build a convincing argument around that claim. For example, consider this claim: *Lawn mowers make a significant contribution to CO_2 emissions in the United States.* Maybe this is something you heard or read somewhere from a reputable source, and it's something you strongly suspect is true. Maybe your instructor asked you to make that argument, or you're writing an opinion piece for an assignment. Conventional research papers are frequently organized from the beginning around a thesis or claim. If that's the kind of project you're working on, now would be a good time to craft a sentence that states your most important assertion or main idea. This may well be refined or even discarded later on as you learn more, but it will help with your research this week.

To generate a *tentative* thesis statement at this point, try finishing one of the following sentences:

1. While most people think _____ about _____, I think _____.
2. The most convincing answer to my research question is _____.
3. The main reason that _____ is a problem is _____, and the best solution is _____.
4. Among the causes of _____, the least understood is _____.
5. Though much has been said about _____, very little attention has been paid to _____.
6. All of the evidence so far about _____ points to _____ as a significant cause/solution/effect/problem/interpretation/factor.

You'll be implementing your research strategy this week and next, looking at sources in the library and on the Web. The exercises that follow will help guide these searches, making sure that you don't overlook some key source or reference. Your instructor may ask you to hand in a photocopy of the exercise as a record of your journey.

Keeping Track of What You Find: Developing a Bibliography

For the next two weeks, you're going to collect a lot of material on your research question: PDF copies of articles, books, bookmarked Web pages, images, and perhaps even audio and video files. You will make your life easier if you don't just collect but *record* what you find. Your options include the following:

■ *Basic bibliography.* This is the minimalist approach. You simply keep a running list, using the appropriate citation method, of information on each source you think you'll use in your essay. If you're using MLA, for example, this will become your Works Cited page. An online citation machine, like bibme (http://www.bibme.org) can help you build it. You can, of course, wait until the last minute to do this but, trust me, you will regret it.

■ *Working bibliography.* This is one step up from the basic bibliography (see Figure 2.7) and is the simplest form of what's called an "annotated bibliography." A working bibliography provides a brief

---

Topic: Theories of Dog Training
Focusing Question: Should dogs be trained using positive reinforcement exclusively?

1. Katz, Jon. "Why Dog Training Fails." *Slate Magazine.*
   N.p. 14 Jan. 2005. Web. 22 Dec. 2010. Web.
      Katz argues that most theories of dog training fail to take into account the realities of raising an animal in a "split-level," not a training compound. He calls his own method the "Rational Theory," which he describes as an "amalgam" of techniques that takes into account the actual situation of both dog and owner.
2. Schilder, Matthijs B. H., and Joanne A.M. van der Borg.
   "Training Dogs with the Help of the Shock Collar: Short and Long Term Behavioural Effects." *Applied Animal Behaviour Science* 85 (2004): 319–334. Medline. Web. 23 Dec. 2010.
      Researchers had two groups of German shepherds, one training with shock collars and the other training without them. They then studied both "direct reactions" of dogs to the shock and their later behavior. Study found that dogs trained with shock collars consistently showed more signs of stress during and after training, including "lower ear positions." Finding "suggests that the welfare of these shocked dogs is at stake, at least in the presence of their owner."
3. Shore, Elise, Charles Burdsal, and Deanna Douglas. "Pet Owners' Views of Pet Behavior Problems and Willingness to Consult Experts for Assistance." *Journal of Applied Animal Welfare Science.* 11.1 (2008): 63–73. Print.
      Study notes that 30 percent of dogs that are given to shelters are there because owners complained of behavior problems; yet only 24 percent of owners surveyed enrolled in obedience classes. Researchers surveyed 170 dog and cat owners and determined that the highest concern was about animals who threatened people, and those owners were most likely to ask for assistance and they mostly turned to the Web unless there was a charge.

FIGURE 2.7   Working Bibliography: An Example

summary of what the source says: what topics it covers and what the basic argument or main ideas are. If you're using a double-entry journal, then you can find the material you need for your summary there. Your annotation may be a brief paragraph or more, depending on the source.

■ *Evaluative bibliography.* In some ways, this is the most useful annotated bibliography of all because it challenges you to not only "say back" what you understand sources to be saying but also to offer some judgments about whether you find them persuasive or relevant. You might comment on what you consider the strengths of the source or its weaknesses. Is writing an evaluative bibliography more work? You bet. But ultimately you are writing your paper as you go because much of the material you generate for the bibliography can be exported right into your essay. Your double-entry journal provides the raw material for these annotations.

Your instructor will tell you what kind of bibliography you should build for this project, but at the very least you should consider maintaining a basic bibliography as you go. Put it on a "cloud," like Google Docs or Evernote, that will store your draft bibliography on the Web and always be available wherever you find a new source—in the library, at home, or in the campus computer lab.

Searching Library Databases for Books and Articles

Despite the appeal of the Web, the campus library remains your most important source of information for academic research. Sure, it can be aggravating. There's that missing book that was supposed to be there or that article that isn't available in full text. You needed that article. Most of all, there's the sense of helplessness you might feel as a relative novice using a large, complicated, and unfamiliar reference system.

In this chapter and the last one, you were introduced to basic library search strategies, knowledge that will help give you some mastery over the university library. Now you'll expand on that knowledge, and at the same time you'll move from a working knowledge of your topic to a deeper understanding, one that will crystallize by reading and writing about what you find.

It's hard for newcomers to the university to fully appreciate the revolution the last decade brought to how we do college research. All you need to know, really, is that finding sources is infinitely easier. And with the growing availability of full-text PDFs of articles, you can end a session of searching with not just a citation but also the printout of the article.

You can't click a mouse and get a digital copy of a book—yet—but with one search you can scour the world, rather just your library, for books on your topic. If the book you want is in a library across the country, you can spend 60 seconds filling out an interlibrary loan form online (see "Interlibrary Loan" on page 78) and get the book you want—often in just a few days.

Find the book you want in your university library the old fashioned way: Journey into the "stacks," which at big schools can be cavernous floor-to-ceiling aisles of books. The trip is well worth it because even if you discover that the book you want isn't right for your project, that book is surrounded by 100 others on your topic or related ones. Browse like you do on Amazon.

You will save time if you know *where* to look for the book you want, and so you must be familiar with how librarians organize books.

Finding Books

There are two systems for classifying books: the Dewey Decimal and the Library of Congress systems. They are quite different. The Dewey system, reportedly conceived in 1873 by an Amherst College undergraduate while daydreaming in church, is numerical, dividing all knowledge into 10 broad areas and further subdividing each of these into 100 additional classifications. Adding decimal points allows librarians to subdivide things even further. Just knowing the *call number* of a book will tell you its subject.

The Library of Congress system, which uses both letters and numbers, is much more common in college libraries. This is the system with which you should become most familiar. Each call number begins with one or two letters, signifying a category of knowledge, which is followed by a whole number between 1 and 9,999. A decimal and one or more Cutter numbers sometimes follow. The Library of Congress system is pretty complex, but it's not hard to use. As you get deeper in your research, you'll begin to recognize call numbers that consistently yield useful books. It is sometimes helpful to simply browse those shelves for other possibilities.

Understanding Call Numbers

The call number, that strange code on the spine of a library book, is something most of us want to understand just well enough to find that book on the shelf. How much do you need to know? First, you should know that there is more than just the alphabet at work in arranging books by their call numbers, and the call numbers tell you more than merely where books are shelved. For example, here's the call number for *The Curious Researcher*:

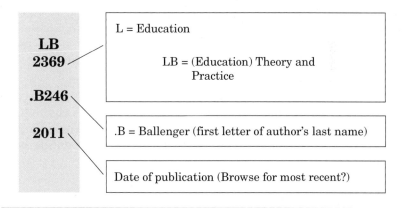

LB
2369

L = Education

LB = (Education) Theory and Practice

.B246

2011

.B = Ballenger (first letter of author's last name)

Date of publication (Browse for most recent?)

FIGURE 2.8   **Deciphering the Call Number Code**

The call number shown in Figure 2.8 tells you the subject area of the book, a little something about its author, and when the book was published. This is useful to know not only because it will help you find the book, but it also might prompt you to find other, possibly more recent, books on the same subject on a nearby shelf. In Figure 2.9, you can see how Library of Congress call numbers determine the arrangement of books on the shelf.

Coming Up Empty Handed?

In the unlikely event that you can't find any books by searching directly using the online catalog, there's another reference you can check that will help locate relevant articles and essays that are *a part* of a book whose title may otherwise seem unpromising. Check to see if your library has a database called the Essay and General Literature Index. Search that database with your keywords or subject and see if it produces something useful. List the relevant results as instructed previously. In addition, Google Book Search

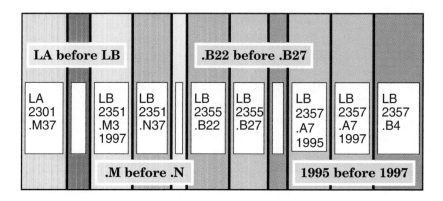

FIGURE 2.9   **How Books Are Arranged on the Library Shelf**

(http://books.google.com) allows users to do full-text searches of many titles. Those books in the public domain (i.e., the rights have lapsed) are available to any user in digital versions. This is a particularly rich resource for older texts, including some dating back hundreds of years.

Checking Bibliographies

One tactic that might lead to a mother lode of sources for your essay is to look at the bibliographies at the back of (mostly) scholarly books (and articles). Don't ever set aside a promising book until you've checked the bibliography! Jot down complete bibliographic information from citations you want to check out later. Keep a running list of these in your research notebook.

Interlibrary Loan

If your library doesn't have the book (or article) you really want, don't despair. Most college libraries have a wonderful low- or no-cost service to students called interlibrary loan. The library will search the collections of other libraries to find what you're looking for and have it sent, sometimes within a week or less. Use the service by checking with the reference desk or your library's Web site.

Article Databases

There are two kinds of article databases at your library: general subject databases that cover multiple disciplines and specialized databases that are discipline specific. Of course, I don't know which of these general databases you have at your library, but here are some of the most common:

GENERAL SUBJECT DATABASES

Academic OneFile

Academic Search

Academic Search Premier

ArticleFirst

IngentaConnect

JSTOR

ProQuest Central

Web of Science

Many of these multidisciplinary databases index popular magazines and some newspapers, and even some scholarly journals, which makes them very useful. For example, Academic Search Premier indexes nearly 8,000 magazines and journals. Increasingly, these databases include full-text articles, an extraordinary convenience for students working from home.

Specialized databases are subject specific. These are usually listed by discipline on your library's Web pages. The advantage of using these databases is that they will produce many more scholarly articles that might be relevant to your research question, though they may not all be full text. For a list of some of these, see the following table.

COMMON SPECIALIZED DATABASES

HUMANITIES	SCIENCE AND TECHNOLOGY	SOCIAL SCIENCES
America, History and Life	AGRICOLA (Agriculture)	Anthropological Index
Arts and Humanities Citation Index	Applied Science & Technology Index	ComAbstracts (Communication)
Historical Abstracts	Biological Abstracts	Contemporary Women's Issues
Humanities Index	CINAHL (Nursing)	Criminal Justice Abstracts
Literature Resource Center	Computer Literature Index	PAIS (Public Affairs)
MLA International Bibliography (Literature and composition)	GeoRef (Geology) Abstracts	PsycINFO
	Health Reference Center	Social Sciences Index
		Social Work
		Sociological Abstracts

(*continued*)

HUMANITIES	SCIENCE AND TECHNOLOGY	SOCIAL SCIENCES
Music Index	MathSciNet	Worldwide Political
Project Muse	Medline (Medicine)	Science Abstracts
Religion and	Web of Science	
Philosophical		
Collection		

BUSINESS	EDUCATION
ABI/Inform	Education Full Text
Business Source Elite	Education Index
FreeEDGAR	ERIC

Finally, certain article databases are focused on certain *types* of publications. The most important of these are indexes to newspapers (see following list, "Newspaper Databases"). They don't index the small-town papers, but they do provide citations to the so-called national newspapers such as the *New York Times,* the *Washington Post,* the *Los Angeles Times,* the *Wall Street Journal,* and the *Christian Science Monitor.* What's good about the national newspapers is that they're among the most authoritative journalistic sources; in other words, because of their large and experienced staffs, the information they provide is more trustworthy than smaller newspapers and online news outlets.

If you're looking for state or local newspapers you have a couple of options. The larger papers (and many magazines, for that matter) also have their own Web sites where you may be able to search their archives and retrieve full-text articles. Some sites charge for this service, though you can usually request them from your campus library for free. A convenient method for searching some of these sites is to use a news search engine that will consult thousands of papers in a few seconds. Two of the best of these search engines are Google News (http://news.google.com) and Yahoo News (http://news.yahoo.com).

Occasionally, the local papers are also indexed online by the university library, and copies are available on microfilm. More and more frequently, however, local papers, like their larger counterparts in major cities, have their own Web sites where you can use keyword searches to scour their archives.

NEWSPAPER DATABASES

Alternative Press Index

Ethnic Newswatch

LexisNexis Academic

National Newspaper Index

National Newspapers
Newspaper Source
ProQuest Central

Saving Search Results

Most online book indexes and article databases allow you to save your search results. Some of these databases allow you to mark the relevant results and then print them out. Some databases and most university libraries also allow you to create an account and a file for your search results. Through the Web page at my library, I can save searches, build a list of books I want to check out, and even publish my bibliographies so others can see them (and I can see theirs). Finally, you can always e-mail your search results page to yourself and organize a bibliography on your own computer.

EXERCISE 2.1

Search Book and Article Databases

Develop your focused knowledge by doing a thorough search using your library's book index and article databases. Unlike in Web and database searches, in book searches it often pays off to begin with broad subject terms. I got better results, for example, when I searched for books on theories of dog training with *animal behavior-canine* than I did with *dog training theories.* Searches that begin broadly might lead you to a relevant chapter in an otherwise irrelevant book.

Choose one of the bibliographies (see pages 73–75) as a way of collecting relevant results. Your instructor may ask you to hand these in to gauge your progress. Remember that online citation machines like bibme.org can help you compile these results in the appropriate format (MLA or APA).

Advanced Internet Research Techniques

I love the word "portal." It summons images of a little window on some vast spaceship that frames the face of an open-mouthed observer looking in wonder at the vast reaches of the universe beyond. Researching on the Internet is a lot like peeping out of that window. There is just so much out there: billions of documents, gazillions of words, each a fragment of electronic data floating in cyberspace, like dust motes in some vast sunbeam. There's useful knowledge for academic writing out there, but it's hard to find and it's easy to get lost.

You're no stranger to the Web, of course, but now, more than ever, your research on the Internet needs to be *efficient*. You need fewer, more focused results and better-quality results. To get these, you need to amp up your Internet search skills by understanding the differences among search engines and what each can do to maximize your penetration of information on the Web.

Types of Search Engines

The most popular search engine is Google, a search engine with an enormous database that is relatively simple to use. It's easy to forget sometimes that Google is in good company; there are plenty of powerful alternatives that may generate some different results. In fact, a recent study showed that each search engine produced unique results *more than 80 percent* of the time.* It obviously pays off for researchers to use more than one.

Here's a partial list of the best of these general research engines.

POPULAR GENERAL SEARCH ENGINES

AltaVista (http://www.altavista.com)

Ask.com (http://www.ask.com)

Bing (http://www.bing.com)

Google (http://www.google.com)

Hotbot (http://www.hotbot.com)

Lycos (http://www.lycos.com)

Yahoo! Search (http://search.yahoo.com)

Google and the others are really quite amazing, but they do have limitations. For one thing, they only index pages on the Web that have hyperlinks pointing to them elsewhere or whose creators have requested they be indexed by a particular search tool. In addition, these databases may not be current.

There are so-called metasearch tools such as Dogpile (http://www.dogpile.com/) that are able to deploy multiple general search engines in the service of a single search (see the following list). These are very useful, particularly at the beginning of an Internet

*"Different Engines, Different Results." *Dogpile.com.* Dogpile. Apr. 2007. Web. 1–26. 4 Jan. 2011.

search on your topic. However, metasearch engines aren't quite as good as they sound because they skim off the top results from each individual search tool so you won't see the range of results you would get if you focus on one of the search engines with its own large database.

METASEARCH ENGINES

Dogpile (http://www.dogpile.com)

Mamma (http://www.mamma.com)

Search.com (http://www.search.com)

SurfWax (http://www.surfwax.com)

Yippy (http://yippy.com)

Finally, there are also specialized search engines (sometimes called "vertical" search engines) that focus on particular subjects such as education, politics, and psychology, as well as search engines that specialize in searching certain *kinds* of content, like finding people, images, blogs, and so on. You probably already use a specialized search engine (and might not know it) when you use a site like Pricegrabber (http://www.pricegrabber.com) to comparison shop online. In the last chapter, you were also introduced to Google Scholar, another example of a search portal that focuses on specialized content, in this case journal articles. There are so many of these that a list—even if it's selective—wouldn't do justice to these focused Web crawlers. One place to visit online to help you find a relevant specialized search engine for your project is Noodletools (http://www. noodletools.com/).

What are the keys to maximizing the efficiency of your Internet research? In the exercise that follows, you'll learn to do the following:

1. Increase your coverage by using multiple search engines, not just your favorite one.
2. If possible, exploit subject directories that allow you to drill down from general to more specific topic categories. These are often put together by people—not software—who are concerned with quality content.
3. Be thoughtful about what and how many keywords you use to search. Generally, the more words—and especially phrases— you use, the more likely you are to generate relevant hits. This contrasts with searching library databases, which respond better to more focused keywords and phrases.

EXERCISE 2.2

Academic Research on the Internet

STEP 1: You already searched on your topic on a general search engine—probably Google—and in the last chapter you tried Google Scholar. Now, using some of the keyword combinations you developed for your topic, try at least two more general search engines from the list on page 82. Remember to play around with keywords, and don't forget the search language you learned earlier in this chapter. The Help button on whatever metasearch tool you use will give you the specifics on what connectors—Boolean or others—it accepts.

STEP 2: Launch a search on one or more of the metasearch engines listed on page 83. Save your relevant results.

STEP 3: Finally, visit Noodletools (http://www.noodletools.com/) and find the link for "Choose the Best Search." Scroll down and find a search engine, perhaps a specialized one, that you haven't tried yet. As before, save relevant results.

STEP 4: Add to your bibliography (see "Keeping Track of What You Find" on page 73) by including Web pages that seem promising, and print copies of them for notetaking. A Web-based citation machine like bibme.org can help you with this.

Living Sources: Interviews and Surveys

Arranging Interviews

A few years ago, I researched a local turn-of-the-century writer named Sarah Orne Jewett for a magazine article. I dutifully read much of her work, studied critical articles and books on her writing, and visited her childhood home, which is open to the public in South Berwick, Maine. My research was going fairly well, but when I sat down to begin writing the draft, the material seemed flat and lifeless. A few days later, the curator of the Jewett house mentioned that there was an 88-year-old local woman, Elizabeth Goodwin, who had known the writer when she was alive. "As far as I know, she's the last living person who knew Sarah Orne Jewett," the curator told me. "And she lives just down the street."

The next week, I spent three hours with Elizabeth Goodwin, who told me of coming for breakfast with the famous author and eating strawberry jam and muffins. Elizabeth told me that many years after Jewett's death, the house seemed haunted by her friendly presence. One time, when Elizabeth lived in the Jewett house as a curator, some unseen hands pulled her back as she teetered at the top of the steep staircase in the back of the house. She likes to believe it was the author's ghost.

This interview transformed the piece by bringing the subject to life—first for me as the writer, and later for my readers. Ultimately, what makes almost any topic compelling is discovering why it matters to *people*—how it affects their lives. Doing interviews with people close to the subject, both experts and nonexperts, is often the best way to find that out.

If you'd like to do some interviews, now is the time to begin arranging them.

Finding Experts

You may be hesitant to consider finding authorities on your topic to talk to because, after all, you're just a lowly student who knows next to nothing. How could you possibly impose on that sociology professor who published the book on anti-Semitism you found in the library? If that's how you feel, keep this in mind: *Most people, no matter who they are, love the attention of an interviewer, no matter who she is, particularly if what's being discussed fascinates them both.* Time and again, I've found my own shyness creep up on me when I pick up the telephone to arrange an interview. But almost invariably, when I start talking with my interview subject, the experience is great for us both.

How do you find experts to interview?

■ *Check your sources.* As you begin to collect books, articles, and Internet documents, note their authors and affiliations. I get calls from time to time from writers who come across my book on lobsters in the course of their research and discover that I am at Boise State University. Sometimes the caller will arrange a phone interview or, if he lives within driving distance, a personal interview.

■ *Check the phone book.* The familiar Yellow Pages can be a gold mine. Carin, who was writing a paper on solar energy, merely looked under that heading and found a local dealer who sold solar systems to homeowners. Mark, who was investigating the effects of sexual abuse on children, found a counselor who specialized in treating abuse victims.

■ *Ask your friends and your instructors.* Your roommate's boyfriend's father may be a criminal attorney who has lots to say about the insanity defense for your paper on that topic. Your best friend may be taking a photography course with a professor who would be a great interview for your paper on the work of Edward Weston. One of your instructors may know other faculty working in your subject area who would do an interview.

■ *Check the faculty directory.* Many universities publish an annual directory of faculty and their research interests. On my campus, it's called the *Directory of Research and Scholarly Activities.* From it, I know, for example, that two professors at my university have expertise in eating disorders, a popular topic with student researchers.

■ *Check the* Encyclopedia of Associations. This is a wonderful reference book that lists organizations with interests ranging from promoting tofu to preventing acid rain. Each listing includes the name of the group, its address and phone number, a list of its publications, and a short description of its purpose. Sometimes such organizations can direct you to experts in your area who are available for live interviews or to spokespeople who are happy to provide phone interviews.

■ *Check the Internet.* You can find the e-mail addresses and phone numbers of many scholars and researchers on the Internet, including those affiliated with your own university and ones nearby. Often, these experts are listed in online directories for their colleges or universities. Sometimes you can find knowledgeable people by subscribing to a listserv or Internet discussion group on your topic. Often an expert will have her own Web page, and her e-mail address will provide a hypertext link. (For more details, see "Finding People on the Internet," later in this chapter on page 90.)

Finding Nonexperts Affected by Your Topic

The distinction between *expert* and *nonexpert* is tricky. For example, someone who lived through 12 months of combat in Vietnam certainly has direct knowledge of the subject, though probably hasn't published an article about the war in *Foreign Affairs.* Similarly, a friend who experienced an abusive relationship with her boyfriend or overcame a drug addiction is, at least in a sense, an authority on abuse or addiction. Both individuals would likely provide invaluable interviews for papers on those topics. The voices and the stories of people who are affected by the topic you're writing about can do more than anything else to make the information come to life, even if they don't have PhDs.

You may already know people you can interview about your topic. Last semester, Amanda researched how mother-daughter relationships change when a daughter goes to college. She had no problem finding other women anxious to talk about how they get along with their mothers. A few years ago, Dan researched steroid use by student athletes. He discreetly asked his friends if they knew anyone who had taken the drugs. It turned out that an acquaintance of Dan's had used the drugs regularly and was happy to talk about his experience.

If you don't know people to interview, try posting notices on campus kiosks or bulletin boards. For example, "I'm doing a research project and interested in talking to people who grew up in single-parent households. Please call 555-9000." Also, poll other students in your class for ideas about people you might interview for your paper. Help each other out.

Making Contact

By the end of this week, you should have some people to contact for interviews. First, consider whether to ask for a face-to face, telephone, or e-mail interview. Though I've never tried it for this purpose, Skype, the free online software that allows users to make a video call anywhere in the world, might be a great interview tool. The personal interview is almost always preferable; you not only can listen, but you can watch, observing your subject's gestures and the setting, both of which can be revealing. When I'm interviewing someone in her office or home, for example, one of the first things I may jot down are the titles of books on the bookshelf. Sometimes, details about gestures and settings can be worked into your paper. Most of all, the personal interview is preferable because it's more natural, more like a conversation.

Be prepared. You may have no choice in the type of interview. If your subject is off campus or out of state, your only options may be the telephone, e-mail, or regular mail.

When contacting a subject for an interview, first state your name and then briefly explain your research project. If you were referred to the subject by someone she may know, mention that. A comment like "I think you could be extremely helpful to me," or "I'm familiar with your work, and I'm anxious to talk to you about it," works well. When thinking about when to propose the interview with an expert on your topic, consider arranging it *after* you've done some research. You will not only be more informed, but you will also have a clearer sense of what you want to know and what questions to ask.

Conducting Interviews

You've already thought about whether interviews might contribute to your paper. If there's a chance that they will, build a list of possible interview subjects and contact several of them. By the end of this week, you should begin interviewing.

I know. You wouldn't mind putting it off. But once you start, it will get easier and easier. I used to dread interviewing strangers, but after making the first phone call, I got some momentum going, and I began to enjoy it. It's decidedly easier to interview friends, family, and acquaintances, but that's the wrong reason to limit yourself to people you know.

Whom to Interview?   Interview people who can provide you with what you want to know. That may change as your research develops. In your reading, you might have encountered the names of experts you'd like to contact, or you may have decided that what you really need is some anecdotal material from someone with experience in your topic. It's still not too late to contact interview subjects who didn't occur to you earlier, but do so immediately.

What Questions to Ask?   The first step in preparing for an interview is to ask yourself, What's the purpose of this interview? In your research notebook, make a list of *specific questions* for each person you're going to interview. Often, these questions are raised by your reading or other interviews. What theories or ideas encountered in your reading would you like to ask your subject about? What specific facts have you been unable to uncover that your interview subject may provide? What don't you understand that he could explain? Would you like to test one of your own impressions or ideas on your subject? What about the subject's work or experience would you like to learn? Interviews are wonderful tools for clearing up your own confusion and getting specific information that is unavailable anywhere else.

Now make a list of more *open-ended questions* you might ask some or all of the people you're going to talk to. Frankly, these questions are a lot more fun to ask because you're likely to be surprised by some of the answers. For example:

- In all your experience with _____, what has most surprised you?
- What has been the most difficult aspect of your work?
- If you had the chance to change something about how you approached _____, what would it be?
- Can you remember a significant moment in your work on _____? Is there an experience with _____ that stands out in your mind?
- What do you think is the most common misconception about _____? Why?
- What are significant current trends in _____?
- Who or what has most influenced you? Who are your heroes?

- If you had to summarize the most important thing you've learned about _____, what would it be?
- What is the most important thing other people should know or understand?

As you develop both specific and open-ended questions, keep in mind what you know about each person—his work in the field and personal experience with your topic. You may end up asking a lot of the same questions of everybody you interview, but try to familiarize yourself with any special qualifications a subject may have or experiences he may have had. That knowledge might come from your reading, from what other people tell you about your subject, or from your initial telephone call to set up the interview.

Also keep in mind the *kinds* of information an interview can provide better than other sources: anecdotes, strong quotes, and sometimes descriptive material. If you ask the right questions, a live subject can paint a picture of his experience with your topic, and you can capture that picture in your paper.

During the Interview. Once you've built a list of questions, be prepared to ignore it. Interviews are conversations, not surveys. They are about human interaction between two people who are both interested in the same thing.

I remember interviewing a lobsterman, Edward Heaphy, on his boat. I had a long list of questions in my notebook, which I dutifully asked, one after the other. My questions were mechanical and so were his answers. I finally stopped, put my notebook down, and talked informally with Edward for a few minutes. Offhandedly, I asked, "Would you want your sons or daughter to get in the business?" It was a totally unplanned question. Edward was silent for a moment, staring at his hands. I knew he was about to say something important because, for the first time, I was attentive to him, not my notepad. "Too much work for what they get out of it," he said quietly. It was a surprising remark after hearing for the last hour how much Edward loved lobstering. What's more, I felt I had broken through. The rest of the interview went much better.

Much of how to conduct an interview is common sense. At the outset, clarify the nature of your project—what your paper is on and where you're at with it. Briefly explain again why you thought this individual would be the perfect person to talk to about it. I find it often helps to begin with a specific question that I'm pretty sure my subject can help with. But there's no formula. Simply be a good conversationalist: Listen attentively, ask questions that your subject seems to find interesting, and enjoy sharing an interest with your subject. Also, don't be afraid to ask what you fear are obvious questions. Demonstrate to the subject that you *really* want to understand.

Always end an interview by making sure you have accurate background information on your subject: name (spelled correctly), position, affiliation, age (if applicable), phone number. Ask if you can call him with follow-up questions, should you have any. And always ask your subject if he can recommend any additional reading or other people you should talk to. Of course, mention that you're appreciative of the time he has spent with you.

Notetaking.   There are basically three ways to take notes during an interview: Use a digital recorder, a notepad, or both. I adhere to the third method, but it's a very individual choice. I like digital recorders because I don't panic during an interview that I'm losing information or quoting inaccurately. I don't want to spend hours transcribing interviews, so I also take notes on the information I think I want to use. If I miss anything, I consult the recording later. It's a backup. Sometimes, I find that there is no recording—the machine decided not to participate in the interview—and at least I have my notes. Again, a backup.

Get some practice developing your own notetaking technique by interviewing your roommate or taking notes on the television news. Devise ways to shorten often-used words (e.g., *t* for *the, imp* for *important,* and *w/o* for *without*).

The E-mail Interview

The Internet opens up new possibilities for interviews; increasingly, experts (as well as nonexperts interested in certain subjects) are accessible through e-mail and even Facebook. While electronic communication doesn't quite approach the conversational quality of the conventional face-to-face interview, the spontaneous nature of e-mail exchanges can come pretty close. It's possible to send a message, get a response, respond to the response, and get a further response—all in a single day. And for shy interviewers and interviewees, an e-mail conversation is an attractive alternative.

Finding People on the Internet.   Finding people on the Internet doesn't have to involve a needle and hay if you have some information on the person for whom you're looking. If you know an expert's name and his organizational affiliation, several search tools may help you track down his e-mail address. You can, of course, Google the person. But there are other methods, too.

For example, an easy way to use the Internet to find someone to interview is through a Web document on your topic. These often include e-mail links to people associated with the site or document. You can also find academics by visiting the Web sites of the universities or colleges where they teach and use the online faculty/staff directories to find their addresses. If you don't know the institutions with which an academic is affiliated, you can often find these listed in their articles, books, or Web page. To find the home pages of hundreds of American universities and colleges, visit the following site: The Yahoo Education Directory (http://dir.yahoo.com/Education/). This search page allows you to find the home pages of universities in the United States. It includes links to a number of sites that also index colleges and universities, as well as their various programs.

Making Contact by E-mail.   Once you find the e-mail address of someone who seems a likely interview subject, proceed courteously and cautiously. One of the Internet's haunting issues is its potential to violate privacy. Be especially careful if you've gone to great lengths in hunting down the e-mail address of someone involved with your research topic; she may not be keen on receiving unsolicited e-mail messages from strangers. It would be courteous to approach any potential interview subject with a short message that asks permission for an online interview. To do so, briefly describe your project and why you think this individual might be a good source for you. As always, you will be much more likely to get an enthusiastic response from someone if you can demonstrate your knowledge of her work on or experience with your topic.

Let's assume your initial contact has been successful and your subject has agreed to answer your questions. Your follow-up message should ask a *limited* number of questions—say, four or five—that are thoughtful and, if possible, specific. Keep in mind that while the e-mail interview is conducted in writing rather than through talking, many of the methods for handling conventional interviews still apply.

The Discussion Board and Listserv Interview.   Discussion or message boards can be good places to find people—and sometimes experts— who are passionately interested in your research topic or question. How do you find one that might be relevant to your project? Try visiting one of the following directories that list these sites by subject.

SEARCH ENGINES FOR DISCUSSION GROUPS

BoardReader (http://boardreader.com)

BoardTracker (http://www.boardtracker.com)

Google Groups (http://groups.google.com)

Yahoo! Groups (http://groups.yahoo.com)

A way to get some help with knowing what to ask—and what not to—is to spend some time following the discussion of list participants before you jump in yourself. You might find, for example, that it would be far better to interview one participant with interesting views than to post questions to the whole list.

But if you do want to query the discussion board, avoid posting a question that may have already received substantial attention from participants. You can find out what's been covered by consulting the list's FAQs (frequently asked questions). The issue you're interested in may be there, along with a range of responses from list participants, which will spare you the need to ask the question at all.

Planning Informal Surveys

Christine was interested in dream interpretation, especially exploring the significance of symbols or images that recur in many people's dreams. She could have simply examined her own dreams, but she thought it might be more interesting to survey a group of fellow students, asking how often they dream and what they remember. An informal survey, in which she would ask each person several standard questions, seemed worth trying.

You might consider it, too, if the responses of a group of people to some aspect of your topic could reveal a pattern of behavior, attitudes, or experiences worth analyzing. Informal surveys are decidedly unscientific. You probably won't get a large enough sample size, nor do you likely have the skills to design a poll that would produce statistically reliable results. But you probably won't actually base your paper on the survey results, anyway. Rather, you'll present specific, concrete information about some patterns in your survey group or, perhaps, use some of your findings to help support your assertions.

Defining Goals and Audience

Begin planning your informal survey by defining what you want to know and whom you want to know it from. Christine suspected that many students have dreams related to stress. She wondered if there were any similarities among students' dreams. She was also curious about how many people remember their dreams and how often and whether this might be related to gender. Finally, Christine wanted to find out whether people have recurring dreams and, if so, what those were about. There were other things she wanted to know, but she knew she had to keep the survey short.

If you're considering a survey, make a list in your research notebook of things you might want to find out and specify the group of people you plan to talk to. College students? Female college students? Attorneys? Guidance counselors? Be as specific as you can about your target group.

Types of Questions

Next, consider what approach you will take. Will you ask *open-ended questions,* which give respondents plenty of room to invent their own answers? For example, Christine might ask, *Describe any dreams that seemed related to stress.* The payoff for open-ended questions is that sometimes you get surprising answers. The danger, which seems real with Christine's question, is that you'll get no answer at all. A more *directed question* might be, *Have you ever dreamed that you showed up for class and didn't know that there was a major exam that day?* Christine will get an answer to this question—yes or no—but it doesn't promise much information. A third possibility is the *multiple-choice question.* It ensures an answer and is likely to produce useful information. For example:

Have you ever had any dreams similar to these?

A. You showed up for a class and didn't know there was a major exam.
B. You're late for a class or an exam but can't seem to move fast enough to get there on time.
C. You were to give a presentation but forgot all about it.

Ultimately, Christine decided to combine the open-ended question about stress and the multiple-choice approach, hoping that if one didn't produce interesting information, the other would (see Figure 2.10). She also wisely decided to avoid asking more than seven questions, allowing her subjects to respond to her survey in minutes.

Survey Design

A survey shouldn't be too long (probably no more than six or seven questions), it shouldn't be biased (questions asked shouldn't skew the answers), it should be easy to score (especially if you hope to survey a relatively large number of people), it should ask clear questions, and it should give clear instructions for how to answer.

As a rule, informal surveys should begin (or end) as polls often do: by getting vital information about the respondent. Christine's survey began with questions about the gender, age, and major of the respondent (see Figure 2.10). Depending on the purpose of your survey, you might also want to know whether respondents are registered to vote, whether they have political affiliations, what year of school

The following survey contains questions about dreaming and dream content. The findings gathered from this survey will be incorporated into a research paper on the function of dreaming and what, if anything, we can learn from it. I'd appreciate your honest answers to the questions. Thank you for your time!

General Subject Information

Gender: ☐ Male   ☐ Female
Age: _____
Major: _____

Survey Questions
(Circle all letters that apply.)

1. How often do you remember your dreams?
   A. Almost every night
   B. About once a week
   C. Every few weeks
   D. Practically never
2. Have you ever dreamt that you were:
   A. Falling?
   B. Flying?
3. Have you ever dreamt of:
   A. Your death?
   B. The death of someone close to you?
4. Have you ever had a recurring dream?
   A. Yes
   B. No
   If yes,   How often? _____
                  What period of your life? _____
                  Do you still have it? _____
5. Have you ever had any dreams similar to these?
   A. You showed up for a class and didn't know there was a major exam.
   B. You're late for a class or an exam but can't seem to move fast enough to get there.
   C. You were to give a presentation but forgot all about it.
6. Do you feel your dreams:
   A. Hold some deep, hidden meanings about yourself or your life?
   B. Are meaningless?
7. Please briefly describe the dream you best remember or one that sticks out in your mind. (Use the back of this survey.)

FIGURE 2.10   Sample Informal Survey
Source: Reprinted with permission of Christine Bergquist.

they're in, or any number of other factors. Ask for information that provides different ways of breaking down your target group.

Avoid Loaded Questions. Question design is tricky business. Biased questions should be avoided by altering language that is charged and presumptuous. Take, for example, the question *Do you think it's morally wrong to kill unborn babies through abortion?* This wording is charged and is also presumptuous (it is unlikely that all respondents believe that abortion is killing). One revision might be *Do you support or oppose providing women the option to abort a pregnancy during the first 20 weeks?* This is a direct and specific question, neutrally stated, that calls for a yes or no answer.

Controversial topics, like abortion, are most vulnerable to biased survey questions. If your topic is controversial, take great care to eliminate bias by avoiding charged language, especially if you have strong feelings yourself.

Avoid Vague Questions. Another trap is asking vague questions. One such question is *Do you support or oppose the university's alcohol policy?* This wording assumes that respondents know what the policy is, and it ignores the fact that the policy has many elements. A revised question might ask about one part of the policy: *The university recently established a policy that states that underage students caught drinking in campus dormitories are subject to eviction. Do you support or oppose this policy?* Other equally specific questions might ask about other parts of the policy.

Drawbacks of Open-Ended Questions. Open-ended questions often produce fascinating answers, but they can be difficult to tabulate. Christine's survey asked, *Please briefly describe the dream you best remember or one that sticks out in your mind.* She got a wide range of answers—or sometimes no answer at all—but it was hard to quantify the results. Almost everyone had different dreams, which made it difficult to discern much of a pattern. She was still able to use some of the material as anecdotes in her paper, so it turned out to be a question worth asking.

Designing Your Multiple-Choice Questions. As you've seen, the multiple-choice question is an alternative to the open-ended question, leaving room for a number of *limited* responses, which are easier to quantify.

The challenge in designing multiple-choice questions is to provide choices that will likely produce results. From her reading and talking to friends, Christine came up with what she thought were three stress-related dreams college students often experience (see question 5, Figure 2.10). The results were interesting (45 percent circled "B"). But Christine wasn't sure about their reliability because she hadn't given respondents a "none of the above" option. How many respondents felt forced to choose one of the dreams listed because there was no other choice? Design choices you think your audience will respond to, but give them room to say your choices weren't theirs.

Using Continuum Questions.   Christine's question 6 has a similar problem in that it asks a direct either/or question: *Do you feel your dreams: (A) Hold some deep, hidden meanings about yourself or your life?* or *(B) Are meaningless?* Phrased this way, the question forces the respondent into one of two extreme positions. People are more likely to place themselves somewhere in between.

A variation on the multiple-choice question is the *continuum,* where respondents indicate how they feel by marking the appropriate place along a scale. Christine's question 6 could be presented as a continuum:

> How do you evaluate the significance of your dreams? Place an "X" on the continuum in the place that most closely reflects your view.

> My dreams always   My dreams are
> hold some meaning   meaningless

Though it is a bit more difficult to tabulate results of a continuum, this method often produces reliable answers if the instructions are clear.

Conducting Surveys

Once you have finalized your questions, using whatever combination of *open-ended, multiple choice,* and *directed* questions you found most appropriate for your purpose, you can make plans to distribute the survey to the target group you defined earlier. Surveys can be administered by phone, in person, or online.

Telephone Surveys.   Surveys administered by telephone have some advantages. People are more likely to be direct and honest over the phone because they are relatively anonymous. Surveys are also more likely to be completed correctly because the answers are recorded by the survey giver. However, making multiple phone calls can be tedious and expensive, if your target group goes beyond the toll-free calling area. But you may have no choice, especially if the target group for your survey isn't exclusively on campus.

In-Person Surveys. One alternative to conducting a telephone survey is to distribute the survey yourself. The university community, where large numbers of people are available in a confined area, lends itself to administering surveys this way. A survey can be distributed in dormitories, dining halls, classes, or anywhere else the people you want to talk to gather. You can stand outside the student union and stop people as they come and go, or you can hand out your survey to groups of people and collect them when the participants have finished. Your instructor may be able to help distribute your survey to classes. I asked a number of my colleagues to distribute Christine's survey in their freshman English classes, a required course representing a relatively random sample of freshmen. Because the survey took only five minutes to fill out, other instructors were glad to help, and in one day Christine was able to sample more than 90 students.

Although an exclusively university audience won't always be relevant, for some research questions it is exactly what's needed. Anna, writing a paper on date rape, surveyed exclusively women on campus, many of whom she found in women's dormitories. For his paper on the future of the fraternity system, David surveyed local "Greeks" at their annual awards banquet.

How large a sample should you shoot for? Because yours won't be a scientific survey, don't bother worrying about statistical reliability; just try to survey as many people as you can. Certainly, a large (say, more than 100) and representative sample will lend more credence to your claims about any patterns observed in the results.

Internet Surveys. You can create an online survey easily using a program like SurveyMonkey (http://surveymonkey.com/). Such programs are remarkably easy to use, walking you through the process of designing questions, posting the survey, and even analyzing the results. For example, SurveyMonkey's free "basic" service will allow you to create a ten-question survey and collect up to 100 responses. You can then post the survey on your blog, send it out to an e-mail address list, or put a link to it on your Web site. The challenge, as usual, is reaching the people you'd like to survey and getting them to respond.

Listservs, discussion boards, and even real-time communication tools such as chat rooms all organize people with similar interests—and in some cases similar demographics. This makes cyberspace a potentially appealing place to conduct survey work. Consider, for example, posting three or four questions on your topic to a relevant discussion group or to a group that may reach an audience you'd like to survey. For example, Marty was working on an essay that explored the extent to which college students felt a generational identity. A search on Google Groups produced a Usenet group (alt.society.generation-x) that proved an ideal forum to respond to her questions.

Fieldwork: Research on What You See and Hear

My daughter Julia, a senior in high school, belonged to the school's theater group, performing in plays and taking theater classes. She enjoyed it. But she also claimed that certain qualities distinguished "theater kids" from other kinds. How did she come to these conclusions? By hanging out with the theater crowd. To use a more academic phrasing, Julia was a "participant-observer," though there was certainly no method involved. We all make judgments about social groups, inferences that come from experience. Usually there's nothing systematic about this process, and sometimes these judgments are unfair.

Yet the data that comes from observation, particularly if we take care to collect and document it, can be a rich vein to mine. This kind of data is also relevant to research in the social sciences and humanities and even relevant to research essays in composition courses. Suppose, for instance, that your research question focuses on comparing crowd behavior at college and high school football games. How can you research that essay *without* observing a few games? If your topic has anything do to with subcultures or social groups—say, international students on your campus or the snowboarding community—fieldwork can be invaluable.

Preparing for Fieldwork

The kind of fieldwork you're able to do for your essay simply won't be the more rigorous and methodologically sophisticated work that academic ethnographers, anthropologists, or sociologists do. For one thing, you don't have the time it requires. But you can collect some useful observations for your paper. There are three tools for this you might find useful:

1. *Notebook.* You can't do without this. For convenience, you might choose a pocket notebook rather than a full-size one.
2. *Digital camera.* Take pictures of the site you're observing and the people participating in an activity for later study. Also photograph

objects (ethnographers call these "artifacts") that have symbolic or practical significance to the people you're observing.
3. *Digital recorder.* Use it for interviews and other recording in the field. (Remember to ask permission to record interviewees.)

Where you go to conduct field observations of course depends on your topic. Typically you choose a physical space in which people in particular social or cultural groups meet to participate in meaningful (to them) activities. If your research is on the high school theater group as a subculture, you might go to rehearsals, auditions, or perhaps a cast party. A researcher interested in adult video gaming addiction might spend a few evenings watching gamers do their thing at someone's home. An essay on Kwanzaa, an African American holiday tradition, might observe some families participating in its rituals.

Notetaking Strategies

What do you look for and how do you document it? Well, that depends on your project. Generally, of course, the task is to watch what people do and listen to what they say. More specifically, though, consider the following:

■ *Look for evidence that confirms, contradicts, or qualifies the theories or assertions you've read about in your research.* Is it true that when they're not playing, adult video gamers can appear irritable and depressed? Do dogs that are punitively corrected during a training class demonstrate submissive behavior?

■ *Look and listen to what people say during moments with particular significance for participants.* How do fans behave when the referee doesn't call the foul? What does one gamer say to another when she beats him?

■ *Describe "artifacts"—things that people in the situation typically use.* A skater's skateboard. The objects in an actor's dressing room. The clothing traditionally worn by women celebrating Kwanzaa.

When you take notes, consider using the double-entry journal system that is discussed in detail in the next chapter. Use the left-facing page of your notebook to scribble your observations and the right-facing page to later freewrite about what strikes you about these observations. Make sure that you clearly indicate when you are quoting someone and when you are describing something.

Using What You See and Hear

Unless your research topic is an ethnography—an investigation that describes and interprets the activities of a cultural group in the field—it's likely that you will use your own fieldwork in your essay in a relatively limited way. Still, it can really be worth the effort. For example, fieldwork can be especially useful to:

- *Give your topic a face.* Nothing makes a problem or idea more meaningful than *showing* how it affects people. Can you use your descriptions of individuals (perhaps along with your interviews) to show rather than simply explain why your topic is significant?

- *Make a scene.* Observations in the field give you the ingredients of a scene: In a particular time and place, people are *doing something.* If what they are doing is significant and relevant to your research question, you can describe the place, the people, the action, and even the dialogue. Few techniques give writing more life.

- *Incorporate images.* Depending on the nature of your project, the digital pictures you take in the field can be powerful illustrations of what you're writing about.

- *Develop a multimodal research essay.* Using the digital recordings you made in the field, and free editing software like Audacity, you can create a podcast of your research essay, even incorporating music. You can use free software like Microsoft Photo Story to use images, text, and voice narration to present your findings.

CHAPTER 3

The Third Week

Writing in the Middle

Tim's inquiry question explores the impact that an adult's addiction to video games has on family and friends. He spends a week collecting research, mostly printing out articles from library databases and Web sites. Tim skims things, underlining a line or a passage from time to time, but for the most part he's like a bear in a blueberry patch, voraciously collecting as much information as he can. This is all in preparation for the writing, which he'll postpone until right before the paper is due.

Sound familiar? This is certainly similar to the way I always did research.

Here's how I would rewrite this scene for Tim: Tim is still hungrily collecting information about video gaming addiction, *but as he does it, he's writing about what he's found.* Tim's notebook is open next to his laptop, and he's jotting down quotations and summaries and maybe an interesting fact or two. He's also marking up the electronic copy, highlighting passages of an article he might want to return to or cutting and pasting relevant passages into an open Word document. Then, when he's done reading the article, Tim writes furiously in his notebook for ten minutes or so, exploring his reaction to what he found.

I now believe that the writing that takes place in the *middle* of the research process—the notetaking stage—may be as important as, if not more important than, the writing that takes place at the end—composing the draft. Writing in the middle helps you take possession of your sources and establish your presence in the draft. It sharpens your thinking about your topic, and it is the best cure for unintentional plagiarism.

I realize I have a sales job to do on this. Writing in the middle, particularly if you've been weaned on notecards, feels like busywork. "It gets in the way of doing the research," one student told me. "I just want to collect as much stuff as I can, as quickly as I can. Notetaking slows me down." Though it may seem inefficient, writing as you read may actually make your research *more* efficient. Skeptical? Read on.

Becoming an Activist Notetaker

Notetaking can and probably should begin your process of writing your paper. Notetaking is not simply a mechanical process of vacuuming up as much information as you can and depositing it on notecards or in a notebook with little thought. Your notes from sources are your first chance to *make sense* of the information you encounter, to make it your own. You do need more time to take thoughtful notes, but the payoff is that you'll write a draft more quickly and produce a paper that reflects your point of view much more strongly.

Writing in the middle is basically something you should do every day: Have a conversation. In this case you're conversing with a stranger who shares your interest in something, and you're talking with texts. The exercise that follows is an opportunity to practice this new kind of dialogue.

EXERCISE 3.1

Getting into a Conversation with a Fact

Mostly, we just collect facts to deploy them in support of a point we're trying to make, conveniently assuming they are true, of course. But facts can ignite thought, if we let them. They can help us discover what we think, refine our point of view, and explore new avenues of thought. But for this to happen, you have to interact with information. Rather than a monologue—simply jotting down what an author is saying—you engage in a conversation—talking *with* an author: questioning, agreeing, speculating, wondering, connecting, arguing. You can do this in your head, but it's far more productive to have this dialogue through writing.

Let's try it.

I'm going to share with you two facts—one at a time—that together start to tell an interesting story about gender, beauty, and culture. Each fact will be a prompt for about five minutes of fast-writing in which you explore your thinking about the fact.

STEP 1: How do women see men's "attractiveness"? *Harper's Magazine* recently reported the following:

Portion of men whose attractiveness is judged by U.S. women to be "worse than average": 4/5

What do you make of this? Does it surprise you? Assuming it's true, how would you explain it? If you doubt it's true, why? Fastwrite your response for five minutes.

STEP 2: Now that you've done five minutes of "thinking through writing" about how women view men, consider how men view women's "attractiveness."

Portion of women whose attractiveness is judged by U.S. men to be "worse than average": 2/5

What do you make of men's more generous attitude toward women? Does this surprise you? How might you explain both "facts"? Together, what does this information say to you about gender and "attractiveness"? Fastwrite for five minutes, exploring these questions.

As you reread your two fastwrites, do you see any consistent line of thought developing? If someone asked you what you thought about these two facts, what would you say?

In a small way, you've just practiced a method of notetaking that can help you make sense of information you encounter when you read for your research project or read any other text you want to think about. Later in this chapter, I'll show you something called the "double-entry journal," which is a system for using this technique. But in this exercise, you have practiced the essence of writing in the middle: seeing information as the beginning of a conversation, not the end of one.

Exploring your reaction to what you read during an open-ended fastwrite is only part of using information to discover what you think. You must also *understand* what you're reading. Most *good* conversations make demands on both speakers. The most important of these is simply to listen carefully to what the other person is saying, even (and perhaps especially) if you don't agree. In couples therapy there's a method to help this along called "say back"—each partner has to listen first and then repeat what he or she heard the other say. Response or reaction comes later. Researchers entering into a conversation with their sources need to engage in the same practice: You need to listen or read carefully, first making an effort to understand a subject or an author's arguments or ideas and then exploring your response to them, as you did in the preceding exercise.

The academic equivalent of "say back" is paraphrasing or summarizing, something we'll look at in more detail later in this chapter. Both are undervalued skills, I think, that require practice. Try your hand at it in the following exercise.

EXERCISE 3 . 2

"Say Back" to a Source

The following passage is from an article by linguist Deborah Tannen on the complexity of communication within families.

> Through talk, we create and shape our relationships. Through talk, we are comforted; through talk we are hurt. We look to family members for come-as-you-are acceptance, but instead of an intimate ally, we sometimes find an intimate critic. A small remark can spark a big conflict because with the family, no utterance stands alone. Every remark draws meaning from innumerable conversations that came before.*

In your notebook, rewrite the passage in your own words in roughly the same length—a *paraphrase.* You'll find it's easier to do if you first focus on understanding what Tannen is trying to say and then on writing without looking much at the passage, if possible. If your instructor assigns this as an in-class exercise, exchange your rewrite with a partner. Then read the following sections on plagiarism.

Plagiarism: What It Is, Why It Matters, and How to Avoid It

Simply put, *plagiarism* is using others' ideas *or* words as if they were your own. The most egregious case is handing in someone else's work with your name on it. Some schools also consider using one paper to meet the requirements of two classes to be a grave offense. But most plagiarism is unintentional. I remember being guilty of plagiarism when writing a philosophy paper my freshman year in college. I committed the offense largely because I didn't know what plagiarism was, and I hadn't been adequately schooled in good scholarship (which is no excuse).

I Read What You Said and Borrowed It, Okay?

Here's another passage from the same article by Deborah Tannen as the passage in Exercise 3.2. In this excerpt she is talking

---

*Tannen, Deborah. "I Heard What You Didn't Say." *Washington Post* 13 May 2001: B1. Print.

about a situation with which we're all familiar. We're talking with a loved one and he or she makes a comment that seems innocuous: "I'll put the dishes in the dishwasher because I can pack more in." But we hear the comment as a larger criticism: "You're not good at housework." There are what seem to be simple messages with equally simple motives, and then there are "metamessages" that we sometimes hear instead of the simple ones. Following the excerpt from Tannen's passage is what seems like a pretty good paraphrase:

> **Original passage:** Distinguishing the message from the metamessage (terms I have adopted from anthropologist Gregory Bateson) is necessary to ensure that family members work things out rather than working each other over. It's frustrating to have the same arguments again and again. But some arguments can be constructive—if family members use them to articulate and understand the metamessages they are intending and hearing.*

> **Paraphrase:** Sometimes family members can have the same argument over and over, not realizing what they're really arguing about. Linguist Deborah Tannen writes that it's important to try distinguishing the message from the metamessage. By articulating what was said and what was heard, arguments can be constructive rather than frustrating.

There are a couple of problems with this paraphrase, but they might, at first glance, be pretty subtle. Notice that the first sentence uses the phrase "have the same argument over and over," which, though worded slightly differently, copies the pattern of Tannen's original "have the same arguments again and again." That won't do.

Worse, the paraphrase fails to include quotation marks around the borrowed phrase "distinguishing the message from the metamessage." It also lifts "constructive" and "frustrating" from the original without quotation marks and uses the word "articulating," which is uncomfortably close to Tannen's "articulate." But the bigger problem is not one I would expect you to notice yet. Even though the paraphrase uses an attribution tag—"Linguist Deborah Tannen writes..."—the paraphrase doesn't include a parenthetical citation, something like "(Tannen 2)," indicating the page of the original passage. We'll talk later about citation, but here's the key thing to remember: *Whenever you quote, paraphrase, or summarize a source, it must always be fully cited, even if you mention the author's name.*

*Tannen, Deborah. "I Heard What You Didn't Say." *Washington Post* 13 May 2001: B2. Print.

What Is Plagiarism?

Each college or university has a statement in the student handbook that offers a local definition. But that statement probably includes most or all of the following forms of plagiarism:

1. Handing in someone else's work—a downloaded paper from the Internet or one borrowed from a friend—and claiming that it's your own.
2. Handing in the same paper for two different classes.
3. Using information or ideas that are not common knowledge from any source and failing to acknowledge that source.
4. Using the exact language or expressions of a source and not indicating through quotation marks and citation that the language is borrowed.
5. Rewriting a passage from a source, making minor word substitutions but retaining the same syntax and structure as the original.

Corrected paraphrase: To get beyond old family arguments and avoid hurting one another, linguist Deborah Tannen writes, it's important for family members to try **"distinguishing the message from the metamessage."** Even old family arguments can be **"constructive,"** says Tannen, if family members are careful to talk openly about the metamessages **(Tannen 2).**

Here are some simple tactics for avoiding plagiarism:

- It's fine to borrow distinctive terms or phrases from a source, but signal that you've done so with quotation marks.
- Make a habit of using attribution tags, signaling to your reader who is the source of the idea, quotation, or fact. These tags include things such as "Tannen argues," "Tannen writes," "According to Tannen," and so on. For a lengthy list of these tags, see the box "Verbs for Discussing Ideas" in Chapter 5.
- *Always* cite borrowed material (more about how to do so in the next chapter).

As a follow-up to Exercise 3.2, return to your paraphrase of the Tannen passage on talk within families. Do you need to edit or alter the

The Common Knowledge Exception

While you always have to tell readers what information you have borrowed and where it came from, things that are "common knowledge" are excluded from this. Everyone knows, for example, that John Kennedy died in Dallas in November 1963. These and other widely known facts need not be cited. Neither do observations that anyone could make or common sayings, such as "home is where the heart is."

paraphrase you wrote to avoid possible plagiarism problems? If you're in class, your instructor may ask you to work in pairs on this. What are the common plagiarism mistakes—almost always unintentional—that students in the class made when they paraphrased the passage in Exercise 3.2? (Forms of plagiarism are summarized in the box "What Is Plagiarism?")

Why Plagiarism Matters

It may seem that concern over plagiarism is just a lot of fuss that reflects English teachers' obsession with enforcing rules. In reality, the saddest days I've ever had as a writing teacher have always been when I've talked with a student about a paper she downloaded from the Internet or borrowed from her roommate. Most instructors hate dealing with plagiarism.

Deliberate cheating is, of course, a moral issue, but the motive for carefully distinguishing between what is yours and what you've borrowed isn't just to "be good." It's really about making a gesture of gratitude. Research is always built on the work that came before it. As you read and write about your topic, I hope that you come to appreciate the thoughtful writing and thinking of people before you who may have given you a new way of seeing or thinking.

Knowledge is a living thing (see Figure 3.1), growing like a great tree in multiple directions, adding (and losing) branches that keep reaching higher toward new understandings and truths. As researchers we are tree climbers, ascending the branches in an effort to see better. It's only natural that as we make this climb, we feel grateful for the strength of the limbs supporting us. Citing and acknowledging sources is a way of expressing this gratitude.`

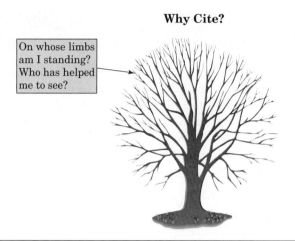

FIGURE 3.1   Like a tree, knowledge in a discipline is a living thing, from time to time losing and adding branches, growing in new directions.

Making Information Your Own: Quotation, Paraphrase, and Summary

Taylor is writing a paper on plastics in the ocean, and from the European Environment Commission Web site, she cuts and pastes the following text into a Word document:

> Marine litter is a global concern, affecting all the oceans of the world. Every year, approximately 10 billion tons of litter end up in the ocean world wide, turning it into the world's biggest landfill and thus posing environmental, economic, health, and aesthetic problems. Sadly, the persistence of marine litter is the result from poor practices of solid waste management, lack of infrastructure, and a lack of awareness of the public at large about the consequences of their actions.*

She likes the passage—it succinctly states the problem of ocean pollution and even includes a powerful statistic: 10 billion tons of garbage end up in the world's oceans each year. Now what does she do with it? Consider her choices:

1. Do nothing. Set the passage aside and hope there will be a place in her paper where she can digitally dump the whole thing or part of it.
2. Rewrite all or part of it in her own words. Set the rewrite aside and hope to weave it into her paper later.

---

*From http://ec.europa.eu/environment/water/marine/pollution.htm. © European Union, 1995–2011. Reproduction is authorized.

Student writers often face this dilemma, and in the digital age, when it's easy to cut and paste text, choice #1 is the odds-on favorite. Just collect and dump. What this usually means in the draft research essay is a quotation. In some cases, this is justified. Perhaps the material *is* so well said that you want the voice of the source to speak for itself. But more often, a cut-and-paste quotation—particularly an extended one—looks like a sign of surrender: Instead of actively guiding a reader through information, the writer opts to take a nap.

What about choice #2? How might Taylor rewrite the passage to establish herself as a reliable guide?

> None of the world's oceans are spared from pollution, notes the European Environment Commission, which also reports that 10 billion tons of garbage are dumped in the world's oceans every year. They now represent "the world's biggest landfill" ("Marine Pollution Awareness").

In the rewrite, Taylor mines the original passage selectively, emphasizing what she thinks is important but without misrepresenting what was said. Here is a writer who is controlling information rather than being controlled by it.

The relationship between a source and a research writer is often complex, for various reasons. Consider how difficult it can be to read someone else's words, make an effort to understand what they mean, and then find your own words to restate the ideas. What's worse is that sometimes the authors are experts who use language you may not easily grasp or use reasoning in ways you can't easily follow. And then there are those authors who write so beautifully, you wonder how you could possibly say it better. Finally, you might fear that somehow you will goof and accidentally plagiarize the source's ideas or words.

One useful, if somewhat crude, way of describing how a writer might take possession of information she gathers is in terms of three approaches you've no doubt heard of before: paraphrase, summary, and quotation. These are useful to learn about, not only so that you know the rules for how to employ them, but, perhaps more important, so you can see each as a different way of interacting with what you read. Ultimately, they are tools that keep you in the game.

Paraphrasing

In Exercise 3.2, you practiced "say back," a technique that helps many married couples who may be headed for divorce. As I mentioned, *paraphrase* is the academic equivalent of this therapeutic method for

How Can I Use That? Four Motives for Using a Source

My daughter Julia wants a pug. This isn't good news because I don't think much of little dogs with sinus problems. I also heard a rumor that if a pug sneezes hard enough its eyes might pop and dangle by the optical nerve until the eyeball is greased and popped back into the eye socket. This posed a research question: *Are pugs typical of overbred dogs that tend to suffer from a range of physiological and psychological problems?*

Because this is a question that goes way beyond my personal experience, I naturally need to turn to outside sources to learn more. When most of us do research for an academic paper, we typically search for sources that exemplify or support a point we want to make. But, especially in an inquiry-based project, you'll want to find sources for reasons other than just supporting your points. For example:

1. *Sources can extend your thinking.* This is an essential motive for doing research, particularly early in the process. You want to learn more about your subject so that you can refine your research question and understand more fully what it is you're asking. For example, in an article in *The Economist* magazine, I learn that kennel clubs, which began in England in the second half of the nineteenth century, have played a key role in "genetic painting" of dog breeds, a euphemism for genetic manipulation (1).* The article goes on to argue that it is

*"It's a Dog's Life." *The Economist* 12 Dec. 2002: 1–5. *Academic Search Premier.* Web. 8 August 2005.

the demands of these associations for a kind of "racial purity" that have contributed to overbreeding (2). Perhaps I should revise my research question: *What role has the Pug Dog Club of America (PDCA) played in promoting or confronting the problem of inbreeding in the dog?*

2. *Sources can provide necessary background.* For a full understanding of your topic, there may be things you—and ultimately your readers—need to know. For example, the *Encyclopedia of Animals** tells me that pugs are one of the oldest breeds and live an average of eight years. The dog's genetic history is a long one, which may be a significant fact. The average life span of a pug means that Julia will go to college before the dog dies, which means her pug will become my pug.

3. *Sources can support or exemplify a point you want to make.* As I just mentioned, this is the motive we usually think of for research. We have a point, claim, or assertion we want to support with the information we've found. For instance, here's a quotation that seems to confirm the claim that kennel clubs have indeed contributed to medical problems in dogs:

> The Kennel Club, the top canine body in Britain, working with breed-specific dog clubs has laid out the "right" looks—a narrow set of desirable characteristics that breeders try to match. "Judges judge against a standard, and it's rewarding and challenging for breeders to try to meet those standards," says Geoff Sampson, a geneticist who works for the Kennel Club. But that kind of judging has too often been unrewarding for the dog. In the quest to create the perfect pooch, close relatives will often be mated, sometimes even brother and sister or mother and son. The danger of this practice is that it increases the likelihood that puppies will inherit genetic diseases—some 400 have now been identified in dogs.†

4. *Sources can present opportunities for analysis and interpretation.* Sometimes you encounter information that raises

(continued)

---

*"Pug." *Encyclopedia of Animals* n.d. *EBSCO Animals.*Web. 8 August 2005.
†Gibson, Helen. "A Flawed Beauty." *Time Europe.* 8 Aug. 2001: 2–3. *MasterFile Premier.* Web. 8 Aug. 2005.

> new questions, and when it does, you have a chance to
> offer your own analysis or interpretation of how that infor-
> mation or assertion might be understood. For example,
> one article asserted that the whole movement to promote
> purebred dogs for show, which originated with the British
> Kennel Clubs in the nineteenth century, might be part of
> a larger, social push toward racial purity in people. That
> dog breeding may have "racist" origins is an explosive and
> fascinating assertion. While I concede this might have been
> true, is it a relevant claim today? Isn't it faulty reasoning
> to infer that the motives of some people 150 years ago nec-
> essarily remain the motives of people today?
>
> By the way, I could not find evidence that pugs blow
> out their eyeballs when they sneeze. Sadly, I can't use that
> as a reason for discouraging Julia about pug ownership
> unless I find some convincing evidence to support it. But
> I'll keep looking.

getting people to listen to each other. Try to say in your own words—
and in about the same length as the author said it—what you understand the author to mean. This is hard, at first, because instead of just
mindlessly quoting—a favorite alternative for many students—you
have to *think*. Paraphrasing demands that you make your own sense
of something. The time is well worth it. Why? Because not only are
you lowering the risk of unintentional plagiarism and being fair to
the source's ideas, *you are essentially writing a fragment of your draft*.
Exercise 3.3 will help you develop these skills.

EXERCISE 3.3

Paraphrase Practice

At the heart of paraphrasing is this very simple idea: *Good
writers find their own way of saying things*. That's your challenge
here. Read each line or passage below until you think you thoroughly
understand it, and then don't look at it again. Paraphrase the line or
passage on a separate piece of paper, finding your own way of saying
what you understand the original to mean. Finally, review your paraphrase to make sure that any borrowed words or phrases from the
original are within quotation marks in your paraphrase.

The lines and passages get progressively harder to paraphrase.

1. For most of the last 500 years, imitation was the sincerest form of architectural flattery.*
2. According to the National Institutes of Health,
   - Percentage of U.S.-born Mexican Americans who have suffered from some psychological disorder: 48
   - Percentage of Mexican immigrants who have: 29
   - Percentage of Mexico City residents who have: 23
3. Houseflies not only defecate constantly but also do so in liquid form, which means they are in constant danger of dehydration.†
4. It should also be understood that the thought content of student recitation or writing need not be original or creative. It's highly unlikely that a freshman will come up with a truly original idea about psychology, economics, or chemistry. But an absolutely original sentence that relates a known fact or logical argument is about the best proof we have of understanding.‡

Exercise 3.3 returns me to my original argument: Thoughtful notetaking pays off in the long run because you're essentially writing your essay in the middle of the process. Imagine what an advantage you'll have over those who wait until the night before the paper is due. Rather than having pages of journal notes that are ripe for the picking, the night-before-it's-due clan is looking at bare branches. In a few pages, I'll suggest several notetaking methods that I think will give you the most to harvest. But first, let's review another listening technique useful for academic writers: summary.

Summarizing

In order to sell a movie to Hollywood, a screenwriter should be able to summarize what it's about in a sentence. "*Juno* is a film about a smart, single, pregnant teenager who finds unexpected humor in her situation but finally finds that her wit is not enough to help her navigate the emotional tsunami her pregnancy triggers in the lives of those around her." That statement hardly does justice to the

*Rybczynski, Witold. "When Architects Plagiarize It's Not Always Bad." *Slate.com.* Slate, 14 Sept. 2005. Web. 15 Sept. 2005.
†Conniff, Richard. "Why Did God Make Flies?" *Wonders.* New York: Owl, 1997. Print.
‡Leamnson, Robert. *Thinking About Teaching and Learning.* Sterling, VA: Stylus, 1999. Print.

film—which is about so much more than that—but I think it basically captures the story and its central theme.

Obviously, that's what a *summary* is: a reduction of longer material into a brief statement that captures a basic idea, argument, or theme from the original. Like paraphrasing, summarizing often requires careful thought. This is especially the case when you're trying to capture the essence of a whole movie, article, or chapter that's fairly complex. Many times, however, summarizing involves simply boiling down a passage—not the entire work—to its basic idea.

E X E R C I S E 3 . 4

Summary Practice

While a summary can never be purely objective, it needs to be fair. After all, each of us will understand a text differently, but at the same time we have to do our best to represent what a source is actually saying without prejudice. That's often a particular challenge when you have strong feelings about a topic. The passage that follows, an excerpt on the debate over gay marriage from the Pew Forum on Religion and Public Life, is itself a summary of sorts; it attempts to capture the sentiments of both sides of the debate.

Carefully read the passage, and write a brief (two to four sentences) summary of its main point. Make sure to summarize in your own words, and if you borrow any words or phrases from the original passage, don't forget those quotation marks.

> Most supporters of same-sex marriage contend that gay and lesbian couples should be treated no differently than their heterosexual counterparts and that they should be able to marry like anyone else. Beyond wanting to uphold the legal principles of nondiscrimination and equal treatment, supporters say there are very practical reasons behind the fight for marriage equity. They point out, for instance, that homosexual couples who have been together for years often find themselves without the basic rights and privileges that are currently enjoyed by heterosexual couples who legally marry—from the sharing of health and pension benefits to hospital visitation rights.
>
> Most social conservatives and others who oppose same-sex marriage argue that marriage between a man and a woman is the bedrock of a healthy society because it leads to stable families and, ultimately, to children who grow up to be productive adults. Allowing gay and lesbian couples to wed,

they contend, will radically redefine marriage and further weaken it at a time when the institution is already in serious trouble due to high divorce rates and a significant number of out-of-wedlock births. Moreover, many predict that giving gay couples the right to marry will ultimately lead to granting people in polygamous and other nontraditional relationships the right to marry as well.*

Quoting

I'll never forget a scene from the documentary *Shoah,* an 11-hour film about the Holocaust, which presents an interview with the Polish engineer of one of the trains that took thousands of Jews to their deaths. As an old man still operating the same train, he was asked how he felt about his role in World War II. He said quietly, "If you could lick my heart, it would poison you."

It would be difficult to restate the Polish engineer's comment in your own words. But more important, it would be stupid even to try. Some of the pain and regret and horror of that time in history is embedded in that one man's words. You may not come across such a distinctive quote as you read your sources this week, but be alert to *how* authors (and those quoted by authors) say things. Is the prose unusual, surprising, or memorable? Does the writer make a point in an interesting way? If so, jot it down in your journal or cut and paste it into a digital file, making sure to signal the borrowed material with quotation marks.

There are several other reasons to quote a source as you're taking notes. Sometimes it's desirable to quote an expert on your topic who is widely recognized in the field. Used to support or develop your own assertions, the voice of an authority can lend credit to your argument and demonstrate your effort to bring recognized voices into the discussion. If your paper is on a literary topic— involving novels, stories, poems, and other works—then purposeful and selective quoting is especially important and appropriate. The texts and the actual language the writers use in them are often central to the argument you're making.

As a general rule, however, the college research paper should contain no more than 10 or 20 percent quoted material. This principle sometimes gets ignored because it's so easy to just copy a passage from a source and paste it into an essay. But keep in mind that a

*Excerpt from "A Contentious Debate: Same-Sex Marriage in the U.S.," *Pew Forum on Religion & Public Life,* http://pewforum.org/Gay-Marriage-and-Homosexuality/ A-Contentious-Debate-Same-Sex-Marriage-in-the-US.aspx. © 2009 Pew Research Center. Reprinted by permission.

writer who quotes may not really need to think much about and take possession of the information, shaping it and allowing herself to be shaped by it. Still, you can retain a strong presence in your work even when using the words of others, if you remember to do the following:

1. *Quote selectively.* You need not use all of the passage. Mine phrases or sentences that are particularly distinctive and embed them in your own prose.
2. *Provide a context.* The worst way to use a quote is to just drop it into a paragraph without attribution or comment. If you're going to bring someone else's voice into your work, you should, at the very least, say who the source is and perhaps why what this person says is particularly relevant to what you're saying.
3. *Follow up.* In addition to establishing a context for a quotation, seize the chance to analyze, argue with, amplify, explain, or highlight what is in a quotation.

As an example of effective use of quotation, consider the following excerpt from Bill Bryson's book *At Home: A Short History of Private Life*. Bryson is especially talented at telling compelling nonfiction stories using research, and here he explains the fears of people in the nineteenth century about being buried alive. In this case, Bryson incorporates a "block quotation"—that is, the passage he quotes is set off and indented, as is required in MLA style for passages of four or more lines.

> According to one report, of twelve hundred bodies exhumed in New York City for one reason or another between 1860 and 1880, six showed signs of thrashing or other postinternment distress. In London, when the naturalist Frank Buckland went looking for the coffin of the anatomist John Hunter at St. Martin-in-the-Fields Church, he reported coming upon three coffins that showed clear evidence of internal agitation (or so he was convinced).... A correspondent to the British journal *Notes and Queries* offered this contribution in 1858:
>
> > A rich manufacturer named Oppelt died about fifteen years since at Reichenberg, in Austria, and a vault was built in the cemetery for the reception of the body by his widow and children. The widow died about a month ago and was taken to the same tomb; but, when it was opened for the purpose, the coffin of her husband was found open and empty, and the skeleton discovered in the corner of the vault in a sitting posture.

For at least a generation such stories became routine in even serious periodicals. So many people became morbidly obsessed with the fear of being interred before their time that a word was coined for it: *taphephobia*.

Notice that Bryson provides a context for his quotation—the name of the source as well as mention of its stature as a "serious publication"—and then follows up the quoted passage by noting that the story it tells is typical of nineteenth-century fears of being buried alive. He also notes that the anecdote is an illustration of what was then called taphephobia. Bryson's book is not an academic work, so you don't see citations, something that you will incorporate into your own essay, but you can see how a powerful quotation can bring the work to life, especially when it's sandwiched within the commentary of the writer who chooses to allow another voice to speak.

Notetaking

There's the skills part of notetaking—knowing how to cite, summarize, paraphrase, and quote correctly—and then there's the more interesting, harder part—making *use* of what you're reading to discover what you think. So far, we've talked about this latter process using the metaphor of conversation. In Exercise 3.1, you tried out this idea, responding in writing to facts about gender and notions of "attractiveness." This conversation metaphor doesn't originate with me. Lots of people use it to describe how all knowledge is made. One theorist, Kenneth Burke, famously explained that we might imagine that all scholarship on nearly any subject is much like a parlor conversation between people in the know (see the box "The Unending Conversation" on the following page). These are the experts who, over time, have contributed to the discussions about what might be true and who constantly ask questions to keep the conversation going.

As newcomers to this conversation, we don't really have much to contribute. It's important that we listen in so that we begin to understand what has already been said and who has said it. But at some point, even novices like us are expected to speak up. We're not there to simply record what we hear. We're writers. We're supposed to discover something to say.

Fortunately, we rarely enter the parlor empty handed. We have experiences and other prior knowledge that is relevant to the conversation we're listening in on. For example, you certainly know something about the subject of Thomas Lord's essay, "What? I Failed? But I Paid

---

The Unending Conversation

Imagine that you enter a parlor. You come late. When you arrive, others have long preceded you, and they are engaged in a heated discussion, a discussion too heated for them to pause and tell you exactly what it is about. In fact, the discussion had already begun long before any of them got there, so that no one present is qualified to retrace for you all the steps that had gone before. You listen for a while, until you decide that you have caught the tenor of the argument; then you put in your oar. Someone answers; you answer him; another comes to your defense; another aligns himself against you, to either the embarrassment or gratification of your opponent, depending upon the quality of your ally's assistance. However, the discussion is interminable. The hour grows late, you must depart. And you do depart, with the discussion still vigorously in progress.

Kenneth Burke

---

for Those Credits! Problems of Students Evaluating Faculty." After all, you've probably filled out an evaluation or two for a course you've taken. But clearly, Lord, as a science educator, has spent considerably more time than you considering whether these evaluations are useful for judging the quality of teaching. Yet college writers, even if they have limited expertise, are expected to speak up on a topic they're writing about, entering the conversation by raising questions, analyzing arguments, speculating, and emphasizing what they think is important.

EXERCISE 3 . 5

Dialogic Notetaking: Listening In, Speaking Up

Drop into the conversation that Thomas Lord has going in his essay, and, drawing on what you've learned so far, use your journal writing to listen in and speak up.

STEP 1:

1. Begin by listening in. Read Thomas Lord's essay once straight through. Underline and mark passages that you think are:
   a. important to your understanding of the article,
   b. puzzling in some way,

c. surprising, or

d. connected with your own initial ideas and experiences.

2. Reread the opening paragraph, the last few paragraphs, and all of your marked passages; then, without looking at the article, compose a two- or three-sentence summary of what you understand to be the most important thing the article is saying. Write this down on the left page of your notebook.

3. Find two passages in the article that you think are good examples of what you state in your summary. Copy these on the left page of your notebook, too. Or if you're doing this on your computer, use the Table function to create two columns, and use the left one.

STEP 2: Now speak up. Use the right side of your notebook to explore your thinking about what Lord is saying. Look on the opposing left pages to remind yourself of some of his ideas and assertions. This is an open-ended fastwrite, but here are some prompts to get you writing and thinking:

- Tell the story of your thinking:
  - *Before I read about this topic, I thought _____, and then I thought _____, and then_____, and then ... but now I think _____.*
- Consider ways you've begun to think differently:
  - *I used to think _____, but now I'm starting to think _____.*
- Try both believing and doubting:
  - *The most convincing points Lord makes in his essay are _____. or Though I don't necessarily agree with Lord, I can understand why he would think that _____.*
  - And then: *The thing that Lord ignores or fails to understand is _____. or The least convincing claim he makes is _____ because _____.*
- Consider questions:
  - *The most important question Lord raises is _____.*
  - *The question that he fails to ask is _____.*

Discuss in class how this notetaking exercise worked. What went well? What was difficult? How did your initial thoughts influence your reading of the article? Did your thinking change? Which of these techniques will you continue to use in your notetaking?

What? I Failed? But I Paid for Those Credits! Problems of Students Evaluating Faculty*

by Thomas Lord

Late one afternoon several days ago, I was startled by a loud rap on my office door. When I opened it, I immediately recognized a student from the previous semester clutching the grade slip he had just received in the mail. Sensing his anger and frustration, I invited him in to discuss his scores. I was surprised that he had not anticipated the failing grade because his exam scores were abysmal, his class work was marginal, and his attendance was sporadic. When I scooted my chair over to my computer to open the course's spreadsheet to review his grade, he told me he didn't have an argument with the test, class, and attendance records. His reason for coming to see me was to ask how he could get his refund. He had, after all, paid for the credits, right? I was astonished. In all my years in higher education, this was the first time I had been asked for a refund.

A day later over lunch, a colleague remarked that with the nation's troublesome economy, many universities have turned to the business model of running the institution. "The business model," he acknowledged, "focuses on financial efficiency while maintaining a quality product."

"Perhaps so," another colleague responded, "but the principal foundation of the business model is the notion of satisfying the customer. Because the products of a college are its graduates, it requires the college to meet their expectations for both a quality education and a gratifying experience. This is nearly impossible if the college wants to retain its integrity and high standards."

Furthermore, what students expect from their college experience varies greatly. A quality, highly respected education is, of course, always desirable, but that's about as common as the expectations get. Some college students relish the liberal challenges universities can provide, some look for a cultural experience, and others simply want to be trained for a career. A large number of undergraduates seek strong intercollegiate athletic or theater programs, and some students are most interested in an exciting social life. This diversity is where the difficulty lies. With such an assortment of demands and expectations, it's simply not possible for any institution to provide it all and maintain a student-as-consumer

*"What? I Failed? But I Paid for those Credits! Problems of Students Evaluating Faculty" by Thomas Lord from *Journal of College Science Teaching,* November/ December 2008. Used by permission of the National Science Teachers Association.

philosophy. Many universities have tried, and in so doing, have undercut their reputation. Several decades ago, education theorist David Reisman (1981) wrote, "This shift from academic merit to student consumerism is one of the two greatest reversals of direction in all the history of American Higher Education; the other being the replacement of the classical college by the modern university a century ago."

Despite Reisman's statement, the student-as-consumer philosophy has become more widely spread in academic institutions over the last two decades, and with it has come a tendency for students to have a stronger voice in higher education (d'Apollonia and Abrami 1997). It is common nowadays for student representatives to serve on university committees. Students are often consulted on ventures that include curriculum, discipline, regulation, and campus construction. In many schools, segments of the institution's governance are shared with students. My institution, for example, retains two students on the University Executive Board.

But by far the greatest number of student voices impacting the institution is in the evaluation of the instructors. The practice was first implemented at Purdue University in 1927, when surveys were distributed to students in a sociology class to solicit their opinions of the course (Remmers 1927). The surveys were not shared with the administration, but were retained by the professors as feedback for self-improvement. Two years later, Remmers revised the surveys to include "student ratings of their instructor's teaching and what they have learned in the course." The researcher reported his finding at a national professional meeting, and soon other universities began soliciting instructor ratings on their campuses. Course and instructor evaluations remained benign until the 1960s, when students discovered the power their united voices could make in higher education. During this time, students began vocalizing their resistance to the war in Vietnam, the ills of the environment, and the materialism of society. It was a time of student free speech about ethical, cultural, and racial issues. Suddenly, evaluations of instructors and courses became more about student satisfaction than about a professor's instructional effectiveness.

. . . .

When the driving mechanism for faculty evaluations shifts from educating to pleasing, many problems occur. "Student evaluations of their professors are impacted heavily by student perception," states Professor Stanley Fish, dean emeritus at the University of Illinois (2007). "When student experiences in classes do not match their prior expectations, they react in negative ways. Students may begin to boycott classes they're unhappy with, they may write complaint letters to administrators, or they may challenge the academic integrity of their professors. Some students may become so disrespectful of the professor that they circulate their feelings in the press, on the internet, and over the airways." In 1965, for example, students at the University of California–Berkeley generated a review of teacher performance in a manual entitled *The Slate Supplement,* and sold it at the campus bookstore. "Most of the opinions in the manual were ill-informed and mean-spirited," recalls Fish. "The opinions weren't from professionals in the field but transient students with little or no stake in the enterprise who would be free (because they were anonymous) to indulge any sense of grievance they happened to harbor in the full knowledge that nothing they said would ever be questioned or challenged. The abuse would eventually affect the careers and livelihoods of faculty members especially the young, nontenured professors" (Selvin 1991). In addition, with the negative exposure, university officials became alarmed that the dissatisfaction would lead to students dropping their courses or leaving the university altogether. With the mounting anxieties, many instructors countered by lowering the expectations in their courses. A survey of faculty found 70% of professors believe that their grading leniency and course difficulty bias student ratings, and 83% admitted making their course easier in response to student evaluations (Ryan, Anderson and Birchler 1980).

This was nicely demonstrated when Peter Sacks, a young journalism instructor, was hired on a tenure track at a small northwest college. At the end of the first semester, Sacks, an accomplished writer but not yet an accomplished teacher, found himself in trouble with student evaluations. When he started, Sacks resolved to maintain a high quality in his courses by emphasizing critical thinking about issues. Although he found it extremely difficult, he stuck with his plan for the entire semester, and as a consequence, received terrible student evaluations. Fearing that he would lose his tenure-track appointment after the spring term, he decided to change his tactics and attempt to achieve higher evaluations by deliberately pandering to his students. At the end of his three-year trial, he had dramatically raised his teaching evaluations and gained tenure. Sacks shamelessly admits he became utterly undemanding and uncritical of his students, giving out easy grades, and teaching to the lowest common denominator (1986). Other researchers have confirmed that lenient grading is the most frequently used faculty strategy to counter abusive student assessment (Howard and Maxwell 1982; Greenwald 1997).

Another problem with the business model is that students truly believe they're paying for their credits and not their education.

Consumers are used to paying for merchandise that can later be returned for a refund with no questions asked. The student confusion over this probably resides in the way universities charge pupils for the credits they're taking (at least for students attending part time or over the summer). If, for example, a high school biology teacher decided to upgrade his or her knowledge of wildflowers and enrolled in a three-credit course at a local college on spring flora, the teacher would be charged for the three credits. If the teacher decided to continue the learning the following semester on summer wildflowers, he or she would again pay for the three credits. It's not hard, therefore, to see how the idea of paying for credits rather than earning them came about.

A final reason why student evaluations are an unreliable way to assess faculty is that most students simply don't know what good teaching is. Undergraduates generally have a vision of how college teaching is conducted from depictions in movies or hearing tales from former students. The most common view is that professors stand before a class and recite, write on the chalkboard, or use PowerPoint slides to get across the information students should know in the lesson (McKeachie 1992).

I asked my students what they thought made a great instructor and was told the best professors move unhurriedly through their notes, speaking at a slow-to-moderate pace, explaining the information the students need to learn. One student told me that good professors don't get sidetracked by superficial chunks of information and don't waste time off the subject. Some students also suggested that competent professors are entertaining when they lecture and frequently use demonstrations and videos to back up their presentations. Many class members said the best professors repeat several times the items that are the most salient and hold review sessions before each exam to reaffirm the important content.

Most contemporary theorists, however, tell us that top instructors don't do most of those things. According to education leaders, competent teachers seldom lecture to a gallery of passive students, but provide experiences and directions that actively challenge class members to think and discover information (Handelsmen et al. 2004). Practiced professors believe understanding is the driving force for learning and spend a great amount of preclass time orchestrating team-based learning situations for the upcoming class. Proponents of student-centered instruction acknowledge that active participation in classes and discovery-based laboratories help students develop the habits of mind that drive science (Udovic et al. 2002). Furthermore, while traditional instructors create factual recall questions for their exams where students reiterate what they were told in class, contemporary teachers challenge students to discover the answers through application, synthesis, or evaluation (Huitt 2004). Quality teachers understand what agronomist George Washington Carver meant in 1927 when he wrote, "I know nothing more inspiring than discovering new information for oneself" (Carver 1998).

Students also believe that the best professors don't expect class members to know information that the professor hasn't covered in lecture. Students don't seem to realize that education is the art of using information, not the art of restating it. College graduates must understand that once they're out of school, they'll depend on their education to get them through life. Often will they have to address unfamiliar questions. As I've stated previously, "Once they're out of college, students can't fall back on the answer, 'I don't know 'cause it wasn't covered by my professor' " (Lord 2007).

Enough has been written on this matter that colleges and universities should justify why they continue to use student evaluations to assess their faculty. "The answer is already known," answers Cahn (1986). "Institutions of higher education provide faculty evaluations to students to assess student satisfaction. Not only are the evaluations easy to grade and inexpensive to administer, but they give the impression of objectivity in comparison with more subjective measures such as letters from observers since student evaluations produce definite numbers."

"The role of the university is leadership, not a servant of consumer demands as the current business model requires," states Wilson (1998). "Universities certainly have a responsibility for the safety, well-being, and satisfaction of the people they serve, but they also have a responsibility to educate the people as well. With their dignity and reputation on the line, the most important responsibility is to certify that their graduates are truly educated. Under the consumer model, the goals of satisfaction and education are sometimes in conflict. It is important, therefore, that the metaphor of students as consumers be replaced by the metaphor of students as apprentices" (Haskell 1997).

References

Cahn, S. 1986. *Saints and scamps: Ethics in academia.* Totowa, NJ: Rowman and Littlefield.

Carver, G.W. 1998. *The all-university celebration.* Iowa City, IA: University Press.

d'Apollonia S., and P. Abrami. 1997. Navigating student ratings of instruction. *American Psychologist* 52 (11): 1198–1208.

Fish, S. 2007. Advocacy and teaching. *Academe* 93 (4): 23–27.

Greenwald, A.G. 1997. Validity concerns and usefulness of student ratings. *American Psychologist* 52 (11): 1182–86.

Handelsman, J., D. Ebert-May, R. Beichner, P. Burns, A. Chang, R. DeHann, J. Gentile, S. Luffefer, J. Stewart, S. Tukgnab, and W. Wood. 2004. Scientific thinking. *Science* 304 (5670): 521–22.

Haskell, R. 1997. Academic freedom, tenure and student evaluation of faculty: Galloping polls in the 21st century. *Education Policy Analysis Archives* 5 (6): 43.

Howard, G., and S. Maxwell. 1982. Linking raters' judgments. *Evaluation Review* 6 (1): 140–46.

Huitt, W. 2004. Bloom et al's taxonomy of the cognitive domain. *Educational Psychology Interactive.* http://chiron.valdosta.edu/whuitt/col/cogsys/bloom.html. Valdosta, GA: Valdosta University Press.

Lord, T. 2007. Putting inquiry to the test: Enhancing learning in college botany. *Journal of College Science Teaching* 36 (7): 56–59.

McKeachie, W. 1992. Student ratings: The validity of use. *American Psychologist* 52 (11): 1218–25

Reisman, D. 1981. *On higher education: The academic enterprise in an era of rising student consumerism.* San Francisco: Jossey Bass.

Remmers, D. 1927. Experimental data on the Purdue rating scale. In *Student ratings of instructors: Issues for improving practice,* eds. M. Theall and J. Franklin. 1990. San Francisco: Jossey Bass.

Ryan, J., J. Birchler, and A. Birchler. 1980. Student evaluation: The faculty responds. *Research in Higher Education* 12 (4): 395–401.

Sacks P. 1986. *Generation X goes to college.* LaSalle, IL: Open Court Press.

Selvin, P. 1991. The raging bull at Berkley. *Science* 251 (4992): 368–71.

Wilson, R. 1998. New research casts doubt on value of student evaluations of professors. *Chronicle of Higher Education* 44 (19): A2–A14.

Udovic, D., D. Morris, A. Dickman, J. Postlethwait, and P. Wetherwax. 2002. Workshop biology: Demonstrating the effectiveness of active learning in an introductory biology course. *Bioscience* 52 (3): 272–81.

Thomas Lord (trlord@grove.iup.edu) *is a professor in the Department of Biology at the Indiana University of Pennsylvania in Indiana, Pennsylvania.*

Notetaking Techniques

In the first edition of *The Curious Researcher,* I confessed to a dislike of notecards. Apparently, I'm not the only one. Mention notecards, and students often tell horror stories. It's a little like talking about who has the most horrendous scar, a discussion that can prompt participants to expose knees and bare abdomens in public places. One student even mailed me her notecards—50 bibliography cards and 53 notecards, all bound by a metal ring and color coded. She assured me that she didn't want them back—ever. Another student told me she was required to write 20 notecards a day: "If you spelled something wrong or if you put your name on the left side of the notecard rather than the right, your notecards were torn up and you had to do them over."

It is true, of course, that some students find recording information on notecards an enormously useful way of organizing information. And some teachers have realized that it's pretty silly to turn notetaking into an exercise that must be done "correctly" or not at all. For these reasons, I included suggestions about how to use notecards effectively in the first edition of this text. But in good conscience, I can't do it anymore. I no longer believe that 3 × 5 or 4 × 6 index cards are large enough to accommodate the frequently messy and occasionally extended writing that often characterizes genuinely useful notes. Little cards get in the way of having a good conversation with your sources.

If conventional notecards encourage a monologue, then what method will encourage dialogue? Basically any notetaking strategy that encourages the things that you've practiced so far in this chapter: listening and responding, collecting and evaluating. It's that movement back and forth between information and what you think of that information, between your observations of things and your ideas about them, between what you once understood and what you *now* understand, that will involve you in the process of *knowledge making,* rather than simple information retrieval and reporting. Now this probably sounds pretty grandiose. Your research essay will probably not earn space in an academic journal. But as you begin to understand the difference between knowledge and information, you will earn yourself a place in an academic community that values people with their own ideas. Isn't that inviting?

I'm convinced that something as seemingly mundane as notetaking can be a key part of becoming a knower rather than a parrot. One method, in particular, seems especially effective at encouraging dialogue between the researcher and his sources: the double-entry journal. You can use your notebook or computer for this technique.

The Double-Entry Journal

The double-entry approach (see Figure 3.2) is basically this: Use opposing pages of your research notebook or opposing columns in a Word document—two columns and one row for each source. At the top of the page for each source, write down the bibliographic information for that source. Then, using the left side or column, compile your notes from

Notes from Source
(left page or column)

- Direct quotations, paraphrases, and summaries of material from the source:
  - of ideas that are important to project
  - of ideas that are surprising or puzzling or generate some emotional response
- Be careful to:
  - include bibliographic information at the top;
  - include the page number from the source.

Fastwrite Response
(right page or column)

- Focused fastwrite in response to material at left
- Tips for fastwrite:
  - Write as long as possible; then look left and find something else to respond to.
  - Try shifting between stances of believing and doubting.
  - Use the questions below.

FIGURE 3.2   Double-Entry Journal Method

a source—paraphrases, summaries, quotes. Put appropriate page numbers in the margin next to borrowed material or ideas. Then on the right side, comment on what you collected from each source. Imagine that the line down the middle of the page—or the spiral binder that divides opposing pages—is a table at which you sit across from an author with something to say about a topic you're interested in. Take care to listen to what the author says through paraphrase, summary, and quotation on the left, and then on the right respond with a fastwrite in which you give your own commentary, questions, interpretations, clarifications, or even feelings about what you heard. Your commentary can be pretty open ended, responding to questions such as the following:

- What strikes you? What was confusing? What was surprising?
- If you assume that this is true, why is it significant?
- If you doubt the truth or accuracy of the claim or fact, what is the author failing to consider?
- How does the information stand up to your own experiences and observations?
- Does it support or contradict your thesis (if you have one at this point)?
- How might you use the information in your paper? What purpose might it serve?
- What do you think of the source?
- What further questions does the information raise that might be worth investigating?
- How does the information connect to other sources you've read?

Refer to this list of questions (and any others that occur to you) as a prompt for the writing on the right side of your journal (or right column of your Word document). There are a variety of ways to approach the double-entry journal. If you're taking notes on the printout of an article or a photocopy from a book, try reading the material first and underlining passages that seem important. Then, when you're done, transfer some of that underlined material—quotes, summaries, or paraphrases—into the left column of your journal. Otherwise, take notes in the left column *as* you read.

While you take notes, or after you've finished, do some exploratory writing in the right column. This territory belongs to you. Here, through language, your mind and heart assert themselves over the source material. Use your notes in the left column as a trigger for writing in the right. Whenever your writing stalls, look to the left. The process is a little like watching tennis—look left, then right, then left, then right. Direct your attention to what the source says and then to what *you* have to say about the source. Keep up a dialogue.

Figures 3.3 and 3.4 illustrate how the double-entry journal works in practice. Note these features:

- Bibliographic information is recorded at the top of the page. Do that first, and make sure it's complete.
- Page numbers are included in the far-left margin, right next to the information that was taken from that page. Make sure you keep up with this as you write.
- While the material from the source in the left column may be quite formal or technical, the response in the right column should be informal and conversational. Try to write in your own voice. Find your own way to say things. And don't hesitate to use the first person: *I*.
- The writers often use their own writing to try to question a source's claim or understand better what that claim might be (e.g., "What the authors seem to be missing here..." and "I don't get this quote at all...").
- Seize a phrase from your source, and play out its implications; think about how it pushes your own thinking or relates to your thesis.
- In Figures 3.3 and 3.4, the writers frequently pause to ask themselves questions—not only about what the authors of the original sources might be saying but what the writers are saying to themselves as they write. Use questions to keep you writing and thinking.

Prior, Molly. "Bright On: Americans' Insatiable Appetite for Whiter-Than-White Teeth Is Giving Retailers Something to Smile About." Beauty Biz 1 Sept. 2005: 36–43. Print.

Teeth are no longer just for eating with — their appearance is becoming more important as a factor in a person's image, and they need to be perfectly white. (36)

Cosmetics companies are now entering territory once reserved for dentists as more and more people care mostly about the aesthetics of their teeth and smile. (36)

"Sephora is so enthusiastic about the [tooth whitening] category, it named 'smile' its fifth retail pillar, joining the four others (makeup, fragrance, skin care and hair care) earlier this year." (37)

"The trend has shed its clinical beginnings and assumed a new identity, smile care. Its new name has been quickly adopted by a growing troupe of retailers, who hope to lure consumers with a simple promise: A brighter smile will make you look younger and feel more confident." (37)

Instead of going to the dentist and taking care of their teeth so they function well, people are investing a cosmetic interest in their teeth. People selling tooth-whitening products hope people associate whiter, more perfect teeth with higher self-esteem and social acceptance. (40)

"What says health, youth and vitality like a great smile?" (40)

I have noticed the increasing amount of importance that people put on the whiteness of their teeth, but this also seems to have increased with the amount of advertising for whitening products on TV and in magazines. I wonder if the whole thing is profit driven: Hygiene companies wanted to make more money, so instead of just selling toothbrushes and toothpaste, they created a whitening product and then worked to produce a demand for it. I almost feel really manipulated, like everyone's teeth were fine the way they naturally existed, and then all the sudden a big company decided it needed to create a new product and sell it by making us feel bad about our smiles, and thus bad about ourselves.

The whole thing is sad, because once something becomes the societal "norm," we start to become obligated to do it. If everyone's teeth are beige, it's no problem when yours are too. But when everyone has sparkling white teeth, then it looks funny if you let yours stay brown. It either says "I don't have the money to whiten my teeth," or "I don't care about my appearance."

Sometimes it feels people might also judge you as being dirty, because white teeth seem healthier and cleaner than brown teeth, or lazy, for not spending the time to whiten your teeth. All those things are negative, and create a negative cloud around our teeth where we once felt good, or at least ambivalent. I don't like the way I'm being told my smile isn't good enough the way it is. I feel like when I smile it should just be about showing happiness and conveying that to others, not a judgment about me as a person.

FIGURE 3.3   Amanda's Double-Entry Journal. Here, Amanda concentrates on thinking through the implications of the summaries and quotations she collected from an article on teeth whitening.

Greenbaum, Jessica B. "Training Dogs and Training Humans: Symbolic Interaction and Dog Training." <u>Anthrozoos</u> 23.2: 129-141. Web. 10 Jan. 2010.

"The 'traditional' dominance-based method of training endorses obedience by using a human-centric approach that places dogs in a subordinate position in order to maintain a space in the family. The 'reward-based' behavior modification method promotes a dog-centric approach that highlights companionship over dominance . . . ." (129)	Article seems to capture the essence of the debate: Is a well-behaved dog a product of dominance or companionship? Why can't it be both? One of the things that always strikes me about these binaries— either/or—is that it ignores both/ and. Dogs will always have some kind of unequal relationship with their owners. Right? They have to. And won't they try to sort out, in their own way, the question of who is in charge?
"The methods we use to train our dogs reflect our perceptions of relationships between human and non-human animals. The socially constructed status of dogs, as pet or companion, influences the philos-ophy, methods, and training skills used." (129)	This seems key: "the socially constructed status of dogs" has an enormous influence on how we construe our relationship with them. Greenbaum draws the distinction as between "pet" and "companion." Behind those general terms is a whole set of ways in which we "socially construct" pets. A pet can be a companion, right? It doesn't necessarily imply subservience? I keep returning to the binaries that theorists draw. This is exactly the same thing that I notice with dog trainers themselves. There is a "right" and "wrong" way, and this divide is typically described as it is here: between positive reinforce-ment and negative reinforcement.
Mead discounted idea that animals can engage in symbolic communication with humans: "the ability to think was the ability to say." But article, using Sanders, argues that in a sense, pet owners "speak for" their animals. Sanders's research on police dogs, however, also highlighted the "ambi-guity" of dog ownership—they are both companions and "tools." Subjective beings and objective things. (130)	This idea that we "speak for ani-mals" strikes home, and I imagine that people like me who constantly give dogs and cats a human voice are more likely to favor "human-centric" methods. How can you put a shock collar on a dog that can talk back? But I never thought about this "ambiguity" between dogs as "tools" and

---

FIGURE 3.4   Double-Entry Journal. Here's a double-entry journal entry that uses Word's Table feature to respond to an article I was reading on theories of dog training. I could copy and paste quotes from the original article, a PDF file, and drop them into the left column. Also notice, however, that I rely on summaries as well. Page numbers in parentheses follow borrowed material.

"companions." Though wouldn't this be mostly true of people who train dogs for particular purposes? Is this ambiguity typical of most pet owners who don't.

Fennel argues that while the principle of modeling training on pack behavior makes sense, the method is often misapplied—correction is too harsh or effort to domesticate too extreme. She thinks this is cause of most behavior problems. "Dog guardians have failed as pack leaders" (131)

Must read Fennel's study. Seems like her argument is much like the one I'm thinking about: It may be that dogs do behave in some ways like wild pack animals, but their trainers aren't exactly alpha dogs, either.

FIGURE 3.4 (Continued)

What I like about the double-entry journal system is that it turns me into a really active reader as I'm taking notes for my essay. That blank column on the right, like the whirring of my computer right now, impatiently urges me to figure out what I think through writing. All along, I've said the key to writing a strong research paper is *making the information your own.* Developing your own thinking about the information you collect, as you go along, is one way to do that. Thoughtful notes are so easy to neglect in your mad rush to simply take down a lot of information. The double-entry journal won't let you neglect your own thinking; at least it will remind you when you do.

The Research Log

The research log is an alternative to the double-entry journal that promotes a similar "conversation" between writer and source but with a few differences. One is that, like Jay Leno, the researcher starts with a monologue and always gets the last word. The standard format of the research log can serve as a template, which can be retrieved whenever you're ready to take notes on another source. Those notes can then be easily dropped into the draft as needed, using the Cut and Paste feature of your word-processing program.

The basic approach is this:

1. Take down the full bibliographic information on the source—article, book chapter, Web page, or whatever (see Figure 3.5). Then read the source, marking up your personal copy in the usual fashion by underlining, making marginal notes, and so on.
2. Your first entry will be a fastwrite that is an *open-ended response* to the reading under the heading "What Strikes Me Most." For example, you might begin by playing the "believing game,"

Project: The Newest Commodity: The Smile

Citation: Tanner, Marty. "American Choppers." *New York Times*. New York Times, 20 Feb. 2005. Web. 4 Apr. 2009.

Date: 4/5/2009

What Strikes Me Most:
A prosthodontist is a dentist who specializes in making teeth look a certain way. While many people are born with smiles they are proud of, a prosthodontist can take any smile and modify it in any way. Unfortunately, more and more people are falling into a trap of believing that there is only one "perfect" smile, and they are asking for their own mouths to be modified to create the perfect smile. This disgusts me because I think there should be as many smiles as there are people. It's becoming like a nose job or a face-lift—some modification people make to their appearance to make it less like the countenance they were born with, and more like that "perfect" face. It makes me sad that another thing that is so distinctive to each person has actually become something we want to normalize. As a woman I feel like I'm told to be a size two; have straight, shiny hair; have a little, cute nose; have perfectly arched eyebrows; and have thick, pink lips. Now, too, I have to have the correct length and width teeth that are a sparkly B1 white. It makes me wonder why our culture goes from accepting one part of ourselves as standard and imperfect but acceptable, and makes it into something we need to modify.

I also think the prosthodontist to the stars, Dr. Levine, is really disingenuous in this article. While his job depends on people being unhappy with the way their teeth look, he tries to play the "good guy" card and say that people's smiles are looking too perfect and that people need to have a great set of choppers, but not overly great. He seems to want to make the polite statement

FIGURE 3.5   Amanda's Research Log

that nobody has a perfect smile, but then, through his profession, his job is to make people believe they can get a perfect smile—and they don't already have one. I think that's kind of slimy.

Source Notes:
"Within certain strict boundaries, Levine likes to see some imperfection because it renders the hand of the dentist invisible. This is his art." Many famous people, like actors and actresses, think of their smile as a sort of symbol of their status that they can flash to attract attention. Many of these smiles are exactly the same, with the golden mean the proportion of the length of their top six front teeth, and with each individual tooth having a width that is 80% of the length. There is even a "perfect" amount of tooth that should show when a person's mouth is closed: around 3.7 mm. Patients can wear a fake set of teeth around their home before they have their smiles modified to see if what they imagine as being perfect actually looks bad. They can test drive their new set of teeth for friends and family so they don't end up with a mistake that looks like a pair of too-perfect dentures.

"Smiles are looking too much alike."

"...the man who credits himself with shaping Christie Brinkley's 'iconic American smile.'"

Reality makeover programs like *The Swan* often use a prosthodontist as part of the makeover.

The Source Reconsidered:
When the article mentions Julia Roberts or the "iconic American smile" I know exactly what it means. In my mind, I truly have an image of that smile, and I realize now that that's because every single starlet and commercial model seems to have that smile. Yet, when I look at my friends and all the people around me, there are so many different smiles. I have one friend with really short, stubby teeth that are pretty brown

---

FIGURE 3.5 (Continued)

around the edges, and I admit that I notice it. But
when she smiles, I tend to look more at the rest of
her face and the fact that she's really happy than I
do at her imperfect teeth. It's like it's turning some
natural human emotion into some mass-produced carbon
copy. That's why the whole smile-care thing really
bothers me. Changing somebody's nose changes only
their nose. Changing someone's smile seems to control
and modify the way they communicate a feeling, and
that is really bothersome. They are modifying something far more personal than just their appearance;
they are changing the way they emote. That's freaky.

FIGURE 3.5 (Continued)

exploring how the author's ideas, arguments, or findings are
sensible and then shift to the "doubting game," looking for gaps,
questions, and doubts you have about what the source says. You
could write a response to any or all of the questions suggested
for the double-entry journal. But as the subheading suggests,
you can also begin with this simple, open-ended question:

What strikes you as the most important thing the author is
trying to say?

3. Next, mine the source for nuggets. Take notes under the heading
"Source Notes." These are quotations, summaries, paraphrases,
or key facts you collect from the reading. They are probably some
of the things you marked as you read the source initially.
4. Finally, follow up with one more fastwrite under the heading
"The Source Reconsidered." This is a second, *more focused* look
at the source in which you fastwrite about what stands out in the
notes you took. Which facts, findings, claims, or arguments that
you jotted down shape your thinking now? If the writing stalls,
skip a line, take another look at your source notes, and seize on
something else to write about.

Narrative Notetaking

This is the simplest method of all. As you read, mark up or annotate your source in the ways you usually do. After you read through
it carefully, you will fastwrite a rapid summary for at least one full
minute, beginning with the following prompt (see Figure 3.6):

What I understand this to be saying is....

Focusing Question: How has cosmetic dentistry changed the way we think of the smile, and what are the repercussions?

Source: Walker, Rob. "Consumed; Unstained Masses." <u>New York Times</u>. New York Times, 2 May 2004. Web. 10 Apr. 2009.

Rapid Summary (one minute):
What I understand this article to be saying is that the American public is getting more and more vain, as evidenced by the fact that tooth whitening is growing in popularity. While only celebrities used to modify the appearance of their teeth, now average people are doing it. Because of the value of appearance in our society, once we realize we can modify the way we look to our advantage, we seem to flock to it quickly. That's what's happening with the whole trend of smile care—we're using whiteners to change the way our teeth look so maybe we will be judged more profitably. And when a large percentage of society decides to buy something, there will always be corporations and retailers standing alongside to reap a profit.

Narrative of Thought (six minutes):
Before I started reading this article I thought that it was the capitalistic profit motive that had introduced whitening products and created a consumer demand for them. Now I understand that all of us as consumers have an equal responsibility with the companies that make and market such products, because we're the ones that buy them and change our standards of beauty. That makes me think that this is a complicated issue. While it's frustrating to feel like I can never be attractive enough, because the standard of attractiveness to which I'm held keeps getting harder and harder to meet, I'm the one that is interested in meeting it in the first place. While it would be easy to denigrate that as vanity, however, I can also see that being judged by others as attractive does have actual benefits, be it a higher salary or better treatment from strangers. In that case I'm put in a tough spot—I can work against the culture that tells me I don't look the right way, and feel negatively judged, or I can conform to it, and feel disappointed that I folded to social pressure. This isn't just an issue about people whitening their teeth for fun, it's about how society changes its standards and how quickly we assimilate to them—and why.

FIGURE 3.6 **Amanda's Narrative Notes**

Skip a line, and begin a second episode of fastwriting. Tell the story of your thinking, a narrative of thought that begins with what you initially might have believed about the topic covered in your source, and then how that thinking was influenced by what you read. This time scribble (or type) for as long as you can without stopping, beginning with this prompt:

When I first began reading this, I thought _____, and now I think _____.

Whenever your writing stalls, repeat the prompt again, inserting another discovery from your reading.

Online Research Notebooks

These days, academic researchers frequently work with digital documents, especially PDF files. While it's always a good idea to print out hard copies of anything you use, it's also convenient to annotate and mark up electronic copies. In addition to highlighting passages, it's also possible with some software to insert comments. These can be much like responses in the double-entry journal.

The problem is that most of the software that can annotate PDF files isn't free. For example, while anyone can download Adobe Reader to read PDF documents, you might need to buy Adobe Acrobat to annotate them. There is, however, some free software that can help you organize your digital research files and attach documents to them. That way you can attach your notes for each source to the digital original. The downside, of course, is that these notes aren't keyed to particular passages in the source, but the software is still useful for researchers. Here's a list of a few you might try:

1. *Zotero* (http://zotero.org). I already mentioned this one earlier in *The Curious Researcher*. This is my favorite software for research because it not only organizes digital documents in project folders but also organizes citation information for each source. Zotero is an add-in that only works on the Firefox browser.
2. *Evernote* (http://evernote.com). You can't annotate documents but you can organize your research sources and associated notes and then upload them so they're accessible everywhere you have an Internet connection. The program also runs on all kinds of devices—iPads, iPhones, PCs, Blackberries, and so on. In addition, Evernote has a function that allows you to search your notes by tags or titles.
3. *Google Docs* (http://google.com). Google Docs is a standard for many users who want to organize (and share) documents, and it's even more useful now that it allows documents like PDFs and Word files to remain in their native formats. As with Evernote, you can access your Google Docs wherever you have an Internet connection. (Google Notebook, which I recommended in the previous edition of *The Curious Researcher*, is no longer supported by the company).

When You're Coming Up Short: More Advanced Searching Techniques

At the end of the third week of the research assignment last semester, Laura showed up at my office, looking pale.

"I spent all night at the library, and I couldn't find much on my topic," she said. "What I *could* find, the library didn't have—it was missing, or checked out, or wasn't even part of the collection. I may have to change my topic."

"I hate libraries!" she said, the color returning to her face.

Laura's complaint is one that I hear often at this point in the research process, especially from students who have dutifully tried to find a narrow focus for their papers, only to realize—they think—that there isn't enough information to make the topic work. They have tried the online catalog, article databases, and the Internet. The students found a few articles but not enough for a ten-page paper. Like Laura, they may decide to broaden their focus or bail out of their topic altogether, even though they're still interested in it.

I always give these frustrated students the same advice: Don't despair yet. And don't give up on your narrow focus or your topic until you've dug more deeply for information. There are still some more specialized databases to try and some nonlibrary sources to consider. You are, in a sense, like the archaeologist who carefully removes the dirt from each layer of a dig site, looking to see what it might reveal. If little turns up, the archaeologist systematically explores the next layer and then the next, until she is convinced she's digging in the wrong place. Student researchers too often give up the dig before they've removed enough dirt, believing too quickly there's nothing there. Some things you might not have considered to help you unearth more useful information are discussed in the following pages.

Advanced Library Searching Techniques

These advanced library searching techniques are listed in the order you might try them.

1. *Vary search terms.* Try using some other search terms suggested by your research so far. You might, for instance, try searching using the names of people who have published on your topic.
2. *Search other databases.* Okay, so you've tried a general subject database like Academic OneFile and even a specialized database like PsycINFO. But have you tried another general database like Academic Search Premier or another specialized database like InfoTrac Psychology? Broaden your coverage.

3. *Check bibliographies.* Academic books and articles always include a list of references at the end. These can be gold mines. Look at all the sources like these that you've collected so far and scan the titles in the bibliographies that seem promising. Find these by searching the library databases.

4. *Consider using interlibrary loan services.* Your campus library will get you that article or book it doesn't have by borrowing the materials from another library. This is an incredibly useful service, often available online. These days delivery of requested materials can take as little as a few days!

5. *Troll government documents.* The U.S. government is the largest publisher in the world. If your research question is related

FIGURE 3.7   USA.gov is a useful starting point for a search of government documents on your topic.

to some issue of public policy, then there's a decent chance you'll find some government documents on the subject. Try the site USA.gov (see Figure 3.7), a useful index to the gazillions of government publications and reports.

6. *Ask a reference librarian for help.* If you do, you won't be sorry.

Advanced Internet Searching Techniques

It's more likely that you've tapped out relevant sources on the Internet before you've tapped out those in the library—most of us like to begin with the Internet. But make sure that you've tried some of the following search strategies on the Web.

1. *Vary search terms.* By now, you've gathered enough information on your topic to have some new ideas about terms or phrases that might yield good results. Say you're researching the origins of American blues music, and you discover that among its many traditions is something called the Piedmont style. Try searching using that phrase in quotation marks. Also consider doing Web searches on the names of experts who have contributed significantly to the conversation on your topic.

2. *Use advanced search features.* Few of us use the advanced search page on Google and other search engines. By habit, we just type in a few terms in the simple search window. But advanced searching will allow you to exploit methods that will give you better results—things like phrase searching in conjunction with Boolean operators like AND and OR.

3. *Use multiple search engines.* Don't call for retreat until you've gone beyond Google. Try Yahoo!, Ask.com, and similar search engines. Also try specialized search engines that are relevant to your subject (see Chapter 2).

Thinking Outside the Box: Alternative Sources

Sometimes you need to be creative. Try finding sources on your research question in places you don't think to look.

1. *Search blogs.* It's easy to dismiss blogs as merely self-indulgent musings of people with nothing better to do, but some blogs are written by people who really know what they're talking about. Bloggers can be vigilant observers of new developments, breaking news stories, and cutting-edge opinion. There are a number of specialized search engines to scour the blogosphere. Perhaps the best is http://technorati.com.

2. *Search images.* Another source of material you may not have thought of is images available on the Internet. A photograph of a collapsed school building following the 2008 earthquake in central China will do much to dramatize your essay on the vulnerability of buildings to such a disaster. Or a historical essay on lynching in the South might be more powerful with a picture of a murder from the Library of Congress archives (especially see http://memory.loc.gov/). Your campus library may also have a collection of digital images relevant to your project. Remember that if you use them in your essay, images need to be cited like any other source.

3. *Archived radio or podcasts.* Suppose your research question focuses on Martin Luther King Jr. Why not listen to an interview of Taylor Branch, the man who wrote a three-volume biography of the civil rights leader? You can find it on NPR.org (see Figure 3.8). National Public Radio is a particularly good source for material for academic projects. There are also a variety of search engines that will help you find podcasts on nearly any subject.

4. *Check out YouTube.* It isn't just about laughing babies anymore. YouTube is a rich archive of video that can provide material on many topics. For the project on Martin Luther King Jr., for example, you might watch a video of his last speech. There are,

FIGURE 3.8   **Searching the Archives at National Public Radio**

of course, other sites that archive video, too. Truveo (http://www.truveo.com/) will help you search them all.

5. *Search iTunes U.* Across the United States, colleges and universities are going online through Apple's iTunes U, putting up video and audio speeches, lectures, and other academic content. You can find iTunes U on iTunes, of course, and you can do a keyword search on multiple sites using "power search." The term "global warming" produced 90 hits, including lectures, opinions, and reports from some of America's top universities.

6. *Local organizations.* The reference librarians on our campus routinely refer students to the state historical society or state law library when relevant to their projects. Local organizations can be rich sources of not only published information but also interviews and artifacts.

Library	Internet	Alternative Sources
• Vary search terms	• Vary search terms	• Search blogs
• Search other databases	• Use advanced search features	• Search images
• Check bibliographies	• Use multiple search engines	• Listen to archived radio and podcasts
• Use interlibrary loan	• Watch videocasts	• Search iTunes U
• Troll government documents		• Visit local organizations or libraries
• Ask a librarian		

FIGURE 3.9   **More Advanced Searching Techniques**

CHAPTER 4

The Fourth Week

Getting to the Draft

It is *not* 2 A.M. Your paper is *not* due in 12 hours but in one or two weeks. For some students, beginning to write a research paper this early—weeks before it's due—will be a totally new experience. An early start may also, for the first time, make the experience a positive one. I know that starting early will help ensure writing a better paper.

Still, there are those students who say they thrive on a looming deadline, who love working in its shadow, flirting with failure. "I work best that way," they say, and they wait until the last minute and race to the deadline in a burst of writing, often sustained by energy drinks or strong doses of caffeine. It works for some students. Panic is a pretty strong motivator. But I think most who defend this habit confuse their relief at successfully pulling off the assignment once again with a belief that the paper itself is successful.

Papers done under such pressure often aren't successful, and that is particularly true of the last-minute research paper, where procrastination is especially deadly. Research writing is recursive. You often have to circle back to where you've already been, discovering holes in your research or looking at your subject from new angles. It's hard to fit in a trip back to the library the night before the paper is due, when you've just started the draft and need to check some information. This book is designed to defeat procrastination, and if, in the past few weeks, you've done the exercises, taken thoughtful notes, and attempted a thorough search for information, you probably have the urge to begin writing.

On the other hand, you may feel as though you don't know enough yet about your topic to have anything to say. Or you may be swamped with information, and your head may be spinning. What do you do with it all?

Exploration or Argument?

What you do with it all depends on what kind of essay you're going to write. Working from an inquiry question, your draft can head in two directions:

1. *Argument.* Your discoveries in the past few weeks may have convinced you that a certain answer to your research question is particularly persuasive. Now you want to prove it. Another way to think about this is to ask yourself whether you think you want your readers to *think* or possibly even *do* something about your research topic.
2. *Exploratory essay.* On the other hand, maybe you're still not ready to make a judgment about the best answer to your research question and you want to use your essay to continue exploring it. You are less concerned with trying to get readers to think or do something than you are with helping them to appreciate what you find interesting or complicated about your topic.

Sometimes your research question will lead you toward one kind of essay or the other. Compare these two questions:

- *What should be done about the problem of smoking on campus?* (Argument)
- *How do smoking bans on college campuses influence social relationships between smokers?* (Exploration)

While both questions involve open-ended inquiry into the topic of campus smoking, one more naturally leads ultimately to a claim that is supported by reasons and evidence, and the other to an exploration of possible effects.

Your instructor may also give you guidance about whether your draft should be exploratory or argumentative. Depending on which it is, your focus this week might be a bit different. But first, gather your thoughts on everything you've learned about your topic so far.

EXERCISE 4.1

Dialogue with Dave

STEP 1: Dave is the reader you imagine when you picture the reader of your essay. He's a pretty nice guy, and smart, too. But first off, like any reader, he wants to know why he should care about the subject you're writing about. Then, once you've got Dave's interest, he has questions about what you're telling him about your topic. Like any conversation, what he asks about depends on the details of what you tell him. This conversation can't be scripted. Just let it develop as you write.

When you assume Dave's persona in this exercise, consider some of the stuff Dave might want to know, like

- Why? Where? Who? When? What?
- What do you mean by _____?
- How do most people see this? How do you see it differently?
- Are you kidding? I didn't know that. What else did you find out?
- Can you give me an example?
- Did that surprise you?
- What other questions does this raise?
- Who does this affect, mostly?
- What should we do about this?
- I'm not sure I believe this. Why do you?
- What do you think we should do about it?

Use the Table feature to format a document on your computer, creating two columns—one for Dave's questions and the other for your answers (see below). Start the conversation with Dave's first question—"What's the big deal about this, anyway?"—and take it from there. *If this is going to be useful, try to keep this conversation going for at least a half hour.*

In Figure 4.1, you can see part of what Mandy did with this exercise. She was exploring how ideas about beauty communicated through the American mass media influence how girls feel about themselves.

STEP 2: Many conversations like this one move toward some kind of conclusion. Reread what you wrote, and finish the exercise by crafting an answer to Dave's final question: *Okay, this is all very interesting. But based on everything you've learned so far, what's your point?*

S.O.F.T.

Many years ago, I was lucky enough to go to graduate school where a wonderful writer and teacher named Donald Murray taught, and he became both a friend and mentor. One of Don's endearing habits was to take a saying about which he was particularly fond

DAVE	MANDY
What's the big deal about this anyway? Why should I care?	In society today, girls at young ages are being influenced by the media and society that they should be culturally beautiful in order to live a happy life and gain social acceptance. Many girls compete in beauty pageants at young ages and grow up to have psychological and mental disorders from this pressure to be beautiful.
What do you mean by culturally beautiful?	Cultural beauty is where the woman appeals to what is considered attractive to the society at the specific time she is being judged. Cultural beauty is basically meeting society's standards; however, biological beauty for a woman means to be healthy and able to reproduce.
Can you give me an example of this cultural beauty affecting girls at a young age?	Beauty, whether it be male or female, will never disappear in society. It is a primitive goal to be considered socially attractive in society and many people will do anything to gain this social acceptance. Plastic surgery and liposuction are two methods women use to keep their beauty. Also this pressure on women can lead to eating disorders at a young age. The age group that has the highest rates of anorexia or bulimia is the female age group of 17 years old to 19 years old. A lot of this can be related back to their childhoods and the influences they had.

FIGURE 4.1   **Mandy's Dialogue with Dave**

and print it out on cardboard, which he would then distribute to his students. "Nulla dies sine linea"—never a day without a line—was one of these. Another was "S.O.F.T." This was an acronym for Say One Fricking Thing. Don believed that every piece of writing should say one fricking thing—it may deal with many ideas, but the writer's job was to find the *one* thing he or she wanted most to say about an essay topic.

More formally, we often understand this to mean that writing—especially academic writing—should have a thesis, a point, a theme, and a main idea. Too often, I'm afraid, writers arrive at this too early in their research—ending the inquiry process prematurely—or they don't arrive at it at all, and the essay or paper seems pointless.

In Exercise 4.1 you moved toward finding your S.O.F.T., and when you did, several things might have happened:

1. You discovered a point, and maybe it was one you didn't expect. Hallelujah! This one might need some fine-tuning but it seems to reflect your understanding of the topic at this point.
2. You arrived at a point, but it doesn't seem quite right. You feel like you're still groping toward a thesis—an answer to your research question—and this one seems forced or too general.
3. You have no clue what might be the S.O.F.T. All you have is more questions. Or perhaps you realize that you simply don't know enough yet to have any idea what you want to say.

If you find yourself in the first situation—you discovered a thesis that seems right—then maybe your draft should be an argumentative essay in which you attempt to prove your point. The second situation might invite you to continue your investigation by writing an exploratory research essay, and the third probably means that you haven't done nearly enough research yet. Actually, you probably need to do more research in every case—and you will as you continue the process.

Organizing the Draft

How you approach writing your first draft this week depends on what you decide about which kind of research essay you think you want to write: an argument or an exploratory essay. Let's look at how the two might differ.

But first the five-paragraph theme. Like a lot of school kids, I learned to write something called the "five-paragraph theme": introduction with thesis; three body paragraphs, each with a topic sentence and supporting details; and conclusion. This was the container into which I poured all of my writing back then. Though it didn't produce particularly interesting writing, the five-paragraph structure was a reliable way to organize things. It was very well suited to out-lines. I vaguely remember this one from sixth grade:

I. China is a really big country.
  A. The population of China is really big.
  B. The geographic size of China is really big.
  C. The economic dreams of China are really big.

What's useful about thinking of structure this way is the notion of hierarchy: Some ideas are subordinated to others, and each idea has some information subordinated under it. A problem with it, however, is the assumption that hierarchy is *always* the best way to organize information. For instance, essays can often make relevant digressions, or they might play with one way of seeing the topic and then another.

Perhaps a more basic problem with forms like the five-paragraph theme is the idea that structure is this kind of inert container that stands apart from the things you put into it and from your particular motives in writing about something.

Yet structure is important. And it's even more important when writers begin a draft with an abundance of information. John McPhee has written popular nonfiction essays on such topics as a guy who still makes birch bark canoes, people who study animal road kill, and his own exploration of Atlantic City using the game Monopoly as a guide. He is a careful and meticulous researcher, accumulating material in multiple binders from his interviews, observations, and reading. By the time he sits down to write, he's looking at pages and pages of notes. McPhee's solution to this problem is to use notecards to organize his information on bulletin boards, moving the cards around until he gets a satisfying arrange-ment. "The piece of writing has a structure inside it," he says, and before he begins drafting he seeks to find it.

If you don't have much information to begin with, structure is less of a problem. You simply end up using everything you have.

I'd like to encourage you, as you start drafting this week, to avoid thinking about the structure of your essay as something set in concrete before you begin. Instead, think of form rhetorically: Who is your audience and what does the assignment say, and what is your purpose in writing about your topic? For example, here are two structures to consider depending on whether your research paper is exploratory or argumentative:

■ *Delayed thesis structure*—characteristic of the exploratory essay
■ *Question-claim structure*—characteristic of the argumentative paper

However you choose to organize it, your research essay will have certain characteristics. For example, nearly any academic research paper includes the following items:

1. A S.O.F.T.—a point, a claim, a thesis—one main thing you are trying to say about the research question
2. A review of what has already been said by others about your topic
3. Specific information—the evidence or data on which your interpretations, conclusions, assertions, and speculations are based
4. A method of reasoning through the question, some pattern of thought—narrative, argument, essaying—that writer and reader find a convincing way to try to get at the truth of things

Delayed Thesis Structure

In an inquiry-based class, you typically choose a topic because you want to learn what you think. As you work through the research process, as I pointed out earlier, either you arrive at what you think is a persuasive answer to your research question and decide you will argue for it or you believe that you have more to learn and decide you will explore further. This second possibility was my motive in writing "Theories of Intelligence," the essay that opened this book. I didn't want to write an argument. I wanted to write an exploratory essay.

Quite naturally, then, I didn't begin my draft with a thesis—an answer to my questions about why I often felt stupid, despite evidence to the contrary—but sought to use my essay to try to sort this out. If you go with the "delayed thesis" structure in writing your essay, you use the information from your research to think through your research question.

In one version of using the delayed thesis structure, you essentially tell the story of your thinking so that your paper is a kind of "narrative of thought." The plot is something like, "This seems to be the problem and this is the question is raises for me. And here's what this person and that person have said about it, and this is what I think of what they said." The story ends with some kind of statement that addresses this question: "What do I understand now about the question I initially asked that I didn't understand when I first asked it, and what in this new understanding is particularly important?" (See Figure 4.2.) This last statement is your delayed thesis. You might also include discussion of questions you would like to further explore. As the arrows in Figure 4.2 show, arriving at a thesis doesn't necessarily mean the end of inquiry. A delayed thesis may end up opening doors rather than closing them.

Figure 4.3 is a more detailed look at a delayed thesis structure. It highlights five parts that a research essay *might* include and lists some specific options for developing each. Figure 4.3 might help you think about how to organize your draft this week.

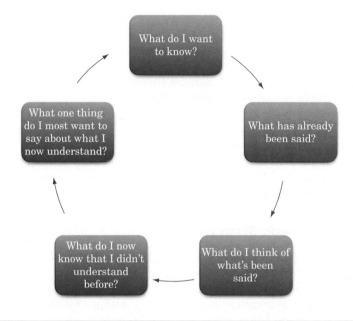

FIGURE 4.2   The Delayed Thesis Structure. This method of thinking through a research question might tell the story of your thinking and of how what you've read and heard has helped you to understand what you didn't understand before about your topic.

Question–Claim Structure

If your initial research question leads you toward an idea about what should be done or what your readers should believe—that is, toward argument—then you'll likely organize your essay differently. Instead of a delayed thesis structure, you might want to use the question–claim structure.

The question–claim structure has some similarities to the delayed thesis structure of the essay—for one thing, it arises from a question—but this method for organizing your draft puts your answer to that question toward the beginning and then proceeds, using your research, to make the most convincing case for that answer (see Figure 4.4). It's a little like the automobile dealer who, after wandering the lot, decides to put the models he or she most wants to sell in the showroom window. You focus your readers' gaze not on the process of discovery but, rather, on the product of that process: the point you want to make.

The question–claim structure may be the form of the research paper with which you're most familiar. Here's one way to think about

I. **Introduce the research problem or question and then your motive for exploring it. For example:**
   - Tell a story that dramatizes the problem.
   - Describe your own experiences with it.
   - What did you read, observe, or experience that made you curious about it?

II. **Establish the significance of the problem or question and why readers should care about it. For example:**
   - How many other people are affected?
   - What difference will it make in people's lives?
   - Why is this *particular* question significant?

III. **Describe and analyze what has already been written or said by others about the problem or question and how this advances your understanding. For example:**
   - Who has made a significant contribution to the conversation about this?
   - What have they said and how does that relate to your research question?
   - What important questions do these other voices raise for you?

IV. **Explain what you find to be the most persuasive or significant answer to the research question. This is your thesis. For example:**
   - In the end, which voices were most convincing? Why?
   - What might you add to the conversation?
   - What do you want to say?

V. **Describe what you've come to understand about the topic that you didn't fully appreciate when you began the project. What is left to explore?**
   - What difference will the discoveries you made about your question make in your life? In your readers' lives?
   - What do you remain curious about?
   - What questions are unresolved and what directions might more inquiry take if you were to continue?

FIGURE 4.3 A Structure for Exploring

organizing your draft using this approach. This structure has five parts (see Figure 4.5), each with various options and considerations. It is a structure that you can adapt to your needs.

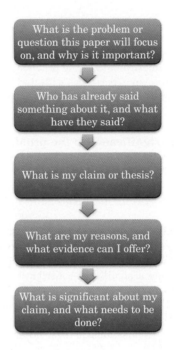

FIGURE 4.4   **The Question–Claim Structure.** This structure, which is characteristic of the argumentative research paper, signals the writer's purpose and point early on and then sets out to prove it.

Exploring or Arguing: An Example

Susan was writing an exploratory research essay on the relationship between attendance at preschool and academic success in elementary school. She decided to introduce her topic by describing her own dilemma with her son, Sam. She wanted to send him to preschool, but as a working college student, she wasn't sure she could afford it. Her personal anecdote highlighted the problem many parents face and the question behind her research: Will children who don't attend preschool be at a disadvantage in primary school or not? In the middle section of her essay, Susan reported on several studies that looked at a range of skills that were affected by preschool experience and discussed which of these she found most significant, particularly in the context of her personal interviews with several local teachers. In the second-to-last section of her draft, Susan concluded that preschool does indeed make a difference, particularly in the areas of reading and reasoning.

I. **Introduce the research question or problem that is the focus of the paper. For example:**
   - Provide factual background.
   - Dramatize with an anecdote.
   - Establish the significance of the problem by citing experts or other observers.

II. **What will be your argument or claim in the paper? This is your thesis.**
   - What do you think your readers should *believe* or what do you think they should *do*? State this thesis clearly.

III. **Review the literature. What have others already said about the question or problem? For example:**
   - Cite published studies, interviews, commentaries, experiments, and so on that are relevant to the question or problem.
   - Which ideas or voices seem most important? Are there identifiable camps in the debate, or certain patterns of argument?
   - Address popular assumptions. What do most people believe to be true?

IV. **What are your reasons for believing what you believe and, for each one, what specific evidence did you find that you thought was convincing?**
   - What kinds of evidence will your readers find most persuasive?
   - Are there various kinds of evidence that can be brought to bear?
   - How do your reasons square with those who might disagree with you?

V. **What is the significance of your claim? What's at stake for your audience? What might be other avenues for research? For example:**
   - What should we do? What might happen if we don't act?
   - How does the thesis or claim that you propose resolve some part of the problem? What part remains unresolved?
   - What questions remain?

FIGURE 4.5 **A Structure for Argument**

Imagine that Susan wanted instead to write an argumentative research paper, a more conventional form for academic research. Would it be organized differently? While she still might begin with a personal anecdote as a way to dramatize the problem, Susan might choose instead to begin with information, highlighting the statistics and arguments that establish the importance of the problem. How many children in the United States attend preschool? How many don't? What are the trends? Are more parents struggling to find affordable preschools? Are fewer preschools available in disadvantaged areas? Is there a shortage of teachers? A significant difference would be where in the paper Susan puts her thesis. In the argumentative paper, the thesis usually appears toward the beginning (see Figure 4.3) and is stated explicitly: "I will argue in this essay that the growing number of children in the United States who are being denied a preschool experience will be at a serious disadvantage in reading and reasoning skills when they enter elementary school." Her essay would then go on to methodically establish the truth of this claim using her research. Susan might end her essay by suggesting how elementary teachers could address the learning deficits these children bring into their classrooms or how more children could be given access to preschool.

Preparing to Write the Draft

If research is a little like soup making, then you want to make something hearty, not thin; that's nearly impossible unless you have a lot of information. If you slacked on developing focused knowledge last week and didn't do enough research on your question, then you'll find that you have to use most everything you *do* have to write the first draft. If that happens, your essay will be unfocused and uninformative. Scanty research is one of the most common problems I see in student work at this stage in the process. Your first decision before beginning the draft is whether you've got what it takes to make at least decent soup.

Refining the Question

But you can't really judge the quality of your information until you feel comfortable with your research question. Are you asking the right question? Is it the question that you find most interesting? Is it focused enough? Did you refine it as you learned more about your topic? Does it incorporate the language or terms you may have learned in your reading? Typically, research questions evolve, especially if you are tackling a topic that you initially didn't know much about.

For these kinds of topics, the research questions we often ask initially are broadly informative or questions of definition:

- *What are the theories of dog training?*

As we learn more about our research topic, the questions frequently become more specific—which is far more helpful in guiding research—and reflect our new understandings of the topic. The next generation of questions often moves beyond questions of fact or definition and reflects a *particular* interest in the topic: Is it any good? What does it mean? What should be done? What might be true? What are important causes? (See Figure 4.6.)

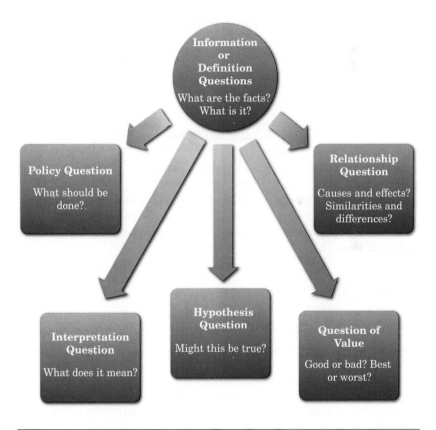

FIGURE 4.6   Categories of Questions. Usually our initial research questions are questions of fact or definition: What is known about this topic? What is it? But a strong research essay needs *to do* something with the facts. One way to think about what a question is trying to do is to place it in one of these additional categories: questions of policy, interpretation, hypothesis, value, or relationship. Before you begin your draft, rethink your question. Can it be more specific? Can you rewrite your question so that it gives you a stronger sense of what you're trying to with your research?

For example, this rewrite of the original research question is a little more specific and also implies value:

- *What are the best theories of dog training?*

The following question is more specific still and incorporates some of the language in the literature:

- *Is there evidence that "dog-centric" approaches to training that reward behavior work better than approaches that emphasize the trainer's dominance over the dog?*

And the following question is even more specific:

- *What is the relationship between the use of shock collars and dog aggression or submission?*

Revisit your research question before you begin your draft. In light of what you've learned about your topic so far, can you rewrite the question so that it provides you with stronger guidance about your purpose in the draft? When you've rewritten your research question, put it on a notecard or sticky note, and put it somewhere on your computer monitor where you can see it as you're writing the draft. Your research question (or thesis) is the sea anchor that will keep you from going adrift.

Refining the Thesis

If you're writing an argumentative essay, then you need to settle on a tentative thesis. It may change as you continue doing the writing and research, but for now you should have a pretty specific statement of what you think. Exercise 4.1 might have helped nudge you in this direction. Now work with your thesis a bit more.

There is considerable talk about thesis statements. Sometimes it seems like a thesis (or S.O.F.T., main point, central claim, organizing idea, etc.) is a kind of club required to beat an essay into submission, forcing every part of the work into obedience. In this view, there is no room for digression, contrary evidence, opposing views, or uncertainty. Much writing—like the world that writers attempt to explore in that writing—is much messier than that, and that complexity is what makes inquiry interesting.

And yet, when writers discover what they want to say—the answer to the question, the realization about what should be done, or the interpretation that makes the most sense—it's essential that they say it clearly, first for themselves and then for their readers. At this stage in the research process, your thesis is very tentative, but if you spend some time refining it, it will reward you later. A well-stated thesis gives you a sense of direction and can help you to organize both your research and your essay. Just don't be slavish about it. A thesis isn't a club. It isn't even a tool. A thesis is a way of seeing that is made of sand, not stone, and it is continually reshaped by what you learn.

What do we know about the qualities of a good thesis? For one thing, we know that they are not overly broad or obvious. Take this statement, for example:

There are many theories about how to train dogs.

Yep, there sure are. This is not a thesis; it's just an observation and a statement of the obvious. What's missing here is a judgment. The kind of judgment you make in your thesis is related to the kind of question you're asking about your topic (see Figure 4.6). The observation that there are many theories of dog training is a statement of fact in response to a question of fact. But a thesis is a tentative answer to another kind of question—a question of policy, interpretation, hypothesis, value, or relationship. So if my research question were "What is the *best* method of dog training?" (a question of value), then my thesis might be something like this:

> *The evidence suggests that "human-centric" approaches to dog training—those that work from the premise that the trainer should be dominant over the dog—are less effective than "dog-centric" approaches, which use positive reinforcement.*

Can you see how your thesis is directly related to your research question?

EXERCISE 4.2

Sharpening Your Point

Even if you're writing an exploratory essay, it's helpful to think about what your thesis might be at this stage in the inquiry process. This is a kind of reality check: What do I think *right now* based on what I've learned? You are invited to change your mind later. If your essay is argumentative, then it's even more important to establish a tentative thesis. The following templates, each based on the kind of question you're asking, might help:

Thesis from a Question of Value

Based on _____, the evidence strongly suggests that _____ is (better / worse, more effective / less effective) than _____.

Example: Based on recent studies comparing how well disciplines teach critical thinking to college students, the evidence suggests that business programs are failing to do a good job teaching reasoning skills to their undergraduates.

Thesis from a Question of Policy

In the debate over _____, I'm persuaded that the most important thing to do is _____.

Example: In the debate over what to do with the overpopulation of wild horses in western rangelands, it's clear that the only effective solution is for the federal agencies to cull the herds.

Thesis from a Question of Interpretation

The pattern in _____ that is most (significant / interesting / obvious) is _____.

Example: Throughout Ken Kesey's *One Flew Over the Cuckoo's Nest*, the character of Nurse Ratched represents everything that sexist men fear: the threat of emasculation by a woman.

Thesis from a Hypothesis Question

Based on my research, the assumption that _____ appears to be (true / false, qualified / unqualified, accurate / inaccurate, difficult to determine / impossible to determine).

Example: My research on Facebook and social intimacy appears to confirm my impression that "friending" can promote connection but can also be used to manipulate and divide.

Thesis from a Relationship Question

There is a (strong / weak) relationship between _____ and _____.

Example: There is a strong relationship between dog owners' views about the need for dominance over their pet and their choice of either "human-centric" or "dog-centric" training methods.

These templates are a bit crude, but try to use them as a starting point to craft a one- or two-sentence thesis that *reflects your current understanding of your topic.* Write this on a sticky note or notecard and, along with your research question, put it on your computer monitor as a reminder when you write the draft.

Deciding Whether to Say *I*

In addition to refining your research question and thesis, there's something else you should wrestle with before you get started: Will you write your essay in first person? You may think that this isn't even a choice. Academic writing is supposed to be faceless, impersonal, and objective, and the best way to maintain this pretense is to religiously avoid ever using the first person in an academic essay.

The ban on the slender "I" from academic prose by teachers and textbooks is based, in part, on the assumption that this is simply the only way to write scholarship, a myth that studies of academic writing prove wrong again and again. Scholarly writing is diverse and discipline specific, and in a number of fields—for example, business, philosophy, English, and linguistics—articles sometimes use the first person and may even include autobiographical material. Another reason that first person is exiled is because it encourages students to write with needless self-references like "I believe that..." or "In my opinion...." As is so often the case with writing, there aren't really "rules" about how things are supposed to be written; these are rhetorical decisions based on your reasons for composing something, to whom you're writing, and what you're writing about.

There are actually good reasons to consider writing this essay in the first person. The most important is this: When a writer stops pretending that the *text* talks instead of the *author* (e.g., "This paper will argue that...") and actually enters into her text, she is much more likely to initiate a genuine conversation with her readers *and* with her sources. This dialogue might very well lead to some new ways of seeing her topic—that is, after all, the purpose of inquiry.

Getting Personal Without Being Personal

Conversation takes place between people, and in writing that embodies conversation, readers sense what Gordon Harvey* called *presence*—an awareness that a writer is making sense of things in his own particular ways, that he has a personal stake in what is being said. This is most easily achieved when the writer *gets* personal by using the first person, sharing personal experiences and perspectives. I hope that you sense my presence in *The Curious Researcher* through my willingness to do such things.

*Harvey, Gordon. "Presence in the Essay." *College English* 56 (1994): 642–54. Print.

Making Your Presence Felt

Here are some ways to establish your presence in your research essay without necessarily using the first person.

- *Control quotation.* Carefully consider how you use the voices of others—where in your essay and for what purpose—as well as what you choose to emphasize in what those voices said.
- *Find your own way of saying things.* Even when talking about what someone else has said, say it in a way that only you can.
- *Find your own way of seeing things.* How do others usually see your topic, and how do you see it differently?
- *Seize opportunities to comment.* More than anything else, what you *do* with information—evaluating it, relating it, defining it, interpreting it, establishing its significance— gives the essay your signature.

But I also want you to see, as Harvey observes, that presence in writing can be registered in ways other than simply talking about yourself. That is, you can write a research essay this week that *doesn't* use the first person or isn't autobiographical and still provides your readers with a strong sense of your presence as an individual writer and thinker. (See the box "Making Your Presence Felt" for some specific suggestions.) This presence may be much more subtle when it's not carried on the first-person singular's sturdy back. But it still makes writing come to life.

Before you begin drafting your essay this week, you'll have to decide how you'd prefer to get personal—explicitly or implicitly. For some of you, the choices may be limited. For instance, if your essay is on the causes of World War I, then integrating your own personal experience with the subject is obviously not an option. Most topics, however, offer the possibility of self-disclosure, and unless your instructor advises otherwise, almost all can accommodate *I*. But when you choose not to get personal in direct ways, you can still establish a strong presence in your essay.

Frankly, one of the best ways to do this isn't self-disclosure *or* first-person writing. The best way to have a strong presence in anything you write is to *find your own way of saying things*. You practice this in your double-entry journal in summaries, paraphrases, and fastwrites. Even if you're borrowing the ideas of someone else—and even bringing their voices into your writing—it is your voice that gives the work your signature.

Starting to Write the Draft: Beginning at the Beginning

John McPhee, whom I mentioned earlier as one of the masters of the research-based essay, gave a talk some years back about beginnings, which vex many writers.

> The first part—the lead, the beginning—is the hardest part of all to write. I've often heard writers say that if you have written your lead you have written 90 percent of the story. You have tens of thousands of words to choose from, after all, and only one can start the story, then one after that, and so forth. And your material, at this point, is all fresh and unused, so you don't have the advantage of being in the middle of things. You could start in any of many places. What will you choose? Leads must be sound. They should never promise what does not follow.

As McPhee said in his talk, "Leads, like titles, are flashlights that shine down into the story."*

Flashlights or Floodlights?

I love this: *"Leads...are flashlights that shine down into the story."* An introduction, at least the kind I was taught to write in high school, is more like a sodium vapor lamp that lights up the whole neighborhood. I remember writing introductions to research papers that sounded like this:

```
There are many critical problems that face soci-
ety today. One of these critical problems is
environmental protection, and especially the con-
servation of marine resources. This paper will
explore one of these resources—the whale—and the
myriad ways in which the whale-watching industry
now poses a new threat to this species' survival.
It will look at what is happening today and what
some people concerned with the problem hope will
```

*McPhee, John. University of New Hampshire, 1977.

```
happen tomorrow. It will argue that new regula-
tions need to be put into effect to reduce boat
traffic around our remaining whales, a national
treasure that needs protection.
```

This introduction isn't that bad. It does offer a statement of purpose, and it explains the thesis. But the window it opens on the paper is so broad—listing everything the paper will try to do—that readers see a bland, general landscape. What's to discover? The old writing formula for structuring some papers—"Say what you're going to say, say it, and then say what you said"—breeds this kind of intro- duction. It also gets the writer started on a paper that often turns out as bland as the beginning.

Consider this alternative opening for the same paper:

```
Scott Mercer, owner of the whale-watching vessel
Cetecea, tells the story of a man and his son
who decide that watching the whales from inside
their small motorboat isn't close enough. They
want to swim with them. As Mercer and his pas-
sengers watch, the man sends his son overboard
with snorkel and fins, and the boy promptly
swims toward a "bubble cloud," a mass of air
exhaled by a feeding humpback whale below the
surface. What the swimmer doesn't know is that,
directly below that bubble cloud, the creature
is on its way up, mouth gaping. They are both
in for a surprise. "I got on the P.A. system and
told my passengers, just loud enough for the guy
in the boat to hear me, that either that swim-
mer was going to end up as whale food or he was
going to get slapped with a $10,000 fine. He got
out of the water pretty fast."
```

I think this lead accomplishes nearly as much as the bland version but in a more compelling way. It suggests the purpose of the paper—to explore conflicts between whale lovers and whales—and even implies the thesis—that human activity around whales needs more regulation, a point that might follow the anecdote. This lead is more like McPhee's "flashlight," pointing out the direction of the paper without attempting to illuminate the entire subject in a paragraph. An interesting beginning will also help launch the writer into a more interesting paper, for both reader and writer.

It's probably obvious that your opening is your first chance to capture your reader's attention. But how you begin your research paper will also have a subtle yet significant impact on the rest of it. The lead starts the paper going in a particular direction; it also establishes the *tone,* or writing voice, and the writer's relationships to the subject and the reader. Most writers at least intuitively know this, which is why beginnings are so hard to write.

Writing Multiple Leads

One thing that will make it easier to get started is to write three leads to your paper, instead of agonizing over one that must be perfect. Each different opening you write should point the "flashlight" in a different direction, suggesting different trails the draft might follow. After composing several leads, you can choose the one that you—and ultimately, your readers—find most promising.

Writing multiple openings to your paper might sound hard, but consider all the ways to begin:

■ *Anecdote*. Think of a little story that nicely frames what your paper is about, as does the lead about the man and his son who almost became whale food.

■ *Scene*. Begin by giving your readers a look at some revealing aspect of your topic. A paper on the destruction of tropical rain forests might begin with a description of what the land looks like after loggers have left it.

■ *Profile*. Try a lead that introduces someone who is important to your topic. Amanda's essay on the relationship between the popularity of tooth whitening and our changing notions of beauty might begin, for example, by describing Dr. Levine, the man who determined with mathematical precision the dimensions of the "perfect smile."

■ *Background.* Maybe you could begin by providing important and possibly surprising background information on your topic. A paper on steroid use might start by citing the explosive growth in use by high school athletes in the last ten years. A paper on a novel or an author might begin with a review of what critics have had to say.

■ *Quotation.* Sometimes, you encounter a great quote that beautifully captures the question your paper will explore or the direction it will take. Heidi's paper on whether *Sesame Street* provides children with a good education began by quoting a tribute from *U.S. News and World Report* to Jim Henson after his sudden death.

■ *Dialogue.* Open with dialogue between people involved in your topic. Dan's paper on the connection between spouse abuse and alcoholism began with a conversation between himself and a woman who had been abused by her husband.

■ *Question.* Pointedly ask your readers the questions you asked that launched your research or the questions your readers might raise about your topic. Here's how Kim began her paper on adoption: "Can you imagine going through life not knowing your true identity?"

■ *Contrast.* Try a lead that compares two apparently unlike things that highlight the problem or dilemma the paper will explore. Dusty's paper "Myth of the Superwoman" began with a comparison between her friend Susan, who grew up believing in Snow White and Cinderella and married at 21, and herself, who never believed in princes on white horses and was advised by her mother that it was risky to depend on a man.

■ *Announcement.* Sometimes the most appropriate beginning *is* one like the first lead on whales and whale-watchers mentioned earlier, which announces what the paper is about. Though such openings are sometimes not particularly compelling, they are direct. A paper with a complex topic or focus may be well served by simply stating in the beginning the main idea you'll explore and what plan you'll follow.

E X E R C I S E   4 . 3

Three Ways In

STEP 1: Compose three different beginnings, or leads, to your research paper. Each should be one or two paragraphs (or perhaps more, depending on what type of lead you've chosen and on the length of your

Here are three openings that Amanda crafted for her draft on our cultural obsession with the "perfect smile." Which do you think is strongest?

1. I haven't felt much like smiling recently. It isn't that I've been particularly melancholy or deprived of necessary joy. I've actually been hesitant to smile because lately I've felt insecure about my teeth. I brush and floss every day and see my dentist twice a year, just like any responsible hygiene patient does—but that doesn't seem to be enough anymore. My teeth need to be white. Now when I feel the corners of my mouth pucker upwards and I start to grin at someone, I can't stop thinking about my teeth. What once was a simple visual expression of happiness has become a symptom of my overall doubts about my appearance.

2. Julie Beatty wants people to look at her as a more confident, strong person, so she's doing the only logical thing. She's shelling out over $12,500 for an overhaul on her teeth. While it sounds completely ridiculous to change a person's oral structure to create a different persona, Julie is a member of a booming group of people who are looking to change their smiles to change their lives. Whether or not Julie's straightening, whitening, and tooth reshaping will change her success as an executive is still unknown, but the popularity of cosmetic dentistry and smile care is an undeniable new phenomenon.

3. I can feel individual molecules of air battering at my teeth. It's the middle of the night, but I can't sleep because of the constant pain in my mouth. Even the weight of my lips pressing down on my teeth is agonizing, like I've spent the day being hit in the mouth with a hammer and have exposed nerves protruding throughout. I haven't been beaten up, though. The cause of all my agony is a 10 percent peroxide gel I've been smearing into trays and putting on my teeth for the past week to whiten them. All this pain is due to my vanity and desire for a bit more pearliness in my pearly whites. As I watch the numbers of the clock roll from 2:00 to 4:00, I wonder why I'm putting up with such dental distress just for a more gleaming smile.

FIGURE 4.7 Amanda's Three Leads*

paper). Think about the many different ways to begin, as mentioned earlier, and experiment. Your instructor may ask you to write the three leads in your research notebook or print them out and bring them to class. (For an example, see Figure 4.7.)

*These excerpts are reprinted with permission of Amanda Stewart.

STEP 2: Get some help deciding which opening is strongest. Circulate your leads in class, or show them to friends. Ask each person to check the one lead he likes best, that most makes him want to read on.

STEP 3: Choose the lead you like (even if no one else does). To determine how well it prepares your readers for what follows, ask a friend or classmate to answer these questions: Based on reading only the opening of the paper: (a) What do you predict this paper is about? What might be its focus? (b) Can you guess what central question I'm trying to answer? (c) Can you predict what my thesis might be? (d) How would you characterize the tone of the paper?

It's easy to choose an opening that's catchy. But the beginning of your paper must also help establish your purpose in writing it, frame your focus, and perhaps even suggest your main point or thesis. The lead will also establish the voice, or tone, the paper will adopt.

That's a big order for one or two paragraphs, and you may find that more than a couple of paragraphs are needed to do it. If you did Exercise 4.3, tentatively select the one opening (or a combination of several) you composed that does those things best. I think you'll find that none of the leads you composed will be wasted; there will be a place for the ones you don't use somewhere else in the paper. Keep them handy.

Writing for Reader Interest

You've tentatively chosen a lead for your paper. You've selected it based on how well you think it frames your tentative purpose, establishes an appropriate tone or voice, and captures your readers' attention. Once you've gotten your readers' attention, you want to keep it. Before you continue writing your draft, take some time to explore the four considerations discussed next. Along with your strong lead, drafting with these considerations in mind will help you craft a lively, interesting paper that will help keep readers turning pages:

1. How does your topic intersect with your readers' experiences?
2. Is there a way to put faces on your topic, to dramatize how it affects or is affected by particular people?
3. Can you find an ending that further clarifies, dramatizes, or emphasizes what you've come to understand about the answers to your research question?
4. Are there opportunities to surprise your readers, with interesting facts or arresting arguments, or highlighting a way of seeing something that is unexpected?

Working the Common Ground

Here's how David Quammen, a nature writer, begins an essay on the sexual strategy of Canada geese:

> Listen: *uh-whongk, uh-whongk, uh-whongk, uh-whongk,* and then you are wide awake, and you smile up at the ceiling as the calls fade off to the north and already they are gone. Silence again, 3 A.M., the hiss of March winds. A thought crosses your mind before you roll over and, contentedly, resume sleeping. The thought is: "Thank God I live here, right here exactly, in their path. Thank God for those birds." The honk of wild Canada geese passing overhead in the night is a sound to freshen the human soul. The question is why.*

If you live in Puerto Rico or anywhere beyond the late-night call of geese flying overhead, this lead paragraph may not draw you into Quammen's article on the birds' sexual habits. But for the many of us who know the muttering of geese overhead, suddenly the writer's question—Why is this a sound "to freshen the human soul"?—becomes our question, too. *We want to know what he knows because he starts with what we both know already:* the haunting sound of geese in flight.

David Quammen understands the importance of working the common ground his readers have with him on his topic. In "The Miracle of Geese," his lead draws on an experience that many of us know, and once he establishes that common ground, he takes us into the less familiar territory he encountered while researching Canada geese. And we willingly go. Quammen gives us a foothold on his topic that comes from our own experience with it.

As you write your draft this week, seize common ground with your readers whenever you can. Ask yourself this:

- *What are my readers' own experiences with my topic?*
- *Is there some way in my paper that I can help them see that it's relevant to them?*
- *How can I help them see what they may already know?*

One of my interests in writing an essay about theories of intelligence—the essay in the Introduction of this book—was the conviction that I'm not alone in wondering whether I'm not all that smart and wondering, too, why these doubts linger despite my success.

---

*Quammen, David. *The Flight of the Iguana.* New York: Delacorte, 1988, 233. Print.

As you draft your research paper, look for ways to work the common ground between your topic and your readers: What typically is their relationship to what you're writing about? What might they know about the topic but not have noticed? How does it touch their world? What would they want to know from their own experiences with your topic?

Steve, writing a paper about the town fire department that services the university, began by describing a frequent event in his dormitory: a false alarm. He then went on to explore why many alarms are not really so false after all. He hooked his readers by drawing on their common experience with his topic.

Some topics, like geese and divorce and alcoholism, may have very real connections to the lives of your readers. Many people have heard geese overhead, seen families broken apart, or watched parents or friends destroy themselves with booze. As you revise your paper, look for opportunities to encourage readers to take a closer look at something about your topic they may have seen before.

Topics for Which Common Ground Is Hard to Find

Some topics don't yield common ground so directly. They may be outside the direct experiences of your readers. For example, Margaret was a history major, and, thankfully, she had never had the bubonic plague. Neither have the rest of us. But she was interested in writing a research essay on the impact of the fourteenth-century epidemic on the lives of European women. This is an age and a disaster that in some ways is beyond the imagining of modern readers, but a skillful writer will look to highlight some of the similarities between our lives and those of the people she's writing about. One of these connections might be the modern AIDS epidemic in Africa, a disaster of truly epic proportions, though it seems largely ignored by many Americans. Margaret might begin her essay with a brief glimpse at the devastation of families in South Africa today as a way of establishing the relevance of her 500-year-old topic.

Literary topics may also present a challenge in establishing common ground with readers, unless the author or work is familiar. But there are ways. When I was writing a paper on notions of manhood in Wallace Stegner's novels *The Big Rock Candy Mountain* and *Recapitulation,* I brought the idea of manhood home to my readers by describing my relationship with my own father and then comparing it to the relationship of two key characters in the books. Comparison to other more popular works that readers may know can also be a way to establish some common ground.

In writing your paper, imagine the ways in which your topic intersects with the life of a typical reader, and then use your insights to bring the information to life.

Putting People on the Page

Essayist E. B. White once advised that when you want to write about humankind, you should write about a human. The advice to look at the *small* to understand the *large* applies to most writing, not just the research paper.

Ideas come alive when we see how they operate in the world we live in. Beware, then, of long paragraphs with sentences that begin with phrases such as *in today's society,* where you wax on with generalization after generalization about your topic. Unless your ideas are anchored to specific cases, observations, experiences, statistics, and, especially, people, they will be reduced to abstractions and lose their power for your reader.

Using Case Studies

Strangely, research papers are often peopleless landscapes, which is one of the things that can make them so lifeless to read. Lisa wrote about theories of child development, citing studies and schools of thought about the topic yet never applying that information to a real child, her own daughter, two-year-old Rebecca. In his paper decrying the deforestation of the Amazon rain forest, Marty never gave his readers the chance to hear the voices of the Indians whose way of life is threatened. *Ultimately, what makes almost any topic matter to the writer or the reader is what difference it makes to people.*

Candy's paper on child abuse and its effect on language development, for example, opened with the tragic story of Genie, who, for nearly 13 years, was bound in her room by her father and beaten whenever she made a sound. When Genie was finally rescued, she could not speak at all. This sad story about a real girl makes the idea that child abuse affects how one speaks (the paper's thesis)—anything but abstract. Candy gave her readers reason to care about what she learned about the problem by personalizing it.

Sometimes, the best personal experience to share is your own. Have you been touched by the topic? Kim's paper about the special problems of women alcoholics included anecdotes about several women gleaned from her reading, but the paper was most compelling when she talked about her own experiences with her mother's alcoholism.

Using Interviews

Interviews are another way to bring people to the page. In "Why God Created Flies," Richard Conniff brought in the voice of a bug expert, Vincent Dethier, who not only had interesting things to say about flies but also said them with humor and enthusiasm. Heidi's paper on *Sesame Street* featured the voice of a school principal, a woman who echoed the point the paper made about the value of the program. Such research essays are filled not just with information about the topic but also with people who are touched by it in some way.

As you write your paper, look for opportunities to bring people to the page. Hunt for case studies, anecdotes, and good quotes that will help your readers see how your topic affects how people think and live their lives.

Writing a Strong Ending

Readers remember beginnings and endings. We already explored what makes a strong beginning: It engages the reader's interest, it's more often specific than general, and it frames the purpose of the paper, defining for the reader where it is headed. A beginning for a research paper should also state its thesis (as in an argumentative essay) or state the question (as in an exploratory essay).

We haven't said anything yet about endings, or "conclusions" as they are traditionally labeled. What's a strong ending? That depends. If you're writing a formal research paper in some disciplines, the basic elements of your conclusion might be prescribed. For example, you might need to summarize major findings and suggest directions for further research. But often, especially if you're writing a less formal research essay, you'll be able select from a wide range of options. For example, in an argumentative research essay, you might end as Figure 4.5 suggests, emphasizing what readers should do about the problem and why it matters. Exploratory essays might end with an anecdote, one that illuminates the understandings the writer has discovered. An ending for either kind of essay might suggest new questions, other avenues for research, or a reconsideration of an initial thesis.

Endings to Avoid

The ending of your research paper could be a lot of things, and in a way, it's easier to say what it should *not* be:

■ Avoid conclusions that simply restate what you've already said. This is the "kick the dead horse" conclusion some of us were taught to write in school on the assumption that our readers probably aren't smart enough to get our point, so we'd better repeat it. This approach annoys most readers, who *are* smart enough to know the horse is dead.

■ Avoid endings that begin with *in conclusion* or *thus.* Words such as these also signal to your reader what she already knows: that you're ending. And they often lead into a very general summary, which gets you into a conclusion such as the one mentioned above: dead.

■ Avoid endings that don't feel like endings—that trail off onto other topics, are abrupt, or don't seem connected to what came before them. Prompting your readers to think is one thing; leaving them hanging is quite another.

In some ways, the conclusion of your research paper is the last stop on your journey; the reader has traveled far with you to get there. The most important quality of a good ending is that it add something to the paper. If it doesn't, cut it and write a new one.

What can the ending add? It can add a further elaboration of your thesis that grows from the evidence you've presented, a discussion of solutions to a problem that has arisen from the information you've uncovered, or perhaps a final illustration or piece of evidence that drives home your point.

Student Christina Kerby's research essay on method acting explores the controversy over whether this approach is selfish, subverting the playwright's intentions about a character's identity and replacing it with the actor's focus on her own feelings and identity. Christina's ending, however, first transcends the debate by putting method acting in context: It is one of several tools an actor can use to tap her emotions for a role. But then Christina humorously raises the nagging question about selfishness once more: Can we accept that Juliet is not thinking about the fallen Romeo as she weeps by his side but about her dead cat Fluffy? Here's Christina's ending:

```
Acting is no longer about poise, voice quality,
and diction only. It is also about feeling the
part, about understanding the emotions that go
into playing the part, and about possessing the
skill necessary to bring those emotions to life
within the character.... Whether an actor uses
Stanislavski's method of physical actions to
unlock the door to her subconscious or whether
she attempts to stir up emotions from deep within
herself using Strasberg's method, the actor's goal
is to create a portrayal that is truthful. It is
```

possible to pick out a bad actor from a mile away,
one who does not understand the role because she
does not understand the emotions necessary to
create it. Or perhaps she simply lacks the means
of tapping into them.

If genuine emotion is what the masses want,
method acting may be just what every star-struck
actress needs. Real tears? No problem. The
audience will never know that Juliet was not
lamenting the loss of her true love Romeo but
invoking the memory of her favorite cat Fluffy,
who died tragically in her arms.*

An ending, in many ways, can be approached similarly to a lead. You can conclude with an anecdote, a quotation, a description, a summary, or a profile. Go back to the discussion earlier in this chapter of types of leads for ideas about types of conclusions. The same basic guidelines apply.

One of the easiest ways to solve the problem of finding a strong ending is to have the snake bite its tail. In other words, find some way in the end of your essay to return to where the piece began. For example, if your research essay began with an anecdote that dramatized a problem—say, the destruction of old growth forests in Washington—you might return to that opening anecdote, suggesting how the solutions you explored in your essay might have changed the outcome. If you pose a question in the first few paragraphs, return to the question in the last few. If you begin with a profile of someone relevant to your topic, return to him or her in the end, perhaps amplifying on some part of your picture of the person. Although this approach is formulaic, it often works well because it gives a piece of writing a sense of unity.

Using Surprise

The research process—like the writing process—can be filled with discovery for the writer if he approaches the topic with curiosity

---

*Reprinted with permission of Christina B. Kerby.

and openness. When I began researching the *Lobster Almanac,* I was constantly surprised by things I didn't know: Lobsters are bugs; it takes eight years for a lobster in Maine to grow to the familiar one-pound size; the largest lobster ever caught weighed about 40 pounds and lived in a tank at a restaurant for a year, developing a fondness for the owner's wife. I could go on and on. And I did, in the book, sharing unusual information with my readers on the assumption that if it surprised me, it would surprise them, too.

As you write your draft, reflect on the surprising things you discovered about your topic during your research and look for ways to weave that information into the rewrite. Later, after you have written your draft, share it with a reader and ask for his ideas about what is particularly interesting and should be further developed. For now, think about unusual specifics you may have left out.

However, don't include information, no matter how surprising or interesting, that doesn't serve your purpose. Christine's survey on the dreams of college freshmen had some fascinating findings, including some accounts of recurring dreams that really surprised her. She reluctantly decided not to say much about them, however, because they didn't really further the purpose of her paper, which was to discover what function dreams serve. On the other hand, Bob was surprised to find that some politically conservative politicians and judges actually supported decriminalization of marijuana. He decided to include more information about who they were and what they said in his revision, believing it would surprise his readers and strengthen his argument.

Writing with Sources

The need for *documentation*—that is, citing sources—distinguishes the research paper from most other kinds of writing. And let's face it: Worrying about sources can cramp your style. Many students have an understandable paranoia about plagiarism and tend, as mentioned earlier, to let the voices of their sources overwhelm their own. Students are also often distracted by technical details: Am I getting the right page number? Where exactly should this citation go? Do I need to cite this or not?

As you gain control of the material by choosing your own writing voice and clarifying your purpose in the paper, you should feel less constrained by the technical demands of documentation. The following suggestions may also help you weave reference sources into your own writing without the seams showing.

Blending Kinds of Writing and Sources

One of the wonderful things about the research essay is that it can draw on all four sources of information—reading, interviews, observation, and experience—as well as the four notetaking strategies discussed earlier—quotation, paraphrase, summary, and the writer's own analysis and commentary. Skillfully blended, these elements can make music.

Look at this paragraph from Heidi's paper on *Sesame Street*:

> There is more to this show than meets the eye, certainly. It is definitely more than just a crowd of furry animals all living together in the middle of New York City. Originally intended as an effort to educate poor, less privileged youth, *Sesame Street* is set in the very middle of an urban development on purpose (Hellman 52). As Jon Stone, one of the show's founders and co-producers sees it, the program couldn't be "just another escapist show set in a tree house or a badger den" (52). Instead, the recognizable environment gave something to the kids they could relate to. "...It had a lot more real quality to it than, say, Mister Rogers.... Kids say the reason they don't like Mister Rogers is that it's unbelievable," says Nancy Diamonti.*

The writing is lively here, not simply because the topic is interesting to those of us who know the program. Heidi has nicely blended her own commentary with summary, paraphrase, and quotation, all in a single paragraph. She has also been able to draw on multiple sources of information—an interview, some effective quotes from her reading, and her own observations of *Sesame Street*. We sense that the writer is *using* the information, and is not being used by it.

---

*Used with permission of Heidi R. Dunham.

Handling Quotes

Avoid the temptation, as Heidi did, to load up your paragraphs with long and unintegrated quotes from your sources. The most common fumble I see with quotations in student papers is what I call "hanging quotes." Embedded in a paragraph is a sentence or two within quotation marks. Though the passage is cited, there's no indication of who said it. Usually this means the writer was uncertain about how to summarize or paraphrase or work *part* of the quotation into his own prose. Here's what I mean:

> The third biggest tattooing movement occurred at the turn of the century: religious tattooing. "When it comes to modern Christian tattoo, it can most likely be traced back to the times of the counterculture movement of the '60s and '70s. While sex, drugs, and rock and roll were waging a war against Christian culture, devoted Christians emerged who wanted to claim back lost Christian territory. One of the ways that they did this was to reclaim the practice of tattoo for God and Jesus, by getting tattoos that were inspired by Christian and religious symbols and images" ("TattooJohnny"). Many Christian preachers and youth group leaders are getting tattoos with Christian themes to combat the satanic images in rock music. Many of the themes include rock-style designs with scripture or crosses that resemble those of the warriors.

Can you see how the long quote just appears in the middle of the paragraph, just floating freely and (aside from a parenthetical citation) unanchored to who said it and why? As a rule, whenever you quote, attribute the source, and *work* with it. Don't just look for opportunities to paraphrase some of it; also comment on what was said: What is interesting about the quote? Why is it significant in the context of what you're talking about? What would you emphasize? (See "Sandwiching Quotes" on page 178.)

Use quotations selectively. And if you can, blend them into your own sentences, using a particularly striking or relevant part of the original source. To see how this might work, contrast the use of quotes in this paragraph and in the reworked paragraph that follows:

> Black Elk often spoke of the importance of the circle to American Indian culture. "You may have noticed that everything an Indian does is in a circle, and that is because the Power of the World always works in circles, and everything tries to be round....The sky is round, and I have heard that the earth is round like a ball, and so are all the stars." He couldn't understand why white people lived in square houses. "It is a bad way to live, for there is not power in a square."

Here the quotes stand out, separate from the writer's own text, but in the revised paragraph they are worked smoothly into the writer's own prose:

> Black Elk believed the "Power of the World always works in circles," noting the roundness of the sun, the earth, and the stars. He couldn't understand why white people live in square houses: "It is a bad way to live, for there is not power in a square."

Although long quotes, especially if unintegrated, should usually be avoided, occasionally it may be useful to include a long quotation from one of your sources. A quotation that is longer than four lines should be *blocked,* or set off from the rest of the text by indenting it an inch from the left margin. Like the rest of the paper, a blocked quotation is also typed double-spaced. For example:

According to Robert Karen, shame is a particularly modern phenomenon. He notes that in medieval times people pretty much let loose, and by our modern tastes, it was not a pretty sight:

> Their emotional life appears to have been extraordinarily spontaneous and unrestrained. From Johan Huizinga's *The Waning of the Middle Ages,* we learn that the average European town dweller was wildly erratic and inconsistent, murderously violent when enraged, easily plunged into guilt, tears, and pleas for forgiveness, and bursting with psychological eccentricities. He ate with his hands out of a common bowl, blew his nose on his sleeve, defecated openly by the side of the road, made love, and mourned with great passion, and was relatively unconcerned about such notions as maladjustment or what others might think.... In post-medieval centuries, what I've called situational shame spread rapidly.... (61)

Note that the quotation marks are dropped around a blocked quotation. In this case, only part of a paragraph was borrowed, but if you quote one or more full paragraphs, indent the first line of each *three* spaces in addition to the inch the block is indented from the left margin. Note, too, that the writer has introduced this long quote in a way that effectively ties it to his own paper.

We'll examine *parenthetical references* more fully in the next section, but notice how the citation in the blocked quotation above is placed *after* the final period. That's a unique exception to the usual rule that a parenthetical citation is enclosed *before* the period of the borrowed material's final sentence.

Quick Tips for Controlling Quotations

From our discussion so far, you've seen the hazards and the benefits of using quotations. Quotations from your sources can definitely be overused, especially when they seem dumped into the draft, untouched and unexamined, or used as a lazy substitute for paraphrase. But when it works, bringing the voices of others into your own writing can bring the work to life and make readers feel as though there is a genuine conversation going on.

You've also seen some basics on how to handle quotes. Here are some specific tips for doing this effectively.

Grafting Quotes

Frequently, the best way to use quoted material is to graft it onto your own prose. Sometimes you just use a word or phrase:

```
Some words for hangover, like ours, refer prosai-
cally to the cause: the Egyptians say they are
"still drunk," the Japanese "two days drunk," the
Chinese "drunk overnight."*
```

In other situations, especially when you want to add emphasis to what a source has said, you might give over parts of several sentences to a source, like this:

```
The makers of NoHang, on their Web page, say what
your mother would: "It is recommended that you
drink moderately and responsibly." At the same
time, they tell you that with NoHang "you can
drink the night away."
```

Sandwiching Quotes

A sandwich without the bread isn't a sandwich. Similarly, when you use a quotation, especially one that is a full sentence or more, it should be surrounded by your comments about it. Introduce the quotation: Who said it, and why is he or she relevant? When did this person say it and in what context? How does the quote relate to the

---

*Acocella, Joan. "A Few Too Many." *New Yorker* 26 May 2008: 32–37. Print.

current discussion in your essay? Follow up the quotation: What do *you* think is important about what was just said? How does it address an important idea or question? What does the person quoted *fail* to say or to see?

Here's an example of what I mean:

> In fact, even back when leeches were held in con-
> tempt by the medical profession, Sawyer had a
> solid rationale for choosing them as his subject.
> Biology, as taught in the United States had left
> him frustrated: "For sex determination, we'd study
> *Drosophilia,* for physiology we'd study frogs, for
> genetics, bacteria. I thought there was more to be
> learned from studying one organism in detail than
> from parts of many." His American professors dis-
> dained this approach as a throw-back to nineteenth
> century biology.*

See how the writer here sets up the quotation? He provides background on the significance of what Sawyer, the leech biologist, was about to say. The guy was frustrated with how organisms were studied. The quotation is then sandwiched with a comment about how the quote reflects Sawyer's reputation as an antitraditionalist.

Billboarding Quotes

Another way you can control quotations is by adding emphasis to billboard parts of a particular quote. Typically you do this by italicizing the phrase or sentence. Here is an example, taken from the end of a block quotation:

> For the sake of Millennials—and, through them,
> the future of America—the most urgent adult task
> is to *elevate their expectations.* (Emphasis added)
> (Howe and Strauss 365)†

---

*Conniff, Richard. *Spineless Wonders.* New York: Holt, 1996. Print.
†Howe, Neil, and William Strauss. *Millennials Rising.* New York: Vintage, 2000. Print.

Notice that the parenthetical note that signals the original quote has been altered to give emphasis.

Splicing Quotes

Sometimes you want to prune away unnecessary information from a quotation to place emphasis on the part that matters most to you or to eliminate unnecessary information. Ellipsis points, those three dots (...) you sometimes see at the beginning, middle, or end of a sentence, signal that some information has been omitted.

Take this passage, for example:

```
During the Gen-X child era, the American family

endured countless new movements and trends—

feminism, sexual freedom, a divorce epidemic,

fewer G-rated movies, child-raising handbooks

telling parents to "consider yourself" ahead of

a child's needs, gay rights, Chappaquiddick, film

nudity, a Zero Population Growth ethic, Kramer vs.

Kramer, and Roe v. Wade. A prominent academic in

1969 proclaimed in the Washington Post that the

family needed a "decent burial."
```

That's a pretty long list of movements and trends, and the reader could get a taste without being served up the whole thing. Ellipsis points can help:

```
During the Gen-X child era, the American family

endured countless new movements and trends—

feminism, sexual freedom, a divorce epidemic...,

[and a] prominent academic in 1969 proclaimed

in the Washington Post that the family needed a

"decent burial."
```

When you have to slightly reword the original text or alter the punctuation for a smoother splice, put the alteration in brackets. In the example, for instance, I turned what was a separate sentence in the original into a compound sentence using the conjunction *and*.

Handling Interview Material

The great quotes you glean from your interviews can be handled like quotations from texts. But there's a dimension to a quote from an interview that's lacking in a quote from a book: Namely, you participated in the quote's creation by asking a question, and in some cases, you were there to observe your subject saying it. This presents some new choices. When you're quoting an interview subject, should you enter your essay as a participant in the conversation, or should you stay out of the way? That is, should you describe yourself asking the question? Should you describe the scene of the interview, your subject's manner of responding, or your immediate reaction to what she said? Or should you merely report what was said and who said it?

Christina's essay, "Crying Real Tears: The History and Psychology of Method Acting," makes good use of interviews. Notice how Christina writes about one of them in the middle of her essay:

> During a phone interview, I asked my acting teacher, Ed Claudio, who studied under Stella Adler, whether or not he agreed with the ideas behind method acting. I could almost see him wrinkle his nose at the other end of the connection. He described method acting as "self-indulgent," insisting that it encourages "island acting." Because of emotional recall, acting has become a far more personal art, and the actor began to move away from the script, often hiding the author's purpose and intentions under his own.*

Contrast Christina's handling of the Claudio interview with her treatment of material from an interview with Dave Pierini later in her essay:

> Dave Pierini, a local Sacramento actor, pointed out, "You can be a good actor without using method, but you cannot be a good actor without

*Reprinted with permission of Christina B. Kerby.

at least understanding it." Actors are perhaps
some of the greatest scholars of the human psy-
che because they devote their lives to the study
and exploration of it. Aspiring artists are told
to "get inside of the character's head." They are
asked, "How would the character *feel*? How would
the character *react*?"

Do you think Christina's entry into her report of the first
interview (with Ed Claudio) is intrusive? Or do you think it adds
useful information or even livens it up? What circumstances might
make this a good move? On the other hand, what might be some
advantages of the writer staying out of the way and simply letting
her subject speak, as Christina chooses to do in her treatment of the
interview with Dave Pierini?

Trusting Your Memory

One of the best ways to weave references seamlessly into your
own writing is to avoid the compulsion to stop and study your sources
as you're writing the draft. I remember that writing my research
papers in college was typically done in stops and starts. I'd write a
paragraph of the draft, then stop and reread a photocopy of an article,
then write a few more sentences, and then stop again. Part of the
problem was the meager notes I took as I collected information. I
hadn't really taken possession of the material before I started writing
the draft. But I also didn't trust that I'd remember what was important from my reading.

If, during the course of your research and writing so far, you've
found a sense of purpose—for example, you're pretty sure your paper
is going to argue for legalization of marijuana or analyze the symbolism on old gravestones on Cape Cod—then you've probably read
purposefully, too. You *will* likely know what reference sources you
need as you write the draft, without sputtering to a halt to remind
yourself of what each says. Consult your notes and sources as you
need them; otherwise, push them aside, and immerse yourself in
your own writing.

Citing Sources

Like most people I knew back then, I took a typing class the
summer between eighth grade and high school. Our instructional

texts were long books with the bindings at the top, and we worked on standard Royal typewriters that were built like tanks. I got up to 30 words a minute, I think, which wasn't very good, but thanks to that class, I can still type without looking at the keyboard. The one thing I never learned, though, was how to turn the typewriter roller up a half space to type a footnote number that would neatly float above the line. In every term paper in high school, my footnotes collided with my sentences.

I'm certain that such technical difficulties were not the reason that most academic writers in the humanities and social sciences have largely abandoned the footnote method of citation for the parenthetical one, but I'm relieved, nonetheless. In the current system, borrowed material is parenthetically cited in the paper by indicating the author of the original work and the page the borrowed material was taken from or the date the work was published. These parenthetical citations are then explained more fully in the "Works Cited" page at the end of your paper where the sources themselves are listed.

By now, your instructor has probably told you which method of citing sources you should use: the Modern Language Association (MLA) style or the American Psychological Association (APA) style. Most English classes use MLA. A complete guide to MLA conventions is provided in Appendix A, and to APA in Appendix B.

Before you begin writing your draft, go to Appendix A or B and read the sections under "Citing Sources in Your Essay." These will describe in some detail when and where you should put parenthetical references to borrowed material in the draft of your essay. Don't worry too much about the guidelines for preparing the final manuscript, including how to do the bibliography. You can deal with that next week.

Driving Through the First Draft

You have an opening, a lot of material in your notes—much of it, written in your own words—and maybe an outline. You've considered some general methods of development, looked at ways to write with sources, and completed a quick course in how to cite them. Finish the week by writing through the first draft.

Writing the draft may be difficult. All writing, but especially research writing, is a recursive process. You may find sometimes that you must circle back to a step you took before, discovering a gap in your information, a new idea for a thesis statement, or a better lead or focus. Circling back may be frustrating at times, but it's natural and even a good sign: It means you're letting go of your preconceived ideas and allowing the discoveries you make *through writing* to change your mind.

It's too early to worry about writing a research paper that's airtight, with no problems to solve. Too often, student writers think they have to write a perfect paper in the first draft. You can worry about plugging holes and tightening things up next week. For now, write a draft, and if you must, put a reminder on a piece of paper and post it on the computer next to your thesis statement or research question. Look at this reminder every time you find yourself agonizing over the imperfections of your paper. The reminder should say, "It Doesn't Count."

Keep a few other things in mind while writing your first draft:

1. *Focus on your tentative thesis or your research question.* In the draft, consider your thesis a theory you're trying to prove but that you're willing to change. If your paper is more exploratory than argumentative, use your focusing question as a reminder of what you want to know. Remember, your question and thesis can change, too, as you learn more about your subject.

2. *Vary your sources.* Offer a variety of different sources as evidence to support your assertions. Beware of writing a single page that cites only one source.

3. *Remember your audience.* What do your readers want to know about your topic? What do they need to know to understand what you're trying to say?

4. *Write with your notes.* If you took thoughtful notes during the third week—carefully transforming another author's words into your own, flagging good quotes, and developing your own analysis—then you've already written at least some of your paper. You may only need to fine-tune the language in your notes and then plug them into your draft.

5. *Be open to surprises.* The act of writing is often full of surprises. In fact, it should be, because *writing* is *thinking,* and the more you think about something, the more you're likely to see. You might get halfway through your draft and discover the part of your topic that *really* fascinates you. Should that happen, you may have to change your thesis or throw away your outline. You may even have to reresearch your topic, at least somewhat. It's not necessarily too late to shift the purpose or focus of your paper (though you should consult your instructor before totally abandoning your topic at this point). Let your curiosity remain the engine that drives you forward.

CHAPTER **5**

The Fifth Week

Revision Is Re-seeing (or Breaking Up Is Hard to Do)

My high school girlfriend, Jan, was bright, warm hearted, and fun, and I wasn't at all sure I liked her much—at least at first. Though we had a lot in common—we both loved sunrises over Lake Michigan, bird watching, and Simon and Garfunkel—I found Jan a little intimidating, a little too much in a hurry to anoint us a solid "couple." But we stuck together for three years, and as time passed, I persuaded myself—despite lingering doubts—that I couldn't live without her. There was no way I was going to break my white-knuckled hold on that relationship. After all, I'd invested all that time.

As a writer, I used to have similar relationships with my drafts. I'd work on something very hard, finally finishing the draft. I'd know there were problems, but I'd developed such a tight relationship with my draft that the problems were hard to see. And even when I recognized some problems, the thought of making major changes seemed too risky. Did I dare ruin the things I loved about the draft? These decisions were even harder if the draft had taken a long time to write.

Revision doesn't necessarily mean you have to sever your relationship with your draft. It's probably too late to make a complete break with the draft and abandon your topic. However, revision does demand finding some way to step back from the draft and change your relationship with it, trying to see it more from the reader's perspective than the writer's. Revision requires that you loosen your grip. And when you do, you may decide to shift your focus or rearrange the information. At the very least, you may discover gaps in information or sections of the draft that need more development. You will certainly need to prune sentences.

Revision, as the word implies, means "re-seeing" or "reconceiving," trying to see what you failed to notice with the first look. That can be hard. Remember how stuck I was on that one picture of the lighthouse? I planted my feet in the sand, and the longer I stared through the camera lens, the harder it was to see the lighthouse from any other angle. It didn't matter that I didn't particularly like what I was seeing. I just wanted to take the picture.

You've spent more than four weeks researching your topic and the last few days composing your first draft. You may find that you've spent so much time staring through the lens—seeing your topic the way you chose to see it in your first draft—that doing a major revision is about as appealing as eating cold beets. How do you get the perspective to "re-see" the draft and rebuild it into a stronger paper?

Global Revision: Revising for Purpose, Thesis, and Structure

Your instinct when you revise may be to take out the microscope rather than the binoculars. But if revision is a process of re-seeing— of not just shutting things down but opening them up—then your rewrite this week should begin with the whole rather than with the details. Rather than trying to "fix" the small things—grammar, citations, diction, and so on—take the large view. Ask these questions: What is my draft trying to do? How well does it do it? And, especially, will it make sense to someone else?

Writer- to Reader-Based Prose

Writing theorist Linda Flower distinguishes between "writer-based prose" and "reader-based prose." When we first start writing about something in notebooks, journals, and sometimes first drafts, we are our own audience. Sure, we might have a vague sense that someone else will be reading what we write, but often our energies are focused on whether it makes sense to us. "Writer-based prose" like this often works from the tacit assumption that readers and writers share the same understanding and knowledge about a topic. As a result, writers may assume that certain things that should be explained don't need to be. Writers may also assume that the things they find interesting or relevant their readers will find interesting or relevant. In "reader-based prose," writers have confronted these assumptions. They have revised their work with their readers in mind.

Reading anything is work. Most of us are willing to do the work if we sense an author is taking us somewhere interesting. More specifically, readers must trust that writers know what they're doing—the writers have a destination in mind, they are reliable guides, and the journey will likely yield something worth knowing or thinking about.

One way to see if your draft research essay is sufficiently "reader-based" is to determine whether it does three things that all essays must do (see Figure 5.1):

- *Have a clear purpose*: What exactly did you want to find out in this investigation of your topic? What is your research question?
- *Establish why the question (and its answer) is significant*: What stake might readers have in your inquiry?
- *Say one main thing*: Among the possible answers to the question you pose, which one seems most persuasive, most significant, or most revealing?

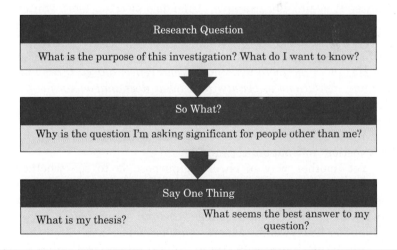

FIGURE 5.1   Three Things the Essay Must Do. As you revise your draft, you can measure your progress by asking whether you've answered these three basic questions: *Is the question I'm asking clear and sufficiently limited? Have I answered the "So what?" question? Is there one most important thing I'm trying to say?* If your draft explicitly answers each of these, then the boat at least will float and have a clear destination.

Is It Organized Around a Clear Purpose?

Purpose, like a torch, lights the way in the darkness. It illuminates one part of your subject, helping to guide you in the direction you want to go. You should determine whether the purpose of your paper is clear and examine how well the information is organized around that purpose.

Presumably, by now you know the purpose of your essay. You know, for instance, whether you're exploring or arguing. But what exactly are you exploring or arguing? Your ability to state this purpose as clearly as you can is a great foundation for revision this week. Try completing one of the following sentences:

For an exploratory essay: The main purpose of my essay on _____ is to explore _____. In particular, I will consider the questions raised by _____ and _____ as well as _____.

For an argument essay: Because of _____ and _____ as well as _____, in this essay I am arguing _____.

Another way of getting at purpose is to clarify your research question, something that you were working on last week. Is it time to revise it again? For example, Amanda's piece on tooth whitening began with this research question: *How has cosmetic tooth whitening changed the way Americans feel about their teeth?* After a few clarifications she made as she learned more, Amanda had this question: *How does the tooth whitening trend reflect our culture's quickly changing definitions of beauty, and what does that mean for people who don't fit that definition?*

Go back to the beginning. What was your initial research question? What is it now? If you're struggling with this, revist "Refining the Question" in Chapter 4, page 154.

Yet another way of checking purpose is to see whether in your draft your sources are all serving your purpose. Writing with research is a wrestling match. You're the 120-pound weakling, who may not have written many college research essays before, trying to take on the heavyweight experts on your topic. You're fighting for your life, trying to use what these authorities say or think for your own purpose, without getting slammed to the floor for meekly submitting a report rather than an essay. The challenge is to get control of the information, to muscle it to the ground using the strength of your purpose. Establishing this control is one of the hardest parts of drafting research papers. Two extreme responses to this problem are giving up entirely and turning your paper over to your sources (letting them do all the talking) and pretending that you're not really wrestling with anyone and writing a paper that includes only your own opinions. Neither option is what you want.

Who won the wrestling match in your draft? To what extent did you have a coherent purpose and succeed in using other people's ideas and information in the service of your purpose? One way to see who is getting the upper hand in the draft is to mark it up, noting where you've given control to your sources and where you've taken it back. Exercise 5.1 can graphically illustrate who is winning the wresting match. To what extent is your purpose in the essay enabling you to *use* the information you've gathered to explore your research question or prove your point? The exercise will also reveal how well you've managed to surround your research with your own analysis, interpretations, arguments, and questions.

EXERCISE 5.1

Wrestling with the Draft*

For this exercise you'll use two highlighters, each a different color.

1. Choose a random page or two of your draft, somewhere in the middle.
2. First mark the parts in which you're a less active author. As you read the page, highlight every sentence that reports facts, quotes sources, or otherwise presents information or ideas that belong to someone else.
3. Now, using the other highlighter, mark the parts in which you're a more active author. Read the same page or pages again, but this time highlight every sentence or paragraph that represents *your* ideas, analysis, commentary, interpretation, definition, synthesis, or claims.
4. Repeat the previous steps with two more pages of your draft.

Which color dominates? Are you turning over too much of the text to your sources? Are you ignoring them and rattling on too much about what you think? Or does your source use seem appropriate to support your purpose?

*This exercise is adapted from one I borrowed from my colleague Dr. Mike Mattison, who borrowed it from his former colleagues at the University of Massachusetts–Amherst. Thanks to all.

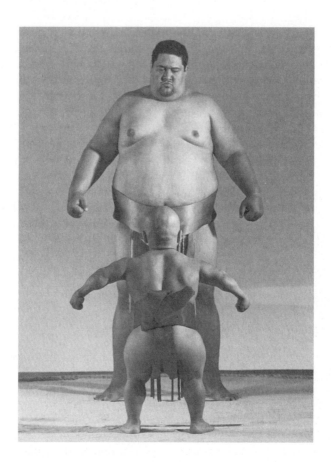

In addition, look at the pattern of color. What do you notice about this pattern? Are you taking turns paragraph by paragraph with your sources, or is your own analysis and commentary nicely blended *within* paragraphs, so that the information is always anchored to your own thoughts? Do you surround quoted passages with your own voice and analysis? Who wins the wrestling match? See Figure 5.2 for an example of this exercise.

Does It Establish Significance?

So what? That's the blunt question here. Any reader will need a *reason* to care about what you have to say. So what reasons might there be for someone to care about a research essay on theories

Our tooth whiteners are safer, and a study by James W. Curtis, DMD, discovered that bleaching through carbamide peroxide actually decreases the amount of plaque on teeth, but we're still doing it for beauty reasons rather than health ones (Nuss 28).

In her article "Bright On," Molly Prior notes that Procter & Gamble and Colgate-Palmolive revolutionized the whitening industry by bringing over-the-counter whiteners to drugstores everywhere at the turn of the twenty-first century (39). No longer did people have to pay high prices for professional whitening — they could do it themselves, at home, for a reasonable cost. In the past, a patient had to eat a bill of $1,000 for a laser whitening treatment, or $10,000 for a full set of veneers; now a package of Crest Whitestrips retails for only $29.99 (Gideonse). Suddenly, whiter teeth were available to everyone. While a shining smile once indicated wealth and the ability to splurge on cosmetic dentistry, it became affordable to the dentally discolored masses eager to emulate the lifestyles of the people they saw in magazines and on television.

Companies didn't create whitening products to fill a demand created by the public for whiter teeth. While Hollywood glitterati did pay high prices for iconic smiles, most people seemed happy with functional teeth. However, companies saw money to be made in creating a whiter norm for teeth, so they barraged the airwaves with advertisements featuring people complaining about the dullness and imperfection of their teeth. Natural teeth were denigrated as ugly. Crest and Colgate-Palmolive wanted to make money, so appealed to the American obsession with beauty to secure a financial reason to smile.

FIGURE 5.2 Amanda Wins the Wrestling Match. The sections of text highlighted in gray are passages from Amanda's sources, and the sections highlighted in blue are passages in which she is commenting, clarifying, asserting, or interpreting. Notice the balance between gray and blue. Clearly Amanda has a strong authorial presence. Also notice how quotations are surrounded by her commentary. By controlling quotations like this, she is also using rather than being used by her sources.

As Jonathan Levine, DDS, notes, "It's lately seeming much harder to go broke by overestimating the vanity of the American public" (Walker). The companies succeeded in making mouthfuls of money, netting $450 million dollars and getting 45 percent of Americans to try some form of whitening (Prior 42). In effect, they appealed to our egos to get to our pocket books.

FIGURE 5.2   (Continued)

of intelligence, or an investigation of video game addiction, or an argument about what should be done about dog poop in city parks? In other words, what stake might readers have in the question you are exploring? Your mother will think nearly anything you write is significant. But what might make someone else consider that you have important things to say? Here are five possible reasons. Do any apply to your draft and, if so, do you emphasize the significance of your inquiry enough?

Readers may find your discussion of a topic significant if:

1. *It raises questions they want to know the answer to*. As a pet owner, I'm interested in theories of dog training because Fred digs in the garden.
2. *It helps them to see what they've seen before in a way they haven't seen it*. Is the destruction of jack pines in Yellowstone National Park really being caused by global warming and not the drought, as I had assumed?
3. *It amplifies what they may already know and care about, leading to new learning*. I play video games and know they're habit forming, but I didn't know what was happening in my brain because I played them.
4. *It moves them emotionally*. The story of the failure of Haitian relief efforts in protecting the health and welfare of children is heartbreaking. Something should be done about it. But what?
5. *It takes a surprising point of view*. The research leads you to believe that decriminalizing marijuana will actually reduce its use.

You should be able to read your draft and see exactly where you establish the significance of your project to your readers, perhaps touching on one or more of the five reasons above. Is this content sufficient or is there more you might say?

Does It Say One Thing?

When I write an exploratory essay, I'm essentially in pursuit of a point and, not infrequently, it playfully eludes me. Just when I think I've figured out exactly what I'm trying to say, I have the nagging feeling that it's not quite right—it's too simplistic or obvious, it doesn't quite account for the evidence I've collected, or it just doesn't capture the spirit of the discoveries I've made. A thesis is often a slippery fish—just when I think I've figured out what I think, I start to think something else.

A thesis can present different problems in an argumentative essay. As we saw in the last chapter, it can become a club—rigid and unyielding—that we use to beat a draft into submission. Yet, the very reason to do research is to *test* your ideas about things, and as your draft evolves, so should your thesis.

Now is a good time to consider revising your thesis again. Does it accurately capture what you're trying to say—or *think* you're trying to say? Is it specific enough? Is it interesting? If you need to, return to "Refining the Thesis" on page 156 in the Chapter 4 to rework your main idea.

Using a Reader

If you wanted to save or improve a relationship, you might ask a friend for advice. Then you'd get the benefit of a third-party opinion, a fresh view that could help you see what you may be too close to see.

A reader can do the same thing for your research paper draft. She will come to the draft without the entanglements that encumber the writer and provide a fresh pair of eyes through which you can see the work. Your reader can tell you what kind of guide you are in the draft: Is it clear where you're headed, why it's significant, and what your most important discovery is?

Your instructor may be that reader, or you might exchange drafts with someone else in class. You may already have someone whom you share your writing with—a roommate, a friend. Whomever you choose, try to find a reader who will respond honestly *and* make you want to write again.

What will be most helpful from a reader at this stage? Comments about your spelling and mechanics are not critical right now. You'll deal with those factors later. For now, the most useful feedback will focus on whether there's a disconnect between what you *intend* in your draft and how a reader understands those intentions.

EXERCISE 5 . 2

Directing the Reader's Response

Though you could ask your reader for a completely open-ended reaction to your paper, the following questions might help her focus on providing comments that will help you tackle a revision:

1. After reading the draft, what would you say is the main question the paper is trying to answer or focus on?
2. In your own words, what is the main point?
3. What did you learn about the topic after reading the paper that you didn't fully appreciate *before* you read it? Is this something you find significant or interesting? If so, why?

How your reader responds to the first two questions will tell you a lot about how well you've succeeded in making the purpose and thesis of your paper clear. The answer to the third question will too, but it may also tell you whether you've established the significance of your project.

Reviewing the Structure

In addition to focusing on your paper in terms of its purpose and thesis, this global revision is also about focusing on structure. If you did Exercise 5.1, about purpose, you've already begun to take a closer look at the structure of your essay. There are various other ways of focusing on structure, including using your thesis.

Using Your Thesis to Revise

The payoff for crafting a stronger thesis is huge. As you will see in Exercise 5.3, a thesis can help you decide what to put in it and what to leave out, and in research-based writing, this is a decision that comes up again and again.

EXERCISE 5 . 3

Cut-and-Paste Revision

Try this cut-and-paste revision exercise (a useful technique inspired by Peter Elbow and his book *Writing with Power*)*:

1. On a notecard or sticky note, write your thesis or main idea. Make sure that it is plainly stated and fully captures what you think you're trying to say in your research essay. Set it aside.

*Elbow, Peter. *Writing with Power*. New York: Oxford University Press, 1981. Print.

2. Photocopy or print two copies of your first draft (one-sided pages only). Save the original; you may need it later.

3. Cut apart a copy of your research paper, paragraph by paragraph. (You may cut it into even smaller pieces later.) Once the draft has been completely disassembled, shuffle the paragraphs—get them wildly out of order so the original draft is just a memory.

4. Retrieve the notecard or sticky note with your thesis on it, and set it before you. Now work your way through the stack of paragraphs and make two new stacks: one of paragraphs that are relevant to your thesis and one of paragraphs that don't seem relevant, that don't seem to serve a clear purpose in developing your main idea. Be as tough as a drill sergeant as you scrutinize each scrap of paper. What you are trying to determine is whether each piece of information, each paragraph, is there for a reason. Ask yourself this question as you examine each paragraph:

> *Does this paragraph (or part of a paragraph) develop my thesis and further the purpose of my paper, or does it seem an unnecessary tangent that could be part of another paper with a different focus?*

For example,

- Does it provide important *evidence* that supports my main point?
- Does it *explain* something that's key to understanding what I'm trying to say?
- Does it *illustrate* a key concept?
- Does it help establish the *importance* of what I'm trying to say?
- Does it raise (or answer) a *question* that I must explore, given what I'm trying to say?

You might find it helpful to write on the back of each relevant paragraph which of these specific purposes it serves. You may also discover that *some* of the information in a paragraph seems to serve your purpose while the rest strikes you as unnecessary. Use your scissors to cut away the irrelevant material, pruning back the paragraph to include only what's essential.

5. You now have two stacks of paper scraps: those that seem to support your thesis and serve your purpose and those that don't. For now, set aside your "reject" pile. Begin to reassemble a very rough draft, using what you've saved. Play with order. Try new leads, new ends, new middles. As you spread out the pieces of information before you, see if a new structure suddenly emerges. *But especially, look for gaps—places where you should add information.* On a piece of paper, jot down ideas for material you might add; then cut up this paper as

well and insert these in the appropriate places. You may rediscover uses for information in your "reject" pile as well. Mine that pile, if you need to.

6. As a structure begins to emerge, reassemble the draft by taping together the fragments of paper, including the ideas for new information and any rejects you've decided to use after all. Don't worry about transitions; you'll deal with those later. When you're done with the reconstruction, the draft might look totally unlike the version you started with.

Examining the Wreckage.   If you did Exercise 5.3, as you dealt with the wreckage your scissors wrought on your first draft, you might have discovered that the information in your draft suggested a revision of your thesis, pointed toward another thesis, or simply suggested your thesis was unworkable.

To your horror, you may have found that your "reject" pile of paragraphs is bigger than your "save" pile. If that's the case, you won't have much left to work with. You may need to reresearch the topic (returning to the library or going online this week to collect more information) or shift the focus of your paper. Perhaps both. But even if your cut-and-paste went well, you will likely need to do more research this week, to fill the gaps you found. That's perfectly normal.

To your satisfaction, you may have discovered that your reconstructed draft looks familiar. You may have returned to the structure you started with in the first draft. If that's the case, it might mean your first draft worked pretty well; breaking it down and putting it back together confirmed that and showed you where you might need to prune and fine-tune.

When Jeff cut up "The Alcoholic Family," he discovered immediately that much of his paper did not seem clearly related to his point about the role outsiders can play in helping the family of an alcoholic. His "reject" pile had paragraph after paragraph of information about the roles that other family members take on when there's an alcoholic in the house. Jeff asked himself, What does that information have to do with the roles of outsiders? He considered changing his thesis to say something about how each family member plays a role in dealing with the drinker. But Jeff's purpose in writing the paper was to discover what *he,* as an outsider, could do to help.

As Jeff played with the pieces of his draft, he began to see two things. First of all, he realized that some of the ways members behave in an alcoholic family make them resistant to outside help; this insight allowed him to salvage some information from his "reject" pile by more clearly connecting the information to his main point. Second, Jeff knew he had to go back to the well: He needed to return to the library and recheck his sources to find more information on what family friends can do to help.

When you slice up your draft and play with the pieces, you are experimenting with the basic architecture of your essay. If the result is going to hold up, certain fundamentals must be in place. You need to be transforming your draft in a direction that is making it more "reader based," with a clear purpose, significance, and point.

Other Ways of Reviewing the Structure

Exercise 5.3, "Cut-and-Paste Revision," invited you to experiment with the organization of your draft by disassembling and then rebuilding your essay, imagining different ways to order information. Its starting point was the thesis. There are other starting points for an examination of structure. Here are a few of these alternative starting points:

Type of Essay. The structure of a research essay is partly a function of the type of essay—of whether you are writing an exploratory or an argumentative essay. Depending on the type of essay you're writing, return to Figure 4.2 or 4.4 in the last chapter for an idea about about how to organize your paper.

Lead. How you begin your paper has a huge influence on how it develops from there. As we discussed in Chapter 4, a lead or introduction should not only draw readers in but also dramatize or introduce the dilemma, problem, question, or argument that is the focus of your inquiry. You might find a stronger lead buried in the middle of your draft. Try it as an alternative introduction and follow it from there.

Logical Structure. In a very general sense, most writing can be said to be structured by either narrative or logic. Essays that focus on the writer's experience tend to rely on some form of narrative structure, though it may not be chronological. Essays that focus on a subject other than the writer often rely on structures that reflect a pattern of reasoning. (And many research essays might employ both types of structures because they can be experiential *and* focused on a subject other than the writer.) Most of us have more experience with narrative structures; after all, part of being human is telling stories. Logical structures are less familiar. They usually spring from either a question or thesis (or both) and are designed to methodically explore a question or prove a point. Consider various ways essays might do this:

- Thesis to proof
- Problem to solution
- Question to answer
- Comparison and conrast
- Cause and effect, or effect and cause
- Known to unknown or unknown to known
- Simple to complex

Review your draft with these possible structures in mind. You may see a way to strengthen it by reshaping its structure to better fit one of these structures. Remember that while your research essay might generally use one of the logical structures, often a piece of writing that generally uses one structure uses others as microstructures. For example, an essay that has a comparison-and-contrast structure might have elements of narrative.

Re-researching

I know. You thought you were done digging. But as I said last week, research is a recursive process. (Remember, the word is *research,* or "look again.") You will often find yourself circling back to the earlier steps as you get a clearer sense of where you want to go. I want to emphasize this. It's actually *unusual*, after you've written a draft, to discover that you're done with research. This means returning to the library databases, trying a different Google search, going back to interview someone, or returning to the field for more observations. You've got the skills now to do this. Make time for it.

As you stand back from your draft, looking again at how well your research paper addresses your research question or thesis, you'll likely see holes in the information. They may seem more like craters. Jeff discovered he had to reresearch his topic, returning to the library to hunt for new sources to help him develop his point. Because he had enough time, he repeated some of the research steps from the third week. This time, though, he knew exactly what he needed to find.

You may find that you basically have the information you need but that your draft requires more development. Candy's draft on how child abuse affects language included material from some useful studies from the *Journal of Speech and Hearing Disorders,* which showed pretty conclusively that abuse cripples children's abilities to converse. At her reader's suggestion, Candy decided it was important to write more in her revision about what was learned from the studies, because they offered convincing evidence for her thesis. Though she could mine her notes for more information, Candy decided to recheck the journal databases to look for any similar studies she may have missed.

Finding Quick Facts

If you're lucky, the holes of information in your research paper draft will not be large at all. What's missing may be an important but discrete fact that would really help your readers understand the point you're making. For example, in Janabeth's draft on the impact of divorce on father–daughter relationships, she realized she was missing an important fact: the number of marriages that end in divorce in the United States. This single piece of information could help establish the significance of the problem she was writing about. And Janabeth could obtain it by simply looking online.

One of the Internet's greatest strengths is its usefulness in searching for specific facts. What are the ingredients in a Big Mac? How high is the Great Wall of China? How many high school kids in Illinois go on to college? What does a map of Brazilian deforestation look like? A quick click or two and the Web can yield a rich harvest of facts and information. Google and similar search engines are naturally where we start looking for that kind of information, and because what you want to know is pretty specific, there's a good chance you'll find what you're looking for. But there are some particularly useful statistical references on the Web that you might want to check out as well.

Facts on the Web

General

- *American Factfinder* (http://factfinder.census.gov). A rich site maintained by the U.S. Census Bureau. It includes data on population and economic trends, both national and local.
- *FedStats* (http://www.fedstats.gov). A superstore of statistical resources that allows users to find information from all U.S. government agencies.
- *Refdesk.com* (http://refdesk.com). Links to the usual references—dictionaries, biographical indexes, encyclopedias, and government information.
- *STATS America* (http://www.statsamerica.org). Search page allows users to find a range of data for states and counties in the United States, including facts on demographics, economics, education, and the workforce.

Subject Specific

Crime

- *National Criminal Justice Reference Service* (http://www.ncjrs.org/search.html). Allows keyword searches to find not just facts but articles on crime, drug abuse, corrections, juvenile justice, and more.

Education

- *National Center for Educational Statisics* (http://nces.ed.gov). The U.S. Department of Education site includes statistics on everything related to schooling in the United States and also features an annual report on the state of education.

Economics

- *Bureau of Economic Analysis* (http://www.bea.gov/). This U.S. Department of Commerce site includes statistics on key economic indicators, trade, corporate profits, and much more.

Energy

- *U.S. Energy Information Administration* (http://www.eia.doe.gov/). Includes use forecasts, environmental impacts, reserves, alternative energy information, and much more.

(continued)

Health

- *National Center for Health Statistics* (http://www.cdc.gov/nchs). Offers information about injuries, diseases, lifestyles, death rates, and more provided by the Centers for Disease Control.

International

- *U.N. Food and Agricultural Organization* (http://www.fao.org/corp/statistics/en/). The FAO site allows users to search for not just statistics on food and hunger but also for information on such topics as world foresty practices and water issues.
- *NationMaster* (http://www.nationmaster.com). Drawing in part from the *CIA Factbook* and UN information, Nation-Master will also generate interesting maps and graphics on a wide range of subjects.

In addition to these Web resources, the standard print texts for researchers hunting down facts and statistics are still quite useful. They include the *Statistical Abstracts of the United States,* the *Information Please Almanac, Facts on File,* and the *World Almanac Book of Facts*—all published annually. A number of these are now available on the Web.

Like the online sources mentioned, these fact books can be especially valuable resources when you need to plug small holes in your draft. But even if you're not sure whether you can glean a useful statistic from one of these sources, they might be worth checking anyway. There's a good chance you'll find something useful.

Local Revision: Revising for Language

Most of my students have the impression that revision begins and ends with concerns about language—that it's about *how* they say it rather than *what* they say. Revising for language is really a tertiary concern (though an important one) to be addressed after the writer has dealt with global revision: clear purpose, significance, and thesis as well as structure.

Once you're satisfied that your paper's purpose is clear, that it provides readers with the information they need to understand what you're trying to say, and that it is organized in a logical, interesting way, *then* focus your attention on the fine points of *how* it is written. Begin with voice.

Listening to the Voice

Listen to your paper by reading it aloud to yourself. You may find the experience a little unsettling. Most of us are not used to actively listening to our writing voices. But your readers will be listening.

As you read, ask yourself: Is this the voice you want readers to hear? Does it seem appropriate for this paper? Does it sound flat or wooden or ponderous in any places? Does it sound anything like you?

If revising your writing voice is necessary for any reason, begin at the beginning—the first line, the first paragraph—and rely on your ears. What sounds right?

You may discover that you begin with the right voice but lose it in places. That often happens when you move from anecdotal material to exposition, from telling a story to explaining research findings. To some extent, a shift in voice is inevitable when you move from one method of development to another, especially from personal material to factual material. But examine your word choices in those passages that seem to go flat. Do you sometimes shift to the dry language used by your sources? Can you rewrite that language in your own voice? When you do, you will find yourself cutting away unnecessary, vague, and pretentious language.

Rewriting in your own voice has another effect, too: It brings the writing to life. Readers respond to an individual writing voice. When I read David Quammen, an author whose work you've read in this text, it rises up from the page, like a hologram, and suddenly I can see him as a distinct individual. I also become interested in how he sees the things he's writing about.

Avoid Sounding Glib

Beware, though, of a voice that calls more attention to itself than the substance of what you're saying. As you've no doubt learned from reading scholarly sources, much academic writing is voiceless, or at least seems to be, partly because what's important is not *who* the writer is but *what* he has to say.

Sometimes, in an attempt to sound natural, a writer will take on a folksy or overly colloquial voice, which is much worse than sounding dry and flat. What impression does the following passage give you?

```
The thing that really blew my mind was that
marijuana use among college students had actually
declined in the past ten years! I was psyched to
learn that.
```

Ugh!

As you search for the right voice in doing your revision, look for a balance between flat prose, which sounds as if it were manufactured by a machine, and folksy prose or flowery prose, or any other style of prose that would distract the reader from what's most important: what you're trying to say.

Tightening Seams Between What You Say and What They Say

One of the basic challenges of writing with sources is integrating them seamlessly. In the past, you may have practiced the "data dump" strategy, or simply dropping factual information into your papers in little or big clumps. Of course, this won't do. Not only does it make the writing horribly dull, but it means that you're not *making use* of the information you worked so hard to find. Surrounding your sources with your own prose and purposes is an important skill you need to learn, and it's something we discussed at length in the Chapter 4 (see "Writing with Sources" on page 173) and looked at Exercise 5.1 earlier in this chapter.

In particular, think about the following points:

■ *Find your own way of saying things.* This is one of the best ways to take possession of information.

■ *Surround factual information with your own analysis.* Provide a context for any quotation you use. Comment on the significance of a fact or statistic. Look for ways to connect any information to your research question or thesis.

■ *Make analogies or comparisons.* Is something like something else? Advocates for addressing climate change, for example, have used an extended analogy of a bathtub to illustrate how easy it is to ignore a problem until it's too late. You start the water running, get involved in, say, a computer game, and then have to decide when to check whether the tub is full. How long do you wait? What goes into this calculation?

Verbal Gestures

Remember Burke's metaphor for the knowledge-making process (see page 118)? He imagined a parlor full of people having an ongoing conversation about what might be true—arguing, agreeing, raising questions, suggesting new ideas, critiquing old ideas, everyone trying to push the conversation along. Any roomful of people in a conversation about things that cause disagreement is also a roomful of gestures. People wave off a point. They nod in assent. They raise a single finger to raise a new question or make a new point. They invite someone to step forward to speak and ask another to step aside.

Similarly, an essay that is a writer's conversation with others about a question that matters to all of them also includes words and phrases that serve as verbal gestures. Some are gestures that invite some people in the room to provide *background* on the question so that everyone understands what has already been said. Other gestures signal *analysis,* or a closer examination and critique of something someone said. Sometimes these verbal gestures signify *speculation*; the writer just isn't quite sure what to think for sure but maybe.... Or they might indicate *agreement or disagreement*—the writer is taking sides with a particular idea, position, or way of seeing.

Consider whether verbal gestures like these will help you manage the conversation about your topic. Go through your draft, and identify those moments in which you seem to be providing background, analyzing something, agreeing or disagreeing, or speculating. Might some of the following language help you signpost that material?

BACKGROUND

Among the most important voices on _____, the most relevant to this inquiry are _____.

Most people _____.

The major sources of controversy are _____.

One idea emerges again and again, and it's _____.

Like most people, I believed that _____.

The unanswered questions are _____.

This much is clear, _____.

_____'s most important contribution is _____.

Most relevant is _____.

ANALYSIS

The most relevant point is _____.

In comparison,...

In contrast,...

What is most convincing is _____.

What is least convincing is _____.

What's most interesting is _____.

The surprising connection is _____.

Paradoxically,...

Actually,...

What isn't clear is _____.

SPECULATION

Perhaps...

Maybe...

It's possible that _____.

AGREEMENT AND DISAGREEMENT

Indeed...

Obviously...

Alternatively...

While others have argued that _____, I think _____.

On balance, the most convincing idea is _____.

What _____ has failed to consider is _____.

The more important question is _____.

Based on my research, _____.

A better explanation is _____.

It's hard to argue with _____.

What I understand now that I didn't understand before is _____.

Scrutinizing Paragraphs

Is Each Paragraph Unified?

Each paragraph should be about one idea and organized around it. You probably know that already. But applying this notion is a particular problem in a research paper, where information abounds and paragraphs sometimes approach marathon length.

If any of your paragraphs seem too long (say, over a page or even verging on a page), look for ways to break them up into shorter paragraphs. Is more than one idea embedded in the long version? Are you explaining or examining more than one thing?

Even short paragraphs can lack unity, so look at those, too. Do any present minor or tangential ideas that belong somewhere else? Are any of these ideas irrelevant? In other words, should the information in the paragraph be moved into another paragraph of your paper, or should the paragraph just be cut? The cut-and-paste exercise (Exercise 5.3) may have helped you with this already.

Scrutinizing Sentences

Using Active Voice

Which of these two sentences seems more passive, more lifeless?

```
Steroids are used by many high school athletes.
```

or

```
Many high school athletes use steroids.
```

The first version, written in the passive voice, is clearly the more limp of the two. It's not grammatically incorrect. In fact, you may have found texts written in the passive voice to be pervasive in the reading you've done for your research paper. Research writing is plagued by passive voice, and that's one of the reasons it can be so mind numbing to read.

Passive voice construction is simple: The subject of the sentence is not the thing *doing the action* of the verb but, rather, the thing *acted upon* by the verb. For instance, in the following pair, the *active voice* sentence has as its subject Clarence, who does the action of kicking, but the passive sentence has the dog as the subject, which was kicked:

```
Clarence kicked the dog.
```

versus

```
The dog was kicked by Clarence.
```

Sometimes, in passive sentences the subject of the corresponding active sentence may be missing altogether, as in:

```
The study was released.
```

Who or *what* released it?

If you have passive sentences, you can remedy the problem by using *active voice* to push the doer of the action up front in the sentence or adding a doer if it is missing. For example:

```
Many high school athletes use steroids.
```

A telltale sign of passive voice is that it usually requires a form of the verb *to be* (*is, was, are, were, am, be, being, been*). For example:

```
Alcoholism among women has been extensively
studied.
```

Search your draft for *be's,* and see if any sentences are written in the passive voice. (Some word-processing programs will search for you.) Unless this is a sentence that is more appropriate in passive voice, make the passive sentence active. To make a sentence active, move its doer from after the verb into subject position or supply the appropriate doer if the sentence doesn't have one.

Using Strong Verbs

Though this may seem like nitpicking, you'd be amazed how much writing in the active voice can revitalize research writing. The use of strong verbs can have the same effect.

As you know, verbs make things happen. Some verbs can make the difference between a sentence that crackles and one that merely hums. Instead of this:

```
The study suggested that the widespread assumption
that oral sex is common among American teenagers
might be wrong.
```

write this:

```
The study shattered the common belief that
American teens increasingly indulge in oral sex.
```

Just because you're writing about people's ideas doesn't mean you can't use strong verbs. See the box "Verbs for Discussing Ideas" on the following page, which was compiled by a colleague of mine, Cinthia Gannett. If you're desperate for an alternative to *says* or *argues,* check out the 135 alternatives this box offers.

Varying Sentence Length

Here's part of a research essay on the promise of wind energy. When you read it, I think you'll find the writing choppy. What's going on? One way to understand the problem is to count the number of syllables in each sentence. That's the number in the parentheses.

Verbs for Discussing Ideas

accepts	critiques	implies	refutes
acknowledges	declares	infers	regards
adds	defends	informs	rejects
admires	defies	initiates	relinquishes
affirms	demands	insinuates	reminds
allows	denies	insists	repudiates
analyzes	describes	interprets	resolves
announces	determines	intimates	responds
answers	diminishes	judges	retorts
argues	disagrees	lists	reveals
assaults	disconfirms	maintains	reviews
assembles	discusses	marshalls	seeks
asserts	disputes	narrates	sees
assists	disregards	negates	shares
believes	distinguishes	observes	shifts
buttresses	emphasizes	outlines	shows
categorizes	endorses	parses	simplifies
cautions	enumerates	perceives	states
challenges	exaggerates	persists	stresses
claims	experiences	persuades	substitutes
clarifies	experiments	pleads	suggests
compares	explains	points out	summarizes
complicates	exposes	postulates	supplements
concludes	facilitates	praises	supplies
condemns	formulates	proposes	supports
confirms	grants	protects	synthesizes
conflates	guides	provides	tests
confronts	handles	qualifies	toys with
confuses	hesitates	quotes	treats
considers	highlights	ratifies	uncovers
contradicts	hints	rationalizes	urges
contrasts	hypothesizes	reads	verifies
convinces	identifies	reconciles	warns
criticizes	illuminates	reconsiders	

Source: Reproduced with permission of Cinthia Gannett.

The idea of alternative energy is sweeping the country and numerous other developed nations. (29) People are beginning to recyle more plastic and metals. (16) They are also more interested in energy efficiency. (16) Wind energy is among the renewable resources sprouting up around the United States. (25) Wind energy affects the environment, wildlife, society, humans, and politics. (23)

It's not hard to see that the sentence length, measured by syllables, doesn't vary much. There are three sentences in the passage that run between 23 and 29 syllables, and the others are both 16. In addition, the structure of these sentences doesn't vary much. Each has just one main clause. Prose that doesn't vary much in sentence length or structure is invariably boring to read. So what can you do about it?

- *Vary sentence length.* Do a syllable count on a paragraph in your draft that seems clunky, and you'll probably find that you need to vary sentence length. Develop the instinct to follow a long sentence, for example, with a short punchy one from time to time.
- *Combine sentences.* This often works wonders. Can you use puncuation or conjunctions like *or*, *but*, and *and* to join separate sentences together? For example, you might take this sequence of sentences in the passage on wind energy:

    People are beginning to recyle more plastic and metals. (16) They are also more interested in energy efficiency. (16)

    and revise it through sentence combining to read like this:

    People are beginning to recycle more plastic and metals, and they're also more interested in energy efficiency. (32)

    Notice that you now have a compound sentence. In varying length, you'll often also be varying structure.

Editing for Simplicity

Thoreau saw simplicity as a virtue. He demonstrated this not only by spending time beside Walden Pond but also by writing prose while living there. Thoreau writes clearly and plainly.

Somewhere, many of us got the idea that simplicity in writing is a vice—that the long word is better than the short word, that the complex phrase is superior to the simple one. The misconception is that to write simply is to be simple minded. Research papers, especially, suffer from this mistaken notion. They are often filled with what writer William Zinsser calls *clutter*.

EXERCISE 5.4

Cutting Clutter

The following passage is an example of cluttered writing at its best (worst?). It contains phrases and words that often appear in college research papers. Read the passage once. Then take a few minutes and rewrite it, cutting as many words as you can without sacrificing the meaning. Look for ways to substitute a shorter word for a longer one and to say in fewer words what is currently said in many. Try to cut the word count by half.

```
The implementation of the revised alcohol policy
in the university community is regrettable at
the present time due to the fact that the admin-
istration has not facilitated sufficient stu-
dent input, in spite of the fact that there have
been attempts by the people affected by this
policy to make their objections known in many
instances.
```
(55 words)

Avoiding Stock Phrases

A place to begin cutting unnecessary clutter in your essay is to hack away at stock phrases. Like many types of writing, the language of the college research paper is littered with words and phrases that find their way to the page as inevitably as drinking root beer prompted my 12-year-old daughter and her friends to hold burping contests. In each case, the one just seems to inspire the other. Following is a list of stock phrases that I often find in research papers. There is nothing grammatically wrong with these. It's simply that they are old, tired phrases, and you can say the same thing more freshly with fewer words. Look for them in your draft and then edit them out.

TIRED PHRASES	BETTER ALTERNATIVES
Due to the fact that...	*Because...*
At this point in time...	*Now...*
In my opinion,...	*(Unnecessary. We know it's your opinion.)*
A number of...	*Many.../Some...*
A number of studies point to the fact that...	*Many/some researchers conclude (or argue)...*
In the event of...	*If...*
In today's society...	*Today we...*
In conclusion,...	*(Omit. If you're at the end of the paper, you're probably concluding.)*
Until such time as...	*Until...*
Referred to as...	*Called...*
It should be pointed out that...	*(Omit. You are pointing it out.)*
Is in a position to...	*Can*
It is a fact that...	*(Omit. Just state the fact, ma'am.)*
It may be said that...	*(Omit. Just say it.)*
There can be little doubt that...	*It's likely...*
It is possible that...	*Perhaps...*

Preparing the Final Manuscript

I wanted to title this section "Preparing the Final Draft," but it occurred to me that *draft* doesn't suggest anything final. I always call my work a draft because until it's out of my hands, it never feels finished. You may feel that way, too. You've spent five weeks on this paper—and the last few days, disassembling it and putting it back together again. How do you know when you're finally done?

For many students, the deadline dictates that: The paper is due tomorrow. But you may find that your paper really seems to be coming together in a satisfying way. You may even like it, and you're ready to prepare the final manuscript.

Considering a "Reader-Friendly" Design

As consumers of texts these days—especially online—we are constantly influenced by visual rhetoric even if we aren't aware of it. "Eye-tracking" studies, for example, suggest that there is a sequence in how we look at a Web page: Most readers typically read a Web page in an upsidedown "L" pattern, reading across the top of the page and then down the left side. Print advertisers are also acutely aware of visual rhetoric for obvious reasons—text works better with images if they are designed to work together.

A research essay like the one you're working on right now would seem to have little to do with visual rhetoric. The form of an academic paper, particularly if the emphasis is on text—and it usually is—seems largely prescribed by the Modern Language Associaton or the American Psychogical Association. Some papers in the social sciences, for example, require certain sections (abstract, introduction, discussion of method, presentation of results, and discussion of results), and these sections need to be clearly defined with subheadings, making it easy for readers to examine the parts they're most interested in. You probably discovered that in your own reading of formal research. You'll likely learn the formats research papers should conform to in various disciplines as you take upper-level courses in those fields.

While you should document your paper properly, you may have some freedom to develop a format that best serves your purpose. As you consider format in revising, keep readers in mind. How can you make your paper more readable? How can you signal your plan for developing the topic and what's important? Some visual devices might help, including:

- Subheadings
- Bulleted lists (like the one you're reading now)
- Graphs, illustrations, tables
- Block quotes
- Underlining and paragraphing for emphasis
- White space

Long, unbroken pages of text can appear to be a gray, uninviting mass to the reader. All of the devices listed help break up the text, making it more "reader friendly." Subheadings, if not overused, can also cue your reader to significant sections of your paper and how they relate to the whole. Long quotes, those over four lines, should be blocked, or indented one inch from the left margin, so they're distinct from the rest of the text. (See Chapter 4, "Writing with Sources," for more on blocking quotes.) Bullets—dots or asterisks preceding brief lines of text—can be used to highlight a list of important information. Graphs, tables, and illustrations also break up the text but, more importantly, they can also help clarify and explain information. (See Section 2.1.5, "Placement of Tables, Charts, and Illustrations," in Appendix A or Section 2.1.8, "Tables and Figures," in Appendix B.)

Using Images

Thanks to digital imaging, it's easier than ever to find pictures and use them in papers. As you probably know, Google allows users to do keyword searching specifically for images. You're writing an essay on the nutritional problems with fast food? You won't have any trouble finding a picture of a Big Mac that you can drop into your essay. Even better, perhaps you're writing your essay on a historical event, a local controversy, or perhaps a profile. With a few clicks you may find a less generic and more relevant image: a photograph of your profile subject or of the Civil War battle that you're analyzing.

You can do this. But should you?

That's up to your instructor, of course. But if she allows it, any visual addition to your essay—and especially an image—needs to do much more than take up space or break up gray text. It must do work. What kind of work can an image do?

■ *Pictures can dramatize a moment, situation, or outcome that you emphasize in your text*: a photograph of the space shuttle's missing insulation in a paper arguing for an end to funding space exploration programs; a picture of the shootings of students on the Kent State campus in 1970 in a paper exploring campus violence.

■ *Pictures can contribute to difficult explanations.* Like a well-crafted analogy, an image can help readers to see more clearly what you're trying to explain. To explain quantitative data, you typically turn to tables and charts. But how can you use pictures? Use images that don't simply reinforce what you say in words but that also amplify what you say. An obvious example: If you're writing about a painting, then surrounding an image of a work with your textual explanations will bring your words to life. Readers simply have more to work with in understanding what you want them to see.

■ *A sequence of pictures can tell a story or illustrate a process.* A disturbing example of this is a series of photos of a meth addict—usually police booking shots—that tell the story of addiction to the drug in the steady deterioration of a user's face. Pictures of Brazilian rainforest before and after logging can help make an argument about loss of biodiversity.

Following MLA Conventions

I've already mentioned that formal research papers in various disciplines may have prescribed formats. If your instructor expects a certain format, he has probably detailed exactly what that format should be. But in all likelihood, your essay for this class doesn't need to follow a rigid form. It will, however, probably adhere to the basic Modern Language Association (MLA) guidelines, described in detail in Appendix A. There, you'll find methods for formatting your paper and instructions for citing sources on your "Works Cited" page. You'll also find a sample paper in MLA style by Ashley Carvalho, "Patching Up Belfast." The American Psychological Association (APA) guidelines for research papers, the primary alternative to MLA guidelines, are described in Appendix B. You'll find a sample paper in APA style by Patricia Urbick, titled "In the Fight: Women and Combat Exclusion."

Proofreading Your Paper

You've spent weeks researching, writing, and revising your paper. You want to stop now. That's understandable, no matter how much you were driven by your curiosity. But before you sign off on your research paper, placing it in someone else's hands, take the time to proofread it.

I was often so glad to be done with a piece of writing that I was careless about proofreading it. That changed about ten years ago, after I submitted a portfolio of writing to complete my master's degree. I was pretty proud of it, especially an essay about dealing with my father's alcoholism. Unfortunately, I misspelled that word— *alcoholism*—every time I used it. Bummer.

Proofreading on a Computer

Proofreading used to necessitate gobbing on correction fluid to cover up mistakes and then trying to line up the paper and type in the changes. Writing on a computer, you're spared from that ordeal. The text can be easily manipulated.

Software programs can, of course, also help with the actual job of proofreading. Most word-processing programs, for example, come with spelling and grammar checkers. These programs will count the number of words in your sentences, alerting you to particularly long ones, and will even point out uses of passive voice. While these style-checkers may not be all that helpful because of their dubious assumptions about what constitutes "good" style, spell-checkers are an invaluable feature. You probably already know that.

Some writers proofread on screen. Others find they need to print out their paper and proofread the hard copy. They argue that they catch more mistakes if they proofread on paper than if they proofread on screen. It makes sense, especially if you've been staring at the screen for days. A printed copy of your paper *looks* different, and I think you see it differently—maybe with fresher eyes and a more energetic attitude. You might notice things you didn't notice before. Decide for yourself how you want to proofread.

Looking Closely

You've already edited the manuscript, pruning sentences and tightening things up. Now proofread for the little errors in grammar and mechanics that you missed. Aside from misspellings (usually typos), some pretty common mistakes appear in the papers I see. For practice, see if you can catch some of them in the following exercise.

EXERCISE 5.5

Picking Off the Lint

I have a colleague who compares proofreading to picking the lint off an outfit, which is often your final step before heading out the door. Examine the following excerpt from a student paper. Proofread it, catching as many mechanical errors as possible. Note punctuation mistakes, agreement problems, misspellings, and anything else that seems off.

> In an important essay, Melody Graulich notes
> how "rigid dichotomizing of sex roles" in most
> frontier myths have "often handicapped and con-
> fused male as well as female writers (187)," she
> wonders if a "universel mythology" (198) might
> emerge that is less confining for both of them.
> In Bruce Mason, Wallace Stegner seems to experi-
> ment with this idea; acknowledging the power of
> Bo's male fantasies *and* Elsa's ability to teach
> her son to feel. It is his strenth. On the other
> hand, Bruces brother chet, who dies young, lost
> and broken, seems doomed because he lacked suffi-
> cient measure of both the feminine and masculine.

```
He observes that Chet had "enough of the old
man to spoil him, ebnough of his mother to
soften him, not enough of either to save him
(Big Rock, 521)."
```

If you did this exercise in class, compare your proofreading of this passage with that of a partner. What did each of you find?

Ten Common Things to Avoid in Research Papers

The following is a list of the ten most common errors (besides misspelled words) made in research papers that should be caught in careful proofreading. A number of these errors occurred in the previous exercise.

1. Commonly confused words, such as *your* instead of *you're*. Here's a list of others:

their/there/they're	advice/advise
know/now	lay/lie
accept/except	its/it's
all ready/already	passed/past

2. Possessives. Instead of *my fathers alcoholism,* the correct form is *my father's alcoholism.* Remember that if a singular noun ends in *s*, still add *'s*: *Tess's laughter*. If a noun is plural, just add the apostrophe: *the scientists' studies.*

3. Vague pronoun references. The excerpt in Exercise 5.5 ends with the sentence, *He observes that Chet....* Who's *he?* The sentence should read, *Bruce observes that Chet....* Whenever you use the pronouns *he, she, it, they,* and *their,* make sure each clearly refers to someone or something.

4. Subject and verb agreement. If the subject is singular, its verb must be, too:

```
The perils of climate change are many.
```

What confuses writers sometimes is the appearance before the verb of a noun that is not really the subject. Exercise 5.5 begins, for example, with this sentence:

```
In an important essay, Melody Graulich notes
how "rigid dichotomizing of sex roles" in most
```

```
frontier myths have "often handicapped and con-
fused male as well as female writers."
```

The subject here is not *frontier myths* but *rigid dichotomizing,* a singular subject. The sentence should read:

```
In an important essay, Melody Graulich notes
how "rigid dichotomizing of sex roles" in most
frontier myths has "often handicapped and con-
fused male as well as female writers."
```

The verb *has* may sound funny, but it's correct.

5. Punctuation of quotations. Note that commas belong inside quotation marks, not outside. Periods belong inside, too. Colons and semicolons are exceptions—they belong *outside* quotation marks. Blocked quotes don't need quotation marks at all unless there is a quote within the quote.

6. Commas. Could you substitute periods or semicolons? If so, you may be looking at *comma splices* or *run-on sentences.* Here's an example:

```
Since 1980, the use of marijuana by college stu-
dents has steadily declined, this was something
of a surprise to me and my friends.
```

The portion after the comma, *this was...,* is another sentence. The comma should be a period, and *this* should be capitalized.

7. Parenthetical citations. In MLA style, there is no comma between the author's name and page number: (Marks 99).

8. Dashes. Though they can be overused, dashes are a great way to break the flow of a sentence with a related bit of information. You've probably noticed I like them. In a manuscript, type dashes as *two* hyphens (- -), not one. Most word-processing programs will automatically turn the hypens into a solid dash, which is what you want.

9. Names. After mentioning the full name of someone in your paper, normally use her *last name* in subsequent references. For example, this is incorrect:

```
Denise Grady argues that people are genetically
predisposed to obesity. Denise also believes
```

```
that some people are "programmed to convert

calories to fat."
```

Unless you know Denise or for some other reason want to conceal her last name, change the second sentence to this:

```
Grady also believes that some people are

"programmed to convert calories to fat."
```

One exception to this is when writing about literature. It is often appropriate to refer to characters by their first names, particularly if characters share last names (as in Exercise 5.6).

10. Colons and semicolons. A colon is usually used to call attention to what follows it: a list, quotation, or appositive. A colon should follow an independent clause. For example, this won't do:

```
The most troubling things about child abuse

are: the effects on self-esteem and language

development.
```

In this case, eliminate the colon. A semicolon should be used as a period, separating two independent clauses. It simply implies the clauses are closely related. Semicolons should not be used as if they were colons or commas.

Using the "Find" or "Search" Function

Use the "Find" or "Search" function in your word-processing program to help you track down consistent problems. You simply tell the computer what word or punctuation to look for, and it will locate all occurrences in the text. For example, if you want to check for comma splices, search for commas. The cursor will stop on every comma, and you can verify if you have used it correctly. You can also search for pronouns to locate vague references or for words (like those listed in item 1) that you commonly misuse.

Avoiding Sexist Language

One last proofreading task is to do a *man* and *he* check. Until recently, sexism wasn't an issue in language. Use of words such as *mankind* and *chairman* was acceptable; the implication was that the terms applied to both genders. At least, that's how use of the terms was defended when challenged. Critics argued that words such as *mailman* and *businessman* reinforced ideas that only men could fill these roles. Bias in language is subtle but powerful. And it's often unintentional. To avoid sending the wrong message, it's worth making the effort to avoid sexist language.

If you need to use a word with a *man* suffix, check to see if there is an alternative. *Congressperson* sounds pretty clunky, but *representative* works fine. Instead of *mankind,* why not *humanity?* Substitute *camera operator* for *cameraman.*

Also check use of pronouns. Do you use *he* or *his* in places where you mean both genders? For example:

```
The writer who cares about his topic will bring it
to life for his readers.
```

Because a lot of writers are women, this doesn't seem right. How do you solve this problem? You can ask your instructor what she prefers, but here are some guidelines:

1. Use *his or her, he or she,* or the mutation *s/he.* For example:

```
The writer who cares about his or her topic will
bring it to life for his or her readers.
```

This is an acceptable solution, but using *his or her* repeatedly can be awkward.

2. Change the singular subject to plural. For example:

```
Writers who care about their topics will bring
them to life for their readers.
```

This version, which also avoids discriminatory language, sounds much better.

3. Alternate *he* and *she, his* and *hers* whenever you encounter an indefinite person. If you have referred to writers as *he* in one discussion, refer to them as *she* in the next. Alternate throughout.

Looking Back and Moving On

This book began with your writing, and it also will end with it. More than a month ago, you began your inquiry project, and even if you're still not happy with your essay, you probably learned some things that influenced the way you think about yourself as a writer, about the nature of research in a university, and how to solve typical problems that arise when you're writing research-based papers.

In this final exercise, you'll do some thinking about all of this in your journal, or perhaps on a class blog or discussion board.

EXERCISE 5.6

Another Dialogue with Dave

You may remember Dave from Chapter 4 (see Exercise 4.1, "Dialogue with Dave"). He's back, and has some things to ask you about your experience with this project. Draw a line down the middle of a blank page in your journal, or create two columns in a Word document. Ask each of Dave's questions by writing them into the left column, and then fastwrite your response in the right column. Spend *at least* three minutes with each question.

DAVE   **YOU**

1. "Hey you, I think you can't really say that one opinion is better than another one. Don't you agree?"
2. "There's all this stuff in the book about research as a process of discovery. What did you discover?"
3. "What do you figure was the most challenging problem you had to solve while working on this research project? How did you solve it?"
4. "After all this work, what do you take away from this experience? What have you learned that you can *use*?"

APPENDIX A

Guide to MLA Style

Appendix A contains guidelines for preparing your essay in the format recommended by the Modern Language Association, or MLA, a body that, among other things, decides documentation conventions for papers in the humanities. The information here reflects the most recent changes by the MLA, as described in the group's definitive reference for students, the *MLA Handbook for Writers of Research Papers,* 7th edition. By the way, the American Psychological Association (APA) is a similar body for the social sciences, with its own documentation conventions. You will find it fairly easy to switch from one system to the other once you've learned both (Table 1, on page 288, summarizes the important differences). Appendix A covers MLA conventions, and Appendix B explains APA conventions.

Checklist Before Handing in a Paper in MLA Style

- My paper has a title but no separate title page (unless my instructor has said otherwise).
- My name, the instructor's name, the course, and the date are in the upper left-hand corner of the first page (see page 235).
- All my pages are numbered using my last name next to the appropriate page number (see page 235).
- My Works Cited list begins on a new page.
- Everything, including my Works Cited page(s), is double-spaced.
- Every page of the paper's text is readable.
- There are no commas in my parenthetical citations between the author's name and the page number (see page 224).
- All my parenthetical citations are *before* the periods at the ends of sentences, unless the citation appears at the end of a blocked quote (see pages 227 and 237–238).
- The entries in my Works Cited page(s) are listed alphabetically, and every line after the first one in an entry is indented a half inch.

Part One of this appendix, "Citing Sources in Your Essay," will be particularly useful as you write your draft; it provides guidance on how to parenthetically cite the sources you use in the text of your essay. Part Two, "Formatting Your Essay," will help you with formatting the manuscript, something you will likely focus on after revising; it includes guidelines for margins, pagination, and tables, charts, and illustrations. Part Three, "Preparing the Works Cited Page," offers detailed instructions on how to prepare your bibliography at the end of your essay; this is usually one of the last steps in preparing the final manuscript. Finally, Part Four presents a sample research essay in MLA style, which will show you how it all comes together.

Directory of MLA Style

Part One: Citing Sources in Your Essay

1.1 When to Cite

Before examining the details of how to use parenthetical citations, remember when you must cite sources in your paper:

1. Whenever you quote from an original source
2. Whenever you borrow ideas from an original source, even when you express them in your own words by paraphrasing or summarizing
3. Whenever you borrow from a source factual information that is *not common knowledge*

The Common Knowledge Exception

The business about *common knowledge* causes much confusion. Just what does this term mean? Basically, *common knowledge* means facts that are widely known and about which there is no controversy.

Sometimes, it's really obvious whether something is common knowledge. The fact that the Super Bowl occurs in late January or early February and pits the winning teams from the American Football Conference and National Football Conference is common knowledge. The fact that President Ronald Reagan was once an actor and starred in a movie with a chimpanzee is common knowledge, too. But what about Carolyn's assertion that most dreaming occurs during rapid eye movement (REM) sleep? This is an idea about which all of her sources seem to agree. Does that make it common knowledge?

It's useful to ask next, How common to whom? Experts in the topic at hand or the rest of us? As a rule, consider the knowledge of your readers. What information will not be familiar to most of your readers or may even surprise them? Which ideas might even raise skepticism? In this case, the fact about REM sleep and dreaming goes slightly beyond the knowledge of most readers, so to be safe, it should be cited. Use common sense, but when in doubt, cite.

1.2 The MLA Author/Page System

The Modern Language Association (MLA) uses the author/page parenthetical citation system. As you can see in Appendix B, the American Psychological Association (APA) uses the author/date system.

The Basics of Using Parenthetical Citation

The MLA method of in-text parenthetical citation is fairly simple: As close as possible to the borrowed material, you indicate in parentheses the original source (usually, the author's name) and the page number in the work that material came from. For example, here's how you'd cite a book or article with a single author using the author/page system:

```
From the very beginning of Sesame Street
in 1969, kindergarten teachers discovered that
incoming students who had watched the program
already knew their ABCs (Chira 13).*
```

The parenthetical citation here tells readers two things: (1) This information about the success of *Sesame Street* does not

---

*This and the following "Works Cited" example are used with permission of Heidi R. Dunham.

originate with the writer but with someone named *Chira,* and (2) readers can consult the original source for further information by looking on page 13 of Chira's book or article, which is cited fully at the back of the paper in the Works Cited. Here is what readers would find there:

```
               Works Cited
   Chira, Susan. "Sesame Street at 20: Taking

       Stock." New York Times 15 Nov. 1989: 13.

       Print.
```

Here's another example of a parenthetical author/page citation, from another research paper. Note the differences from the previous example:

```
   "One thing is clear," writes Thomas Mallon,

   "plagiarism didn't become a truly sore point

   with writers until they thought of writing as

   their trade. . . . Suddenly his capital and iden-

   tity were at stake" (3-4).
```

The first thing you may have noticed is that the author's last name—Mallon—was omitted from the parenthetical citation. It didn't need to be included because it had already been mentioned in the text. *If you mention the author's name in the text of your paper, then you only need to parenthetically cite the relevant page number(s).* This citation also tells us that the quoted passage comes from two pages rather than one.

Placement of Citations.   Place the citation as close as you can to the borrowed material, trying to avoid breaking the flow of the sentences, if possible. To avoid confusion about what's borrowed and what's not—particularly if the material you're borrowing spans more than a sentence—when possible mention the name of the original author *in your paper* in a way that clarifies what you've borrowed. Note that in the next example the writer simply cites the source at the end of the paragraph, not naming the source in the text. As a result, it is hard for the reader to figure out whether

Citations That Go with the Flow

There's no getting around it: Parenthetical citations can be like stones on the sidewalk. Readers stride through a sentence in your essay and then have to step around the citation at the end before they resume their walk. Yet citations are important in academic writing because they help readers know who you read or heard that shaped your thinking. And you can write your citations in such a way that they won't trip up readers. As a result, your essay will be more readable. Try these techniques:

- Avoid lengthy parenthetical citations by mentioning the name of the author in your essay. That way, you usually only have to include a page number in the citation.
- Try to place citations where readers are likely to pause anyway—for example, at the end of the sentence or right before a comma.
- Remember you *don't* need a citation when you're citing common knowledge or referring to an entire work by an author.
- If you're borrowing from only one source in a paragraph of your essay, and all of the borrowed material comes from a single page of that source, don't repeat the citation over and over again with each new bit of information. Just put the citation at the end of the paragraph.

Blager is the source of the information in the entire paragraph or just in part of it:

> Though children who have been sexually abused
> seem to be disadvantaged in many areas,
> including the inability to forge lasting
> relationships, low self-esteem, and crippling
> shame, they seem advantaged in other areas.
> Sexually abused children seem to be more
> socially mature than other children of their
> same age group. It's a distinctly mixed
> blessing (Blager 994).

In the following example, notice how the ambiguity about what's borrowed and what's not is resolved by careful placement of the author's name and parenthetical citation in the text:

> Though children who have been sexually abused seem to be disadvantaged in many areas, including the inability to forge lasting relationships, low self-esteem, and crippling shame, they seem advantaged in other areas. According to Blager, sexually abused children seem to be more socially mature than other children of their same age group (994). It's a distinctly mixed blessing.

In this latter version, it's clear that Blager is the source for one sentence in the paragraph, and the writer is responsible for the rest. When you first mention authors, use their full name, and when you mention them again, use only their last names. Also note that the citation is placed *before* the period of the sentence (or last sentence) that it documents. That's almost always the case, except at the end of a blocked quotation, where the parenthetical reference is placed *after* the period of the last sentence. The citation can also be placed near the author's name, rather than at the end of the sentence, if it doesn't unnecessarily break the flow of the sentence. For example:

> Blager (994) observes that sexually abused children tend to be more socially mature than other children of their same age group.

1.2.1 WHEN YOU MENTION ONE AUTHOR

It's generally good practice in research writing to identify who said what. The familiar convention of using attribution tags such as "According to Fletcher,…" or "Fletcher argues…" and so on helps readers attach a name with a voice or an individual with certain claims or findings. As just discussed, when you mention the author of a source in your sentence, the parenthetical citation includes only the page number. For example,

> Robert Harris believes that there is "widespread uncertainty" among students about what consti- tutes plagiarism (2).

As was also discussed, the page number could come directly after the author's name.

> Robert Harris (2) believes that there is "wide- spread uncertainty" among students about what constitutes plagiarism.

1.2.2 WHEN YOU MENTION MORE THAN ONE AUTHOR

Often your sources will have more than one author. If the book or article has two or three authors, list all their last names in the parenthetical citation, with *and* before the final author; for example:

> (Oscar and Leibowitz 29)

If your source has more than three authors, you can either list them all or use the first author and *et al.*:

> (Kemp et al. 199)

1.2.3 WHEN THERE IS NO AUTHOR

Occasionally, you may encounter a source whose author is anonymous—that is, who isn't identified. This isn't unusual with pamphlets, editorials, government documents, some newspaper arti- cles, online sources, and short filler articles in magazines. If you can't parenthetically name the author, what do you cite?

Most often, cite the title (or an abbreviated version, if the title is long) and the page number. If you abbreviate the title, begin with the word under which it is alphabetized in the Works Cited list. For example:

> Simply put, public relations is "doing good and getting credit" for it (*Getting Yours* 3).

Here is how the publication cited above would be listed at the back of the paper:

Works Cited

Getting Yours: A Publicity and Funding Primer

    for Nonprofit and Voluntary Organizations.

    Lincoln: Contact Center, 2008. Print.

As with other sources, for clarity, it's often helpful to mention the original source of the borrowed material in the text of your paper. Refer to the publication or institution (e.g., the American Cancer Society or Department of Defense) you're citing or make a more general reference to the source. For example:

An article in *Cuisine* magazine argues that the
best way to kill a lobster is to plunge a knife
between its eyes ("How to Kill" 56).

or

According to one government report, with the
current minimum size limit, most lobsters end up
on dinner plates before they've had a chance to
reproduce ("Size" 3-4).

Note the abbreviation of the article titles; for example, the full title for "How to Kill," listed in the Works Cited, is "How to Kill a Lobster." Note also that article titles are in quotation marks and book titles are italicized.

1.2.4 WORKS BY THE SAME AUTHOR

Suppose you end up using several books or articles by the same author. Obviously, a parenthetical citation that merely lists the author's name and page number won't do because it won't be clear *which* of several works the citation refers to. In this case, include the author's name, an abbreviated title (if the original is too long), and the page number. For example:

The thing that distinguishes the amateur from
the experienced writer is focus; one "rides off
in all directions at once," and the other finds

```
one meaning around which everything revolves
```
```
(Murray, Write to Learn 92).
```

The Works Cited list would show multiple works by one author as follows:

```
                    Works Cited
```
```
Murray, Donald M. Write to Learn. 8th ed. Boston:
```
```
     Heinle, 2004. Print.
```
```
---. A Writer Teaches Writing. Boston:
```
```
     Heinle, 2004. Print.
```

It's obvious from the parenthetical citation which of the two Murray books is the source of the information. Note that in the parenthetical reference, no punctuation separates the title and the page number, but a comma follows the author's name. If Murray had been mentioned in the text of the paper, his name could have been dropped from the citation.

How to handle the Works Cited list is explained more fully later in this appendix, but for now, notice that the three hyphens used in the second entry signal that the author's name in this source is the same as in the preceding entry.

1.2.5 WORKS BY DIFFERENT AUTHORS WITH THE SAME NAME

How do you distinguish between different authors who have the same last name? Say you're citing a piece by someone named Lars Anderson as well as a piece by someone named Kelli Anderson. The usual in-text citation, which uses the last name only (Anderson 2), wouldn't help the reader much. In this situation, add the author's first initial to the citation: (L. Anderson 2) or (K. Anderson 12).

1.2.6 INDIRECT SOURCES

Whenever you can, cite the original source for material you use. For example, if an article on television violence quotes the author of a book and you want to use the quote, try to hunt down the book. That way, you'll be certain of the accuracy of the quote and you may find some more usable information.

Sometimes, however, finding the original source is not possible. In those cases, use the term *qtd. in* to signal that you've quoted or paraphrased material that was quoted in your source and initially appeared elsewhere. In the following example, the citation signals that the quote from Bacon was in fact culled from an article by Guibroy, rather than from Bacon's original work:

```
Francis Bacon also weighed in on the dangers of
imitation, observing that "it is hardly possible
at once to admire an author and to go beyond
him" (qtd. in Guibroy 113).
```

1.2.7 PERSONAL INTERVIEWS

If you mention the name of your interview subject in your text, no parenthetical citation is necessary. If you don't mention the subject's name, cite it in parentheses after the quote:

```
The key thing when writing for radio, says one
journalist, is to "write to the sound if you've
got great sound, and read your stuff aloud"
(Tan).
```

Regardless of whether you mention your subject's name, you should include a reference to the interview in the Works Cited. In this case, the reference would look like this:

```
                    Works Cited
Tan, Than. Personal interview. 28 Jan. 2011.
```

1.2.8 SEVERAL SOURCES IN A SINGLE CITATION

Suppose two sources both contributed the same information in a paragraph of your essay. Or, even more likely, suppose you're summarizing the findings of several authors on a certain topic—a fairly common move when you're trying to establish a context for your own research question. How do you cite multiple authors in a single citation? Use author names and page numbers as usual, and separate them with a semicolon. For example,

```
A whole range of studies have looked closely at
the intellectual development of college stu-
dents, finding that they generally assume
```

```
"stages" or "perspectives" that differ from sub-
ject to subject (Perry 122; Belenky et al. 12).
```

Sample Parenthetical References for Other Sources

MLA format is pretty simple, and we've already covered some of the basic variations. You should also know the following five additional variations:

1.2.9 AN ENTIRE WORK

If you mention an author's name and his or her work in the text but don't refer to specific details, no citation is necessary. The work should, however, be listed in the Works Cited. For the following example, Edel's book would be listed in the Works Cited.

```
Leon Edel's Henry James is considered by many to
be a model biography.
```

1.2.10 A VOLUME OF A MULTIVOLUME WORK

If you're working with one volume of a multivolume work, it's a good idea to mention which volume in the parenthetical reference. The citation below attributes the passage to the second volume, page 3, of a work by Baym and other authors. The volume number is always followed by a colon, which is followed by the page number:

```
By the turn of the century, three authors
dominated American literature: Mark Twain,
Henry James, and William Dean Howells (Baym
et al. 2: 3).
```

1.2.11 A LITERARY WORK

Because so many literary works, particularly classics, have been reprinted in so many editions, and readers are likely using different editions, it's useful to give readers information about where a passage can be found regardless of edition. You can do this by listing not only the page number but also the chapter number—and any other relevant information, such as the section or volume—separated from the page number by a semicolon. Use arabic rather than roman numerals.

```
Izaak Walton warns that "no direction can be
given to make a man of a dull capacity able to
make a Flie well" (130; ch. 5).
```

When citing poems or plays, instead of page numbers, cite line numbers for poems and act, scene, and line numbers, separated with periods, for plays. For example, (Othello 2.3.286) indicates act 2, scene 3, line 286 of that play.

1.2.12 AN ONLINE SOURCE

If you're using material from a book on your Kindle or iPad, you'll notice that there are "location numbers" or percentages rather than page numbers. (Other e-text devices may have page numbers.) And you've probably already noticed that many online documents don't have page numbers or don't have permanent ones. What should you do when you want to cite sources that don't have page numbers?

When a document or Web page lacks permanent page numbers, you can cite just the author, but you may be able to alert readers to a more general location: "In the first chapter, Payne argues that...." If the source is authorless, the citation would just include a title, as in this citation of an article from the Web:

```
Many women who wait to begin a family may won-
der if prior birth control choices negatively
affect their fertility. It's not uncommon, for
instance, for a woman to take oral contracep-
tives for 10 years or longer. The birth control
pill itself doesn't affect long-term fertility
("Infertility: Key Q and A").
```

On the other hand, PDF files frequently have permanent pagination, particularly if the document is a copy of the original article. In that case, the page numbers should be used in your citation.

Part Two: Formatting Your Essay

2.1 The Layout

There is, well, a certain fussiness associated with the look of academic papers. The reason for it is quite simple—academic disciplines generally aim for consistency in format so that readers of scholarship know exactly where to look to find what they want to know. It's a matter of efficiency. How closely you must follow the MLA's requirements for the layout of your essay is up to your instructor, but it's really not that complicated. A lot of what you need to know is featured in Figure A1.

2.1.1 PRINTING

Print your paper on white, 8½ × 11-inch paper. Make sure the printer has sufficient ink or toner.

2.1.2 MARGINS AND SPACING

The old high school trick is to have big margins so you can get the length without the information. Don't try that trick with this paper. Leave one-inch margins at the top, bottom, and sides of your pages. Indent the first line of each paragraph a half inch, and indent

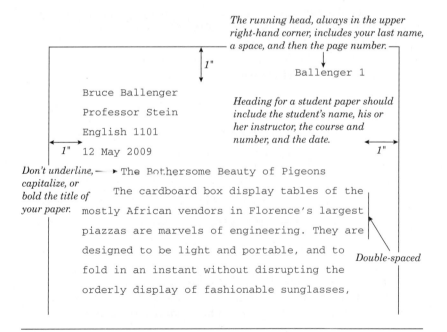

FIGURE A1   The Basic Look of an MLA-Style Paper

blocked quotes an inch. Double-space all of the text, including blocked quotes and Works Cited.

2.1.3 TITLE

Your paper doesn't need a separate title page; the title will go on your first page of text. On that page, one inch from the top on the upper left-hand side, type your name, your instructor's name, the course name and number, and the date. Below that, type the title, centered on the page. Begin the text of the paper below the title. For example:

```
Karoline Ann Fox

Professor Dethier

English 401

15 December 2008
              Metamorphosis, the Exorcist,
                   and Oedipus
Ernst Pawel has said that Franz Kafka's The
Metamorphosis...*
```

Note that everything is double spaced. The title is not italicized (although italics would be used for the name of a book or other work that should be italicized), underlined, or boldfaced.

2.1.4 HEADER WITH PAGINATION

Make sure that every page is numbered. That's especially important with long papers. Type your last name and the page number in the upper right-hand corner, flush with the right margin: `Ballenger 3`. Don't use the abbreviation *p.* or a hyphen between your name and the number.

2.1.5 PLACEMENT OF TABLES, CHARTS, AND ILLUSTRATIONS

With MLA format, papers do not have appendixes. Tables, charts, and illustrations are placed in the body of the paper, close to the text that refers to them. Number tables and charts consecutively (Table 1, Table 2, and so on; Fig. 1, Fig. 2, and so on; notice the abbreviation of "Figure"). Place the title of a table above it, flush left. Place the caption for a chart or illustration below it. For tables, charts, and illustrations that are borrowed, give full citations. This

---

*Reprinted with permission of Karoline A. Fox.

Table 1
Percentage of Students Who Self-Report Acts of Plagiarism

Acts of Plagiarism	Never/ Rarely	Some- times	Often/ Very Freq.
Copy text without citation	71	19	10
Copy paper without citation	91	5	3
Request paper to hand in	90	5	2
Purchase paper to hand in	91	6	3

Source: Scanlon, Patrick M., and David R. Neumann; "Internet Plagiarism among College Students," *Journal of College Student Development* 43.3 (2002): 379. Print.

FIGURE A2   Example of Format for a Table.

information goes at the bottom of a table or at the end of a caption for a chart or illustration. See Figure A2 for an example of a table formatted according to MLA guidelines.

2.2 Some Style Considerations

2.2.1 HANDLING TITLES

The general MLA rule for capitalization of titles is that the writer should capitalize the first letters of all principal words in a title, including any that follow hyphens. Words not capitalized include articles (*a, an,* and *the*), prepositions (*for, of, in, to*, and so on), coordinating conjunctions (*and, or, but, for*), and *to* in infinitives. However, these words are capitalized if they appear at the beginning or end of the title.

In May 2008, the MLA updated its citation style, and among the changes is a no-brainer in this era of word processing: a shift to *italicizing* titles of works rather than <u>underlining</u> them. The APA figured this out about a decade ago.

The new rules for deciding whether to italicize a title or place it in quotation marks (the usual alternative) makes this distinction:

1. If the work is "published independently," italicize it. These works are typically books, Web sites, online databases, TV broadcasts, plays, periodicals, and so on.
2. If the title is part of a larger work—say, an article in a periodical or an episode of a TV program—then place it in quotation marks.

Here are some examples:

The Curious Researcher (book)

A Streetcar Named Desire (play)

"Once More to the Lake" (essay in a collection)

New York Times (newspaper)

"Psychotherapy" (encyclopedia article)

"Funny Talking Animals" (YouTube clip)

2.2.2 STYLE RELATED TO SOURCES AND QUOTATIONS

Names. Though it may seem as if you're on familiar terms with some of the authors you cite by the end of your research project, it's not a good idea to call them by their first names. Give the full names of people you cite when you first mention them, and then give only their last names if you mention them again.

Ellipsis Points. Those are the three dots (or four if the omitted material comes at the end of a sentence where they join a period) that indicate you've left out a word, phrase, or even whole section of a quoted passage. It's wise to use ellipsis points and omit material when you want to emphasize part of a quotation and don't want to burden your reader with unnecessary information, but be careful to preserve the basic intention and idea of the author's original statement. Ellipsis points can come at the beginning of a quotation, in the middle, or at the end, depending where it is you've omitted material. For example,

> "After the publication of a controversial picture that shows, for example, either dead or grieving victims . . ., readers in telephone calls and in letters to the editor, often attack the photographer for being tasteless . . ." (Lesser 56).

Quotations. Quotations that run more than four lines long should be blocked, or indented one inch from the left margin. The first sentence of any paragraphs within a blocked quotation should be indented an additional quarter inch. The quotation should be double spaced. Quotation marks should not be used. The parenthetical citation is placed *after* the period at the end of the quotation. A colon is a customary way to introduce a blocked quotation. For example,

> Chris Sherman and Gary Price, in *The Invisible Web*, contend that much of the Internet, possibly most, is beyond the reach of researchers who use conventional search engines:
>
>> The problem is that vast expanses of the Web are completely invisible to general-purpose search engines like AltaVista, HotBot, and Google. Even worse, this "Invisible Web" is in all likelihood growing significantly faster than the visible Web that you're familiar with. It's not that search engines and Web directories are "stupid" or even badly engineered. Rather, they simply can't "see" millions of high-quality resources that are available exclusively on the Invisible Web. So what is this Invisible Web and why aren't search engines doing anything about it to make it visible? (xxi)

Part Three:
Preparing the Works Cited Page

The Works Cited page ends the paper. (This may also be called the "References Cited" or "Sources Cited" page, depending on the preference of your instructor.) Occasionally, instructors may want another kind of source list along with or instead of a Works Cited list: An "Annotated List of Works Cited" includes a brief description of each source; a "Works Consulted" list includes not only the sources you cited but also others that shaped your thinking; a "Content Notes" page, keyed to superscript numbers in the text of the paper, lists short asides that are not central enough to the discussion to be included in the text itself.

The Works Cited page is the workhorse of most college papers. Works Cited is essentially an alphabetical listing of all the sources you quoted, paraphrased, or summarized in your paper. If you have used MLA format for citing sources, your paper has numerous parenthetical references to authors and page numbers. The Works Cited page provides complete information on each source cited in the text for the reader who wants to know. (In APA format, this page is called "References" and is slightly different in how items are listed. See Appendix B for APA guidelines.)

3.1 Format

Alphabetizing the List

Works Cited follows the text of your paper on a separate page. After you've assembled complete information about each source you've cited, put the sources in alphabetical order by the last name of the author. If the work has multiple authors, alphabetize by the last name of the first one listed. If the source has no author, then alphabetize it by the first key word of the title. If you're citing more than one source by a single author, you don't need to repeat the name for each source; simply place three hyphens followed by a period (- - - .) for the author's name in subsequent listings.

Indenting and Spacing

Type the first line of each entry flush left, and indent subsequent lines of that entry (if any) a half inch. Double-space between each line and each entry. For example:

```
                                              Hall 10

                    Works Cited

Biernacki, Patrick. Pathways from Heroin Addic-

     tion. Philadelphia: Temple UP, 1986. Print.

Brill, Leon. The De-Addiction Process. Spring-

     field: Thomas, 1972. Print.

Epstein, Joan F., and Joseph C. Gfroerer. "Heroin

     Abuse in the United States." National Clear-

     inghouse for Alcohol and Drug Information.
```

US Dept. of Health and Human Services,
Aug. 1997. Web. 24 Nov. 2008.

Hall, Lonny. Personal interview. 1 Mar. 2009.

Kaplan, John. *The Hardest Drug: Heroin and Public Policy.* Chicago: U of Chicago P, 1983. Print.

"Methadone." *Encyclopaedia Britannica.* 1999 ed. 1999. CD-ROM.

Shaffner, Nicholas. *Saucerful of Secrets: The Pink Floyd Odyssey.* New York: Dell, 1992. Print.

Strang, John, and Michael Gossop. *Heroin Addiction and Drug Policy: The British System.* New York: Oxford UP, 1994. Print.

Swift, Wendy, et al. "Transitions between Routes of Heroin Administration: A Study of Caucasian and Indochinese Users in South-Western Sydney, Australia." *Addiction* (1999): 71-82. Print.

3.2 Citing Books, in Print and Online

You usually need three pieces of information to cite a book: the name of the author or authors, the title, and the publication information. Information you need to cite for an online text depends on whether the book is also available in print. The following chart shows the basics for citing in-print and electronic books.

CITING A BOOK IN PRINT	CITING AN E-BOOK
1. Author(s)	1. Author(s)
2. *Title*	2. *Title*
3. Edition and/or volume (if relevant)	3. Edition and/or volume (if relevant)

(continued)

4. Where published, by whom, and date	4. If also in print, where published, by whom, and date; in any case, sponsoring organization, date of electronic publication
5. Medium: Print	5. Medium: Web
	6. Date of access

SAMPLE CITATION: BOOK IN PRINT	SAMPLE CITATION: E-BOOK (WEB ONLY)
Donald, David H. *Lincoln*. New York: Simon & Schuster, 1995. Print.	Lincoln, Abraham. *The Writings of Abraham Lincoln*. B & R Samizdat Express, 2009. Web. 28 Jan. 2011.

Author(s).   Authors' names should appear as they do in the source. Only list an author's name with initials if it appears that way on the title page. You don't need to include titles or degrees that sometimes follow an author's name (e.g., Diana Rosenstein PhD).

Title.   As a rule, the titles of books are italicized, with capitalization of the first letters of the first word and all principal words, including in any subtitles. Titles that are not italicized are usually those of pieces found within larger works, such as poems and short stories in anthologies. These titles are set off by quotation marks. Titles of religious works (the Bible, the Koran) are neither italicized nor enclosed within quotation marks. (See the guidelines in "Handling Titles," in Part Two.)

Edition.   If a book doesn't indicate any edition number, then it's probably a first edition, a fact you don't need to cite. Look on the title page. Signal an edition like this: *2nd ed., 3rd ed.,* and so on. If you're citing a multivolume work, include the total number of volumes in the citation following the book's title, using the abbreviation *vols.* (e.g. 2 vols.).

Publication Information.   For any book that has been published in print, this includes place, publisher, and date. Look on the title page to find out who published the book. Publishers' names are usually shortened in the Works Cited list; for example, *St. Martin's Press, Inc.,* is shortened to *St. Martin's*.

What publication place to cite may be unclear when several cities are listed on the title page. Cite the first one. For books published outside the United States, add the country name along with the city to avoid confusion.

The date a book is published is usually indicated on the copyright page. If several dates or several printings by the same publisher are listed, cite the original publication date. However, if the book is a revised edition, give the date of that edition. One final variation: If you're citing a book that's a reprint of an original edition, give both dates. For example:

> Stegner, Wallace. *Recapitulation*. 1979. Lincoln:
>
> U of Nebraska P, 1986. Print.

This book was first published in 1979 and then republished in 1986 by the University of Nebraska Press.

Online books also often appear in print, and in such cases your citation will include all the usual print publication information. For all online books you must give the date of electronic publication and the organization that is sponsoring the electronic text. These organizations range from commercial sponsors like Amazon to nonprofit groups like Project Gutenberg. You can usually find the name of the sponsor either on the text itself or on the Web page from which you downloaded it.

Medium.   Following the publication information, you indicate the medium—Print or Web. Capitalize the word and follow it with a period.

Date of Access.   For electronic sources, the citation also includes the date you accessed the title. In the example that follows, notice the form for the date, as well as the print publication information and the sponsoring organization:

> Badke, William. *Research Strategies: Finding*
>
> *Your Way Through the Information Fog*.
>
> Lincoln: Writers Club P, 2000. *iUniverse*.
>
> Web. 12 July 2008.

Page Numbers.   Normally, you don't list page numbers of a book in your Works Cited. The parenthetical reference in your paper specifies the particular page or pages the material you borrowed is from. But if you use only part of a book—an introduction or an essay— list the appropriate page numbers following the publication date.

A period should follow the page numbers. Notice in this example that if the author(s) or editor(s) of the entire work also wrote the introduction or essay you're citing, the second mention in that citation uses last name only:

> Lee, L. L., and Merrill Lewis. Preface. *Women,*
>   *Women Writers, and the West.* Ed. Lee and
>   Lewis. Troy: Whitston, 1980. v-ix. Print.

Sample Book Citations

The examples that follow show the form for some common variations on the basic book citation format just shown. Although most of the examples are for printed books, the corresponding online sources work in much the same way. Remember that for an online source you would give print publication information if the source has also been published in print and would in any case give the sponsoring organization and date of electronic publication, indicate Web as the medium, and give the date of access.

3.2.1 A BOOK WITH ONE AUTHOR

> Armstrong, Karen. *The Spiral Staircase.* New
>   York: Knopf, 2004. Print.

In-Text Citation: (Armstrong 22)

3.2.2 A BOOK WITH TWO OR THREE AUTHORS

If a book has two authors, give the second author's names uninverted.

> Ballenger, Bruce, and Michelle Payne. *The Curi-*
>   *ous Reader.* New York: Longman, 2006. Print.

In-Text Citation: (Ballenger and Payne 14)

Cite a book with three authors like this:

> Bloom, Lynn Z., Donald A. Daiker, and Edward M.
>   White, eds. *Composition Studies in the New*

```
Millenium. Carbondale: Southern Illinois
    UP, 2003.
```

In-Text Citation: (Bloom, Daiker, and White 200)

3.2.3 A BOOK WITH MORE THAN THREE AUTHORS

If a book has more than three authors, you may list the first and substitute the term *et al.* for the others.

```
Jones, Hillary, et al. The Unmasking of Adam.
    Highland Park: Pegasus, 1992. Print.
```

In-Text Citation: (Jones et al. 21-30)

3.2.4 SEVERAL BOOKS BY THE SAME AUTHOR

```
Baldwin, James. Tell Me How Long the Train's Been
    Gone. New York: Dell-Doubleday, 1968. Print.
---. Going to Meet the Man. New York: Dell-
    Doubleday, 1948. Print.
```

In-Text Citation: (Baldwin, *Going* 34) or (Baldwin, *Tell Me How Long* 121)

3.2.5 AN ENTIRE COLLECTION OR ANTHOLOGY

```
Crane, R. S., ed. Critics and Criticism: Ancient
    and Modern. Chicago: U of Chicago P, 1952.
    Print.
```

In-Text Citation: (Crane xx)

3.2.6 A WORK IN A COLLECTION OR ANTHOLOGY

The title of a work in a collection should be enclosed in quotation marks. However, if the work was originally published as a book, its title should be italicized.

```
Jones, Robert F. "Welcome to Muskie Coun-
    try." The Ultimate Fishing Book. Ed. Lee
```

Eisenberg and DeCourcy Taylor. Boston:
Houghton, 1981. 122-34. Print.

In-Text Citation: (Jones 131)

Bahktin, Mikhail. *Marxism and the Philosophy of
Language. The Rhetorical Tradition.* Ed.
Patricia Bizzell and Bruce Herzberg. New
York: St. Martin's, 1990. 928-44. Print.

In-Text Citation: (Bahktin 929-31)

3.2.7 AN INTRODUCTION, PREFACE, FOREWORD, OR PROLOGUE

Scott, Jerie Cobb. Foreword. *Writing Groups:
History, Theory, and Implications.* By Ann
Ruggles Gere. Carbondale: Southern Illinois
UP, 1987. ix-xi. Print.

In-Text Citation: (Scott x-xi)

Rich, Adrienne. Introduction. *On Lies, Secrets,
and Silence.* By Rich. New York: Norton,
1979. 9-18. Print.

In-Text Citation: (Rich 12)

3.2.8 A BOOK WITH NO AUTHOR

Merriam-Webster Dictionary Online. Encyclopedia
Britannica, 2011. Web. 8 Feb. 2011.

In-Text Citation: (*Merriam-Webster* 444)

3.2.9 AN ENCYLOPEDIA ARTICLE

"City of Chicago." *Encyclopaedia Britannica.*
1999 ed. Print.

In-Text Citation: ("City of Chicago" 397)

For online encyclopedias, as for other online sources, include the name of the sponsor of the Web site and the date you accessed the site. Notice the in-text citation for this source without page numbers.

"Diarrhea." *Columbia Encyclopedia Online.* 6th

ed. Columbia UP, 2008. Web. 10 June 2008.

In-Text Citation: ("Diarrhea")

Wikipedia raises eyebrows among many academics who don't consider it a particularly authoritative source, but should you need to cite it, include the date and time of the latest revision of the page you're citing. You can find that date at the bottom of the page.

"Flesh Fly." *Wikipedia.* Wikimedia Foundation, 27

January 2011. Web. 28 January 2011.

In-Text Citation: ("Flesh Fly")

3.2.10 A BOOK WITH AN INSTITUTIONAL AUTHOR

Hospital Corporation of America. *Employee Bene-*

fits Handbook. Nashville: HCA, 2004. Print.

In-Text Citation: (Hospital Corporation of America
5-7)

3.2.11 A BOOK WITH MULTIPLE VOLUMES

If you are using material from more than one volume of a multi-volume work, include the number of volumes in the work between the title and publication information. In your in-text citations, indicate the relevant volume.

Baym, Nina, ed. *The Norton Anthology of American*

Literature. 6th ed. 2 vols. New York:

Norton, 2002. Print.

In-Text Citation: (Baym 2: 3)

If you use only one volume of a multivolume work, indicate which one along with the page numbers. The in-text citation includes only the page number.

Baym, Nina, ed. *The Norton Anthology of American Literature*. 6th ed. Vol 2. New York: Norton, 2002. Print.

In-Text Citation: (Baym 1115)

3.2.12 A BOOK THAT IS NOT A FIRST EDITION

Check the title page to determine whether the book is an edition other than the first (2nd, 3rd, 4th, etc.); if no edition number is mentioned, assume it's the first. Put the edition number right after the title.

Ballenger, Bruce. *The Curious Researcher*. 5th ed. Boston: Longman, 2007. Print.

In-Text Citation: (Ballenger 194)

Citing the edition is necessary only for books that are *not* first editions. This includes revised editions (*Rev. ed.*) and abridged editions (*Abr. ed.*).

3.2.13 A BOOK PUBLISHED BEFORE 1900

For a book published before 1900, it's usually unnecessary to list the publisher.

Hitchcock, Edward. *Religion of Geology*. Glasgow, 1851. Print.

In-Text Citation: (Hitchcock 48)

3.2.14 A TRANSLATION

Montaigne, Michel de. *Essays*. Trans. J. M. Cohen. Middlesex: Penguin, 1958. Print.

In-Text Citation: (Montaigne 638)

3.2.15 GOVERNMENT DOCUMENTS

Because of the enormous variety of government documents, citing them properly can be a challenge. Because most government documents do not name authors, begin an entry for such a source with the level of government (United States, State of Illinois, etc., unless it is obvious from the title), followed by the sponsoring agency, the title of the work, and the publication information. Look on the title page to determine the publisher. If it's a federal document, then the Government Printing Office (abbreviated *GPO*) is usually the publisher.

```
United States. Bureau of the Census. Statistical
     Abstract of the United States. Washington:
     GPO, 1990. Print.
```

In-Text Citation: (United States, Bureau of the Census 79-83)

3.2.16 A BOOK THAT WAS REPUBLISHED

A fairly common occurrence, particularly in literary study, is to find a book that was republished, sometimes many years after the original publication date. In addition, some books first appear in hard cover and then are republished in paperback. To cite one, put the original date of publication immediately after the book's title, and then include the more current publication date, as usual, at the end of the citation. Do it like so:

```
Ballenger, Bruce, and Barry Lane. Discover-
     ing the Writer Within: 40 Days to More
     Imaginative Writing. 1989. Shoreham:
     Discover Writing P, 2008. Print.
```

In-Text Citation: (Ballenger and Lane 31)

3.3 Citing Articles, in Print and Online

Citations for articles from periodicals—magazines, newspapers, journals, and other such publications that appear regularly—are similar to those for books but include somewhat different information.

As with books, citations for online articles have their own special requirements. The following chart shows, in the appropriate order, the elements for citations for a print article and an article from the Web or your library's online databases. As the following pages show, the elements actually included vary a bit depending on specifics of the source.

PRINT ARTICLE	ARTICLE FROM A DATABASE OR THE WEB
1. Author(s)	1. Author(s)
2. "Article Title"	2. "Article Title"
3. *Periodical Title*	3. *Periodical Title*
4. Volume and issue	4. Volume and issue
5. Date published	5. Date published
6. Page numbers	6. Page numbers, if any (usually present in versions also in print)
7. Medium: Print	7. *Database* or Sponsor
	8. Medium: Web
	9. Date of access
SAMPLE CITATION: PRINT ARTICLE	**SAMPLE CITATION: DATABASE ARTICLE**
Martinello, Marian L. "Learning to Question for Inquiry." *Educational Forum* 62 (1998): 164-71. Print.	Greenebaum, Jessica B. "Training Dogs and Training Humans: Symbolic Interaction and Dog Training." *Anthrozoos: An Interdisciplinary Journal of the Interactions of People & Animals* 23.2 (2010): 129-41. *ArticleFirst*. Web. 28 Jan. 2011.

Author(s).   List the author(s)—one, two, or three or more—as you would for a book citation.

Article Title.   Unlike book titles, which are italicized, article titles are usually enclosed in quotation marks. Capitalize same as book citations.

Periodical Title.   Italicize periodical names, dropping introductory articles (*Aegis,* not *The Aegis*). Capitalize as for book citations. If you're citing a newspaper your readers may not be familiar with, include in the title—enclosed in brackets but not italicized—the city in which it was published. For example:

```
MacDonald, Mary. "Local Hiker Freezes to Death."
    Foster's Daily Democrat [Dover, NH] 28 Jan.
    1992: 1. Print.
```

Volume Number. Most academic journals are numbered as volumes (or, occasionally, feature series numbers); the volume number should be included in the citation. Popular periodicals sometimes have volume numbers, too, but these are not included in the citations. Indicate the volume number immediately after the journal's name. Omit the tag *vol.* before the number.

Issue Number. Most scholarly journals have issue numbers as well as volume numbers. Include the issue number in your citation if one is given. Follow the volume number with a period and then the issue number, with no spaces. Volume 12, issue 1, would appear in your citation as "12.1."

Date(s). When citing popular periodicals (newspapers, magazines, and so on), include the day, month, and year of the issue you're citing—in that order—following the periodical name. Academic journals are a little different. Because the issue number indicates when the journal was published within a given year, just indicate that year. Put it in parentheses following the volume number and before the page numbers. For example,

```
Elstein, David. "Training Dogs to Smell Off-
    Flavor in Catfish." Agricultural Research
    52.4 (2004): 10.
```

Electronic-source citations usually include two dates: the date of publication and the date of access (when you visited the site and retrieved the document). There is a good reason for listing both dates: Online documents are changed and updated frequently—when you retrieved the material matters.

Page Numbers. The page numbers of the article follow the volume and issue or date. Just list the pages of the entire article, omitting abbreviations such as *p.* or *pp.* It's common for articles in newspapers and popular magazines *not* to run on consecutive pages. In that case, indicate the page on which the article begins, followed by a "+": (12+).

Newspaper pagination can be peculiar. Some papers wed the section (usually a letter) with the page number (A4); other papers simply begin numbering anew in each section. Most, however, paginate continuously. See the following sample citations for newspapers for how to deal with these peculiarities.

Online sources, which often have no pagination at all, present special problems. If the article you're using from an online source also appeared in print, then you'll often find the same page numbers that are in the print version. But if an article appeared only online and has no page numbers, all you can do is signal that's the case, using the abbreviation *n. pag.* (no pages).

Databases. The availability of full-text versions of many articles through the campus library's databases makes it possible for researchers to retrieve materials without hiking to the library. In recent years these databases have evolved to be highly user friendly, not only enabling researchers to easily search multiple databases at once but also offering them nifty features like citation formatting. Earlier in *The Curious Researcher* we explored the wide range of general and subject databases available to you. Citations for an article you've found on such a database should contain the same information as one for the print version, with the addition of the name of the database (in italics). Here's an example:

> Winbush, Raymond A. "Back to the Future: Campus Racism in the 21st Century." *Black Collegian* Oct. 2001: 102-03. *Expanded Academic ASAP.* Web. 12 Apr. 2002.

In-Text Citation: (Winbush 102)

When citing an abstract from a library database, include the word "abstract" in the citation. For example,

> Erskine, Ruth. "Exposing Racism, Exploring Race." *Journal of Family Therapy* 24

(2002): 282-97. Abstract. *EBSCO Online*

Citations. Web. 3 Dec. 2002.

In-Text Citation: (Erskine)

Medium. As with books, indicate the medium of the source (Print, Web).

Sample Periodical Citations

3.3.1 A JOURNAL OR MAGAZINE ARTICLE

Cite articles from print magazines like this (notice that for a monthly magazine only the month and year are given):

Oppenheimer, Todd. "The Computer Delusion."

Atlantic Monthly July 1997: 47-60. Print.

In-Text Citation: (Oppenheimer 48)

Zimmer, Marc. "How to Find Students' Inner

Geek." *Chronicle of Higher Education* 12

Aug. 2005: B5. Print.

In-Text Citation: (Zimmer B5)

Cite print journal articles like this:

Allen, Rebecca E., and J. M. Oliver. "The

Effects of Child Maltreatment on Language

Development." *Child Abuse and Neglect* 6.2

(1982): 299-305. Print.

In-Text Citation: (Allen and Oliver 299-300)

Online articles usually come from either a library database or a periodical's Web site. The key thing you need to know is whether the article is online only or also appeared in print, as in the latter case you need to include information on the print version as well.

Cite an article that appeared online only like this:

Beyea, Suzanne C. "Best Practices of Safe Medi-
    cine Administration." *AORN Journal* Apr.
    2005. Web. 26 Aug. 2005.

In-Text Citation: (Beyea)

For this document without page or paragraph numbers, simply
give the author's name. Or avoid parenthetical citation altogether
by mentioning the name of the source in your essay (for example:
"According to Suzanne Beyea, medications are . . .").

Cite an online article that also appeared in print like this (this
example is from a library database):

Liu, Eric Zhi Feng, and Chun Hung Liu. "Devel-
    oping Evaluative Indicators for Educa-
    tional Computer Games." *British Journal*
    of Educational Technology 40.1 (2009):
    174-78. *Academic Search Complete.* Web.
    5 Feb. 2009.

In-Text Citation: (Liu and Liu 174)

3.3.2 A NEWSPAPER ARTICLE

Some newspapers have several editions (late edition, national
edition), each of which may contain different articles. If an edition is
listed on the masthead, include it in the citation.

Mendels, Pamela. "Internet Access Spreads to
    More Classrooms." *New York Times* 1 Dec.
    1999, late ed.: C1+. Print.

In-Text Citation: (Mendels C1)

Some papers begin numbering pages anew in each section. In
that case, include the section number if it's not part of pagination.

```
Brooks, James. "Lobsters on the Brink." Portland
     Press 29 Nov. 1999, sec. 2: 4. Print.
```

In-Text Citation: (Brooks 4)

Increasingly, full-text newspaper articles are available online using library databases such as Newspaper Source or through the newspapers themselves. As when citing other online articles, you'll need to include the database in italics if you used a database (e.g., *Newspaper Source*) and the date of access.

Cite a newspaper article from a database like this:

```
"Lobsterman Hunts for Perfect Bait." AP Online 7
     July 2002. Newspaper Source. Web. 13 July
     2008.
```

In-Text Citation: ("Lobsterman")

An entry for an article from a newspaper's Web site would include both the title of the online site (in italics) and the name of the publication, even if they're the same, as in this example:

```
Wiedeman, Reeves. "A Playwright Whose Time Seems
     to Be Now." New York Times. New York Times.
     9 Feb. 2011. Web. 10 Feb. 2011.
```

In-Text Citation: (Reeves)

3.3.3 AN ARTICLE WITH NO AUTHOR

```
"The Understanding." New Yorker 2 Dec. 1991:
     34-35. Print.
```

In-Text Citation: ("Understanding" 35)

3.3.4 AN EDITORIAL

```
"Paid Leave for Parents." Editorial. New York
     Times 1 Dec. 1999: 31. Print.
```

In-Text Citation: ("Paid Leave" 31)

To cite an editorial found online, include date of access. Unsigned editorials would begin with the title.

McGurn, William. "Obama, Religion, and the Pub-
    lic Square." Editorial. *WSJ.com.* Wall Street
    Journal. 8 June 2008. Web. 10 June 2008.

In-Text Citation: (McGurn)

3.3.5 A LETTER TO THE EDITOR

Ault, Gary Owen. "A Suspicious Stench." Letter.
    Idaho Statesman 18 Aug. 2005: 14. Print.

In-Text Citation: (Ault 14)

Wood, Bradford. "Living with a Disability, in a
    Caring Setting." Letter. *Washington Post.*
    27 Jan. 2011. Web. 28 Jan. 2011.

In-Text Citation: (Wood)

3.3.6 A REVIEW

Page, Barbara. Rev. of *Allegories of Cinema:
    American Film in the Sixties*, by David E.
    James. *College English* 54 (1992): 945-54.
    Print.

In-Text Citation: (Page 945-46)

O'Connell, Sean. "Beauty Is as Bardam Does."
    Rev. of *Biutiful. WashingtonPost.com.*
    Washington Post. 28 Jan. 2011. Web. 28
    January, 2011.

In-Text Citation: (O'Connell)

3.3.7 AN ABSTRACT

It's usually better to have the full text of an article for research purposes, but sometimes all you can come up with is an abstract, or short summary of the article that highlights its findings or summarizes its argument. Online databases frequently offer abstracts when they don't feature full-text versions of an article.

To cite an abstract, begin with information about the full version, and then include the information about the source from which you got the abstract. Unless the title of the source makes it obvious that what you are citing is an abstract (i.e., as with *Psychological Abstracts*), include the word "abstract" after the original publication information, but don't italicize it or put it in quotation marks. In this example, the source of the abstract is a periodical database:

> Edwards, Rob. "Air-raid Warning." *New Scientist*
>
>   14 Aug. 1999: 48-49. Abstract. *MasterFILE*
>
>   *Premier*. Web. 1 May 2009.

In-Text Citation: (Edwards)

The following citation is from the print version of *Dissertation Abstracts International,* a useful source of abstracts (notice that the word "abstract" isn't needed because this source just contains abstracts):

> McDonald, James C. "Imitation of Models in the
>
>   History of Rhetoric: Classical, Belletris-
>
>   tic, and Current-Traditional." U of Texas,
>
>   Austin. DAI 48 (1988): 2613A. Print.

In-Text Citation: (McDonald 2613A)

3.4 Citing Web Pages and Other Online Sources

3.4.1 A WEB SITE OR PAGE FROM A WEB SITE

If you're citing a Web site, you're referring to either the entire site or a particular page. A citation for an entire Web site includes the author's name, though it's rare for an entire site to have identifiable authors. Lacking an author or compiler, begin with the Web site's name (in italics), the sponsoring organization and date published, medium of publication, and date of access. For example,

> *Son of Citation Machine*. Landmark Project, 2009.
>
>   Web. 12 Feb. 2009.

> *In-Text Citation:* (*Son of Citation Machine*)

More commonly, though, you'll be citing a page on a Web site, and this must include, along with all the Web site information mentioned above, the title of the Web page itself (in quotation marks). Begin with the author of the Web page, if there is one, as in this example:

> Rogers, Scott. "The Stupid Vote." *The Conserva-*
>
>   *tive Voice*. Salem Web Network, 7 June 2008.
>
>   Web. 10 June 2008.

> *In-Text Citation:* (Rogers)

Here's a citation for a page with an institutional sponsor rather than an author:

> "ESL Instructors and Students." *The OWL at*
>
>   *Purdue*. Purdue Online Writing Lab, 2011.
>
>   Web. 8 Feb. 2011.

> *In-Text Citation:* ("ESL Instructors")

Finally, here is a citation for a Web page with no author or institutional sponsor (notice it begins with the title of the Web site):

> "Urban Wildlands." Center for Biological
>
>   Diversity, n.d. Web. 28 Jan. 2011.

> *In-Text Citation:* ("Urban Wildlands")

3.4.2 AN ONLINE POSTING

An online post can be a contribution to an e-mail discussion group like a listserv, a post to a bulletin board or usenet group, or an entry on a WWW forum. The description "Online posting" is included if there is no title. (The title is usually drawn from the message subject line). List the author's name, Web site name, the date the material was posted, the medium, and the access date, as you would for other online citations.

> Justin, Everett. "Team Teaching in Writing-
>
> Intensive Courses in a Science Context."
>
> *Writing Program Administration Listserv*
>
> Arizona State University, 29 Jan. 2011.
>
> Web. 8 Feb. 2011.

In-Text Citation: (Justin)

3.4.3 AN E-MAIL MESSAGE

> Kriebel, David. "Environmental Address." Message
>
> to the author. 8 June 2008. E-mail.

In-Text Citation: (Kriebel)

3.4.4 A SOUND CLIP OR PODCAST
Cite an audio clip from a Web site like this:

> Gonzales, Richard. "Asian American Political
>
> Strength." *Morning Edition*. Natl. Public
>
> Radio, 27 May 2008. Web. 12 July 2008.

In-Text Citation: (Gonzales)

A citation for a podcast should explicitly say that is the medium. For example,

> Johnson, Roberta. "Climate Changes, People
>
> Don't." *This American Life*. Natl.
>
> Public Radio, 14 Jan. 2011. Podcast.
>
> 8 Feb. 2011.

In-Text Citation: (Johnson)

3.4.5 AN ONLINE VIDEO

"Daughter Turns Dad In." Online video clip. *CNN.*
    com. Cable News Network, 4 Apr. 2008. Web.
    10 Apr. 2008.

In-Text Citation: ("Daughter Turns")

Shimabukuro, Jake. "Ukelele Weeps by Jake Shima-
    bukuro." Online video clip. *YouTube.* You
    Tube, 4 Apr. 2008. Web. 6 Apr. 2008.

In-Text Citation: (Shimabukuro)

3.4.6 AN INTERVIEW

Boukreev, Anatoli. Interview. *Outside.* Mariah
    Media, 14 Nov. 2007. Web. 27 May 2008.

In-Text Citation: (Boukreev)

3.4.7 A BLOG ENTRY OR BLOG COMMENT

For a blog entry, include the author's name (or screen name), title of the entry, the phrase "Weblog entry," name of the blog, sponsoring organization (if any), date of update, the medium, and your date of access.

Dent, Shirley. "Written on the Body: Literary
    Tattoos." Weblog entry. *The Blog: Books.*
    Guardian News and Media, 9 June 2008. Web.
    10 June 2008.

In-Text Citation: (Dent)

If you want to cite a comment on a blog—and sometimes they're pretty interesting—then include the author's name (or screen name); a title, if there is one, or the first few words of the post if there isn't one; "Weblog comment"; and the date it was posted. Then include the information on the blog that is the subject of the comment.

MargotBlackSheep. "Tattoos Exist in Every Cul-
      ture." Weblog comment. 10 June 2008. Dent,
      Shirley. "Written on the Body: Literary
      Tattoos." *The Blog: Books.* Guardian News
      and Media, 9 June 2008. Web. 10 June 2008.

In-Text Citation: (MargotBlackSheep)

3.4.8 AN ONLINE IMAGE

Online images often don't give you much to go on. If there is a
name of the artist and a title of the image, include them. If not, at
least describe the image, and include the name of the sponsoring
organization or site and when you downloaded it.

"China Town Engulfed." Online image. 12 May 2008.
      BBC News. BBC, 8 June 2008. Web. 10 June
      2008.

3.5 Citing Other Sources

3.5.1 AN INTERVIEW

If you conducted the interview yourself, list your subject's name
first, indicate what kind of interview it was (telephone interview,
e-mail interview, or personal interview), and provide the date.

Hall, Lonny. Personal interview. 1 Mar. 2005.

In-Text Citation: (Hall)

Or avoid parenthetical reference altogether by mentioning the
subject's name in the text: According to Lonny Hall, . . .
   If you're citing an interview done by someone else (perhaps from
a book or article) and the title does not indicate that it was an interview, you should include it after the subject's name. Always begin the
citation with the subject's name.

Stegner, Wallace. Interview. *Conversations with*
      Wallace Stegner. By Richard Eutlain and
      Wallace Stegner. Salt Lake: U of Utah P,
      1990. Print.

In-Text Citation: (Stegner 22)

3.5.2 SURVEYS, QUESTIONNAIRES, AND CASE STUDIES

If you conducted the survey or case study, list it under your name and give it an appropriate title.

```
Ball, Helen. "Internet Survey." Boise State U,

    1999. Print.
```

In-Text Citation: (Ball)

3.5.3 RECORDINGS

Generally, list a recording by the name of the performer and italicize the title. Also include the recording company, and year. (If you don't know the year, use the abbreviation *n.d.*. Include the medium (CD, Audiocassette, LP, etc.).

```
Orff, Carl. Carmina Burana. Cond. Seiji Ozawa.

    Boston Symphony. RCA, n.d. CD.
```

In-Text Citation: (Orff)

When citing a single song from a recording, put it in quotation marks:

```
Larkin, Tom. "Emergence." Oceans. Enso,

    1997. CD.
```

In-Text Citation: (Larkin)

3.5.4 TELEVISION AND RADIO PROGRAMS

List the title of the program (italicized), the station, and the date. If the episode has a title, list that first in quotation marks. You may also want to include the name of the narrator or producer after the title.

```
All Things Considered. Interview with Andre

    Dubus. Natl. Public Radio. WBUR, Boston,

    12 Dec. 1990. Radio.
```

In-Text Citation: (All Things Considered)

```
"U.S. to Limit Sales Related to Amphetamine

    Scourge." All Things Considered. Natl.
```

Public Radio. WBUR, Boston, 18 Aug. 2005.

Radio.

In-Text Citation: ("U.S. to Limit")

3.5.5 FILMS, VIDEOS, AND DVDS

Begin with the title (italicized), followed by the director, the distributor, and the year. You may also include names of writers, performers, or producers. End with the date and any other specifics about the characteristics of the film or video that may be relevant (length and size).

Saving Private Ryan. Dir. Steven Spielberg.

Perf. Tom Hanks, Tom Sizemore, and Matt

Damon. Paramount, 1998. Videocassette.

In-Text Citation: (*Saving*)

You can also list a video or film by the name of a contributor you'd like to emphasize.

Capra, Frank, dir. *It's a Wonderful Life*. Perf.

Jimmy Stewart and Donna Reed. RKO Pictures,

1946. Film.

In-Text Citation: (Capra)

3.5.6 ARTWORK

List each work by artist. Then cite the title of the work (italicized), the year of its creation, and where it's located (institution and city). If you've reproduced the work from a published source, include that information as well.

Homer, Winslow. *Casting for a Rise*. 1889. Hirschl

and Adler Galleries, New York. *Ultimate*

Fishing Book. Ed. Lee Eisenberg and DeCourcy

Taylor. Boston: Houghton, 1981. Print.

In-Text Citation: (Homer 113)

3.5.7 AN ADVERTISEMENT

To cite an advertisement in a periodical, first list the company behind the ad, then the word "Advertisement," and then the publication information.

```
Volkswagen. Advertisement. Men's Health August
     2005: 115. Print.
```

In-Text Citation: (Volkswagen)

3.5.8 LECTURES AND SPEECHES

List the name of the speaker, followed by the title of the address (if any) in quotation marks, the name of the sponsoring organization, the location, and the date. Also indicate what kind of address it was (lecture, speech, etc.).

```
Naynaha, Siskanna. "Emily Dickinson's Last
     Poems." Sigma Tau Delta, Boise, 15 Nov.
     2011. Lecture.
```

In-Text Citation: Avoid the need for parenthetical
     citation by mentioning the speaker's name
     in your text.

     In her presentation, Naynaha argued that
Dickinson...

3.5.9 PAMPHLETS

Cite a pamphlet as you would a book.

```
New Challenges for Wilderness Conservationists.
     Washington: Wilderness Society, 1973.
     Print.
```

In-Text Citation: (New Challenges)

Note: If no page numbers are listed, use *n. pag.*

Part Four:
Student Paper in MLA Style

Ashley Carvalho's essay, "Patching Up Belfast," is a compelling research essay on the innovations in trauma care that emerged from decades of death during the conflict between Catholics and Protestants in Northern Ireland. During a semester abroad in Ireland, Ashley experienced the legacy of the conflict firsthand—through the colorful murals on public buildings, the lingering tension on the faces of Belfast residents, and, most of all, the words of several of the doctors who cared for victims. She combines first-hand observations, interviews, and other research to tell an amazing story of the courage and inventiveness of Belfast's health care providers, particularly those at Royal Victoria Hospital, which was at the epicenter of the violence. "Patching Up Belfast" is an inspiring example of how a writer can take a personal experience and use research to make it richer and more meaningful for both reader and writer.

Ashley Carvalho

Prof. Jill Heney

English 201

10 November 2010

Patching Up Belfast

It was May of 1972, and from his van-
tage point in a pub on the Malone Road,
Colin Russell saw the thick, inky pall of
smoke erupt and curdle blackly over Belfast city center. Mere seconds had gone
by when, right on cue, the pub's telephone trilled. Before the barman could
answer, before his ruddy face could pale
slightly, and even before his eyes could
flash uneasily to Colin and his mouth
could speak the words "Dr. Russell, it's
for you," Colin knew by the sinking feeling in his gut that it was the hospital,
calling him in despite the fact he was
off duty. It wasn't the first time this
scenario had happened, and, disturbingly,
it wouldn't be the last. "Tell them I'm
on my way"—and Colin was out the door,
leaving behind an untouched pint and a
pubful of people expecting the worst.

Take a walk down any major West
Belfast thoroughfare, particularly
near the Catholic Falls and Protestant
Shankill roads, and you'll see Northern Ireland's history splashed vividly

Ashley uses a "scene lead" (see page 163) to dramatize the purpose of her essay—an examination of the medical innovations that came from the tragedy of northern Ireland's "Troubles."

Carvalho 2

onto walls, sides of houses and buildings, like so many pages torn from a giant coloring book. The infamous political
murals of West Belfast illustrate a range
of visceral emotions: vengeance, hatred,
sorrow, desperation, and, above all, fe-
rocious pride. Even before the Troubles,
mural-painting had been a conduit of
self-expression for Belfast natives, but
the way these sentiments are expressed
has changed over the years. At the height
of the conflict, the sentiments behind
the murals that sprang up almost overnight were those of aggression and anger.
Nowadays, new murals continue to appear
almost weekly, but most focus on moving
toward a brighter, more peaceful future,
not only for Belfast, but also for the
world (see fig. 1).

Just as art can be inspired by tragedy, the violence and wartime atmosphere
of the Troubles have also resulted in the
creation of some of the most innovative
medical treatments the world has seen, and
it is this violence that provided a stimulus to Northern Ireland's hospitals to
make progress in medicine. Like the mural
painters, Northern Ireland's doctors and
surgeons expressed their frustration and

Carvalho 3

Fig. 1 Graffiti, Peace Wall, Belfast.

despair through their work. From something bad, they created good.

   Although the deep-seated divide
between Catholics and Protestants frequently put Northern Ireland in national
news headlines from 1968 onward, the
roots of sectarianism—the opposition
between Nationalist Catholics and Unionist Protestants in Northern Ireland—date
back to the seventeenth century, to the
time of Oliver Cromwell. In 1649, Cromwell led English forces in an invasion of
Ireland to suppress Catholic power, and,

*Images can
enhance a
paper if they
add something
to the discus-
sion. See page
213 for things
to consider
about using
pictures.*

Carvalho 4

within three years, Cromwell's forces
defeated the major Irish cities and their
armies (Bardon 140-1). This paved the way
for English and Scottish Protestants to
begin settling in the North of Ireland,
alongside the Irish Catholics who already
inhabited the area. With the close proximity of Catholics and Protestants concentrated in the North, the stage was set
for the sectarianism that fueled the fire
of the Troubles, and still lingers in
today's Belfast.

Throughout the Troubles, Catholics
and Protestants were seemingly at logger-
heads, pitted against one another, which
leads to the common misconception that
the Troubles was primarily a religious
conflict. But the religious identity of
these groups is a secondary association;
the conflict is predominantly political.
Republican and Nationalist parties
envision a united Ireland that includes
Northern Ireland and is independent
of British influence, whereas Loyalists
and Unionists desire Northern Ireland
to remain a part of the powerful
United Kingdom and separate from the
Republic of Ireland (McKittrick and
McVea 26-28).

Here Ashley addresses an assumption that she believes most readers share about her topic. It's not that simple, she suggests, and then explains why.

Carvalho 5

In 1968, the violence of the Troubles began with several small sparks born from a housing allocation dispute that soon became a full-fledged conflagration, and Northern Ireland's history was to be forever transformed (McKittrick and McVea 40-4). Over the next three decades, violence raged in streets and city centers throughout Northern Ireland, resulting in casualties of a type and scale previously unseen in Northern Ireland's hospitals. In a setting where only one murder had been recorded in the preceding decade, Northern Ireland's hospitals were suddenly inundated with Troubles victims as the civil conflict became a part of daily life (D'Sa 51). Over the thirty-year period of the Troubles, nearly 3,600 people were killed, and over ten times that number injured as a result of the violence (McKittrick and McVea 324-8). From a medical perspective, numbers of this magnitude are difficult to cope with in any capacity, and Northern Ireland's hospitals had to quickly mobilize the resources, personnel, and expertise to face the violence of the Troubles head-on.

Dr. Colin Russell is not a superhero, and he doesn't claim to be. As a surgeon who worked in Belfast's Royal Victoria

Carvalho 6

Fig. 2 Royal Victoria Hospital, Belfast.

Hospital (see fig. 2) during the peak of the Troubles, Russell witnessed almost daily the tragedy of lives left wrecked by human hands, but rarely does he lose his composure speaking about his memories. In fact, I can't help but smile along with him as he remembers not the horror but the exhilaration, the sheer thrill of playing a healing role in the Troubles. In the sitting room of his spacious, secluded South Belfast home, Russell and his wife, Pat, sit opposite me. "I would be dishonest if I denied that there was an excitement about working during the Troubles." Russell says, opting for a conversational interview rather than a rigid question-and-answer session.

If you use figures or tables in your paper, make sure you refer to them in the text.

Carvalho 7

"At night, there was an almost wartime atmosphere prevailing in the hospital. We were only people, confined together, under pressure, and emotions ran high. But us doctors, we were not immune to getting upset" (Russell).

In his mid-seventies now, Russell's face still retains a youthful quality, a perpetual, boyish eagerness for education and understanding. For Russell, the time of the Troubles was a hands-on learning experience. He began his postgraduate schooling not as a surgeon, but as a dentist. After completing a five-year dentistry course at Queen's University Belfast, Russell realized as the course progressed that the aspect of dentistry that interested him most was surgery. Upon gaining a post as a dental surgeon in the Royal Victoria Hospital, Russell became increasingly frustrated; with his dental degree, he simply didn't have enough education and expertise to work in the hospital's surgical wards. So, in 1967, he went back to Queen's University, this time as a medical student. Graduating in 1971, just as the brewing political turmoil began to froth and boil over, Russell was appointed to the surgical house staff of the Royal Victoria, and the

bulk of his surgical training and career
was spent at the Royal Victoria during the
height of the Troubles—specifically, the
1970s and early 1980s.

The outbreak of the Troubles was a
critical moment, a point of no return, not
only for Russell but also for countless
other medical trainees working in Belfast's hospitals at the turn of the decade. Speak to any of these individuals,
and the odds are that they can pinpoint
the exact moment when, for them, everything changed. Siobhan,* a doctor at both
the Royal Victoria and Belfast City hospitals, attributes her life-changing moment to the introduction of internment. On
August 9, 1971, Northern Ireland's prime
minister demanded the large-scale arrest
and imprisonment, without trial, of suspected IRA members in the hopes that civil
violence would lessen with the IRA locked
away. Siobhan, only a junior doctor at the
time, recalls what August 9, 1971, symbolized for her:

> I remember looking out from the second
> floor of the West wing of the Roy-
> al Victoria, where my bedroom was at

*Name has been changed at the request of the interviewee.

Carvalho 9

that time, and seeing scores of troop
carriers arrive silently, in the dead
of night. One minute, Dunville Park
across the road was as it ever was.
The next moment, it was surrounded
by a host of camouflaged vehicles,
silently moving in and taking their
places in a massed migration influx.
My life, our lives, would never be
the same again. Like seeing Kennedy
shot, like seeing a man land on the
moon, like seeing the Twin Towers
falling, it was a salient moment in
history, one which I will never forget.

Quotations that are four or more sentences are "blocked" by indenting one inch from the left margin. And, by the way, what a great quotation!

As the largest and best-equipped
hospital in all of Northern Ireland, the
Royal Victoria experienced a recurring influx of patients injured in riots, and
the hospital's proximity to the Falls Road
meant that it was often the center
of the riot zones. In the nearly thirty
years of violence, the Royal Victoria accommodated victims of rioting
episodes almost nightly (Clarke 114-8).
These were peppered in between frequent
terrorist bombings, and the combination
of the two types of incidents produced a
steady stream of casualties. Secondly, and

Carvalho 10

equally problematic, was the need for the hospital and its employees to remain neutral throughout the conflict. This proved difficult for some, particularly during the many high-stress, emotionally charged incidents the violence of the Troubles produced. Many of the injured that arrived in the hospital's Accident and Emergency Department following a bombing or shooting were friends or relatives of the medical personnel. Still others who sought medical care from the hospital were paramilitaries or members of a wrongdoing sectarian gang. Within the highly politicized milieu of the Troubles, where one's religious and political views could be figured out just by learning one's name (during the Troubles and even today, a Gerald O' Callahan or an Aisling Murphy would be categorized as a Republican Irish Catholic while a Richard Carrington or an Elizabeth Montgomery would be assumed a Unionist Protestant), shrugging off the shroud of politics and throwing on the neutrality cloak wasn't exactly easy. But healthcare providers in Northern Ireland sidestepped this difficulty and continued to provide high-quality, nonbiased healthcare to the injured.

Carvalho 11

In the hospital ward, medical personnel looked after civilians, terrorists, freedom fighters, innocent bystanders, policemen, and soldiers alike, curious but never aware of who was who, or who fired the deadly bullet or detonated the lethal bomb, or who was Catholic or Protestant. In tense situations, Siobhan focused on her work: "I learned very early on to be apolitical and to never, ever comment on any political incident one way or another, to my colleagues or to my patients. My role was to care always and to cure if possible."

The most catastrophic weapon appeared on the stage of the Troubles at the end of 1971. Worried that the British army would not be able to contain the IRA, and wanting to exercise their newfound strength, the loyalist Ulster Volunteer Force (UVF) in conjunction with the Ulster Defense Association (UDA) placed a fifty-pound bomb in a small North Belfast Catholic pub called McGurk's Bar. The explosion killed fifteen people and injured many more (McKittrick and McVea 75). This incident marked the debut of the bomb as a means for paramilitary organizations to influence Belfast's street politics.

Carvalho 12

Bombings provided a sizeable stimulus to Belfast's healthcare services in two ways: first, to develop a system that could provide comprehensive care to the sheer numbers of those injured in a bombing incident and, second, to create new methods of treatment to address the variety of injuries produced in a bomb blast. For example, the McGurk's Bar bombing resulted in a wide range of injury patterns, the worst of which included crush injuries, burn injuries, cranial injuries, lacerations from projectiles, and carbon monoxide poisoning (Gillespie 37-40).

A sentence like this firmly reattaches the essay to its thesis much like a tack pins down loose fabric so that it keeps its shape.

Regarded as the most violent year of the Troubles, 1972 brought with it an unparalleled level of violence, and the state of civil conflict in Northern Ireland closely resembled civil war. The events of this year placed a higher strain on Belfast's hospital services than any other year of the Troubles, not necessarily because the incidents of violence were the most catastrophic, but because they occurred with an unpredictable and terrifying frequency. One month into the year, the infamous Bloody Sunday in Londonderry left thirteen dead and another thirteen injured when British troops openly fired upon a

Carvalho 13

large illegal march. Enraged, Republican supporters bolstered the IRA with money, guns, and men, and violence was loosed upon the streets throughout Northern Ireland (Coogan 674-5). Riots, shootings, and bombings began to occur with alarming regularity. On March 4th, the IRA slipped a six-pound bomb inside one of the shopping bags carried by two sisters. Having decided to stop for tea, the girls, unknowingly carrying the bomb, entered the Abercorn, a popular restaurant in Belfast city center. The girls were killed immediately and at least one hundred others were injured (Gillespie 47-9). For the first time in its history, the Royal Victoria used a documented disaster plan to care for the masses of the injured (McKittrick and McVea 78).

Bomb injuries presented an entirely new set of challenges to Belfast's hospitals. Colin Russell, who worked in the Royal Victoria that day, recalled that mass-casualty on this large a scale was an entirely new experience, one that the hospital and its staff weren't totally ready for. "There were horrific injuries," Russell remembers. Making matters worse, this particular bomb was designed to explode outward, rather than upward as

Carvalho 14

most bombs do, and the shockwaves from
the blast careened along the Abercorn's
wooden floors. Trying to contain my horror, I winced inwardly as Russell showed
me some slides containing photographs of
the horrific injuries that came into the
Royal that day: a chair leg shot through
someone's thigh, pieces of an amputated
limbs placed on green towels in the surgical wards, unable to be reunited with
the bodies of their owners, faces charred
beyond recognition. But none of this prepared me for the emotional shock that came
next from Russell's memories: "I remember
the senior anesthetist who was on call at
the time, working on one of the victims
of the bombing in the operating room. He
was completely unaware of the fact that
the two sisters who were carrying the bomb
and who were killed in the blast were his
daughters" (Russell).

The medical progress made in Northern
Ireland's hospitals during the Troubles
speaks to the remarkable ability of the
medical personnel to rise to the challenges posed by the civil violence.
Developments in disaster planning, triage,
and organization in Northern Ireland's
hospitals went hand-in-hand with the

Carvalho 15

creation of specific medical treatments
to address the needs of civil violence
victims. Throughout the Troubles, paramilitary violence generated casualties that
varied greatly in the type and pattern of
injury as well as in the numbers of injured, calling attention to the need for
a comprehensive, all-encompassing system
of treatment. In Northern Ireland's hospitals, the seamless joining of the methods
of disaster planning and the methods of
medical treatment enabled these hospitals
to meet the demands of mass casualty terrorist incidents head-on throughout the
decades of civil violence.

The innovation of Belfast's medics is clearly seen in the treatment of
punishment injuries. These injuries were
different from other types of injury seen
during the Troubles because they were
completely nonsectarian; in a bizarre
twist of vigilante justice, Protestants
would shoot Protestants, and Catholics
would shoot Catholics, usually for some
sort of wrongdoing on the victim's part.
A certain subset of punishment injury
termed "kneecapping," whereby the victim
was shot from close range in the back of
the legs, is unique to Northern Ireland

This paragraph is a typical example of how well Ashley reports information from her research but finds her own way of saying things (e.g. "in a bizarre twist of vigilante justice") and characterizing them.

Carvalho 16

alone and, as such, necessitated a unique form of surgical treatment (Nolan 405-6). If an individual were suspected of a serious crime, such as rape or murder, he would be punished with gunshots through the elbows and ankles in addition to the knees—the proverbial "six pack"—although this type of punishment was much less common.

Throughout the thirty-year period of violence, some 2,500 people in Northern Ireland sustained a kneecapping injury (Williams 79). The high prevalence of this type of injury and the severe destruction of knee vasculature that it caused presented a whole host of challenges to trauma surgeons during the Troubles, and it wasn't long before they developed effective methods of treatment. Belfast's trauma surgeons learned to reconnect the damaged blood vessels in the knee using an ingenious system of shunts and vein grafts, and toward the end of the Troubles most kneecapping injuries were repaired successfully and quickly, the victim up and walking within a matter of months (D'Sa 38-9).

But however clever Belfast's trauma surgeons proved to be, the paramilitary organizations tried to be more clever. In response to the surgical developments made by trauma surgeons during the Troubles, the IRA changed its methods of kneecapping in order to cause further damage and to hinder surgeons in repairing the knee vasculature, which in turn prompted surgeons to again reinvent treatment methods in reaction.

The method created in Belfast to restructure severely fractured skulls might be the most resourceful of all medical developments during the Troubles. This method was created in the mid 1970s and was the brainchild of a dental surgeon, George Blair, and a neurosurgeon, Derrick Gordon, in the Royal Victoria. Skull fractures like the ones seen during the Troubles posed a real challenge to neurosurgeons, not least because of the bony defects that resulted in the skull, but also the fact that pieces of the skull were often lost, leaving the underlying brain layers completely exposed. Gordon and Blair devised a method of treatment in which a material used to make impressions of the teeth called alginate was poured into a light metal cap, which was placed on the patient's head to make an impression of the fractured skull. Then, titanium metal was poured into the impression to make a plate, which was fitted into the patient's skull. Titanium, as a fairly light yet inert metal, was perfect for the job. Later research showed that the success rate for this procedure was at least 90 percent (Roy 544). Today, this treatment method is used in hospitals worldwide.

Even today, the tension isn't completely gone from Belfast's streets. It will still take another couple of generations for the emotional sting of the Troubles to lose its poignancy and for the painfully sharp memories of the violence to soften around the edges. But even now, the hope of Belfast's overwhelming majority is one of peace, of moving away from a violent, harrowing past and toward a brighter future. In terms of the developments and progress in medicine achieved by Northern Ireland's healthcare workers, Northern Ireland's medics left a legacy of tenacity, determination, and strength of spirit. Just as the mural-painters fought the Troubles by expressing themselves through art, the medics fought the Troubles in their

Carvalho 19

Fig. 3 Rainbow in a Troubled Sky, Belfast.

own way: by patching up Belfast and healing the city. In finding a silver lin-
ing within the black stormclouds of the
Troubles, placing a rainbow (see fig. 3)
in Belfast's perpetually grey skies, and
creating good from bad, these medics are
truly remarkable.

Carvalho 20

Works Cited

Bardon, Jonathan. *A History of Ulster*. Belfast:

    The Blackstaff Press, 1992. Print.

Clarke, Richard. *The Royal Victoria Hospital*

    Belfast: A History 1797-1997. Belfast:

    Blackstaff, 1997. Print.

Coogan, Tim Pat. *The Troubles: Ireland's Ordeal*

    and the Search for Peace. New York:

    Palgrave, 1996. Print.

D'Sa, Airres Barros. "Symposium Paper: Manage-

    ment of Vascular Injuries of Civil Strife."

    British Journal of Accident Surgery 14.1

    (1982): 51-57. Print.

---. "A Decade of Missile-Induced Vascular

    Trauma." *Annals of the Royal College of*

    Surgeons of England 64 (1982): 37-44.

    Print.

Gillespie, Gordon. *Years of Darkness: The Trou-*

    bles Remembered. Dublin: Gill & Macmillan,

    2008. Print.

McKittrick, David, and McVea, David. *Making Sense*

    of the Troubles. London: Penguin, 2001.

    Print.

Nolan P. C., and G. McCoy. "The Changing Pat-

    tern of Paramilitary Punishments in North-

    ern Ireland." *Injury* 27.6 (1996): 405-06.

    Print.

The Works Cited list begins a new page at the end of your paper.

Carvalho 21

Roy, Douglas. "Gunshot and Bomb Blast Injuries: A
     Review of the Experience in Belfast." *Jour-
     nal of the Royal Society of Medicine* 75.7
     (1982): 542-45. Print.

Russell, Colin. Personal interview. Oct. 2010.

Siobhan. Personal interview. Sept. 2010.

Williams, John. "Casualties of Violence in North-
     ern Ireland." *International Journal of
     Trauma Nursing* 3.3 (1997): 78-82. Print.

APPENDIX B

Guide to APA Style

The American Psychological Association (APA) style is, like MLA style, commonly used for documenting and formatting college papers. APA style is the standard for papers in the social and behavioral sciences as well as in education and business. In those disciplines, the currency of the material cited is often especially important. Therefore, APA style's author/date citation system emphasizes the date of publication, in contrast to MLA's author/page system.

Checklist Before Handing in a Paper in APA Style

- My paper is double spaced throughout, including the References list (see pages 296, 298, and 301).
- I have a running head (see pages 296–297) on each page, including a page number in the upper right-hand corner.
- I've cited page numbers in my paper whenever I've quoted a source.
- I've "blocked" every quotation that is longer than 40 words (see page 300).
- Whenever possible, I've mentioned the names of authors I cite in my paper and put the date of the appropriate publication next to their names.
- I've doubled-checked the accuracy of DOIs and URLs of electronic sources that I included in my References.
- The References begin on a new page and are organized alphabetically by the authors' last names.
- In article and book titles cited, only the first words of titles and subtitles are capitalized; the remaining words are not capitalized unless they would ordinarily be capitalized.

I think you'll find APA style easy to use, especially if you've had some practice with MLA. Converting from one style to the other is easy (for some key differences between the two, see Table 1). Appendix B covers what you need to know about APA style, including how and when to cite sources in your essay (Part One) and how to assemble the References page (Part Three). The discussion of conventions for formatting your paper (Part Two) offers guidance on pagination, layout, and various specifics of style. Finally, you can see what APA style looks like in a paper like the one you're writing (Part Four).

TABLE 1   Key Differences Between MLA and APA Formats

MLA	APA
Capitalizes most words in book and article titles on Works Cited page.	Capitalizes only the first word and proper nouns in book and article titles on References page.
Uses author's full first and last name on Works Cited page.	Uses author's last name along with first and middle initials on References page.
Uses the word "and" to combine authors' names in in-text citations and on Works Cited page if there is more than one author for a source.	Uses an ampersand (&) to combine authors' names in in-text citations and on References page if a source has more than one author.
In-text citations use author's last name and pages cited.	In-text citations use author's last name and date; page numbers aren't required except for quotations.
In-text citations use no punctuation between author's name and page number.	In-text citations use a comma between author's last name and date.
Page numbers are listed simply as a number in in-text citations.	Page numbers are denoted with a "p." or "pp." in in-text citations.
There is no separate title page.	There is a title page with running head.
Running head contains author's last name and the page number.	Running head contains the first words of the paper's title and the page number.
No subheadings occur within the paper.	Subheadings often occur within the paper. Paper often begins with an abstract.
Tables and figures are integrated into the body of the paper.	Tables and figures can be integrated or in an appendix.

The *Publication Manual of the American Psychological Associa-tion** is the authoritative reference on APA style, and the sixth edition, published in 2010, features some updates, including some new guidelines for referencing electronic sources. The APA Web site now includes some free tutorials on the citation style, narrated by a guy who seems really excited about it. Though the information in the section that follows should answer your questions, check the manual when in doubt.

Directory of APA Style

(continued)

**Publication Manual of the American Psychological Association.* 6th ed. Washington DC: APA, 2010. Print.

Part One:
Citing Sources in Your Essay

1.1 The APA Author/Date System

The Basics of Using Parenthetical Citation

The author/date system is pretty uncomplicated. If you mention the name of the author in text, simply place the year her work was published in parentheses immediately after her name. For example:

```
Herrick (2006) argued that college testing was
biased against minorities.
```

If you mention both the author's name and the date in the text of your essay, then you can omit the parenthetical citation altogether. For example:

```
In 2006, Herrick argued that college testing was
biased against minorities.
```

If you don't mention the author's name in the text, then include that information parenthetically. For example:

```
A New Hampshire political scientist (Bloom,
2008) recently studied the state's presidential
primary.
```

Note that the author's name and the year of her work are separated by a comma.

When to Cite Page Numbers.   If the information you're citing came from specific pages (or chapters or sections) of a source, that information may also be included in the parenthetical citation, as in the example below. Including page numbers is essential when quoting a source.

```
The first stage of language acquisition is
called caretaker speech (Moskowitz, 1985,
pp. 50–51), in which children model their
parents' language.
```

Or, if the author's name is mentioned in the text:

```
Moskowitz (1985) observed that the first stage
of language acquisition is called caretaker
speech (pp. 50-51), in which children model
their parents' language.
```

1.1.1 A WORK BY ONE AUTHOR

```
Herrick (2006) argued that college testing was
biased against minorities.
```
or
```
One problem with college testing may be bias
(Herrick, 2006).
```

1.1.2 A WORK BY TWO AUTHORS
When a work has two authors, always mention them both whenever you cite their work in your paper. For example:

```
Allen and Oliver (1998) observed many cases of
child abuse and concluded that maltreatment
inhibited language development.
```

Notice that if the authors' names are given in a parenthetical citation, an ampersand is used:

```
Researchers observed many cases of child abuse
and concluded that maltreatment inhibited lan-
guage development (Allen & Oliver, 1998).
```

1.1.3 A WORK BY THREE TO FIVE AUTHORS

If a source has three to five authors, mention them all the first time you refer to their work. However, in any subsequent references give the name of the first author followed by the abbreviation *et al.* For example, here's what a first mention of a multiple author source would look like:

```
The study found that medical students sometimes
responded to an inquiry-based approach by becom-
ing more superficial in their analyses (Balas-
oriya, Hughes, & Toohey, 2011).
```

Subsequent mentions use the convention *et al.*:

```
Though collaboration is supposed to promote
learning, in one case it actually hindered it
(Balasoriya et al., 2011).
```

1.1.4 A WORK BY SIX OR MORE AUTHORS

When citing works with six or more authors, *always* use the first author's name and *et al.*

1.1.5 AN INSTITUTIONAL AUTHOR

When citing a corporation or agency as a source, simply list the year of the study in parentheses if you mention the institution in the text:

```
The Environmental Protection Agency (2007)
issued an alarming report on global warming.
```

If you don't mention the institutional source in the text, spell it out in its entirety, along with the year. In subsequent parenthetical citations, abbreviate the name. For example:

```
A study (Environmental Protection Agency [EPA],
2007) predicted dire consequences from continued
global warming.
```

And later:

```
Continued ozone depletion may result in wide-
spread skin cancers (EPA, 2007).
```

1.1.6 A WORK WITH NO AUTHOR

When a work has no author, cite an abbreviated title and the year. Place article or chapter titles in quotation marks, and italicize book titles. For example:

```
The editorial ("Sinking," 2007) concluded that
the EPA was mired in bureaucratic muck.
```

1.1.7 TWO OR MORE WORKS BY THE SAME AUTHOR

Works by the same author are usually distinguished by the date; these would rarely be published in the same year. But if they are, distinguish among works by adding an *a* or *b* immediately following the year in the parenthetical citation. The References list will also have these suffixes. For example:

```
Douglas's studies (1986a) on the mating
habits of lobsters revealed that the females
are dominant. He also found that the female
lobsters have the uncanny ability to smell a
loser (1986b).
```

This citation alerts readers that the information came from two works by Douglas, both published in 1986.

1.1.8 AUTHORS WITH THE SAME LAST NAMES

In the rare case that you're using sources from different authors with the same last name, distinguish between them by including the first initials of each author whenever you mention them in your paper, even if the publication dates differ:

```
M. Bradford (2010) and L. S. Bradford (2008)
both noted that Americans are more narcissistic.
```

1.1.9 SEVERAL SOURCES IN A SINGLE CITATION

Occasionally, you'll want to cite several sources at once. Probably the most common instance is when you refer to the findings of several relevant studies, something that is a good idea as you try to establish a context for what has already been said about your research topic. When listing multiple sources within the same parenthetical citation, order them as they appear in the References and separate them with semicolons. For example:

```
A number of researchers have explored
the connection between Internet use and
depression (Sanders, Field, & Diego, 2000;
Waestlund, Norlander, & Archer, 2001).
```

1.1.10 INDIRECT SOURCES

If you discover, say, a great quotation or idea from someone who is mentioned in another author's book or article, try to track down the original source. But when you can't find it, signal parenthetically that you're using an indirect source, using the phrase *as cited in*.

```
De Groot's study on chess expertise (as cited in
Kirschner, Sweller, & Clark, 2006) is...
```

The only source you'll include in your References list is the source you used; it isn't necessary to include the indirect source.

1.1.11 NEW EDITIONS OF OLD WORKS

For reprints of older works, include both the year of the original publication and that of the reprint edition (or the translation).

Pragmatism as a philosophy sought connection between scientific study and real people's lives (James, 1906/1978).

1.1.12 INTERVIEWS, E-MAIL, AND LETTERS

Interviews and other personal communications are not listed in the references at the back of the paper, because they are not *recoverable data,* but they are parenthetically cited in the text. Provide the initials and last name of the subject (if not mentioned in the text), the nature of the communication, and the complete date, if possible.

Nancy Diamonti (personal communication, November 12, 1990) disagrees with the critics of *Sesame Street.*

   In a recent e-mail, Michelle Payne (personal communication, January 4, 2011) complained that....

1.1.13 A WEB SITE

When referring to an *entire* Web site, cite the address parenthetically in your essay. Do not include a citation for an entire Web site in your References list.

The Centers for Disease Control (http://www.cdc .gov) is a reliable source for the latest health information.

If you're quoting from a Web site, you should cite the date of online publication, if available, and the page number, if available. (When simply referring to a part of a Web site, just use the date, if available, not the page number.) However, most Web documents that aren't also available in print do not have page numbers. What do you do in that case? If you can, use a heading or short title from the source that helps readers to locate the part of the document where they can find the material you cited. Then add a paragraph number using the abbreviation *para.*

> According to Cesar Milan (2010), it's essential
> that dog owners establish themselves as "pack
> leaders" ("Why Does CDC Teach Wolf Pack Theory?"
> para. 2).

Part Two: Formatting Your Essay

2.1 Formatting the Essay and Its Parts

2.1.1 PAGE FORMAT AND HEADER

Papers should be double spaced, with at least 1-inch margins on all sides. Number all pages consecutively, beginning with the title page; using the header feature in your word processor, put the page number in the upper right-hand corner. In the upper left-hand corner of each page, beginning with the title page, give an abbreviated title of the paper in uppercase letters. As a rule, the first line of all paragraphs of text should be indented five spaces or a half inch.

2.1.2 TITLE PAGE

Unlike a paper in MLA style, an APA-style paper sometimes has a separate title page. The title page includes the title of the paper, the author, and the author's affiliation (e.g., what university she is from). As Figure B1 shows, this information is double spaced, and each line is centered. The upper left of the title page has the abbreviated title in uppercase letters, preceded by "Running head" and a colon, and the upper right has the page number.

2.1.3 ABSTRACT

Though it's not always required, many APA-style papers include a short abstract (between 150 to 250 words) following the title page. See Figure B2. An abstract is essentially a short summary of the paper's contents. This is a key feature, because it's usually the first

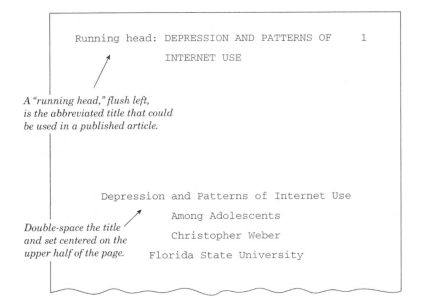

Running head: DEPRESSION AND PATTERNS OF   1
INTERNET USE

A "running head," flush left, is the abbreviated title that could be used in a published article.

Depression and Patterns of Internet Use
Among Adolescents
Christopher Weber
Florida State University

Double-space the title and set centered on the upper half of the page.

FIGURE B1   **Title Page in APA Style**

An abstract usually follows the title page. This is a concise (no longer than 250 words) summary of the article and its thesis, purpose, or findings.

DEPRESSION AND PATTERNS OF INTERNET USE   2

Abstract

Continue the page header.

With the growth of the Internet as both a source of information and entertainment, researchers have turned their attention to the psychology of Internet use, particularly focusing on the emotional states of high Internet users. This project focuses on the relationship between patterns of Internet use and depression in adolescent users, arguing that

FIGURE B2   **The Abstract Page**

thing a reader encounters. The abstract should include statements about what problem or question the paper examines and what approach it follows; the abstract should also cite the thesis and significant findings. Type the title "Abstract" at the top of the page. Type the abstract text in a single block, without indenting.

2.1.4 BODY OF THE PAPER

The body of the paper begins with the centered title, followed by a double space and then the text. Like all pages, the first page of the body will have an abbreviated title and a page number ("3" if the paper has a title page and abstract). See Figure B3.

If your paper is fairly formal, you might need to divide it into specific sections, each with its own heading—for example, "Introduction," "Method," "Results," and "Discussion." Check with your instructor about whether to follow this format. If you do not need to follow it, you can create your own headings to clarify the organization of your paper.

In the formal structure mentioned, which is typical in academic journals, the sections would include content such as the following:

- Introduction: Why does your research question matter? What has already been said about it? What is the hypothesis you'll be exploring?

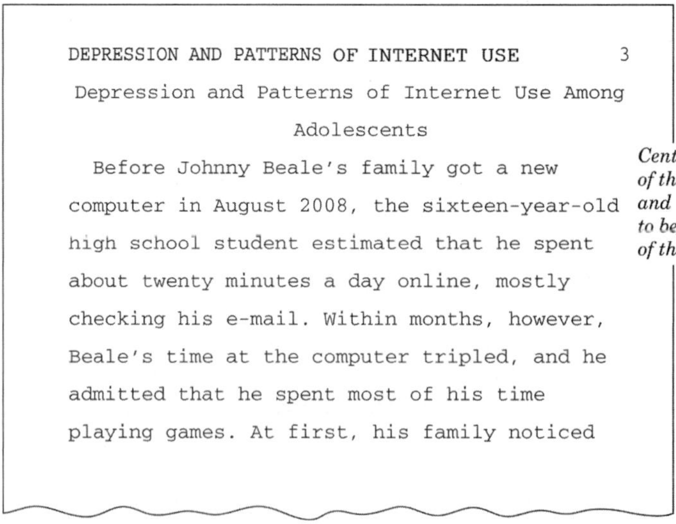

```
DEPRESSION AND PATTERNS OF INTERNET USE          3

Depression and Patterns of Internet Use Among

                  Adolescents

     Before Johnny Beale's family got a new

computer in August 2008, the sixteen-year-old

high school student estimated that he spent

about twenty minutes a day online, mostly

checking his e-mail. Within months, however,

Beale's time at the computer tripled, and he

admitted that he spent most of his time

playing games. At first, his family noticed
```

Center the title of the paper and double-space to begin the body of the text.

FIGURE B3   **The Body of the Paper in APA Style**

- Method: How did you test your hypothesis? What you say here depends on the kind of study you're doing.
- Results: What did you find?
- Discussion: How do you interpret the findings? To what extent do they support—or fail to support—your initial hypothesis? What are the implications of these discoveries?

2.1.5 HEADINGS

If you use headings, the APA specifies the following hierarchy:

Centered, Boldface, Uppercase and

Lowercase (Level 1)

Flush Left, Boldface, Uppercase and

Lowercase (Level 2)

Five levels of headings

    Indented, boldface, lowercase, ending with period, running into paragraph. (Level 3)

    Indented, boldface, italicized, lowercase, ending with period, running into paragraph. (Level 4)

    Indented, italicized, lowercase, ending with a period, running into paragraph. (Level 5)

A paper, particularly a short one, will rarely use all five levels of headings. In fact, it's much more common for a student paper to use just two or possibly three.

2.1.6 HANDLING QUOTED MATERIAL

When you borrow words, phrases, or passages from another author, typically the material must be contained in quotation marks. Usually, it is smoothly integrated with attribution (*According to Ballenger,…*) and parenthetical citation including page numbers, into your own sentences and paragraphs. For example,

According to Ellison, Steinfeld, and Lampe
(2007), Facebook and other social networ-
king sites offer researchers an "ideal"

```
chance to investigate "offline and online
connection" (p. 12).
```

But if the quoted material is longer than 40 words, it should be "blocked." Indent the entire quoted passage five spaces or a half inch from the left margin, and omit the quotation marks. For example,

```
According to Perfetti's (2003) book on women in
the Middle Ages and laughter,
```

```
    Laughter is both a defense mechanism and
    a weapon of attack, essential to groups
    struggling to be taken seriously by the
    rest of society. But it is perhaps women,
    more than any other group, who have had the
    most complicated relationship with humor
    in Western culture. People of every reli-
    gion, nationality, ethnicity, class, and
    occupation have at some time found them-
    selves the butt of an offensive joke and
    told to lighten up because "it's just a
    joke." But it is women who have been told
    that their refusal to laugh at jokes made
    at their expense shows that they don't have
    a sense of humor at all. So a woman has to
    assert her right not to laugh at offensive
    jokes but simultaneously prove that she is
    capable of laughter or risk being seen as
    a humorless spoilsport: a balancing act
    requiring a quick wit. (p. viii)
```

Notice that blocked quotations are double spaced and that the parenthetical reference is placed *after* the period rather than before it.

If you omit material from an original source—a common method of using just the relevant information in a sentence or passage—use *ellipsis points* (...). For example,

The study (Lampe, 2010) noted that "student athletes in U.S. universities are highly visible.... They are often considered to be representatives of the university, and may be the most visible spokespeople for, in some cases..." (p. 193).

2.1.7 REFERENCES LIST

All sources cited in the body of the paper are listed alphabetically by author (or title, if anonymous) in the list titled "References," as shown in Figure B4. This list should begin a new page, and it is double spaced throughout. The first line of each entry is flush left; subsequent lines are indented a half inch. Explanation of how to cite various types of sources in the References list follows (see "Part Three: Preparing the References List").

2.1.8 TABLES AND FIGURES

Should you include a table, chart, or photograph in your paper? Sure, if you're certain that it adds something to your discussion and if the information it presents is clear and understandable. If you use a table (and with programs like Excel and Word they are incredibly easy to generate), place it in the manuscript as close as

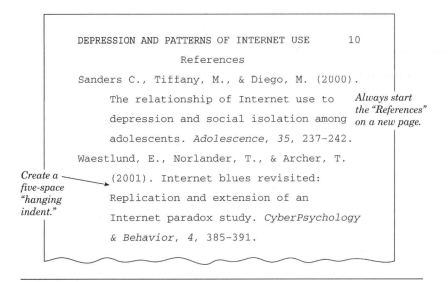

FIGURE B4   **The References Page**

you can to where you mention it. Alternatively, you can put your tables and figures in an appendix. Tables should all be double spaced. Type a table number at the top, flush left. Number tables "Table 1," "Table 2," and so on, corresponding to the order in which they are mentioned in the text. The title, in italics, should be placed on the line below the number. Tables that you put in an appendix should be labeled accordingly. For example, Table 1 in Appendix A would be numbered Table A1.

Figures (graphs, charts, photographs, and drawings) are handled similarly to tables. They are numbered consecutively beginning with "Figure 1." This figure number, below the figure itself, is followed by a title and, if needed, a caption (see Figure B5). Captions are often helpful to explain a chart, photograph, drawing, or other figure. As with tables, insert figures in your paper as close as you can to where you refer to them or, alternatively, put them in an appendix.

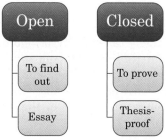

Figure 1. Two Broad Categories of Writing Assignments. Open-ended and more closed writing assignments each are characterized by a different motive and result in a different genre.

FIGURE B5   **Example of Format for a Figure**

2.1.9 APPENDIX

This is a seldom-used feature of an APA-style paper, though you might find it helpful for presenting specific material that isn't central to the discussion in the body of your paper: a detailed description of a device described in the paper, a copy of a blank survey, a table, or the like. Each item, placed at the end of the paper following the References page, should begin on a separate page and be labeled "Appendix" followed by "A," "B," and so on, consecutively.

2.1.10 NOTES

Several kinds of notes might be included in a paper. The most common is *content notes*, or brief commentaries by the writer keyed to superscript numbers in the body of the text. These notes are useful for discussion of key points that are relevant but might be distracting if explored in the text of your paper. Present all notes, numbered consecutively, on a page titled "Footnotes" (placed after the References page but before any appendixes) or at the bottom of the relevant page. Notes should be double spaced. Begin each note with the appropriate superscript number, indented like the first line of a paragraph; subsequent lines of a note are not indented.

2.2 Some Style Considerations

2.2.1 USE OF ITALICS

The APA guidelines for *italicizing* call for its use when:

- Giving the titles of books, periodicals, films, and publications that appear on microfilm.
- Using new or specialized terms, but only the first time you use them (e.g., "the authors' *paradox study* of Internet users...").
- Citing a phrase, letter, or word as an example (e.g., "the second *a* in *separate* can be remembered by remembering the word *rat*").

Use quotation marks around the titles of articles or book chapters mentioned in your essay.

2.2.2 TREATMENT OF NUMBERS

Numbers 9 and below that don't represent precise measurements should be spelled out, and numbers 10 and above should be expressed as numerals. Any numbers that begin a sentence or represent a commonly used fraction (e.g., "one-quarter of the sample") should be spelled out.

Part Three: Preparing the References List

All parenthetical citations in the body of the paper correspond to a complete listing of sources in the References list. The format for this section was described earlier in this appendix (see "References List" in Part Two).

3.1 Order of Sources and Information

Order of Sources

List the references alphabetically by author last name or by the first key word of the title if there is no author. This alphabetical principle has a few complications:

- You may have several sources by the same author. If these sources weren't published in the same year, list them in chronological order, the earliest first. If the sources were published in the same year, include a lowercase letter to distinguish them. For example:

  Lane, B. (2007a). Verbal medicine . . .

  Lane, B. (2007b). Writing . . .

- Because scholars and writers often collaborate, you may have several references in which an author is listed with several *different* collaborators. List these alphabetically using the second author's last name. For example,

  Brown, M., Nelson, A. (2002)

  Brown, M., Payne, M. (1999)

Order of Information

A Reference list entry for a periodical or book includes this information, in order: author, date of publication, book title or, for articles, article title followed by periodical title, and publication information. Here are some basics about each of these entry parts; details and examples follow. Remember that all entries should be double spaced and that the first line of each should begin flush left and all subsequent lines should be indented.

Author or Authors.   List all authors—last name, comma, and then initials. Invert all authors' names. Use commas to separate authors' names; add an *ampersand* (&) before the last author's name. When citing an edited book, list the editor(s) in place of the author, and add the abbreviation *Ed.* or *Eds.* in parentheses after the last editor's name. End the list of names with a period.

Date.   After the last author's name, in parentheses list the year the work was published. If the source is a magazine or newspaper, also include the month and day; for example "(2011, April 4)." If a source doesn't list any date, use the abbreviation *n.d.* in parentheses. Add a period after the closing parenthesis.

Book Title or Article Title.   Use a period at the end of each title, and style titles as follows:

- **Book titles** are italicized. Only the first word of titles and subtitles are capitalized; all other words are lowercase unless ordinarily capitalized. For example:

  The curious researcher: A guide to writing

      research papers.

  Sound reporting.

- **Article titles** are given without italics or quotation marks. As with book titles, capitalize only the first word of the title and any subtitle.

  Student athletes on Facebook.

  Oyster apocalypse? Truth about bivalve

      obliteration.

Periodical Title and Publication Information.   Periodical titles are italicized, like book titles; unlike book and article titles, they use both uppercase and lowercase. Add the volume number (if any), also italicized and separated from the title with a comma. If each issue of the periodical starts with page 1, then also include the issue number in parentheses immediately after the volume number. End the entry, following a comma, with the page numbers of the article. For example, you might have *Journal of Mass Communication, 10*, 138–150. Use the abbreviation *p.* (for one page) or *pp.* (for more than one page) only if you are citing a newspaper.

Publication Information for Books.   List the city and state or country of publication (use postal abbreviations for states) and then, following a colon, the name of the publisher, followed by a period.

Bringing these elements together, a print book citation would look like this in APA style:

Blakeswell, S. (2010). *How to live or a life of*

    Montaigne. New York, NY: Other Press.

And a print periodical citation would look like this:

```
Alegre, A. (2011). Parenting styles and
     children's emotional intelligence. What do
     we know? The Family Journal, 19, 56-62.
```

Digital Sources.   In many ways citing an electronic source is the same as citing a print one—you'll include author, title, and publication information. But there are also some significant differences. Online material may appear in different versions—say, as a talk and an article based on that talk—and because electronic sources may come and go, it's hard to be certain that readers will be able to find a particular source. APA has been making changes in an effort to meet the special challenges posed by online material. Basically, the organization recommends that you identify where the article or document is located using one of two methods:

1. Include the URL (Web address)

Or, preferably,

2. Cite the DOI (digital object identifier)

The digital object identifier is a unique number that is assigned to an electronic document. Journal articles these days almost all have a DOI, which is often listed on the first page of a document. Because these numbers are stable and unique to each source, they are the preferred method of citing the location of an electronic source.

For example, here's a typical citation of an online document that has no DOI.

```
Perina, K, Flora, P., & Marano, H. P. (2011,
     January 1). Who are you? (And what do you
     think of me?) Psychology Today. Retrieved
     from http://www.psychologytoday.com
     /articles/201012/who-are-you-and-what
     -do-you-think-me
```

A journal article with a DOI would be cited like this:

```
O'Neil, J. (2011). The privatization of
     public schools in New Zealand. Journal
     of Education Policy, 26, 17-31. doi:
     10.1080/02680939.2010.493227
```

3.2 Citing Books, in Print and Online

3.2.1 A BOOK WITH ONE AUTHOR

Cite a print book like this:

Barry, J. M. (2004). *The great influenza: The epic story of the deadliest plague in history*. New York, NY: Viking.

In-Text Citation: (Barry, 2004) *or* According to Barry (2004),...

Cite a book that only appears electronically like this:

Burnheim, J. (2006). *Is democracy possible? The alternative to electoral politics*. Retrieved from http://setis.library.usyd .edu.au/democracy/index.html

In-Text Citation: (Burnheim, 2006) *or* According to Burnheim (2006),...

For an electronic book that is also available in print, include information in brackets about how it appeared digitally. For example,

Gwynne, S.C. (2010). *Empire of the summer moon* [iBook version]. Retrieved from http:// www.apple.com/us/ibooks

In-Text Citation: (Gwynne, 2010) *or* According to Gwynne (2010),...

3.2.2 A BOOK WITH TWO AUTHORS

Graff, G., Birkenstein, C., & Durst, Russell (2009). *They say, I say*. New York, NY: Norton.

In-Text Citations: (Graff, Birkenstein, & Durst, 2009); after first citing all the names, you can subsequently use the first author's name followed by *et al.*

3.2.3 A BOOK WITH THREE TO SEVEN AUTHORS

> Belenky, M., Clinchy B. M., Goldberger, N. R.,
>
>   & Tarule, J. M. (1986). *Women's ways of*
>
>   *knowing: The development of self, voice,*
>
>   *and mind.* New York, NY: Basic Books.

In-Text Citation: (Belenky, Clinchy, Goldberger, &
Tarule, 1986) when mentioned first, and (Belenky
et al., 1986) thereafter.

3.2.4 A BOOK WITH EIGHT OR MORE AUTHORS

For a work with eight or more authors, give the first six authors
followed by an ellipsis (...) and the final author. For example,

> Jones, B., Doverman, L. S., Shanke S., Forman,
>
>   P., Witte, L. S., Firestone, F. J., ...
>
>   Smith, L. A. (2011). *Too many authors spoil*
>
>   *the soup.* New York, NY: Oyster Press.

In-Text Citation: (Jones et al., 2011)

3.2.5 A BOOK WITH AN INSTITUTIONAL AUTHOR

> American Red Cross. (2007). *Advanced first aid*
>
>   *and emergency care.* New York, NY: Doubleday.

In-Text Citation: (American Red Cross, 2007)

or

> The book *Advanced First Aid and Emergency Care*
>
>   (2007) states that...

3.2.6 A BOOK WITH NO AUTHOR

> *The Chicago manual of style* (16th ed.). (2010).
>
>   Chicago, IL: University of Chicago Press.

In-Text Citations: `(Chicago Manual of Style, 2010)`

or

`According to the` *Chicago Manual of Style* `(2010),...`

3.2.7 AN ENCYCLOPEDIA ENTRY

Cite an article from a print encyclopedia like this:

`Hansen, T. S. (2003). Depression. In` *The new encyclopaedia Britannica* `(Vol. 12, pp. 408-412). Chicago, IL: Encyclopaedia Britannica.`

In-Text Citations: `(Hansen, 2003)` *or* `Hansen (2003) defines depression as...`

Cite an article from an online encyclopedia like this:

`Diarrhea. (2008). In` *Columbia encyclopedia* `(6th ed.). Retrieved from http://www .encyclopedia.com/doc/1E1-diarrhea.html`

In-Text Citations: `("Diarrhea," 2008)` *or* `According to the Columbia Encyclopedia (2008), diarrhea...`

3.2.8 A CHAPTER IN A BOOK

`Kuhn, T. S. (1996). The route to normal science. In` *The structure of scientific revolutions* `(pp. 23-34). Chicago, IL: University of Chicago Press.`

In-Text Citations: `(Kuhn, 2006)` *or* `Kuhn (2006) argues that...`

3.2.9 A BOOK WITH AN EDITOR

`Crane, R. S. (Ed.). (1952).` *Critics and criticism.* `Chicago, IL: University of Chicago Press.`

In-Text Citations: (Crane, 1952) *or* In his preface,
Crane (1952) observed that...

3.2.10 A SELECTION IN A BOOK WITH AN EDITOR

McKeon, R. (1952). Rhetoric in the Middle Ages.
    In R. S. Crane (Ed.), *Critics and criticism*
    (pp. 260-289). Chicago, IL: University of
    Chicago Press.

In-Text Citations: (McKeon, 1952) *or* McKeon (1952)
argued that...

3.2.11 A REPUBLISHED WORK

James, W. (1978). *Pragmatism*. Cambridge, MA:
    Harvard University Press. (Original work
    published 1907).

In-Text Citations: (James, 1907/1978) *or* According
to William James (1907/1978),...

3.2.12 A GOVERNMENT DOCUMENT

U.S. Bureau of the Census. (1991). *Statistical*
    abstract of the United States (111th ed.).
    Washington, DC: U.S. Government Printing
    Office.

In-Text Citations: (U.S. Bureau, 1991) *or* According
to the U.S. Census Bureau (1991),...

3.3 Citing Articles, in Print and Online

3.3.1 A JOURNAL ARTICLE

Cite a print journal article like this:

Blager, F. B. (1979). The effect of intervention
on the speech and language of children.
Child Abuse and Neglect, 5, 91–96.

In-Text Citations: (Blager, 1979) *or* Blager (1979)
stated that . . .

For a journal article, include the DOI, if available:

Wang, F., McGuire, P., & Pan, E. (2010). Applying technology to inquiry-based learning
in early childhood education. *Early Childhood Education Journal, 37,* 381–389. doi:
10.1007/s10643-009-0634-6

In-Text Citations: When first mentioned cite all three
(Wang, McGuire, & Pan, 2010) *or* Wang, McGuire,
and Pan (2010) argue that. . . Subsequent mentions
can use *et al.*: (Wang et al., 2010).

For a journal article with no DOI, include the URL of the database or the online journal's homepage:

Kaveshar, J. (2008). Kicking the rock and the
hard place to the curb: An alternative and
integrated approach to suicidal students in
higher education. *Emory Law Journal, 57*(3),
651–693. Retrieved from http://find
.galegroup.com/itx/start.do?prodId=AONE

In-Text Citations: (Kaveshar, 2008) *or* According to
Kaveshar (2008), . . .

3.3.2 A JOURNAL ARTICLE NOT PAGINATED CONTINUOUSLY

Most journals begin on page 1 with the first issue of the year
and continue paginating consecutively for subsequent issues. A
few journals, however, start on page 1 with each issue. For these,

include the issue number in parentheses following the italicized
volume number:

> Williams, J., Post, A. T., & Strunk, F. (1991).
>
>   The rhetoric of inequality. *Attwanata*,
>
>   *12*(3), 54-67.

In-Text Citation: (Williams, Post, & Strunk, 1991)
or Williams, Post, and Strunk (1991) argue
that . . .   When first mentioned, cite all three authors and
subsequently you can use *et al.*: (Williams et al.,
1991).

3.3.3 A MAGAZINE ARTICLE

To cite print articles, include the year, month, and (if present)
day published.

> Moore, Peter. (2003, August). Your heart will
>
>   stop. *Men's Health*. 142-151.

In-Text Citations: (Moore, 2003) *or* Moore (2003)
observed that . . .

Cite online articles like this:

> O'Hehir, A. (2008). Beyond the multiplex. *Salon.*
>
>   *com*. Retrieved from http://www.salon.com
>
>   /ent/movies/btm/

In-Text Citations: (O'Hehir, 2008) *or* According to
O'Hehir (2008), . . .

3.3.4 A NEWSPAPER ARTICLE

Cite print articles like this:

> Honan, W. (1991, January 24). The war affects
>
>   Broadway. *New York Times*, pp. C15-16.

In-Text Citations: (Honan, 1991) *or* Honan (1991)
said that "Broadway is a battleground" (p. C15).

Cite online articles like this:

Englund, W., DeYoung, K., & Willgoren, D.
(2011, February 4). Huge protests continue for 11th day as Obama administration
weighs Egypt options. *The Washington Post.*
Retrieved from http://www.washingtonpost.com

In-text Citations: (Englund, DeYoung, & Willgoren,
2011) *or* According to Englund et al.,...

3.3.5 AN ARTICLE WITH NO AUTHOR

If there is no author, a common situation with newspaper articles, alphabetize using the first significant word in the article title.
For example:

New Hampshire loud and clear. (1998, February 19).
The Boston Globe, p. 22.

In-Text Citations: ("New Hampshire," 1998) *or*
In the article "New Hampshire loud and
clear" (1998),...

3.3.6 AN ARTICLE ON A WEB SITE

Note that this citation includes the abbreviation *n.d.* because
the article did not include a date.

Lopez, M. (n.d.). Intellectual development of
toddlers. *National Network for Childcare.*
Retrieved from http://www.nncc.org/Child
.Dev/intel.dev.todd.html

In-Text Citations: (Lopez, n.d.) *or* According to
Lopez (n.d.),...

3.3.7 AN ABSTRACT

The growth of online databases for articles has increased the
availability of full-text versions and abstracts of articles. While it is
almost always better to use the full article, sometimes an abstract

itself contains some useful information. Typically, there are two situations in which you might choose to cite just an abstract: when you're working with an original print article or when you've culled the abstract from a database like *Biological Abstracts.* In the first case, include the term *Abstract* in brackets following the title and before the period.

For example,

```
Renninger, A. K. (2009). Interest and identity

     development in instruction: An inductive

     model [Abstract]. Educational Psychologist,

     44, 105-118.
```

In-Text Citation: (Renninger, 2009) *or* Renninger (2009) claims that . . .

If the abstract was from a database or some other secondary source, include the name of that source. The term *Abstract* in brackets isn't necessary in this case. For example,

```
Garcia, R. G. (2002). Evolutionary speed

     of species invasions. Evolution, 56,

     661-668. Abstract retrieved from Biological

     Abstracts.
```

In-Text Citations: (Garcia, 2002) *or* Garcia (2002) argues that . . .

3.3.8 A BOOK REVIEW

Cite a review that's in print like this:

```
Dentan, R. K. (1989). A new look at the brain

     [Review of the book The dreaming brain

     by J. Allen Hobsen]. Psychiatric Journal,

     13, 51.
```

In-Text Citations: (Dentan, 1989) *or* Dentan (1989) argued that . . .

Cite an online review like this:

Benfey, C. (2008). Why implausibility sells
     [Review of the book *Painter in a savage*
     land by Miles Harvey]. *Slate*. Retrieved
     from http://www.slate.com/id/2193254/

In-Text Citations: (Benfey, 2008) *or* Benfey (2008)
argued that . . .

3.3.9 AN EDITORIAL

Editorial: Egypt's agonies. [Editorial] (2011,
     February 2). *The New York Times*. Retrieved
     from http://www.nytimes.com/2011/02/04
     /opinion/04fr1.htm

In-Text Citations: ("Egypt's Agonies," 2011) *or The*
New York Times (2011) argued . . .

3.3.10 A LETTER TO THE EDITOR

Hill, A. C. (1992, February 19). A flawed his-
     tory of blacks in Boston [Letter to the
     editor]. *The Boston Globe*, p. 22.

In-Text Citations: (Hill, 1992) *or* Hill (1992) complained that . . .

3.3.11 A PUBLISHED INTERVIEW

Personal interviews are usually not cited in an APA-style paper.
Published interviews are cited as follows:

Cotton, P. (1982, April). [Interview with
     Jake Tule, psychic]. *Chronicles Magazine*,
     pp. 24–28.

In-Text Citations: (Cotton, 1982) *or* Cotton (1982)
noted that . . .

3.4 Citing Other Sources

3.4.1 AN ENTIRE WEB PAGE

If you're referring to an entire Web site in the text of your essay,
include the address parenthetically. However, there is no need to
include it in the Reference list. For example:

The Google Scholar search engine (http://scholar
.google.com) is considered good for academic
research.

3.4.2 A FILM, DVD, OR ONLINE VIDEO

Hitchcock, A. (Producer & Director). (1954).

   Rear window [Film]. United States: MGM.

In-Text Citations: (Hitchcock, 1954) *or* In *Rear Window*, Hitchcock (1954) . . .

Here's how to cite an online video:

Price, P. (Writer).(2008, April 4). *Research-

   ing online: Five easy steps* [Video file].

   Retrieved from http://www.youtube.com/watch?

   v=Ylp9nJpGak4&feature=related

In-Text Citations: (Price, 2008) *or* In *Researching
Online*, Price (2008) . . .

3.4.3 A TELEVISION PROGRAM

Burns, K. (Executive producer). (1996). *The

   West* [Television broadcast]. New York,

   NY, and Washington, DC: Public Broad-

   casting Service.

In-Text Citations: (Burns, 1996) *or* In Ken Burns's (1996) film, . . .

3.4.4 AN AUDIO PODCAST

Kermode, M. (2008, June 20). The edge of

love. *Mark Kermode and Simon Mayo's Movie*

Reviews [Audio podcast]. Retrieved from

http://www.bbc.co.uk/fivelive/entertainment

/kermode.shtml

In-Text Citations: (Kermode, 2008) *or* In his latest review, Kermode (2008) decried . . .

3.4.5 A BLOG

Shen, H. (2008, June 4). Does your password

meet the test? [Web log post]. Retrieved

from http://googleblog.blogspot.com/2008

/06/does-your-password-pass-test.html

In-Text Citations: (Shen, 2008) *or* Our passwords are vulnerable, says Shen (2008), because . . .

3.4.6 A WIKI

How to use Audacity for podcasting. (n.d.).

Retrieved from http://sites.google.com/a

/biosestate.edu/podcasting-team/Home

In-Text Citation: ("Audacity," n.d.)

3.4.7 ONLINE DISCUSSION LISTS

These include listservs, electronic mailing lists, newsgroups, and online forums, with the method of citation varying slightly depending on the specific type of source. For example,

Hord, J. (2002, July 11). Why do pigeons lift
   one wing up in the air? [Online forum
   comment]. Retrieved from rec://pets.birds
   .pigeons

In-Text Citations: (Hord, 2002) *or* Hord asks (2002)...

Note that the citation includes the subject line of the message as the title, and bracketed information about the source, in this case an online forum comment. For listservs use "[Electronic mailing list message]."

3.4.8 A MUSICAL RECORDING

Wolf, K. (1986). Muddy roads [Recorded by
   E. Clapton]. On *Gold in California* [CD].
   Santa Monica, CA: Rhino Records. (1990).

In-Text Citations: (Wolf, 1986, track 5) *or* In
Wolf's (1986) song, ...

Part Four: Student Paper in APA Style

Patricia Urbick has set her sights on a career in the Air Force, and so her research essay on military policies that limit women's roles in combat has personal meaning. In "In the Fight," Patricia calls for an end to combat exclusion policies, arguing that such policies ignore the key roles military women are already playing in combat situations. Her essay, written in APA style, is a traditional argument, organized around a claim that Patricia sets out to prove. It's a deeply personal essay, nonetheless, because, among other reasons, the ultimate outcome of the argument has huge implications for Patricia's military career. For those of us who aren't in the armed forces, "In the Fight" lifts a curtain on an issue that deserves more attention.

IN THE FIGHT   1

In the Fight: Women and Combat Exclusion

Patricia Urbick

Boise State University

A running head is an abbreviated title. This will appear, along with page numbers, on every page, including the title page.

IN THE FIGHT   2

Abstract

    Polling data suggest that while most
Americans support women in the military,
they are deeply divided over whether women
should have combat roles. Current military
policies exclude women from combat though
unofficially they are assuming a greater
role on the front lines. The policies that
deny women an opportunity to serve alongside men in combat should be changed so
female service members receive the recognition and benefits they deserve.

In the Fight: Women and Combat Exclusion

> "Women are in the military, and there they will remain."
>
>   —Retired U.S. Navy Commander
>   Darlene M. Iskra, PhD

The presence of women in the military elicits responses ranging anywhere from absolute condemnation to enthusiastic support. An 83-percent majority of the American public is supportive of women serving in noncombatant military roles; however, approval ratings dip 30 points once the topic of women serving in combatant roles is broached. Older Americans, in particular, are against women serving in combat (CBS News, 2010).

While this poll does demonstrate that a slight majority of Americans overall approve of women in combat (a lukewarm 53 percent), I think that support would increase if Americans knew that women are already involved in day-to-day combat operations in our current conflicts. There is a pressing need to eliminate the combat exclusion laws because military women deserve the recognition and care that come with their service.

The most virulent opponents of women's military service claim that since

IN THE FIGHT   4

the integration of women in 1948 there
has been a dangerous "feminization" of
the U.S. military, with military readiness and effectiveness sacrificed to a
pernicious social experiment (Mitchell,
1998, pp. xv-xvii). To some, this could
appear to be a viable objection. After
all, Department of Defense (DoD) policies
on things like living quarters, rations,
and families have evolved drastically
since the integration of women began more
than 60 years ago. However, this is not
a softening of the DoD's expectations of
its troops. Better food and quarters indeed *followed* women into military life,
and these were necessary changes demanded
by women who wanted to improve provisions
for all military personnel, not just
women (Holm, 1992).

    As a member of the military myself,
I can testify that current members owe a
debt of gratitude to these women who had
everyone's health and comfort in mind.
The physical conditions that my comrades-
in-arms and I are often required to serve
under can be difficult and uncomfortable
enough. Without the initiative for better food and housing as begun by military women in the 1940s, these operating
conditions could be far less tolerable.

Here Patricia makes a move that is char- acteristic of a well-crafted argument: She presents the claims of critics of her thesis.

This self- disclosure makes Patricia's argument even more persua- sive because it establishes her credibility. She speaks with authority about the military because she serves.

There has also been dramatic transformation in policies concerning military women's families—and military families in general—since female integration; however, these changes were necessary so the military could retain qualified women in its ranks. Before 1975, DoD regulations stipulated that "women [be] forced out of the military if they became pregnant or even if they married someone with children. . . . If an unmarried woman became pregnant, she would receive a punitive discharge and little to no support for her prenatal care" (Iskra, 2010, pp. 26, 41). These antiquated policies contributed to unnecessarily high rates of women leaving the military and made the lives of those who wished to stay needlessly complicated. For example, when my own mother became pregnant while in the military in 1979, she was counseled to have an abortion. She joined the Air Force at the age of 17 and was already a competent electrician. And although regulations had changed four years prior, much of the mindset within the workplace had not; so because my mother was at the time a scared 19-year-old with few advisors and fewer options, she did as she was told

IN THE FIGHT   6

(J. Anderson, personal communication,
November 9,2010).

　　Eventually, the Department of Defense
adjusted its policies. By the mid-1970s,
DoD recognized that forcing a woman to
choose between having a career and having
a family was preposterous, especially
in light of the women's rights movements of the sixties and seventies. More
importantly, the DoD changed its policies because it saw the benefit of allowing
women who were experts in their fields to
remain in their jobs after the birth of
their first child. Clearly, when making
demographic decisions, the military leadership is more concerned with what benefits
national security than in orchestrating any
kind of social change. As Commander Iskra
(2010) observes, "The military reflects
social change—it does not initiate it" (p. 24).

　　Women have been allowed to participate in air and surface naval combat since
1992 and 1994, respectively (Iskra, 2010).
Since the mid-1990s, women have repeatedly
proven themselves in countless naval and
aviation missions. One example of many is
the accomplishments of Air Force Colonel
Martha McSally. As the first woman fighter
pilot in combat for the United States

Note that per-sonal interviews are cited in the text of your paper but aren't included in the list of references.

Air Force, she has distinguished herself as a top A-10 pilot in both Kuwait and Afghanistan beginning in the mid-1990s; she became the first female squadron commander of a fighter squadron while stationed at Davis-Monthan Air Force Base in Tucson, Arizona; in 2006 she was selected to attend the Air War College, which trains senior personnel in strategic air and space forces employment; and she continues to contribute extensively to the security missions of the U.S. armed forces (Bergquist, 2010).

Colonel McSally is just one of many women who have proven their dedication and capability in the air and on the sea. Women have demonstrated the same courage, skill, and honor as their male counterparts. It stands to reason, then, that women will display the same character traits in ground combat as they have in air and naval combat. It's time for legislation allowing for the official inclusion of women in every aspect of ground combat operations.

Critics of such a move would cite aeronautical disasters such as the fatal crash of Navy pilot Kara Hultgreen in 1994 or any number of adulterous cases

IN THE FIGHT   8

involving female aviators as evidence that
women cannot be trusted with multimillion-
dollar machinery (or co-ed work environments) and, by extension, that women
cannot be trusted with the lives of their
comrades-in-arms (Mitchell, 1998). However, it is important to remember that fatal
crashes and adulterous affairs occurred
long before women came onto the scene and
that the well-publicized weaknesses of a
few should not be used to judge the abilities and potentials of such a diverse
group as American military women.

  The challenges in today's military
conflicts demand the best of every soldier, sailor, and airman, regardless of
gender. Military women have proven on the
Army's and Marines' training grounds that
they handle the same tasks as men. As a
group, women's average scores are five
percent higher than men's average scores
(Burke, 2004). By policy, however, commanders are not allowed to deploy some of
their most talented soldiers for no other
reason than that they are women. As Marine
Brigadier General Thomas V. Draude said,
"These units deploy with the best men,
but not necessarily the best Marines" (as
cited in Iskra, 2010, p. 3).

Patricia nicely makes an asser-tion—that commanders can't use some of their best soldiers simply because they are women—and then uses a quotation from a commander that supports the assertion.

   Some commanders recognize that
combat exclusion laws are outdated, and
they already employ women on combat missions, but under different official guis-
es. Currently, when a commander needs to
use a woman on a mission, she will be
placed in the combat unit under the official status of a "temporary assignment"
or "combat support," all the while performing the same duties and service as
her male counterparts (Iskra, 2010).

   Women in combat and forward-operating
units aren't just there because they're
good soldiers. They are also needed in
some conflicts because men are forbidden
by local law and custom to touch native
women for any reason. Women soldiers and
Marines are needed on many missions to
conduct business involving native wom-
en and children, whether it is performing personal searches, guarding them,
or calming them down after a distress-
ing event (McLachlan & Sommers, 2008).
These women execute the same tasks, fight
in the same battles, and run the same
risks as their brothers-in-arms yet do
not receive the same benefits as the men
do. They may be denied combat pay, combat
recognition in the form of awards and

decorations, opportunities for promotion, and, most importantly, care for combat-related stress and injuries. Put simply, women are already engaged in combat. Why not make it legal?

In the changing terrain of twenty-first century warfare, the time has come to eliminate combat exclusion laws. Women who already engage in combat deserve the recognition and treatment that accompany combatant status, and women of the future military deserve the chance to prove them-selves on the battlefield and further their careers just as their brothers-in-arms have done for centuries. This will not result in some fictional "feminization" of the military but will allow it to use the best minds rather than a select group based on gender. Women are needed on the battlefields of America's wars, not as a dangerous social experiment but because they provide additional talent and flex-ibility to execute vital missions. It is time to recognize the abilities and poten-tial of American military women by passing legislation that gives them the rights and responsibilities that every male soldier takes part in. It is time to repeal the combat exclusion laws.

IN THE FIGHT   11

References

Bergquist, C. (2010). Air Force Lt.

    Col. Martha McSally: First female

    pilot in combat reflects on career.

    The Face of Defense (Dec. 6, 2006).

    Retrieved from http://www.defense

    .gov/home/faceofdefense/fod/2006-12

    /f20061207a.html

Burke, C. (2004). *Camp all-American, Hanoi*

    Jane, and the high-and-tight: Gender,

    folklore, and changing military culture.

    Boston, MA: Beacon Press.

CBS News (Producer). (15 Aug. 2009). Poll:

    53% support women in combat roles. *CBS*

    News. Retrieved from http://www.cbsnews

    .com/stories/2009/08/15/opinion/polls

    /main5244312.shtml

Holm, J. (1992). *Women in the military:*

    An unfinished evolution. Novato, CA:

    Presidio.

Iskra, D. (2010) *Women in the United States*

    Armed Forces: A guide to the issues.

    Santa Barbara, CA: Praeger Security

    International.

McLaclan, M., & Sommers, D. (Directors).

    (2008). *Lioness* [Film]. United States:

    Chicken and Eggs Production.

Mitchell, Brian. (1998). *Women in the*

    military: Flirting with disaster.

    Washington, DC: Regnery Publishing.

Always begin the references on a new page.

APPENDIX C

Understanding Research Assignments

About 15 years ago, in a dark, dimly lit basement floor of the University of New Hampshire library, I discovered the textbook that may have had the very first research paper assignment for undergraduates. Charles Baldwin's 1906 *A College Manual of Rhetoric* encouraged students to write essays based on reading that emphasized "originally" compiling facts so that the writer gives "already known" information his "own grouping and interpretation." In an article that year, Baldwin noted that "from the beginning a student should learn that his use of the library will be a very practical measure of his culture."

In the century since Baldwin's book, the college research paper has become probably the most common genre of student writing in the university. It is a fixture in composition classes and many other courses that require a "term paper." Naturally, this is why there are books like *The Curious Researcher*—to help students understand these assignments and give them guidance in the process of writing them. As you know, this book emphasizes the research *essay* rather than the formal research paper. My argument is that this more exploratory, possibly less formal, researched piece is the best way to introduce you to the spirit of inquiry that drives most academic research. The habits of mind that come from essaying, along with the research and writing skills that essaying develops, should help you whenever you're asked to write a paper that involves research.

There's another skill that's invaluable when you encounter a research paper assignment in another class: knowing how to interpret what exactly you're being asked to do. This involves reading your writing assignment rhetorically. In other words, analyze the *situation* for each assignment: How does it fit into other writing projects in the course? What particular purpose does this assignment have? What do you know about the instructor's particular attitudes about research and about writing? How do you figure out the best approaches to the research project? Apparently, this analysis can pose a huge problem for students. In one study, for example, 92 percent of students said that the most frustrating part of doing research was figuring out what their professor wanted.*

Instructors aren't trying to be obtuse. They want you to understand the assignment, and most have made an effort to be clear. While there's not much you can do about *how* the assignment is conceived or described, you can be savvier at analyzing the assignment's purpose and guidelines.

I've recently conducted a review of research paper assignments from courses across the disciplines, and actually there are striking similarities among them. I tried to read them as a student would, actively looking for guidance about how to approach the assignment and also alert to subtleties that students might miss. In the following sections, I break this rhetorical analysis into parts, drawing on what I learned.

Analyzing the Purpose of the Assignment

One of the things I hear most often from my students who have research assignments in other classes is that the instructor "doesn't want my opinion in the paper." Frankly, I'm often skeptical of this. College writing assignments typically are about what or how you think. But because research papers involve considerable time collecting and considering the ideas of others, it's easy to assume that you're supposed to be a bystander.

Actually, even some instructors seem to equate the term "research paper" with merely reporting information. "This is not a research paper," said one assignment. "The idea here is not to pack in as much information as you can, but instead to present a thoughtful and clearly written analysis." Another noted that "although this is a research paper, the focus is fundamentally on your own analysis and interpretation...."

*Head, Alison. "Beyond Google: How Do Students Conduct Academic Research?" *First Monday* 12.8, 6 Aug. 2007. Web. 30 Mar. 2008.

What these instructors are at pains to point out is that, contrary to what you might think, they are actively interested in what you think. They want students to *do* something with the information they collect. But merely having an opinion isn't enough. As one assignment put it, "You are not being graded on your opinion, but your ability to communicate and support a point of view (your thesis)."

Writing a convincing, well-supported paper is straightforward enough. But why do the project in the first place? What is the purpose of writing a research paper? The assignments I reviewed sometimes talk about encouraging "critical thinking" or helping students enter "a scholarly conversation." A few talk about "advancing your knowledge" about a topic or learning the conventions of research writing in a particular discipline. But many, unfortunately, just focus on a requirement that your paper make an argument.

Argumentative Research: Open or Closed?

The language that research assignments use to emphasize argument is quite often very explicit: "You are to write a research paper in which you make an argument related to some aspect of life in Southeast Asia." Not much ambiguity there. Similarly, some assignments ask that you "take a position" on a topic. Argumentative research papers are most often organized around a thesis, and some assignment descriptions go to great lengths to explain what makes a strong one (usually, sufficiently narrow, addressing a significant question, and explicitly stated).

What may not be obvious, however, is how much latitude you have in letting your research revise your thesis or even dramatically change your initial point of view. Most often, instructors *expect* the research to change your thinking, and they often use the term "working thesis" to describe your initial position. These are the more open-ended assignments that might specify that the crafting of a final thesis can occur late rather than early in the research process. These are also assignments that emphasize a focus on a *research question* much like we've discussed in this book.

More rarely, an assignment will imply a closed approach: First identify a thesis, and then seek evidence from your research that will support it. This is the conventional thesis-support model in which the expectation is that you will use your thesis, and not your research question, to dictate not just the structure of your paper but also the goal of your research. These kinds of assignments tend not to mention that a thesis might be revised and are silent on how it arises from a research question or problem. Always ask your instructor about whether your reading of the assignment as more closed-ended is accurate. The key questions are these:

Questions to Ask Your Instructor About the Thesis

- Where should the thesis in this assignment come from?
- What process do you suggest for arriving at it?
- Finally, might it be revised—even substantially—later in the process?

In a more open-ended research paper, the inquiry-based methods of *The Curious Researcher* directly apply. For example, crafting a researchable question is an important route to coming up with a strong working thesis, and the dialogue or double-entry journal can help you think through how your research might develop or revise that thesis. The strict thesis-support paper seems to have little opportunity for inquiry. Indeed, the emphasis in these assignments is frequently on the formal qualities of the paper—how well it's organized around and supports a thesis, the proper use of citations, and mechanical correctness. Developing an outline at the front end of the project is usually helpful. However, there's no reason that after developing working knowledge of your topic you can't use exercises like "Dialogue with Dave" or "Sharpening Your Point" (Exercises 4.1 and 4.2) in Chapter 4, or "Using Your Thesis to Revise" in Chapter 5, on p. 194. All of these sections will help you come up with a strong thesis that is based on what you've discovered in your research.

Audience

For whom are you writing? So much hinges on the answer to this question: the tone of the paper, how specialized its language might be, the emphasis you give on providing background on the research question, and the degree to which you stress reader interest. Despite the importance of audience, research paper assignments frequently fail to mention it at all. This omission can often mean that you are writing for your instructor. But it actually might surprise you how often this isn't intended to be the case. Particularly if your assignment includes peer review of drafts or class presentations, you may be writing for a more general audience. Sometimes this is explicit: "Your paper should be understood by a broader audience than scholars in your field. You will have to explain concepts and not expect your audience to understand in-house jargon." If the audience for your paper isn't clear, ask your instructor this simple question:

Question to Ask Your Instructor About the Audience

- Who is the audience for this assignment—readers like the instructor who are knowledgeable about the topic and/or readers who are not?

Extent of Emphasis on Formal Qualities

An essay like "Theories of Intelligence" in the Introduction of this book is relatively informal: It's casual in tone, has a strong individual voice, and is structured to explore a question—*to find out* rather than *to prove*. It certainly has a thesis, but it is a delayed thesis, appearing not in the introduction but toward the end of the essay. The essay is organized around the writer's questions, not around making a point and logically providing evidence to support it. It does, however, have some formal qualities, including careful citation and attribution, the marshalling of appropriate evidence to explore the topic, and a sensible organization that moves from question to answers.

Research paper assignments in other classes are likely to put considerably more emphasis on a structure based on logic and reasoning. Put another way, these papers differ from an exploratory essay like "Theories of Intelligence" in that they report the *products* of the process of thinking about and researching the question, rather than describe the *process* of thinking and researching the question. The chief product, of course, is your thesis—the thing you are trying to say—and typically you're expected to place this in the introduction of your paper. Fairly often, research paper assignments instruct you to state your thesis or position explicitly in a sentence. Along with a thesis, however, many assignments, in keeping with the approach of this book, ask that you develop a research question from which the thesis then emerges. These are the open assignments we discussed earlier. As one put it, "[The] introduction should make three points: It should briefly introduce your question and its significance, state your answer, and orient the reader regarding your way of proceeding. This is the place to say, 'I'm going to argue....'" Patricia Urbick's essay in Appendix B, in which she argues that the policies that exclude military women from combat should be abolished, is a great example of this kind of paper

Also pay close attention to what context the assignment asks you to establish for your research question—course discussion, literature review, or both. Some instructors are keen on having you write a paper that in some way extends the course's readings or discussion points. Others want you to become familiar with the scholarly conversation that might extend beyond the class. Here's a question to ask about this:

Question to Ask Your Instructor About the Context

- What is the more important context for establishing the significance of my research question or thesis—what we talked about in class or what I discover when I review the relevant literature?

The logical structure of an argumentative research paper doesn't vary much (see the discussion about this in Chapter 4), although in some disciplines you will be instructed to use the organizational conventions of the field; for example, scientific papers might require an abstract, introduction, methods, results, discussion, and conclusion, in that order. Generally, the body of your paper must draw on evidence from your research to support your thesis, though frequently your assignment requires that you also consider opposing points of view. How are they misguided? In what ways do they fail to address your research question? Also pay attention to whether your assignment asks you to tightly tether each paragraph to the thesis using topic sentences that address how that paragraph supports it.* If so, you might find it useful to outline the topic sentences before you draft your essay.

Because one of the aims of teaching research writing is to help you understand its conventions, assignments almost always discuss the need for proper citation, correct format, a required number of scholarly sources, and so on, as well as attention to grammar and mechanics. You need to determine the relative importance of these conventions. Some research paper assignments, for example, devote much more ink to describing the required format—location of page numbers, font, margins—and the need for "perfect" grammar than they do a discussion of the research process, formulating a thesis, or the larger goals of the assignment. In this case, you might give these

---

*Some instructors heavily stress the use of topic sentences in paragraph writing, though there is considerable evidence that much writing, including academic prose, doesn't consistently feature topic sentences.

conventions more attention. If you're not sure how to weigh them, ask this question:

Question to Ask Your Instructor About the Importance of Formal Qualities

- When you evaluate the paper, what is the relative importance of getting the format right? Do you give that concern as much weight as the quality of my thesis or the soundness of my thinking?

As you know, *The Curious Researcher* encourages essays in which writers have a strong presence. The easiest way to do this is to enter the text directly by using the first person, though in Chapter 4 we explored other ways to do this. Research paper assignments rarely mention whether you can use "I." Silence on this question usually means that you should not. One of the conventions of much academic writing is a more formal register, the sense that the paper speaks rather than the writer. Yet a considerable number of the assignments I reviewed encouraged students to write with "voice" and lively, vigorous prose. The most effective way to inject voice into your research writing is to find your own way of saying things, something that "writing in the middle"—the notetaking strategies encouraged in this book—should help you with. Assignments that say nothing about voice or style probably expect what one assignment described as writing that is "formal in tone, working to establish an authoritative, critical, and analytical voice." If you're unsure about this, consider asking your instructor the following question:

Question to Ask Your Instructor About Tone

- Should the voice in my paper mimic the scholarly sources I'm reading, or can it be somewhat less formal, perhaps sounding a bit more like me?

Types of Evidence: Primary or Secondary

As you move from a general audience (people who may know little about your topic) to a more specialized audience (people who know more), the tone and structure of your paper will change. So will the types of evidence that will make your argument persuasive. In popular writing—say, articles in *Wired* or *Discover* or op-ed pieces in the newspaper—the types of evidence that writers use to convince readers are quite varied. Personal experience and observation, for instance, are often excellent ways to support a point. But as you begin writing research papers in academic disciplines, you need to pay attention to what your instructor considers *appropriate* evidence in that field and for that particular assignment. Scientific papers, for example, often rely on experimental data. Literature papers lean most heavily on evidence culled from the literary text you're writing about. Papers in anthropology might rely on field observations.

Sometimes assignments explicitly talk about appropriate evidence for your paper. More often they do not. Generally speaking, research papers that are assigned in lower-division courses won't require you to conduct experiments or generate field notes. They will likely ask you to draw evidence from already published, or secondary, sources on your topic. But this isn't always the case. A history paper, for example, might require that you study a primary text, perhaps letters by historical figures, political documents, or archived newspapers. This is something you need to know. If the types of evidence you should use in your paper aren't clear, ask this question:

Question to Ask Your Instructor About Evidence

- What types of evidence should I rely on for this paper? Primary or secondary sources? And is personal experience and observation, if relevant, appropriate to use?

In the spirit of writing a conventional conclusion, let me restate what might be apparent by now: The most important thing you must do when you get a research assignment is read the handout carefully, considering what you've already learned in the class about writing in that discipline. I read a lot of research paper assignments, and they usually provide very good guidance. But if they don't, that's never an excuse for floundering. Ask, ask, ask. Your instructor wants you to.

Index